GOLDSMITH: THE CRITICAL HERITAGE

THE CRITICAL HERITAGE SERIES

GENERAL EDITOR: B. C. SOUTHAM, M.A., B.LITT. (OXON.)
Formerly Department of English, Westfield College, University of London

---

For a list of books in the series see the back end paper

GOLDSMITH

THE CRITICAL HERITAGE

Edited by
G. S. ROUSSEAU
*Associate Professor of English, University of California,
Los Angeles*

ROUTLEDGE & KEGAN PAUL : LONDON AND BOSTON

First published in 1974
by Routledge & Kegan Paul Ltd
Broadway House, 68-74 Carter Lane,
London EC4V 5EL and
9 Park Street,
Boston, Mass. 02108, U.S.A.
ISBN 0 7100 7720 3
Library of Congress Catalog Card No. 73-87318

Printed in Great Britain
by W & J Mackay Limited, Chatham

ad patrem philologum

General Editor's Preface

The reception given to a writer by his contemporaries and near-contemporaries is evidence of considerable value to the student of literature. On one side we learn a great deal about the state of criticism at large and in particular about the development of critical attitudes towards a single writer; at the same time, through private comments in letters, journals or marginalia, we gain an insight upon the tastes and literary thought of individual readers of the period. Evidence of this kind helps us to understand the writer's historical situation, the nature of his immediate reading-public, and his response to these pressures.

The separate volumes in the *Critical Heritage Series* present a record of this early criticism. Clearly, for many of the highly productive and lengthily reviewed nineteenth- and twentieth-century writers, there exists an enormous body of material; and in these cases the volume editors have made a selection of the most important views, significant for their intrinsic critical worth or for their representative quality – perhaps even registering incomprehension!

For earlier writers, notably pre-eighteenth century, the materials are much scarcer and the historical period has been extended, sometimes far beyond the writer's lifetime, in order to show the inception and growth of critical views which were initially slow to appear.

In each volume the documents are headed by an Introduction, discussing the material assembled and relating the early stages of the author's reception to what we have come to identify as the critical tradition. The volumes will make available much material which would otherwise be difficult of access and it is hoped that the modern reader will be thereby helped towards an informed understanding of the ways in which literature has been read and judged.

B.C.S.

Contents

CONTENTS

Preface

This book is divided into two parts. Part one, comprising Nos 1–36, presents the critical heritage of Goldsmith's seven most important works; part two, containing Nos 37–86, incorporates a chronological assortment of statements concerning the author and his works, from William Rider's early remarks in 1762, considered in fact to be the first critique about Goldsmith as an author, to Frederic Harrison's in 1883 and 1912.

In a collection such as this, chronological arrangement of items is decidedly a requisite, especially since Goldsmith wrote in many different genres. With this in mind it seemed advantageous to present the critical heritage of his most important works individually in part one, positioning these works by date of publication, and proceeding for each work to list its reviews and criticisms chronologically. Consequently *The Traveller*, having been published in 1764, heads the list, together with Nos 1–4, reviews and criticisms of this work in chronological sequence; *The Vicar of Wakefield*, published in 1766, together with Nos 5–15—comments about this work—is next; and so on. Part two is a conglomerate of remarks, criticisms, comments, etc., ranging from short statements to full essays about the author's life and his works. These are allocated strictly by date.

The eighty-six items have been gathered from many different sources: reviews, diaries, memoirs, letters, autobiographies, biographies, prefaces, and, not least, brief introductions to editions of the works of Oliver Goldsmith. Inasmuch as many of these statements are by little known authors of obscure works, I thought it judicious to provide brief headnotes telling the reader something about each. In some cases, such as No. 67 by the German critic Wilhelm Adolf Lindau, I deemed it desirable to inform the scholar where a copy may be found. These headnotes, some admittedly long, have been intended primarily for the student who wishes to pursue the item further. In many instances, items have been abbreviated without loss of identity, while others, because of spatial restriction, have been reduced virtually to a point of non-recognition. An example of the latter is No 65 in which John Keats with a maximum of brevity comments to Fanny on Goldsmith's poetry; in view of Keats's stature I felt it would be remiss to omit this remark, for very often a brief utterance by a great thinker carries more weight than a full essay by a mediocre personality. The decision to include items such as Keats's remark was well calculated in order to provide the reader, within the limits of space set by this series, with a broader scope rather than a few lengthy items.

Yet, there is no need, as I have explained in the Introduction, for a complete 'critical heritage'; no reason to record every pedestrian comment made about Goldsmith, such as Henry MacKenzie's silly remark to Betty Rose about *The Deserted Village*, or Melville's snappy comment in chapter 55 of *Moby Dick* calling *Animated Nature* 'that popular work.' 'Other critical heritages'—Rowlandson's twenty-four engravings of *The Vicar*, Dalziel's illustrations, numerous paintings that silently glance at Goldsmith's poetic landscapes—are worthy of preservation, especially in the case of an author with as many beauties and faults as Goldsmith, but for many reasons it has not been possible to record them here. Finally, there are the 'oblique heritages' and 'unprinted heritages' about which every scholar dreams: much of Crabbe's poetry, especially *The Village*, which never refers to Goldsmith by name, the tea-talk and table-talk of families and individuals who never recorded their sentiments. How to record these 'other' heritages? They cannot adequately be recorded, or described, and it is therefore best to leave them where they began: unrecorded.

Yet, in each case an attempt has been made to retain the essence of the critic's thought, and at the same time eliminate a repetition of facts. Even in instances of radical abbreviation—as in the outstanding case of Sir James Prior's *Life of Goldsmith* (No. 75)—every effort has been made to preserve the author's original intent. Footnotes have been deleted from many items, again for purposes of conserving space, but other brief footnotes have been provided to explain difficult references and allusions. Typographical errors in the original items have been silently corrected, except where a question persisted about the author's original intention. When I refer to Boswell's *Life of Johnson* it is always to the edition by G. B. Hill and L. F. Powell, 6 vols, Oxford, 1934–50.

The long form of 's' which was used in many of the documents has been normalized; single quotation marks have been used in place of double; and the titles of works by Goldsmith have been given throughout in italics.

Acknowledgments

For permission to reprint materials from books and manuscripts in their collections I would like to thank the British Museum, the Bodleian Library, the Cambridge University Library, the Edinburgh University Library, the Harvard University Library, the Yale University Library, the combined libraries of the University of California at Los Angeles, the Huntington Library, and the University of Heidelberg Library.

I wish to express my thanks to the publishers for permission to reprint copyright material from the following books: Macmillan Publishing Co. Inc. for *Life of Samuel Johnson* by Sir John Hawkins edited by Bertram H. Davis © Bertram H. Davis, 1961; John Murray (Publishers) Ltd for *Byron: Letters and Diaries 1798-1824* volume II edited by Peter Quennell, 1950; the Cambridge University Press and the University of Chicago Press for *The Correspondence of Edmund Burke* volume II by Edmund Burke edited by Lucy S. Sutherland, 1960 and for *The Correspondence of Edmund Burke* volume IV by Edmund Burke edited by John A. Woods, 1963; the Yale University Press for *The Yale Edition of Horace Walpole's Correspondence* edited by Wilmarth Sheldon Lewis *et al.*; and to McGraw Hill for allowing me to cite material from Boswell's private papers printed in *Portraits of Sir Joshua Reynolds*, edited by Frederick W. Hilles, 1952.

Thanks are also due to Ian Willison, Caroline Jakeman, Christina M. Hanson, Robert Collison, and Robert Shackelton, who graciously permitted me the use of their collections. David Johnson, Robert Bennett, Michael Ponsor, Linda Kaplan—all of Harvard—and Frances Funaro, Sally Hambridge, and Jane Flick—of UCLA—helped to collect materials. Roger Hambridge assisted in various matters, as did several of my colleagues, Marga Contini-Jones, Frank A. Lewis, Evelyn Mohr, Barbara Killian, Claus-Peter Clasen, and Philip Levine. Bernhard Fabian, Michael Baumann, and Rudolf Sühnel helped me obtain documents, especially secondary sources, from Germany, and Elizabeth Weinruth assisted with the translation of Wilhelm Adolf Lindau's essay. John Neubauer helped me explore the possibility of interest in Goldsmith in late eighteenth-century Hungary, as did P. G. Boucé for France.

During the early stages of this project, Walter Jackson Bate encouraged me and gave me the benefit of his vast knowledge of eighteenth-century literature. Arthur Friedman, dean of Goldsmith scholars, shared with me his unrivalled knowledge of Goldsmith and discussed ways of organizing this volume. Professor Mario Praz spent long hours discussing with me Goldsmith's reputation on the Continent, and suggested avenues of exploration.

But my greatest debt remains to my father, who has guided me through many periods of storm and stress, especially when I was 'harnessed to the dull duty of an editor.' I have tried to express some of my debt to him in the dedication.

Los Angeles   G. S. R.

Chronological Table

1730[?]	Born 10 November, probably at Pallas, Co. Wesmeath. Second son of the Rev. Charles Goldsmith who shortly after Oliver's birth moves to Lissoy as curate-in-charge of the parish of Kilkenny West. The year torn away in the entry of Oliver's birth in the family Bible.
ca. 1737–45	Attended the Diocesan School at Elphin and schools at Athlone near Lissoy and Edgeworthstown, Co. Longford.
1745	Admitted to Trinity College, Dublin on 11 June, as sizar.
1747	Death of his father. Oliver publicly admonished on 21 May for his part in a student riot.
1750	Graduated B.A. in February.
1750–2	Fails to be ordained in the Church. Employed as tutor to Flinn family in Co. Roscommon. Makes unsuccessful journeys to Cork, possibly hoping to migrate to America, and to Dublin, intending to study law in London.
1752	Enters University of Edinburgh in September to study medicine.
1754	Leaves Edinburgh about 10 February to study medicine at Leyden University. Remains until early 1755.
1755	Sojourns across Flanders to Paris, through Germany and Switzerland to Italy (Padua, Venice, Florence), returning to England across France. Begins writing *The Traveller* in the summer of this year.
1756	Lands at Dover about 1 February, and travels to London.
1756–7	Works as assistant to an apothecary, as a physician in Southwark (probably at this time applying for a medical degree from Trinity College, Dublin), possibly as a proof-reader in Samuel Richardson's printing-house, and as usher at a boys' school at Peckham, Surrey, run by the Rev. John Milner.

1757   Contributes articles to the *Monthly Review* while living with Ralph Griffiths, its editor and proprietor.

1758   Publication in February of his translation of Jean Marteilhe's *Mémoires d'un Protestant*. He is temporarily back at Peckham in charge of the school. In August he is promised post of civilian physician with the East India Company on the coast of India; but fails to reach his destination when on 21 December does not obtain post as hospital-mate on ship to India.

1759   Starts contributing to Smollett's *Critical Review* in January. Gives up plan of travelling to India when he learns of French victories there. Publishes *An Enquiry into the Present State of Learning in Europe* on 2 April. Henceforth known as 'Dr Goldsmith', and his increasing literary acquaintance soon includes Percy, Smollett, Murphy, Burke, Young, and Johnson. He writes *The Bee* between 6 October and 24 November.

1759–60   Contributes essays to the *Busy Body*, the *Weekly Magazine*, the *Royal Magazine*, the *British Magazine*, and *Lady's Magazine*.

1760   Begins to contribute his 'Chinese Letters' on 24 January to John Newbery's *Public Ledger*, and continues until 14 August 1761. Moves during the summer from Green Arbour Court to No. 6 Wine Office Court, off Fleet Street.

1761   Percy describes meeting with Goldsmith and Johnson. Goldsmith probably meets Joshua Reynolds at this period.

1762   Contributes essays to *Lloyd's Evening Post*, including 'The Revolution in Low Life', concerned with depopulation. The 'Chinese Letters' published in book form as *The Citizen of the World* on 1 May. This marked the virtual end of Goldsmith's journalistic period and the beginning of his career as compiler and hack-writer, mainly for Newbery.

First printed comment on Goldsmith as an author in Rider's *Historical Account of the Living Authors of Great Britain*. On 14 October *The Life of Richard Nash* published. Collins, a bookseller in Salisbury, buys from Newbery a third share in *The Vicar of Wakefield*.

Johnson instrumental in having Newbery purchase share of *The Vicar* after Goldsmith's arrest brought on by his poverty. Goldsmith, late in the year, moves to Canonbury House, Islington, to live with Newbery.

1764   A founder member of The Club, with Johnson, Reynolds, Burke, Garrick, and others.

On 26 June publishes *An History of England in a Series of Letters from a Nobleman to his Son.*

Moves during September to No. 2 Garden Court in the Temple. Sells his oratorio libretto *The Captivity* to Newbury and Dodsley on 31 October. Publishes on 19 December *The Traveller, or A Prospect of Society.*

1765   On 3 June publishes his *Essays*, collected from earlier publications. Moves to No. 3 King's Bench Walk in the Temple.

1766   On 27 March *The Vicar of Wakefield* published at Salisbury. In December publishes an anthology, *Poems for Young Ladies*, dated 1767.

1767   Friendship grows with Reynolds and his coterie, including Mrs Horneck, a widow, and her two daughters.

Publishes an anthology, *The Beauties of English Poesy.*
Completes his comedy, *The Good Natured Man.*
John Newbery dies in December.

1768   *The Good Natured Man*, produced by Colman and performed at Covent Garden on 29 January.

His brother, Henry, dies in May.

Moves to No. 2 Brick Court in the Temple. Acquires a cottage at Edgware with a friend, Edward Bott.

1769   Contracts to write 'a new Natural History of Animals, etc.' for Griffin.

The Roman History published on 18 May.

Contracts to write a history of England for Davies on 13 June.

Appointed Professor of Ancient History at the Royal Academy.

1770   *The Deserted Village* published by Griffin on 26 May.
His *Life of Parnell* prefixed to edition of Parnell's *Poems.*
He journeys to Paris with the widow Horneck and daughters from July to early September.

Writes *The Haunch of Venison*, addressed to his friend, Lord Clare.

1771 Stays at a cottage near Hyde, writing his *History of England*, and a new comedy.

History of England . . . to the Death of George II published on 6 August.

1772 *Threnodia Augustalis* performed on 20 February.

Bladder infection causes serious illness.

1773 Contributes essays on the theatre, and other articles to the *Westminster Magazine* from January to March.

On 15 March, *She Stoops to Conquer* produced by Colman at Covent Garden.

Completes first volume of *Grecian History* by 22 June.

1774 Garrick's satiric epitaph on Goldsmith read during meeting of club at St James's Coffeehouse prompts latter to write *Retaliation*, unfinished at his death.

On 25 March, seriously ill with kidney trouble.

Dies at the Temple on 4 April.

Retaliation posthumously published on 19 April.

History of the Earth, and Animated Nature posthumously published on 1 July.

Abridged *History of England* posthumously published on 2 July.

Grecian History posthumously published on 15 July.

1776 Johnson's Latin epitaph placed on monument by Nollekens erected in Westminster Abbey.

The Haunch of Venison posthumously published.

'Whether, indeed, we take him as a poet,—as a comick writer,—
or as an historian, he stands in the first class.'

Boswell, *Life of Johnson*,
30 April 1773

Introduction

Goldsmith's critical heritage is neither fruitful nor sanguine. It has preoccupied itself so consistently with the author's personal weaknesses and so triflingly with his strictly literary attainments, that one wonders —especially an editor—whether the 'heritage' is worth compiling. Throughout my search for relevant materials I continued to hope that enough documents would present themselves to make the arduous road worth travelling. But as I compiled, it became painfully clear that Goldsmith-the-writer, as opposed to the 'other Goldsmiths' (the pauper, the unlucky Irishman, the down-trodden hack), had attracted a paucity of thinkers: Goethe, Johnson, Scott, Thackeray, Hunt— a handful of important names but not nearly enough to constitute a tradition, a school, and, much less, a genuine 'critical heritage.' The scarcity of important criticism was so overwhelming that I could not help believe, in advance as it were, that those reviewers who would savage me, would have good reason. Other volumes in this series had already experienced a sad fate at the hand of reviewers,[1] despite the fact that the critical heritage of their authors had been much more impressive than Goldsmith's.

In one area alone could I find encouragement: Goldsmith's critical heritage proved, once again, that criticism essentially subserves the tides of taste, and will never achieve the rank of pure science.[2] If certain Victorians, for example, thought long and hard about Goldsmith's writings, they nevertheless did not think as we do today: their values, emphases, and sense of greatness in English literature were altogether different. This is stated not to derogate from their achievement but to note that their thinking will not satisfy us, nor vice versa. Early reviewers of Goldsmith's works satisfied their audiences as did his critics in the Regency, Victorian and Edwardian epochs, but this will not do for us. The fact that all this criticism combined must be rejected by us today as gossip, persiflage, and anecdotal scandal lends further credence to the old quip that each age seeks only to satisfy itself, and shows no concern for subsequent ages. Take this often-quoted statement by Sir Walter Scott:[3]

We read *The Vicar of Wakefield* in youth and in age—We return to it again and again, and bless the memory of an author who contrives so well to reconcile us to human nature. Whether we choose the pathetic and distressing incidents of the fire, the scenes at the jail, or the lighter and humorous parts of the story, we find the best and truest sentiments enforced in the most beautiful language; and perhaps there are few characters of purer dignity [who] have been described than that excellent pastor, rising above sorrow and oppression, and labouring for the conversion of those felons, into whose company he had been thrust by his villainous creditor.

It was deemed brilliant in his own time and repeated again and again by Goldsmith's critics as an *aperçu* worthy of emulation. Today it would probably be marked in red pencil by some house editor who would ask for historical evidence, factual support, footnoted documentation, and a less rhetorical manner (we live in an anti-Carlylean age in which 'overwriting' is the greatest vice).

As I concluded my editorial work on this volume, I persuaded myself that the task had not been in vain, no matter what the reviewers would say. Several aspects, after all, were clear: (1) only a half dozen, or so, items in this volume say anything significant about Goldsmith's writing; (2) such scarcity of significant utterance must confirm a slightly different point of view from the one this series (i.e., *The Critical Heritage*) has espoused, namely, that this heritage is worth preserving *because* it embraces great criticism; on the contrary, it is important to preserve because it proves, however laboriously, that criticism is really in its infancy—that we are just beginning to ask the right questions and posit partial solutions; (3) finally, it became clear as I waded through hundreds of documents that repetition was the greatest sin: so firm was this conviction that I have omitted whole documents that one might otherwise expect to find in a reference book of this nature, on grounds of repetition.[4] It is better to spare the inquiring reader from tedium than satisfy the demands of some pedantic reviewer that each and every document pertaining to Goldsmith, whether original or not, be included. Such avid Goldsmithians could quench their thirst by combing the *New Cambridge Bibliography of English Literature* and by index-hunting, but they would turn up nothing fresh, nothing original, nothing that has not been said here; and the sorry state (sorry from our vantage in this decade) is that truly original thinking about Goldsmith has been limited to the handful of names mentioned above. This volume, therefore, could certainly have been abbreviated further, but it would not under that treatment satisfy the demands of the series.

At the heart of the problem—and it *is* a problem—lies Goldsmith's life. Virtually every critic believed it was tragic and wished to pause, ponder, and meditate on this tragedy. Poor and rich alternately, a victim of booksellers and jealous rivals, and dead by the tender age of about forty-four, Goldsmith-the-man has interested critics more than Goldsmith-the-writer. And authors writing about Goldsmith have deemed it necessary to commiserate with his sufferings, to weep for his untimely demise, and to shed a tear at his memory. Upon regaining their composure and dismissing their nostalgia, these very critics have attacked Goldsmith for not writing more prolifically, for indulging so heavily in ephemeral writing and periodical literature, and for not pursuing his greatest forte, poetry. Goldsmith's critical heritage thus displays a truly schizoid nature: his critics have been overly sentimental about his *life* (there have been sadder lives by far: Chatterton, Mozart, Keats, Rimbaud) and unrealistically harsh about his *writings*. If they had considered the disparity of their angles of vision regarding his life and writings, they would have undoubtedly concluded that they had been unjust. Statements such as the following one by Goethe are rare and separated by long intervals of time:[5]

The delineation of this character [the vicar] on his course of life through joys and sorrows, and the ever increasing interest of the plot, by the combination of what is quite natural with the strange and the wonderful, make this romance one of the best which has ever been written; besides this, it has the great superiority of being quite moral, nay, in a pure sense, Christian, for it represents the reward of good intentions and perseverance in the right, it strengthens an unconditional confidence in God, and asserts the final triumph of good over evil, and all this without a trace of cant or pendantry. The author was preserved from both of these by an elevation of mind that shows itself throughout in the form of irony, by reason of which this little work must appear to us as wise as it is amiable. The author, Dr. Goldsmith, has without question great insight into the moral world, into its strength and its infirmities; but at the same time he may thankfully acknowledge that he is an Englishman, and reckon highly the advantages which his country and nation afforded him.

No one since 1766 has been more profoundly stirred by *The Vicar of Wakefield* than Goethe, and at the heart of this enthusiasm, expressed in a letter to his friend Zelter, lies Goldsmith's ironic way of seeing things. As Goethe himself says:

The influence Goldsmith . . . exercised upon me, just at the chief point of my development, cannot be estimated. This high, *benevolent irony* [italics mine], this just and comprehensive way of viewing things, this gentleness to all opposition, this equanimity under every change, and whatever else all the kindred virtues may be termed,—such things were a most admirable training for me, and surely, these are the sentiments, which in the end lead us back from all the mistaken paths of life.

This perception is truly keen, and exciting as well. Recently, an American critic, Professor Robert Hopkins, wrote a full-length study[6] devoted to Goldsmith's ironic mode, especially the satiric element present in much of his writing. Such a work, like Goethe's brief comment in his autobiography, heralds a breakthrough in Goldsmith's critical heritage: it looks at writings and tries not to indulge in moral weeping over a tragic life.[7] One may not agree with its conclusions, but nevertheless it tackles the problem sensibly, unlike most of Goldsmith's critics.

Another huge stumbling block is Goldsmith's 'age,' the most hated of all epochs in literary history by the nineteenth century. And since Goldsmith's critical heritage must necessarily deal with the period 1780–1880, it is impossible for this dislike to be overlooked. Nowhere does this distaste for the 'Age of the Wits' loom larger than in the writings of Goldsmith's Victorian biographers, James Prior, John Forster, and Lord Macaulay, but it is also evident in the argument of commentators like George Craik, Leigh Hunt, George Lewes, and David Masson. 'Literature and the writing of literature was then in a sorry state,' says one of these commentators, and this remark could aptly express the thinking of all these Victorian commentators. This estimate should come as no surprise: Matthew Arnold called Goldsmith's epoch an 'Age of Prose,' and Frederic Harrison, Arnold's disciple, who is the last author included in this volume, restates the position with especial attention to Goldsmith:[8]

It was essentially the age of prose . . . Its imaginative genius spoke in prose and not in verse. There is more poetry in the *Vicar of Wakefield* than in the *Deserted Village*, in *Tom Jones* than in Pope's *Iliad*, and the death of Clarissa Harlowe is more like Sophocles than the death of Addison's Cato. The age did not do well in verse . . .

How can critics with a bias of such distorted proportions assess the writings of Goldsmith, especially his poetry? If the entire epoch was foredoomed to an 'Age of Prose,' then it follows, as Arnold and Harrison contend, that its poetry was prosaic. QED. We should therefore expect the largest number of Goldsmith's critics to assault his poetry on one ground in particular, its prosaicness, and this tallies

4

precisely with what we discover. But not only the poetry of Goldsmith's epoch suffered at the hands of nineteenth-century critics. Every form of literature was discredited, the novel perhaps least of all, and authors themselves (Johnson, Boswell, Goldsmith, Sterne) were viewed as unreal persons writing as machines for a larger machine, Grub Street. There was little, if any, attempt to understand the social milieu in which Goldsmith and his contemporaries wrote, and most critics tended to view the epoch as limited to writers' feuds, jealousies, and embroglios.

The third and final impediment hindering a balanced view of Goldsmith involves the variety of 'literary kinds' or genres in which he composed. Again and again, one finds in his critical heritage bewilderment about his achievement in each genre: poetry, drama, the novel, essays, history, philosophy, and so on. One reads repeatedly that he, after Johnson, was the most versatile author of the age, and that few authors could distinguish themselves in so many genres as did Goldsmith. Pope, the argument goes, wrote poor prose and never attempted the drama, while Fielding and Sterne were no poets. Smollett may have explored all genres but he never soared, it is supposed, in any. And Boswell, however perfect his memoirs and *Life of Johnson*, never assumed the role of the muse of poetry or the sock. Johnson alone remains Goldsmith's peer, and while one might believe this a valid reason for a strong critical heritage, just the opposite is the case. Most critics, whether rightly or not, found it impossible to equate Goldsmith as Johnson's peer,[9] and once this conclusion was reached, they set about to differentiate among the various genres in which Goldsmith wrote. In other words, if a critic could show that Goldsmith's poetry was mediocre, and that his plays were pedestrian, he (the critic) could still contend that *The Vicar of Wakefield* was the greatest novel ever written without any scruples about Goldsmith and Johnson as peers. I labor this point not to note the obvious (Goldsmith did write in almost all known literary genres yet remains a lesser writer than Johnson), but to assert my belief that if Goldsmith and Johnson had not been contemporaries, had not been close literary friends and members of the same literary club, Goldsmith's critical heritage might have fared better.[10]

These pronounced tendencies—concern with Goldsmith's life, confusion in view of his diversity in writing, constant comparison with Johnson—resulted in a paltry critical heritage. Though Johnson, Burke, Scott, and Thackeray highly praised Goldsmith's writing, the same cannot be said of numerous other great authors who wrote criticism during 1780–1880. Carlyle, in an essay on Goldsmith, had a few words of praise for him,[11] yet most of his contemporaries remained silent. The early Romantic poets viewed Goldsmith as the last member of the 'School of Pope,' but few took his poetry seriously. Keats uttered one, solitary, brief remark to Fanny, 'I think you will like Goldsmith'[12] (meaning his poetry), and Coleridge had a favourable word for *The Vicar of Wakefield* only. Shelley said nothing and one can accurately predict that Blake's opinion of Goldsmith (had he uttered one), would have been a sequel to his 'Mock on Voltaire.' Byron was amused at Schlegel's high estimate of *The Vicar*[13], but nothing more than amused, as evidenced by his failure to write anything to express his own view. The French and German reception of our author is not far different from that of the English. A large number of inferior critics and translators, many romantically inspired by all things British, sang Goldsmith's praises as they had extolled Richardson and Fielding before him; yet in contrast, a minuscule part of the genuinely influential critics (Schlegel, Herder, Goethe), gave him their staunch support. And in such fashion, Goldsmith's critical heritage plodded on: attracting some renowned English and European literary critics but repelling most. Still sadder, in a sense, is an aspect of his critical heritage that is less tangible than the one described in this volume; it is the absence of influence of Goldsmith's writings on other writers. There are however two outstanding exceptions worthy of mention.

We note first the rather unique reception of *The Vicar of Wakefield* and its influence on such novelists as Jane Austen, George Eliot, and Henry James; and secondly, the effect of Goldsmith's two descriptive landscape poems, *The Traveller* and *The Deserted Village*, on subsequent landscape poets (frequently of greater stature than Goldsmith), Wordsworth, Crabbe, Arnold, and even some early nineteenth-century American poets.[14] While both influences are subtle and often elusive, they are evident. In some instances, such as George Eliot's conception of narrative art in prose or Henry James's sense of first person narrative and tone in fiction, the influence is relatively easy to demonstrate. But in other cases, for example, the influence of Goldsmith's poetry on Wordsworth's landscapes, or the effect of Goldsmith's prose style on Jane Austen's, such demonstration is difficult, if not impossible. I shall discuss these topics at greater length in connection with individual works by Goldsmith, even though such aspects of Goldsmith's critical heritage must play a smaller role than the critics' statements themselves.

Finally, a word must be said about the evolution of Goldsmith's critical heritage. His reputation as an author reached its zenith in the 1820s. Before that, too little time had elapsed since his death in 1774 to permit critics to know their own minds, and so their appraisals were often impulsive. After the 1820s his renown slowly began to decline, slowly proceeding downhill throughout the Victorian era with but a few exceptions,[15] and reaching its nadir in the 1880s, as may be gleaned from Frederic Harrison's observations.[16] My decision to end this volume basically in the 1880s was not arbitrary; it was instead a calculated judgment that this century of criticism (1780–1880) has very clearly delineated and encompassed his rise and fall. Harrison's later observations on Goldsmith, published in 1912, are included because they express a positive note on which to end the book and because they reveal the schizoid thinking, mentioned earlier, of the Victorians:[17]

In all English prose, no one to my mind can beat Goldsmith. I take *The Vicar of Wakefield* to be the high-water mark of English . . . To me dear 'Goldie' is the Mozart of English prose—the feckless, inspired ne'er-do-well of eighteenth-century art . . .

Not an exceptionally astute comment but one well worth including. Harrison, like so many of his Victorian contemporaries, did not change his mind about Goldsmith: contrarily, he firmly adhered to the view that the eighteenth century was an 'Age of Prose' and that Goldsmith, consequently, could not have soared in poetry. But Harrison's comment of 1912 is merely an addendum, a grace note, and ought not to be construed as part of the time span of the critical heritage set forth here. But if Goldsmith's critical heritage *were* extended beyond the 1880s, one would readily see that his fame had not risen much above the nadir point. No doubt, it has risen to a degree: witness the editorial care lavished on him in this century by Arthur Friedman, and the fascination that continued throughout his life to grip R. S. Crane, one of the greatest scholars of our times, for all Goldsmith's works. These, however, are isolated cases and are atypical of Goldsmith's general reception since the 1880s. Those in the literary world know, after all, that scholarly evaluation cannot be counted on as an accurate gauge of an author's reputation. The most obscure writers of the past have in this century been dredged up as the subject of forlorn doctoral dissertations; and arcane authors, never before heard of, have suddenly been called great writers by certain scholars. But an assessment of Goldsmith by a critic of repute has been as rare as the discovery of a Hope diamond. Such men as Yeats, Eliot, Pound, F. R. Leavis, Georg Lukács, R. P. Blackmur, and a few continental critics have offered little or nothing. No promethean revaluations and recantations, as Eliot on Milton, and even when a prominent critic like Eliot *has* spoken out, his utterance still bears the vestiges of the old Arnoldian view of the eighteenth century as an 'Age of Prose.' 'Of Goldsmith and Johnson,' writes T. S. Eliot, 'we can say the same; their verse is poetry partly because it has the virtues of good prose.'[18] And when Eliot tells in the same essay of Goldsmith's originality, he speaks so half-heartedly, using so many clichés and worn phrases, critical tags empty of meaning, that one cannot take seriously his brief pronouncement:[19]

The originality of Goldsmith as a poet consists in his having the old and the new in such just proportion that there is no conflict; he is Augustan and also sentimental and rural without discordance. Of all the eighteenth-century poets, Goldsmith and Johnson deserve fame because they used the form of Pope beautifully, without ever being mere imitators. And from the point of view of the artisan of verse, their kind of originality is as remarkable as any other: indeed, to be original with the minimum of alteration is sometimes more distinguished than to be original with the maximum of alteration.

Once again the tattered comparison of Goldsmith and Johnson, and the oft repeated remark that Goldsmith was of the School of Pope. Would Eliot himself believe this precept about greatness and alteration? Who are the great poets with 'minimum of alteration'? Wordsworth, for example, is known to have composed verse by building on the lyricists of the age before his (1750–90), by studying the poetry of Gray, Collins, Goldsmith, and Cowper; but he was still a great innovator in form, still altered the poetic mold of his predecessors by radically injecting new intellectual content and revising their whole notion of poetry itself. Even Eliot-the-poet fundamentally altered, turned away from Swinburne and his contemporaries, and found his voice by consulting unusual sources, at once classical, mythical, philosophical, anthropological, and religious. Could Eliot-the-critic say of Eliot-the-poet that he deserved fame because he used the form of Hardy or Hopkins or D. H. Lawrence, 'without being a mere imitator'? Emphatically not, but he states this mindless observation about Goldsmith in relation to Pope and seems to believe in its absolute validity. Eliot's comment serves as an example of Goldsmith's 'second critical heritage' from 1880 to the present—one that is not much more inspiring or perceptive than that of the first hundred years of criticism nor which rescues from near obscurity its maligned victim.

I

The Vicar of Wakefield

Unquestionably *The Vicar* has been considered Goldsmith's greatest work virtually from the date of its publication in 1766 until the end of the Victorian epoch; and every modern critic knows that it has been an enduring source of European pathos. Some critics have even regarded it as the finest novel in the language, as evidenced in the passage by Frederic Harrison cited above. Inasmuch as this work, in the eyes of most critics, surpasses all his others by so vast a margin, it behooves me to explicate its lure. Dr Johnson, one of its earliest appraisers, did indeed believe it would not have much success: 'No, madam,' he told Fanny Burney,[20] 'it is very faulty; there is nothing of real life in it, and very little of nature.' But Johnson's view was pure bias from the outset: his previous attacks on fiction, especially romance, were *prima facie* evidence of his aversion to this type of literature. However, it was Henry James at the other end of the critical heritage, rather than Johnson who expressed the preponderant view, and did so most eloquently in a short introduction to a new edition of *The Vicar*. He approached the novel with a hushed sense of mystery and awe, maintaining that its success was 'a mystery and a riddle.'[21] While James had absolutely no doubt about its being a masterpiece, his reservations betray only mild complaint. In all, his judgment is overwhelmingly positive, even to the extent of rapture: 'it has succeeded by incomparable amenity'; 'the spoiled child of our literature'; 'the tone is exquisite and that's the end of it'; 'the frankness of his sweetness and the beautiful ease of his speech'; 'optimism of the purest water'; etc. James's search for metaphors to describe the incomparable beauty of this miracle of prose fiction ends on a skeptical note: 'criticism does not get near the thing at all.' Why not? James provides no clue. He knows what he knows and understands only so much; and when we recall that his essay is merely an introduction to a new edition of *The Vicar*, we must be grateful for whatever pittance is thrown our way. James's remark represents no hardened view; he would have been the first to modify his rhapsodic tone and caution the reader about his overstatements. Nevertheless, it is representative of nineteenth-century critics.

Criticisms uttered in the interval between Johnson and James reveal no consistent or predictable pattern, except that there has been more praise than blame. Its first reviewers were puzzled, could not understand its literary form or rhetorical mold. While the anonymous *Monthly* reviewer exercised caution by listing merits and defects,[22] the *Critical* reviewer was less favourable, charging Goldsmith with a lack of 'variety in his characters,' a dearth of satire, and an improbable plot, especially 'the passing of the catastrophe.' But other critics expressed no such censure. Lady Sarah Pennington, that willowy universal mother advising all the Pamelas alive, forebade her own daughters from reading 'romances' but broke her rule with *The Vicar* because that novel alone is 'equally entertaining and instructive.'[23] Other Bluestockings were equally impressed, although their degree of excitement varied: Jane West viewed it as a sort of moral *vade mecum* and Clara Reeve found in it a perfect balance of 'great merits and great faults.'[24] Edward Mangin adored its genteel satire, praised its 'true sensibility,' and predicted that it would be 'understood as long as the [English] language is read.'[25] Throughout the Regency and Victorian periods one discovers critics vacillating between enraptured praise and mild approbation. Some, like Hazlitt,[26] were brief and insipid in their comments; others like George Craik,[27] reflected serious thinking and wrote profusely upon it. A few must be counted as anomalies, since their ideas are either too eccentric to be credited or too erroneous to be taken seriously. An example is Henry Crabb Robinson's indictment of first-person narrative in *The Vicar* on grounds that it is unsuitable to self-disclosure. This is an obtuse judgment of the first order. What could be more appropriate to the vicar's tale, or Moll Flanders' for that matter, than first-person narrative? Perhaps one expects mindless observations from a Robinson, but, alas, instances of men of intelligence who likewise disappointed their readers, also prevail. Carlyle couldn't get aroused by this work and called it 'the best of all Idyls . . . but nothing more,'[28] and Thackeray, who often rose to critical perspicuity, when writing about *The Vicar* consulted his frailest emotions without also consulting his deepest intelligence. Even Washington Irving, whose essay on the novel remains among the lengthiest, had nothing new to say.

In contrast, Goethe, Leigh Hunt, George Eliot, and, of course, Henry James have enhanced the critical fortunes of *The Vicar*. All four were excited by Goldsmith's sweetness of tone, perfect morality, simplicity of prose style, pathetic suffering of his characters, and—emphatically contravening Johnson's opposite view—his fidelity to nature as it really is. Later, the German romanticists of the mid and late nineteenth century were to allude to *The Vicar* as an example of the philosophy of things as they really are, *wie es eigentlich gewesen*, but they rarely wrote *about The Vicar*.[29] The four authors just mentioned all aimed at a description of these five rare qualities they believed Goldsmith to possess. He was unique in this regard, they believed, and their judgment was cushioned by wide reading in eighteenth-century prose. Hunt can be called a common spokesman for all. He considered Goldsmith the most consummate prose stylist of the Georgians and a man 'vain of his genius.'[30] Dwelling on the 'apparent unconsciousness . . . which afterwards proved to be Goldsmith's best originality' in *The Vicar*, he focused his intelligence on questions of tone, plot, prose rhythm: 'in no novel is there an assemblage of characters so equally natural'; 'the morality is unexceptional'; 'domestic pathos'; 'dry simplicity of style'; 'a perfectly elegant prose style to be aimed at'; 'this end [i.e., union of the elegant and the vigorous] seems to have been attained more nearly by Goldsmith than by any single writer.'

Hunt, like the other three critics mentioned, believed in Goldsmith's absolute uniqueness in *The Vicar*; and in every stylistic category he examined, Hunt discovered his basic assumption buttressed. The plot was unlike any other plot (i.e., Richardson, Fielding, Sterne, Smollett): it was fable aspiring to the status of myth. *The Vicar* is considerably shorter than other novels, he noticed, and its sentences so pure and simple, that they typify Wordsworth's demand, in the Preface to the *Lyrical Ballads*, for language understood by the common man. Goldsmith's 'sweetness of tone' especially excited his best critics, although they were vague about its role in the book. It pervades the whole work and seems intrinsically tied to the vicar's religious character, they maintained; it was *au fond* a religious, almost metaphysical, type of *sweetness*, contributing to the idyllic ambience of *The Vicar* in much the same way as shades of light influence the picturesque paintings of David or Caspar Friedrich. The Victorians, unlike Dr Johnson, were sensitive to this moral *sweetness* of tone and fully credited its author for discovering it. The novels and romances of Goldsmith's contemporaries appeared colorless by contrast, and they certainly failed to create the pastoral, idyllic world of Wakefield. Thus, there was a tendency, but no more, to view *The Vicar* as part of the tradition of prose idyll and even poetic pastoral; to locate it as an analogue to such works as Marlowe's *The Passionate Shepherd* and Burns's realistic narrative *The Cotter's Saturday Night*. Victorian and Edwardian emphasis on this tonal sweetness usually excluded any focus on the vicar's Jobian qualities, on his moral determination and almost naive religious tenacity, on the varieties of his exile. It would be interesting to learn what Blake, himself a commentator on *The Book of Job*,[31] would have said about Dr Primrose's Jobian traits—Blake's successors in the nineteenth century were unconcerned; not one noted the parallel.

Finally, something must be said about Goldsmith's satirical impulses in *The Vicar* for his critical heritage speaks out clearly on the subject. His contemporaries found no satire, as the early reviews printed in this volume reveal.[32] They were impressed with it as an attempt to elevate the status of prose fiction and refine the dubious morality reflected in the narratives of his contemporaries. Those critics at the turn of the nineteenth century who still revered primitivistic narratives and wallowed in idyllic pastoral landscapes, concentrated on Goldsmith's faithfulness to Nature, at least one version of it. They were charmed by his local expressiveness and picturesque descriptions. But no intimation of a satiric intention on Goldsmith's part entered their writing. Even in the nineteenth century critics such as James Prior (Goldsmith's first Victorian biographer) and Leigh Hunt, failed to note the presence of satire. True, Goethe, perhaps Goldsmith's most understanding student, discovered at the heart of *The Vicar* a 'high, *benevolent irony*,'[33] but the emphasis here is clearly on Goldsmith's magnanimous loftiness, on his munificent benevolence and certainly not on his will to lash the often naive, and seemingly idiotic, parson, as some twentieth-century critics assert to be the case for Swift in Book IV of *Gulliver's Travels*.[34] Goldsmith-the-harsh-satirist is unknown to the critics in the heritage studied here, i.e., 1780–1880. To these authors, ranging from Johnson to George Eliot and Henry James, such a reading of *The Vicar* would be perverted and would introduce an element virtually absent in any sizeable degree in this book. The story of how *The Vicar* metamorphosed into a satiric attack on parsonical naïveté must be told elsewhere;[35] in any case it occurred after the time limit set here and plays no part whatsoever in early criticism of *The Vicar*.

However great Goldsmith's prose fiction was thought to be, there existed sharp criticism of it and it would be inappropriate to leave the reader without mentioning at least one or two. The attacks were almost always by minor critics with picayunish minds that had no sense of poetic license or fictive liberty. A perfect example is George Craik,[36] a man of limited intelligence and less imagination whose criticism usually balanced strengths and weaknesses in order to arrive at a fair conclusion. While he conceded that *The Vicar* is 'our first genuine novel [i.e., in English] of domestic life,' he also stressed the contradictions, absurdities, and inconsistencies of the story. I suppose some twentieth-century critics[37] would construe this emphasis as an inchoate form of their own view of *The Vicar* as a satire, but close reading of Craik shows no such profundity of insight. 'Finally,' Craik concludes his essay, 'the humour of the book is all good-humour. There is scarcely a touch of ill-nature or even of *satire* in it from beginning to end—nothing of either acrimony or acid.'[38] Typical of the pedestrian-minded Craik always looking for consistency in narrative detail. 'Never was there a story put together in such an artificial, thoughtless, blundering way,' he maintains. Even George Eliot had been troubled by aspects of Goldsmith's story, especially the relation of the beginning to its middle and end, but she never carped about literal inconsistency. The gray area between an author's intention to satirize and his uncon-scious lapse of fact and narrative consistency, is indeed murky; and perhaps precisely this nebulous area ought to concern Goldsmith's critics in the future; but looking backwards, it received no attention at all and when it was casually consulted, it appears in foolish dress. To most men it seemed perfectly clear, as Goethe wrote, that *The Vicar* 'asserts the final triumph of Good over Evil.' And *sans* satire.

II

GOLDSMITH AS POET

'As a poet, Goldsmith ranks higher than any other English author who has written so little, with the exception, perhaps, of Gray.' Thus wrote Henry Bohn in 1848 in his preface to an edition of Goldsmith's works.[39] An insidious compliment in 'who has written so little'? Not really, Bohn believes that Gray and Goldsmith divide the lion's share among poets of the third rank. Obviously, Goldsmith was no Chaucer or Milton, nor did he write enough to qualify among the second rank of great poets, Spenser, Dryden, Pope, Wordsworth. Bohn's view represents a continuing refrain in Goldsmith's critical heritage: that what he wrote, however little, was most distinguished, that his poetry dealt with the best of many possible topics, and that he would have risen to the status of a genuinely great poet (Spenser or Dryden) if he had written more.

Early in the century of criticism studied here, some attitudes clearly emerged and were repeated numerous times. *The Deserted Village* was thought generally to be a greater poem, more original than *The Traveller*. Goldsmith received *kudos* for writing in the 'School of Pope.'[40] His poetic appeal was believed to lie in the attractiveness of his poetic images (purple passages) rather than in the sheer intellectual force or logical organization of his arguments. Although the 'Hermit' (i.e., *Edwin and Angelina*) received some attention, especially during the first quarter of the nineteenth century, Goldsmith's reputation was firmly made on the two poems just mentioned. Some critics were troubled by questions relating to comparisons between his prose and poetry, i.e., was he a better writer in one or the other and to what extent? Having thoroughly surveyed his critical heritage up to about 1880, one can fairly state that critics of his poetry (John Hawkesworth, John Scott, Edward Mangin, Thomas Percy, Southey, Hazlitt) tend to be not so distinguished in their own reputations as were critics of his prose (Washington Irving, Leigh Hunt, Thackeray, George Eliot, Henry James); but ironically their criticism is often more penetrating. At least there is more agreement about Goldsmith's poetic strengths and weaknesses than in comments about his prose.

Goldsmith's recognition as a considerable poet dates from the point that Johnson told Boswell 'there has not been so fine a poem [as *The Traveller*] since Pope's time.'[41] Some critics during Goldsmith's own lifetime, such as John Langhorne, and others afterwards, John Scott and Edward Mangin, questioned his ideas about luxury within an agrarian society quickly industrializing; still others, like Leigh Hunt, harped continuously on the disparity between his prosaic ideas and poetic language:[42]

If *The Traveller* had been written in prose, or were stripped of its poetical ornament, it would allure no readers at all; and I am afraid that with the same alteration many an argument in Dryden and Pope would share the same fate. The nearer logic is allied to poetry, the faster it loses its strength to the greater power.

But most critics, even those like Hunt in whose thought the Romantic conception of poetry prevailed, agreed on Goldsmith's permanent niche in the pantheon of poetry. He deserved a place in the Hall of Fame, they reasoned, because he chose a mighty theme (the evils of luxury) in both poems and endowed his subject with beautiful poetic images. They liked the fact that he could 'paint' as a descriptive poet,[43] that he looked to Nature for the greatest truths, used images and similes every man could understand, maintained sublime thoughts while stressing the essential importance of moral feelings. 'In descriptive poetry Goldsmith has few superiors,' his first reviewer wrote,[44] and later critics showed, sometimes with good reason, how he had glanced backwards at Addison and learned from Pope. Edmund Burke, admittedly no astute critic of English poetry, maintained that Goldsmith's pastoral images 'beat all Pope and Philips and Spenser too in my opinion.'[45] The opulent pastoral content of both poems was adjudged to be a virtue, not a limitation—not a surprising fact of literary history when we recall the different kinds of revivals of pastoral poetry then (ca. 1780–1830) under way.

Both Goldsmith's poems naturally influenced the course of landscape poetry for about fifty years. As Robert A. Aubin has suggested, it is an influence that may not be terribly exciting nor one that inspired great poetry, but it remains central to the literary history of the English Industrial Revolution:[46]

It is this intrusion of the Industrial Revolution and its problems into the local poet's reflections that particularly distinguishes Goldsmith's poem [The Deserted Village]. Assuming that 'sweet Auburn' stands for Lissoy, county Westmeath (or some other actual locality), we may consider it topographical; as such it consists of an opening salutation to the village, childhood recollections, a vague account of several features of interest, even less definite historical retrospection, the retirement theme, genre pictures, a pronounced personal note, and prolix economic propaganda. Reflective rather than descriptive, it avoids much of the machinery of local poetry and works out from Thomsonian scientific, extroitive wordpainting toward the sentimental afternoon glow of Gainsborough. Chief among Goldsmith's imitators were two ladies. Susanna Blamire, the 'Muse of Cumberland,' constructs 'Stoklewath; or, The Cumbrian Village' on the ideal day scheme with genre scenes galore and . . . the other, Hannah Cowley . . . Mrs. Cowley, who disliked the Industrial Revolution . . . naturally dreaded and indeed deprecated comparison of her poem [Scottish Village; or, Pitcairne Green] with Goldsmith's; but by adopting the form of a dialogue between a Sage and a Genius she partially concealed indebtedness.

The Deserted Village, even more so than The Traveller, inspired better poets than Blamire and Cowley,[47] especially during the period of enclosure of many villages and towns in the first two decades of the nineteenth century. John Clare is perhaps the best example of a good poet clearly imitating Goldsmith, although several lesser topographical poets were also indebted. Clare himself admits that *The Deserted Village* was his model when composing *Helpstone* (1809), a poem about the effects of enclosure; and John Barrell, Clare's most learned student in recent times, affirms that Clare's long poem *The Parish* is also indebted to Goldsmith, although it glances rhetorically at Crabbe.[48] Luxury and the battle against it no less than the theme of exile were subjects that appealed to didactic poets as well as cultural historians and philosophers, and Goldsmith's poems were too central to the heart of the debates about luxury to avoid. If Smollett, who was in 1770 putting the final touches on *Humphry Clinker*, could have read *The Deserted Village*, then just published, there is no doubt he would have agreed with its central thesis about the ill effects of luxury; Smollett's own extensive passages about luxury[49] were probably composed slightly before the year 1770 but he was too much in agreement with Goldsmith to overlook his poems. And others felt the same way, especially landscape poets who studied *The Deserted Village* because it captured the essence of a landscape. 'The poets were influenced,' Barrell has written,[50] 'in the descriptions they made of places, very little by the accidental knowledge they [i.e., the poets] might happen to have about them [particular landscapes], and in particular they had very little sense of what can perhaps be called the "content" of a landscape—I mean they gave little evidence of caring that the topography of a landscape was a representation of the needs of the people who had created it.' But they cared about the *order* of a landscape, and for this they looked repeatedly to Goldsmith. Richard Payne Knight and Uvedale Price, two important theorists, may not have explicitly commented about Goldsmith's two poems, but these men were as aware of their influence on landscape poets as economists were sure that Goldsmith's ideas about luxury had pierced through economic thinking.[51]

But we must remain sober to the totality of late eighteenth-century English poetry, a vast expanse covering much more than topography. Smart, the visionary thinker and writer of religious dreamlike poetry, was to prove a far greater influence on the best future poetry than Goldsmith. Blake, Shelley, and Coleridge had nothing in common with poems like *The Deserted Village*. If Goldsmith's two poems had been satires, the story might be otherwise especially regarding Byron; but Goldsmith was temperamentally no satirist, as Dryden and Pope had been, and he didn't possess the moral gravity to write a *Vanity of Human Wishes*. Temperamentally 'the sad historian of the pensive plain' was a lyricist, in the Wordsworthian sense, deeply imbued with a sense of specific place and setting. But he wrote two poems only, as his early critics noted, and this just wasn't sufficient to establish a reputation of his being anything more than a bard limited in subject matter. Scholars and pedants, the John Scotts, Edward Mangins, and Percival Stockdales,[52] were impressed but they had been equally awed by such dwarfs as Dyer, Shenstone, and Richard Jago. True, Keats later wrote to Fanny, 'I think you will like [his poems].'[53] But he wasn't necessarily emphasizing the Goldsmithian aspect; he may have been talking directly to Fanny about Fanny, i.e., you are the kind of girl who will enjoy that sort of poetry. Nothing, certainly, in the total corpus of Keats's poetry suggests the slightest affinity with Goldsmith's poetry; nor did Keats's colleagues, Byron and Shelley, learn about Nature from Goldsmith. Some critics at the turn of the century noted that Goldsmith, like Milton and Wordsworth, was a 'nature poet' (how could they not?) and that his two poems were similar (thereby elevating them to greatness) to the Lavinia episodes, for example, in *The Seasons*. They further enhanced his distinction by commenting that he modestly displayed 'the general melancholy of moralists,'[54] though not so profoundly or religiously as Johnson in *The Vanity of Human Wishes*.

Lacking in all this praise was significant commentary about Goldsmith's poetic craft. Critics were quick to note how extensively he revised his couplets and how much he was indebted to the 'School of Pope' without following Pope's rhetorical mold, syntactic structures, dense allusiveness, or artificial Latinate inversions. But critics, especially the radical 'New Critics' of the time, Wordsworth, Coleridge, and the German romantic philosophers, discovered nothing original *to poetry*,[55] neither new ideas nor new poetic forms. This was tantamount to their saying that Goldsmith had not innovated, could teach young aspiring poets little, if anything. Later on, in the Victorian age, many critics looked back to Goldsmith as a poet exemplifying the rural bard in a still pastoral landscape, untainted, unperverted by the lure of the big city, still as pure as his vicar. But these critics, almost never poets themselves, said nothing about *The Traveller* or *The Deserted Village* in relation to the evolution of great English poetry—not even in comparison to other great short poems, Gray's *Elegy,* Collins' *Odes,* Crabbe's *Village,* or Wordsworth's *Tintern Abbey.*

By the middle and late Victorian period, the poetic scene had altered and a new type of poetry, meditative, personal, and expressive, was in vogue. Relatively 'conventional' landscapes like Goldsmith's were spurned and the idea of primitivism *sans* luxury found repulsive. Lord Macaulay, arch-Victorian whose poetic sense was never highly developed, lost no opportunity in his brief life of Goldsmith[56] to set the record straight. Gone is the old precept, evident at the turn of the century, that *The Deserted Village* was the finest English poem since *The Dunciad.* And Macaulay, 'shocked by one unpardonable fault which pervades the whole,' gives his reason: 'A poet may easily be pardoned for reasoning ill; but he cannot be pardoned for describing ill, for observing the world in which he lives so carelessly that his portraits bear no resemblance to the originals, for exhibiting as copies from real life monstrous combinations of things which never were and never could be found together.' The charge of *incongruity* and outright *impossibility* ('What would be thought of a painter who should mix August and January in one landscape, who should introduce a frozen river into a harvest scene?') was levelled again and again at Goldsmith, not only by Macaulay but by his contemporaries, especially distinguished professors of literature like David Masson at Cambridge and George Saintsbury at Edinburgh.

Goldsmith-the-poet had fallen, never again to rise, in the twentieth century. His other poems, usually described as versified gossip (it would be farcical here to speak of *major* and *minor*), had never received serious commentary, and the two main ones were now buried forever. Historians of the Industrial Revolution, like J. H. Plumb,[57] and critics of the literature produced by that revolution, like Raymond Williams,[58] have looked at *The Traveller* and *Deserted Village en passant.* But others, poets most of all, have forgotten them, don't read them, and probably never will again.

III

THE DRAMA

Goldsmith's two comedies, *The Good Natured Man* (1768) and *She Stoops to Conquer* (1773), are still read and performed, perhaps enjoyed today more than his prose or poetry. Ironically, they were severely criticized when first viewed, although it was universally understood

INTRODUCTION

that Goldsmith's purpose in writing them was to depose sentimental
comedy from its stronghold. Critics during 1768–75 never wrote
explicitly about the prevalence of sentimental comedy in comparison
to the number of other dramas performed,[59] but they were reasonably
certain about Goldsmith's anti-sentimentalism. Virtually every critic
reviewing the two plays commented on this aspect; in fact, the tradition
soon hardened, and by the turn of the century textbooks and other
guides to the English drama, singled out Goldsmith for his tether in
turning the tide of the prevalent brand of sentimentalism. His own
essay *A Comparison between Laughing and Sentimental Comedy*, published
shortly before *She Stoops to Conquer*, reinforced this view, as did the
writings of others, for example John Pinkerton (Robert Heron) in
Letters of Literature (1785).

Part of Goldsmith's success, early critics wrote, was his *bravura* in
attempting to challenge 'that Monster called sentimental Comedy,'[60]
especially 'considering the strength of the enemy.' In other words he
wasn't receiving accolades for any attainment in dramatic form, as
will become clear in a moment, but for an ingenious idea closer to
intuition than to artistic achievement. If early critics felt impelled to
comment that Goldsmith understood the *vis comica*, they were much
quicker to note that he loathed sentimental comedy of the Hugh Kelly
and Richard Cumberland variety. Goldsmith, they argued, was closest
to Arthur Murphy but he possessed a more highly developed sense of
comic mirth. This native understanding of levity was not apparent in
the loose and faulty structure of *The Good Natured Man* but was very
evident in *She Stoops to Conquer*, and Sheridan's following in Goldsmith's
footsteps, especially in *The Rivals* and *The School for Scandal*, added
weight to Goldsmith's original attempt to stem the false delicacy of
weeping comedies.

Nevertheless, these early critics, most of them used to comedies
inducing either laughter or sentimental weeping, were not terrifically
impressed by Goldsmith's dramatic craft. If *She Stoops to Conquer* had
appeared first, the situation might have been otherwise; *The Good
Natured Man* was, however, a technical failure and the critics viewed
it as such. 'Though we condemn his gen'ral plan,'[61] one began and
another, writing six decades later,[62] could offer only a lukewarm
appraisal. With this play Goldsmith established himself as a dramatist
and his reviewers did not forget their ominous predictions when he
brought out his second play five years later. 'Most of the incidents are
offenses against nature and probability,' the highly irritated William

Woodfall wrote,[63] and then lamented the shame of it all because Goldsmith was, after all, talented. The anonymous author of the *Critical Review* was no more receptive, nor was the aristocratic Horace Walpole who found it 'the lowest of all farces' and bellowed from Strawberry Hill that 'what disgusts me most, is that though the characters are very low, and aim at low humour, not one of them says a sentence that is natural or marks any character at all.'[64] During the spring of 1773 and throughout the next calendar year the newspapers continued to debate the essential questions: whether the play was a comedy or farce; whether it violated the unities; the efficacy of its incongruous characters (an old lady setting out on a forty-mile journey in the middle of the night); the inconsistency of some minor details; the manners depicted.

Johnson, that arbiter of taste, had liked it from the outset[65] and maintained, unlike the jealous Colman the Elder, that he knew 'of no comedy for many years that has so much exhilarated an audience, that had answered so much the great end of comedy.'[66] This view eventually prevailed, and even critics like Sir Joshua Reynolds who were put off by its 'coarseness,' came round to applauding it. Decades later, in the first half of the nineteenth century, the status of comedy altered and Goldsmith, like Congreve and Farquhar before him, was appreciated for his dramatic achievement, although dissenters from this view existed. One of them, Henry Neele, admitted that Goldsmith's comedies were 'the greenest spots in the Dramatic waste of the period,' but he could say nothing good about Goldsmith's contemporaries in *Lectures on English Poetry* (1827) and maintained no critical theories about Goldsmith's plays. Moving ahead in time, one can't expect the Victorians to have cherished this play as they enjoyed Shakespeare's comedies or those of the Greeks; indeed it was not until the last quarter of the century that comedy came back into its own; but they still continuously performed it along with six or seven other masterpieces of comic literature and thought of it as a permanent part of the comic repertory. In this century, with its penchant for Aristophanic and Plautine farcical moods, it has been among the most popular plays in the theatre.

IV

CONCLUSION

Goldsmith's other works require no comment in this brief sketch of his heritage. His periodical literature, *The Bee*, *The Citizen of the World*, especially his 'Chinese Letters' included in the latter, remain interesting primarily to eighteenth-century specialists. It is naturally exciting to explore his prose style in these occasional pieces in relation to previous authors writing in a similar vein, Addison in the *Spectator*, and to such later writers as appeared in Griffiths' *Monthly Review*. But space does not permit such luxury in a volume devoted to Goldsmith's best known works. Nor can much be said about his role in the history of other subjects: literary patronage, authors 'to be let,' writing as a professional occupation, his almost uncanny sense of vocation in the field of letters, and, of course, his role as a hack in Grub Street, or as one modern scholar has called it, in that most fascinating of eighteenth-century 'subcultures.'[67] Moreover, it would be enlightening to explore Goldsmith's 'other' critical heritages: the statements of painters and art critics, especially during the fifty years after his death, regarding the possible influence of his poetry on English landscape painting;[68] Regency and Victorian historians on his hackneyed histories of Greece, Rome, and England, so quickly tossed off by their author; scientists, like John Aikin,[69] on Goldsmith-the-naturalist and as the author of *A History of the Earth and Animated Nature*; and his views on luxury and mercantilism within the history of economic theory, Adam Smith to Ricardo and Marx.

Levin L. Schücking, a German sociologist of literary taste, has commented on Goldsmith's almost unique role in the history of the liberation of writers.[70] Such a perspective perhaps suggests some new avenues of approach for future investigation. One aspect about Goldsmith's past, however, is clear: he pleased thousands of readers with relatively few works, *The Vicar of Wakefield*, two poems, and *She Stoops to Conquer*. True, these do not add up to a large number and no one would wish to maintain that Goldsmith ranks in the first class of writers, but readers during the century 1780–1880 didn't hold this against him—they were still grateful for having them.

But serious criticism of these four works did not flourish in the century studied here, and has barely subsisted on a mere pittance in this century. We today are just beginning to ask the right questions about these works, questions for example about the secret of Goldsmith's calculated and exquisitely *simple* prose style in *The Vicar* or his curious blend of discriminately selected autobiographical materials and the detached ironic vision found in this book.[71] Let us not assume that the first century of his critical heritage has answered the big and important questions. Without unduly disparaging Goldsmith's early critics, it is fair to say that most of the time they didn't ask questions—with a few exceptions they merely recollected, repeated hearsay, retold anecdotes, and regurgitated what they had heard in school or read in books. As I suggested at the outset, this early critical heritage is neither fruitful nor sanguine, and is herein presented as prime evidence that much remains to be said.

NOTES

1 A good example is the *TLS* review (30 April 1971, p. 500) of R. P. Draper's *D. H. Lawrence* volume (1970), which stirred controversy in their correspondence columns. But there have been many other negative reviews. Unless stated otherwise, the place of publication of all works cited is London.

2 Harry Levin has demonstrated this in his little book *Why Literary Criticism Can Never Be a Science* (Cambridge: Harvard University Press, 1968); however true this is, critics still aspire today towards making it scientific.

3 Scott, *Biographical and Critical Notices of Eminent Novelists* (1827), p. 178. Since most of the critical observations quoted or referred to in this essay appear in the below volume, notes will refer to the number of the *item only* and not to full titles or page references. E.g., the reference in this note is merely No. 70.

4 An example is Thomas Percy's important *Memoir of Goldsmith*, No. 59, which repeats so much of the biographical material appearing during 1775–1800; and for this reason much of it has been omitted. Other examples, listed chronologically, include *Humorous Anecdotes of Dr. Goldsmith* in *Westminster Magazine* (March 1773), Glover's *Authentic Anecdotes* in *Universal Magazine* (May 1774), many short anecdotes printed in the *European Magazine* (1792–1793), a few brief items by William Cooke, Isaac Reed's *Life of Goldsmith* (1795) cribbed from Malone and Davies, John Evans' *Anecdotes of Goldsmith* (1804), R. H. Newell's remarks on *The Deserted Village* published in *Poetical Works of Goldsmith* (1811), R. A. Wilmott's 'Goldsmith and Gray,' in *Church of England Quarterly*, I (1837) and many others. The writings of unknown authors such as Daniel Hayes, James Tytler, Barton Coutts, Philip Parsons, William Tasker and other contemporaries of Goldsmith were combed, but produced no more than one or two brief opinions not worth quoting.

5 See No. 79.

6 Robert Hopkins, *The True Genius of Oliver Goldsmith* (Baltimore: Johns Hopkins University Press, 1969). See also the important review by D. J. Greene in *Studies in Burke and his Time*, xii (1971), 1933–6.

7 In somewhat similar fashion to the New Critics of the 1930s, I. A. Richards, F. R. Leavis *et al.*, although these men seem never to have grown interested in Goldsmith, nor did critics such as Ivor Winters, Allen Tate, or R. P. Blackmur.

8 See No. 86a.

9 For various reasons: he was personally a fool, obnoxious to boot, wrote for the highest bidder, possessed little learning, and had no influence on important dignitaries—so the argument goes. For some modern comparisons, see Ricardo Quintana, *Oliver Goldsmith: A Georgian Study* (New York, 1967), pp. 89–90.

10 Johnson's Club needs revaluation, especially the relation of its members. Hopefully James M. Osborn's forthcoming study will clarify Goldsmith's position within it.

11 See No. 73.

12 See No. 65.

13 See No. 13.

14 For a discussion of these writers as landscape poets and some mention of Goldsmith, see: John Barrell, *The Idea of Landscape and the Sense of Place 1730–1840* (Cambridge, 1972); Edward Malins, *English Landscaping and Literature 1660–1840* (Oxford, 1966); Alan Roper, *Arnold's Poetic Landscapes* (Baltimore: Johns Hopkins University Press, 1969); Leo Marx, *The Machine and the Garden: Technology and the Pastoral Idea in America* (New York, 1964); John Gloag, *Georgian Grace: A Social History of Design from 1660–1830* (1956).

15 E.g., his biographers James Prior and John Forster, who had a vested interest in rescuing Goldsmith, Leigh Hunt, Thackeray, and a few others. De Quincey, for example, could not quite make up his mind, although he seems to have esteemed *The Vicar* (see Françoise Moreux, *Thomas de Quincey: la vie, l'homme, l'oeuvre*, Paris, 1964, p. 402). Bulwer-Lytton, on the other hand, wrote about Goldsmith (*Goldsmith, Miscellaneous Prose Works*, 1868, i, pp. 69–70) as if he had a schoolboy crush; his comments are so gushy and sentimental, so devoid of any analytic incisiveness, as not to be worth reprinting even if they were written at greater length. But most Victorian critics, like George Lillie Craik (see No. 78) and Allan Cunningham (*Biographical and Critical History of the British Literature of the Last Fifty Years*, Paris, 1834), were disparaging. The present volume could have been swelled by including the statements, usually terse but dispraising, by such Victorians as William Spalding, Thomas Arnold, William Rushton, Charles Duke Young, Henry Morley, and W. J. Courthope.

16 See No. 86a.

17 See No. 86b.

18 T. S. Eliot, 'Poetry in the Eighteenth Century,' in Boris Ford (ed.), *From Dryden to Johnson* (1957), iv, p. 273.

19 T. S. Eliot, *ibid.*, iv, p. 272.

20 See No. 48.

21 All quotations in this paragraph from James's essay are found in No. 15.

22 See Nos 5 and 6.

23 See No. 8.

24 See Nos 11 and 10.

25 See No. 26.

26 See No. 46b. Roy Park, *Hazlitt and the Spirit of the Age, Abstraction and Critical Theory* (Oxford, 1971), pp. 175, 188–9, has made a case for Hazlitt's genuine appreciation of Goldsmith's prose that seems overstated to me. Undoubtedly Hazlitt *did* enjoy the sincerity and gusto of eighteenth-century prose from Addison to Goldsmith and Johnson, but it remained little more than detached fondness, never elevating itself to the importance it held, for example, for Goethe. Hazlitt's neat pronouncement about Goldsmith and Johnson is well known: 'Goldsmith was a fool to Dr. Johnson in argument; that is, in assigning the specific grounds of his opinion. Dr. Johnson was a fool to Goldsmith in the fine tact, the airy, intuitive faculty with which he skimmed the surfaces of things' (*Works*, 1930–4, viii, p. 32).

27 See No. 78.

28 See No. 73 and, for Thackeray, No. 83. Thackeray's sentimental rhetoric is captured in nostalgic exclamations: 'Think of him reckless, thriftless, vain if you like—but merciful, gentle, generous, full of love and pity. He passes out of life, and goes to render his account beyond it.'

29 This school of objective historicism was founded by Leopold von Ranke (1795–1886). As L. M. Price has shown in his important study *The Reception of English Literature in Germany* (Berkeley, California, 1932), the Germans responded to Goldsmith's novel more quickly and favourably than other Europeans, but the matter is complicated, on balance, by numerous German romantic critics (Wincklemann, Novalis, Schiller, and many others) who paid no attention at all to *The Vicar*. For further comment on Goethe in Germany, see Carl Hammer, Jr, 'Goethe's Estimate of Oliver Goldsmith,' *JEGP*, xliv (1945), pp. 131–8 and Karl Vietor, 'Goethe, Goldsmith und Merck,' *Jahrbuch des freien Deutschen Hochstiffs*, xxi (1916), pp. 78–94. The pathos which moved the Germans failed to excite the Italians, as Maurice le Breton shows in 'Goldsmith et l'Italie,' *Caliban*, iii (1967), pp. 29–56. The French were quick to translate *The Vicar* (in a popular edition that appeared in 1767), but seemed not to understand it; this is made perfectly clear by the anonymous notes in the first French translation of 1767, *Le Ministre de Wakefield*. Nor does any critical commentary appear in writing in France during 1770–1820—a case almost of oblivion. C. E. Engel finds no interest in Goldsmith in late eighteenth-century Switzerland; see 'English Novels in

Switzerland in the xviii century,' *Comparative Literature Studies*, xiv–xv (1944), pp. 2–8. Nor do I discover any interest in *The Vicar* in Scandinavia. But the illustrations of Goldsmith's novel are an essential part of his critical heritage and ought to be studied, especially those included in the translations mentioned here. This has not been possible here.

30 See No. 80.

31 S. Foster Damon and Andrew Wright have recently written explications of Blake's attitude to the Biblical figure—and these shed light on the point made here. Goldsmith's sweetness impressed several romantics including Robert Southey, who wrote in 1808 to Neville White that 'Goldsmith threw a *sunshine* over all his pictures.'

32 See Nos 5–7, 9, 12.

33 See No. 71. This slippery *irony* has continued to puzzle scholars since the 1820s, although earlier critics never mention it. Some recent studies include: Ricardo Quintana, 'Oliver Goldsmith, Ironist to the Georgians,' in *Eighteenth-Century Studies in Honor of Donald Hyde*, ed. by W. H. Bond (New York: Grolier Club, 1970), pp. 297–310; R. J. Jaarsma, 'Satiric Intent in *The Vicar of Wakefield*,' *Studies in Short Fiction*, v (1968), pp. 331–41, and R. Hopkins, *The True Genius of Goldsmith* (Baltimore, 1969).

34 His supposed ridicule of Gulliver and the Houyhnhnms; see M. P. Foster (ed.), *A Casebook on Gulliver among the Houyhnhnms* (New York, 1961).

35 It has not yet been told, although the position has recently been argued forcefully by Robert Hopkins in *The True Genius of Oliver Goldsmith* (1969). Most nineteenth-century critics, including Austin Dobson in his *Life of Goldsmith* (1888), never dreamed there could be such hidden elements in Goldsmith's *Vicar*; see, for example, Prior's treatment (No. 75): 'The style is peculiarly easy, perspicuous, and simple, free from all attempt at fine writing or ambitious ornament, and without even one of those epigrammatic smartnesses which the apprehension of being considered dull led him occasionally to introduce into his essays.' Oddly enough, none of these critics focused his discussion on Goldsmith's concept of the *family* in *The Vicar*, a somewhat surprising development when one considers the vast changes in family structure underway in Victorian England as a consequence of industrialization. See Peter Laslett, *The World We Have Lost* (1965), index under 'Family, familial relationships.'

36 See No. 78 and the biographical headnote.

37 Hopkins, *Genius of Goldsmith* (1969), has used statements such as these to argue that his interpretation of *The Vicar* as a satire is not absolutely radical.

38 See No. 78.

39 See No. 82.

40 Critics meant by this that he wrote stylized couplets and not the blank verse of Thomson, the sublime Pindarics of Gray and Collins, the didactic poetry of Armstrong and Erasmus Darwin, or the bizarre lyrics of Smart. This lineage was clear, they argued, from Pope to Johnson, Churchill and

Goldsmith. Much recent literature has discussed Goldsmith in this context including: John Arthos, *The Language of Natural Description in Eighteenth-Century Poetry* (Ann Arbor: Michigan, 1949); John Chalker, *The English Georgic* (1969); R. Quintana, '*The Deserted Village*: Its Logical and Rhetorical Elements,' *College English*, xxvi (1964), pp. 204–14; R. J. Griffin, 'Goldsmith's Augustanism: A Study of his Literary Works' (University of California, Berkeley, Doctoral Dissertation, 1965).

41 Boswell, *Life of Johnson*, ed. G. B. Hill, rev. by L. F. Powell (1934), ii, p. 5. Johnson spoke highly of the poem on several other occasions, and even wept on one when reading Goldsmith's character of the English. His critical estimate (see No. 1) glanced backward: 'such is the poem, on which we now congratulate the public, as on a production to which, since the death of Pope, it will not be easy to find anything equal.' If Johnson had written a biography of Goldsmith in his *Lives of the English Poets*, there is no doubt it would contain unconditional encomium. As it is, he wrote praisingly of him in the *Life of Parnell* (*Lives*, ii, p. 49): 'a man of such variety of powers and such felicity of [literary] performance that he always seemed to do best that which he was doing; a man who had the art of being minute without tediousness, and general without confusion; whose language was copious without exuberance, exact without constraint, and easy without weakness.' Johnson wrote this statement after Goldsmith's death, at a time when he could view all Goldsmith's writings in perspective and weigh his total achievement.

42 See No. 80. Elsewhere in his essay, Hunt commented that no poet writing in English had been stylistically so 'unchangeably vigorous,' but he failed to comprehend what Goldsmith's ideas were all about, the old mechanical conception of Nature, the difference among nations, the perils of exile, the evils of wealth, creeping industrialization.

43 See, for example, Prior's comment (No. 75), 'one of the most admirable pieces of poetical painting in the whole range of ancient and modern literature.'

44 See No. 18; attribution is impossible here.

45 See No. 24.

46 Robert A. Aubin, *Topographical Poetry in XVIII-Century England* (New York, 1936), pp. 178–9.

47 A long list of imitations, panegyrics, and similar poems could be compiled but no one has done so as yet.

48 John Barrell, *The Idea of Landscape and the Sense of Place* (Cambridge, 1972), p. 196.

49 See *Humphry Clinker* (1771), Matt Bramble to Dr Lewis, 29 May.

50 Barrell, *The Idea of Landscape and the Sense of Place*, p. 59.

51 Not contemporaries of Goldsmith like Adam Smith, John Brown (*An Estimate . . . of the Times*, 1757), and David Hume but slightly later economic thinkers like Butel-Dumont (*Théorie du luxe*, 1771, preface), Percival

Stockdale (*Three Discourses, Two against Luxury and Dissipation* . . ., 1773), Ricardo, and, much later, J. S. Mill. Some ideas about luxury and anti-luxury in Goldsmith's age are discussed by Raymond Williams in 'Literature and Rural Society,' *Listener*, 16 November 1967, p. 631 and in his book *Culture and Society 1780–1950* (1958), chap. 1.

52 See Nos 24, 25, and Percival Stockdale, *An Enquiry into the Nature and Genuine Laws of Poetry* (1778), pp. 3–11. Such critics were more concerned about their own abilities in analyzing a poem than about the worth of the poem itself. Today, nobody reads their academic exercises in verbal gymnastics.

53 See No. 65.

54 See No. 80.

55 Their vision of the world had undergone a kind of Copernican revolution, especially as a result of works like Kant's *Critique of Pure Reason* (1781) and German philosophers like Schiller and Novalis. One can almost divide English Romantic poets *ca.* 1800–30 into two camps, i.e. according to their reception of poets like Goldsmith. But the problem is that a vast ocean lies between the pronouncements of a poet and the actual ideas he uses. Wordsworth, Coleridge, Keats, Blake, Shelley, Byron; not one of these authors looks to Goldsmith for poetic illumination. Aspects of the changes in poetry from Goldsmith to Wordsworth are described in Paul van Tieghem's *Le Préromantisme* (Paris, 1924–30), especially vol. ii, and Meyer Abrams, *Natural Supernaturalism: Tradition and Revolution in Romantic Literature* (New York, 1971).

56 See No. 84. For the sake of brevity, the Victorian reception of Goldsmith's poetry has been kept to a minimum in this volume, but much more could be included. For example, Thomas B. Shaw's statement in *Outlines of English Literature* (1847), p. 275 and E. A. Duyckinck, *Portrait Gallery of Eminent Men* (1873), i, p. 39.

57 *England in the Eighteenth Century* (rev. ed., Pelican History, 1963), p. 100.

58 *Culture and Society 1780–1950* (1958).

59 Robert D. Hume, 'Goldsmith and Sheridan and the Supposed Revolution of "Laughing" against "Sentimental Comedy," ' *Studies in Change and Revolution*, ed. P. J. Korshin (York: Scolar Press, 1972), pp. 237–76, has recently argued that much less sentimental drama was performed during these years than scholars have thought; and he supports his thesis with statistical evidence from *The London Stage Part IV: 1747–1776*, to the effect that only about 20 percent of the total London performances from 1750 onwards were devoted to sentimental comedies. The problem is surely complicated and depends on the definition of *sentimental*, both then and now. But Hume's sound thesis doesn't change Goldsmith's early dramatic reception one bit—his critics *thought* he thoroughly opposed sentimental comedy and only that matters. Theoretical debates about the role of sentiment in the theater are too well documented to be discussed here.

60 Both phrases appear in No. 28. Many early reviews of *The Good Natured Man* have been omitted on grounds of repetition and in keeping with the general plan of this volume, i.e. to prune repetition as much as possible. I could see no point in the inclusion of nine or ten early reviews which repeat each other, often cribbing from one another. Two prime examples are the unfavorable review in the *Monthly Review*, xxxviii (April 1768), pp. 159–60, in which the anonymous author merely says that the play has faults and does not act well; and an unsigned notice in the *Gentleman's Magazine*, xxxviii (February 1768), pp. 78–80, slightly more favorable and hinting that the characters are admirably drawn. See also *London Magazine*, xxxvii (March 1768), pp. 270–1; *Theatrical Monitor*, xi (6 February 1768); *Lloyd's Evening Post* (10–12 February 1768); *St. James's Chronicle* (28 January–2 February 1768); *European Magazine*, xxiv (March 1793), pp. 94–5; all of which are brief and contribute nothing to Goldsmith's critical heritage about this play.

61 See No. 16.

62 George Daniel, No. 17.

63 See No. 27a.

64 See No. 27b.

65 See No. 47.

66 Boswell, *Life of Johnson*, ii, p. 233. According to Boswell, Johnson also said '[it] borders on farce. The dialogue is quick and gay, and the incidents are so prepared as not to seem improbable.' William Woodfall (No. 27a), taking his cue from Johnson, also commented on the excellence of Goldsmith's dialogue, although he disliked the play in general: 'This [dialogue] is why the Reader must peruse the present Comedy without pleasure, while the representation of it may make him laugh.' For Reynolds, see No. 43; although Johnson esteemed Goldsmith-the-author higher than other members of the Club did, Reynolds understood Goldsmith-the-man best.

67 Pat Rogers, *Grub Street: Studies in a Subculture* (1972).

68 Arnold Hauser, the German art historian, has mentioned Goldsmith in this connection; see *The Social History of Art: Rococo, Classicism, Romanticism* (1951; New York: Vintage Books, 1960), pp. 66, 208.

69 See No. 58 and Aikin's *An Essay on the Application of Natural History to Poetry* (1777). After consulting dozens of scientific works written during the period of Priestley's eminence, *ca.* 1770–1800, I discover that not one of them took seriously Goldsmith's *Animated Nature*.

70 *The Sociology of Literary Taste* (Chicago, 1966), p. 17; Schücking's important work originally appeared in 1923 as *Die Soziologie der literarischen Geschmacksbildung* (Munich).

71 Curiously, no significant psychoanalytic interpretation has been made of *The Vicar*, a surprising development considering the suitability of Goldsmith's life to such treatment. The essays published in Frederick Crews' *Psychoanalysis and Literary Process* (Cambridge: Winthrop, 1970) are an example.

THE TRAVELLER,
OR A PROSPECT OF SOCIETY

December 1764

1. Dr Johnson, *Critical Review*

December 1764, xviii, 458–62

It is fitting, as well as symbolic, that Samuel Johnson should write a review of that work which first put Goldsmith in the public limelight. It is doubly fitting because Goldsmith cultivated the company of Dr Johnson and even copied aspects of his manner. According to Boswell in *The Life of Johnson*: 'He [Goldsmith] had sagacity enough to cultivate assiduously the acquaintance of Johnson, and his faculties were gradually enlarged by the contemplation of such a model. To me and many others it appeared that he studiously copied the manner of Johnson, though, indeed, .upon a smaller scale.'

THE author has, in an elegant dedication to his brother, a country clergyman, given the design of his poem:— 'Without espousing the cause of any party, I have attempted to moderate the rage of all. I have endeavoured to shew, that there may be equal happiness in other states, though differently governed from our own; that each state has a peculiar principle of happiness; and that this principle in each state, particularly in our own, may be carried to a mischievous excess.'

That he may illustrate and enforce this important position, the author places himself on a summit of the Alps, and, turning his eyes around, in all directions, upon the different regions that lie before him, compares, not merely their situation or policy, but those social and domestic manners which, after a very few deductions, make the sum total of human life.

> 'Remote, unfriended, melancholy, slow,
> Or by the lazy Scheld, or wandering Po;
> Or onward, where the rude Carinthian boor
> Against the houseless stranger shuts the door;
> Or where Campania's plain forsaken lies,
> A weary waste expanded to the skies.
> Where'er I roam, whatever realms to see,
> My heart untravell'd fondly turns to thee;
> Still to my brother turns, with ceaseless pain,
> And drags at each remove a lengthening chain.——
> Even now, where Alpine solitudes ascend,
> I sit me down a pensive hour to spend;
> And, plac'd on high above the storm's career,
> Look downward where an hundred realms appear;
> Lakes, forests, cities, plains extended wide,
> The pomp of kings, the shepherd's humbler pride.
> When thus creation's charms around combine,
> Amidst the store, 'twere thankless to repine.
> 'Twere affectation all, and school-taught pride,
> To spurn the splendid things by heaven supply'd.
> Let school-taught pride dissemble all it can,
> These little things are great to little man;
> And wiser he, whose sympathetic mind
> Exults in all the good of all mankind.'

The author already appears, by his numbers, to be a versifier; and by his scenery, to be a poet; it therefore only remains that his sentiments discover him to be a just estimator of comparative happiness.

The goods of life are either given by nature, or procured by ourselves. Nature has distributed her gifts in very different proportions, yet all her children are content; but the acquisitions of art are such as terminate in good or evil, as they are differently regulated or combined.

> 'Yet, where to find that happiest spot below,
> Who can direct, when all pretend to know?
> The shudd'ring tenant of the frigid zone
> Boldly asserts that country for his own,
> Extols the treasures of his stormy seas,
> And live-long nights of revelry and ease;
> The naked Negro, panting at the line,

Boasts of his golden sands and palmy wine,
Basks in the glare, or stems the tepid wave,
And thanks his Gods for all the good they gave.——
　　Nature, a mother kind alike to all,
Still grants her bliss at Labour's earnest call;
And though rough rocks or gloomy summits frown,
These rocks, by custom, turn to beds of down.
　　From Art more various are the blessings sent;
Wealth, splendours, honor, liberty, content:
Yet these each other's power so strong contest,
That either seems destructive of the rest.
Hence every state, to one lov'd blessing prone,
Conforms and models life to that alone.
Each to the favourite happiness attends,
And spurns the plan that aims at other ends;
Till, carried to excess in each domain,
This favourite good begets peculiar pain.'

This is the position which he conducts through Italy, Swisserland,
France, Holland, and England; and which he endeavours to confirm
by remarking the manners of every country.

Having censured the degeneracy of the modern Italians, he proceeds
thus:

'My soul turn from them, turn we to survey
Where rougher climes a nobler race display,
Where the bleak Swiss their stormy mansions tread,
And force a churlish foil for scanty bread;
No product here the barren hills afford,
But man and steel, the soldier and his sword.
No vernal blooms their torpid rocks array,
But winter lingering chills the lap of May;
No Zephyr fondly sooths the mountain's breast,
But meteors glare, and stormy glooms invest.
Yet still, even here, content can spread a charm,
Redress the clime, and all its rage disarm.
Though poor the peasant's hut, his feasts though small,
He sees his little lot, the lot of all;
Sees no contiguous palace rear its head
To shame the meanness of his humble shed;
No costly lord the sumptuous banquet deal
To make him loath his vegetable meal;
But calm, and bred in ignorance and toil,
Each with contracting, fits him to the soil.'

31

But having found that the rural life of a Swiss has its evils as well as comforts, he turns to France.

> 'To kinder skies, where gentler manners reign,
> We turn; and France displays her bright domain.
> Gay sprightly land of mirth and social ease,
> Pleas'd with thyself, whom all the world can please.——
> Theirs are those arts that mind to mind endear,
> For honour forms the social temper here.——
> From courts to camps, to cottages it strays,
> And all are taught an avarice of praise;
> They please, are pleas'd, they give to get esteem,
> Till, seeming blest, they grow to what they seem.'

Yet France has its evils:

> 'For praise too dearly lov'd, or warmly sought,
> Enfeebles all internal strength of thought,
> And the weak soul, within itself unblest,
> Leans for all pleasure on another's breast.——
> The mind still turns where shifting fashion draws,
> Nor weighs the solid worth of self-applause.'

Having then passed through Holland, he arrives in England, where,

> 'Stern o'er each bosom reason holds her state,
> With daring aims, irregularly great,
> I see the lords of human kind pass by,
> Pride in their port, defiance in their eye,
> Intent on high designs, a thoughtful band,
> By forms unfashion'd, fresh from Nature's hand.'

With the inconveniences that harrass the sons of freedom, this extract shall be concluded.

> 'That independence Britons prize too high,
> Keeps man from man, and breaks the social tie;
> See, though by circling deeps together held,
> Minds combat minds, repelling and repell'd;
> Ferments arise, imprison'd factions roar,
> Represt ambition struggles round her shore,
> Whilst, over-wrought, the general system feels
> Its motions stopt, or phrenzy fires the wheels.
> Nor this the worst. As social bonds decay,
> As duty, love, and honour fail to sway,
> Fictitious bonds, the bonds of wealth and law,

Still gather strength, and force unwilling awe.
Hence all obedience bows to these alone,
And talent sinks, and merit weeps unknown;
Till time may come, when, stript of all her charms,
That land of scholars, and that nurse of arms;
Where noble stems transmit the patriot flame,
And monarchs toil, and poets pant for fame;
One sink of level avarice shall lie,
And scholars, soldiers, kings unhonor'd die.'

Such is the poem, on which we now congratulate the public, as on a production to which, since the death of Pope, it will not be easy to find any thing equal.

2. Unsigned notice, *Gentleman's Magazine*

December 1764, xxiv, 594

WE congratulate our poetical readers on the appearance of a new poet so able to afford refined pleasure to true taste as the writer of the *Traveller*: After the crude and virulent rhapsodies upon which caprice and faction have lavished an unbounded praise, that if known to any future time will disgrace the present, it is hoped this poem will come with some advantage, and that a general encouragement of real merit will shew, that we have not totally lost the power to distinguish it.

It is an epistle to Mr *Henry Goldsmith*, the author's brother, from *Switzerland*, and intended to shew that there may be happiness in other states equal to that of our own, though differently governed, and that each state has a peculiar principle of happiness, which, however, may be carried to a mischievous excess; this principle is illustrated by a comparison of *Italy* with *Switzerland*, and *France* with *Holland*, the pictures of which, receive great beauty from the *Contrast*; it concludes with an apostrophe to *England*, in which the author has shewn a warm love for his country, without deviating into either bigotry or enthusiasm. We should chuse to exhibit as a specimen the prospect of *Italy* and *Switzerland*; but as the extract would be too long for our work, we shall select only that of *Britain*. Having named his native country in the preceeding line, the author instantly adopts it as his theme . . . [quotations follow].

3. Unsigned notice, *London Chronicle*

18-20 December 1764, 539

It has been for some time justly objected to our Poets, that they have been unable to solicit the attention of the Public in any extraordinary degree, without leaning upon party for support. The writer of the poem we have under consideration, borrows no aid from prejudice, but builds upon a nobler and more extensive plan.

It were injustice to this ingenious gentleman not to allow him a degree of poetical merit beyond what we have seen for several years, and we must acknowledge him possessed of a strength and connexion of thought which we little expected to see.

As a specimen of his abilities, take the following description of England and Holland . . .

> To men of other minds my fancy flies,
> . . . and learns to venerate himself as man.

4. John Langhorne, *Monthly Review*

January 1765, xxxii, 47–55

Almost every species of affectation has its origin in vanity, and that with which Authors are so justly chargeable, when they pretend to be unconcerned about the success of their works, is derived from no other source. While they bear before them a negligence of praise, their whole aim is to persuade us, that they should be equally careless of censure; and thus, by a kind of preposterous opposition to attacks which they have not felt, their fastidious indifference exposes them the more. It is in vain that the Author of this poem tells us, he is 'not much solicitous to know what reception it may find.'—No Writer was ever yet indifferent to the reputation of his works; and if Mr. Goldsmith finds himself unconcerned for the success of the poem before us, we should think him, at best, an unnatural parent, to be negligent of the interests of so beautiful an offspring:—for the *Traveller* is one of those delightful poems that allure by the beauty of their scenery, a refined elegance of sentiment, and a correspondent happiness of expression. Thus the Author addresses his brother, to whom the poem is inscribed:

> Where'er I roam, whatever realms I see,
> My heart untravell'd fondly turns to thee;
> Still to my brother turns, with ceaseless pain,
> And drags at each remove, a lengthening chain.

It is impossible not to be pleased with the 'untravell'd heart,' and the happy image of 'the lengthening chain;' nevertheless, it may be somewhat difficult to conceive how a heart *untravell'd*, can, at the same time, make farther removes.

The following simile is equally just and magnificent; and is one of those real beauties in imagery, which have the power of pleasing universally, by being at once obvious to the mind, and, at the same time, possessing native dignity enough, to secure them from that indifference with which things frequently contemplated are beheld.

> Impell'd with steps unceasing to pursue
> Some fleeting good that mocks me with the view,

35

That, like the circle bounding earth and skies,
Allures from far, yet, as I follow, flies.

The Traveller *sits him down* (as he sometimes inelegantly expresses it) on an eminence of the Alps, and from thence takes a view of the several kingdoms that lie around him; not with the contracted eye of a Monastic, but with the liberal spirit of a man, who rightly considers, and embraces, the general blessings of Providence:

When thus Creation's charms around combine,
Amidst the store, 'twere thankless to repine.
'Twere affectation all, and school-taught pride,
To spurn the splendid things by Heaven supply'd.
Let school-taught pride dissemble all it can,
These little things are great to little man;
And wiser he, whose sympathetic mind
Exults in all the good of all mankind.
Ye glittering towns, with wealth and splendour crown'd,
Ye fields, where summer spreads profusion round,
Ye lakes, whose vessels catch the busy gale,
Ye bending swains, that dress the flow'ry vale,
For me your tributary stores combine;
Creation's Heir, the world, the world is mine.

He then enquires whether superior happiness be the lot of any particular country; but concludes that, though every man thinks most favourably of his own, Nature has, in general, observed an equality in the distribution of her bounties:

Yet, where to find that happiest spot below,
Who can direct, when all pretend to know?
The shudd'ring tenant of the frigid zone,
Boldly asserts that country for his own,
Extols the treasures of his stormy seas,
And livelong nights of revelry and ease;
The naked Negroe, panting at the Line,
Boasts of his golden sands, and palmy wine,
Basks in the glare, or stems the tepid wave,
And thanks his Gods for all the good they gave.
Nor less the Patriot's boast, where'er we roam,
His first best country ever is at home.

And yet, perhaps, if states with states we scan,
Or estimate their bliss on Reason's plan,
Though Patriots flatter, and though Fools contend,
We still shall find uncertainty suspend;

> Find that each good, by Art or Nature given,
> To these, or those, but makes the balance even:
> Find that the bliss of all is much the same,
> And patriotic boasting Reason's shame.

Yet though this patriotic Boasting may not have its foundation in truth, it is amongst those pleasing errors that contribute to our happiness; and he who should labour to undeceive us in this instance, would be employed in the *triste Ministerium*[1] of making us miserable. We ought, indeed, never so far to cherish an attachment to our native country, as to shut out the inhabitants of different nations from our benevolence or good opinion, but while our innocent enthusiasm only indulges a preference of suns and soils, it will always be our prudence to retain it.

> Nature, a mother kind alike to all,
> Still grants her bliss at Labour's earnest call;
> And though rough rocks, or gloomy summits frown,
> These rocks, by custom, turn to beds of down.

Nothing is more true; but is not the Author's proposition controvertible, in which he maintains, that there is in every state a peculiar principle of happiness?

> Hence every state to one lov'd blessing prone,
> Conforms and models life to that alone.
> Each to the favourite happiness attends,
> And spurns the plan that aims at other ends;
> 'Till, carried to excess in each domain,
> This favourite good begets peculiar pain.

it is certain that every individual has a peculiar principle of happiness; but does it therefore follow, that a state composed of these individuals should have the same? rather the contrary, where there must necessarily be so many different opinions concerning the very existence of happiness. It is, in truth, with states as with private men; they appear to be actuated rather by casual circumstances, than to pursue the general good upon any established principle. We find that what is the object of public attention in one reign, is totally changed in another; and that as interest, power, and caprice prevail, political sagacity is for ever varying its principles and practice. The character of a people is not always the same: as they vary, their ideas of happiness are varied too, and that in so great a degree, that they can scarcely be said to have

[1] I.e., the sad office.

any fixed or determined principle. But though our Author makes no great figure in political Philosophy, he does not fail to entertain us with his poetical descriptions:

> Far to the right, where Appennine ascends,
> Bright as the summer, Italy extends;
> Her uplands sloping deck the mountain's side,
> Woods over woods, in gay theatric pride;
> While oft some temple's mould'ring top between,
> With venerable grandeur marks the scene.

> Could Nature's bounty satisfy the breast,
> The sons of Italy were surely blest.
> Whatever fruits in different climes are found,
> That proudly rise, or humbly court the ground,
> Whatever blooms in torrid tracks appear,
> Whose bright succession decks the varied year;
> Whatever sweets salute the northern sky,
> With vernal lives that blossom but to die;
> These here disporting, own the kindred soil,
> Nor ask luxuriance from the Planter's toil;
> While sea-born gales their gelid wings expand,
> To winnow fragrance round the smiling land.

> But small the bliss that sense alone bestows,
> And sensual bliss is all this nation knows.
> In florid beauty groves and fields appear,
> Men seem the only growth that dwindles here,
> Contrasted faults through all their manners reign,
> Though poor, luxurious, though submissive, vain;
> Though grave, yet trifling, zealous, yet untrue,
> And even in penance planning sins anew.
> All evils here contaminate the mind,
> That opulence departed, leaves behind;
> For wealth was theirs, nor far remov'd the date,
> When commerce proudly flourish'd through the state:
> At her command the palace learnt to rise,
> Again the long-fall'n column sought the skies;
> The canvass glow'd beyond even Nature warm,
> The pregnant quarry teem'd with human form.
> But, more unsteady than the southern gale,
> Soon Commerce turn'd on other shores her sail;
> And late the nation found, with fruitless skill,
> Their former strength was now plethoric ill.

Yet, though to fortune lost, here still abide
Some splendid arts, the wrecks of former pride;
From which the feeble heart and long fall'n mind
An easy compensation seem to find.
Here may be seen, in bloodless pomp array'd,
The paste-board triumph and the cavalcade;
Processions form'd for piety and love,
A Mistress or a Saint in every grove.
By sports like these are all their cares beguil'd,
The sports of children satisfy the child;
At sports like these, while foreign arms advance,
In passive ease they leave the world to chance.

    When struggling Virtue sinks by long controul,
She leaves at last, or feebly mans the soul;
While low delights, succeeding fast behind,
In happier meanness occupy the mind:
As in those domes, where Cæsars once bore sway,
Defac'd by time, and tottering in decay,
Amidst the ruin, heedless of the dead,
The shelter-seeking peasant builds his shed,
And, wond'ring man could want the larger pile,
Exults, and owns his cottage with a smile.

The description of the people of Italy is not less just than that of their country is picturesque and harmonious: but has not the Author, towards the conclusion, laid open a redoubt which the Moralist ought never to give up, when he represents the Italians as a happier people when fallen from their virtue?

When struggling virtue sinks by long controul,
She leaves at last, or feebly mans the soul;
While low delights succeeding fast behind,
In happier meanness occupy the mind.

How very unfavourable to the interests of Virtue to conclude, that low delights have power, even in their meanness, to make us happier; for if happiness be the end and aim of our Being, who would not seek it through those paths by which it appeared most accessible? The truth, however, is, that Happiness, like every thing else, is to be estimated according to its quality. The Author has declared, that sensual bliss is all that the Italians know; but will he consequently maintain, that those low delights, this meanness of enjoyment, could make the Italians happier than the conscious pleasures of that virtue which they had lost, and the higher and more rational satisfactions of the mind?—We are sorry to find such an argument deducible from his poem. The instance he adduces of a peasant's finding himself happy in a cottage formed out of the ruins of an imperial palace affords no proof in this case; for it doth not appear, that the peasant had fallen from his virtue: moreover, there is not the least similitude in the circumstances.

Let us now accompany the Traveller in his prospect of a very different people:

> —————— —————— Turn we to survey
> Where rougher climes a noble race display,
> Where the *bleak* Swiss their stormy mansions tread,
> And force a churlish soil for scanty bread;
> No product here the barren hills afford,
> But man and steel, the soldier and his sword.
> No vernal blooms their torpid rocks array,
> But winter lingering chills the lap of May;
> No Zephyr fondly sooths the mountain's breast,
> But meteors glare, and stormy glooms invest.
> Yet still, even here, Content can spread a charm,
> Redress the clime, and all its rage disarm.
> Though poor the peasant's hut, his feasts though small,
> He sees his little lot, the lot of all;
> Sees no contiguous palace rear its head,
> To shame the meanness of his humble shed;
> No costly Lord the sumptuous banquet deal,
> To make him loath his vegetable meal;
> But calm, and bred in ignorance and toil,
> Each wish contracting, fits him to the soil.
> Chearful at morn he wakes from short repose,
> Breasts the keen air, and carols as he goes;
> With patient angle trolls the finny deep,
> Or drives his vent'rous plough-share to the steep;
> Or seeks the den where snow-tracks mark the way,
> And drags the struggling savage into day.
> At night returning, every labour sped,
> He sits him down the monarch of a shed;
> Smiles by his chearful fire, and round surveys
> His childrens looks, that brighten at the blaze:
> While his lov'd partner boastful of her hoard,
> Displays the cleanly platter on the board;
> And haply too some Pilgrim, thither led,
> With many a tale repays the nightly bed.

Thus every good his native wilds impart,
Imprints the patriot passion on his heart.
Dear is that shed to which his soul conforms,
And dear that hill which lifts him to the storms;
And as a babe, when scaring sounds molest,
Clings close and closer to the mother's breast;
So the loud torrent, and the whirlwind's roar,
But bind him to his native mountains more.

These are the charms to barren states assign'd;
Their wants are few, their wishes all confin'd.
Yet let them only share the praises due,
If few their wants, their pleasures are but few;
Since every want that stimulates the breast,
Becomes a source of pleasure when redrest.
Hence from such lands each pleasing science flies,
That first excites desire, and then supplies;
Unknown to them, when sensual pleasures cloy,
To fill the languid pause with finer joy;
Unknown those powers that raise the soul to flame,
Catch every nerve, and vibrate through the frame.
Their level life is but a smould'ring fire,
Nor quench'd by want, nor fan'd by strong desire;
Unfit for raptures, or, if raptures chear,
On some high festival of once a year,
In wild excess the vulgar breast takes fire,
Till, buried in debauch, the bliss expire.

But not their joys alone thus coarsly flow:
Their morals, like their pleasures, are but low.
For, as refinement stops, from sire to son
Unalter'd, unimprov'd their manners run,
And love's and friendship's finely pointed dart,
Fall blunted from each indurated heart;
Some sterner virtues o'er the mountain's breast
May sit like falcons cow'ring on the nest;
But all the gentler morals, such as play
Through life's more cultur'd walks, and charm our way,
These far dispers'd, on timorous pinions fly,
To sport and flutter in a kinder sky.

It would be superfluous to point out the beauties of this description:
they are so natural and obvious, that no eye can overlook them—
Whether the severity of a Helvetian winter chills the lap of May,
when no Zephyr soothes the breast of the mountain; whether the

hardy Swiss sees his little lot, the lot of all; breasts the keen air, and carols as he goes; drives his plowshare to the steep, or drags the struggling savage into day—the whole is beautiful————Whether he sits down the monarch of a shed, and surveys his childrens looks, that brighten at the blaze; or entertains the pilgrim, whose tale repays the nightly bed—the whole is still beautiful—but the simile of the babe is something more; there is a grandeur as well as beauty in the application of it.

Those moral and intellectual refinements, which at once embellish and add to the happiness of life in cultivated societies, could not be expected among such a people as this: the want of them, and of those various inferiour pleasures they bring along with them, is very properly considered in this elegant description.

But behold a people almost of a different species !

> To kinder skies, where gentler manners reign,
> We turn; and France displays her bright domain.
> Gay sprightly land of mirth and social ease,
> Pleas'd with thyself, whom all the world can please,
> How often have I led thy sportive choir,
> With tuneless pipe, beside the murmuring Loire?
> Where shading elms along the margin grew,
> And freshen'd from the wave the Zephyr flew;
> And haply, tho' my harsh touch faltering still,
> But mock'd all tune, and marr'd the dancer's skill;
> Yet would the village praise my wond'rous power,
> And dance, forgetful of the noon-tide hour.
> Alike all ages. Dames of ancient days
> Have led their children through the mirthful maze,
> And the gay grandsire, skill'd in gestic lore,
> Has frisk'd beneath the burthen of threescore.
>
> So blest a life these thoughtless realms display,
> Thus idly busy rolls their world away:
> Theirs are those arts that mind to mind endear,
> For honour forms the social temper here.
> Honour, that praise which real merit gains,
> Or even imaginary worth obtains,
> Here passes current; paid from hand to hand,
> It shifts in splendid traffic round the land:
> From courts to camps, to cottages it strays,
> And all are taught an avarice of praise;
> They please, are pleas'd, they give to get esteem,
> Till, seeming blest, they grow to what they seem.

> But while this softer art their bliss supplies,
> It gives their follies also room to rise:
> For praise too dearly lov'd, or warmly sought,
> Enfeebles all internal strength of thought,
> And the weak soul, within itself unblest,
> Leans for all pleasure on another's breast.
> Hence ostentation here, with tawdry art,
> Pants for the vulgar praise which fools impart;
> Here Vanity assumes her pert grimace,
> And trims her robes of frize with copper lace;
> Here beggar pride defrauds her daily cheer,
> To boast one splendid banquet once a year;
> The mind still turns where shifting Fashion draws,
> Nor weighs the solid worth of self-applause.

There is something whimsical in the former part of this description, where the Author represents himself as playing upon some instrument, and the French dancing to it: but whether this were fact or fancy, is of little consequence. The characteristics in the passage beginning with 'so blest a life,' are very just, and ingeniously struck out; yet neither is the description of the French nation, nor that of any other introduced in this poem, full, or perfect. The Author has contented himself with exhibiting them in a single point of view; such an one, indeed, in which they are generally beheld: but the lights are much strengthened by the powers of poetic genius.

The Poet next makes a transition to Holland, and from thence proceeds to Britain; but we must now refer the Reader to the poem itself, which we cannot but recommend to him as a work of very considerable merit.

THE VICAR OF WAKEFIELD

27 March 1766

5. Unsigned notice, *Monthly Review*

May 1766, xxxiv, 407

Some of the reasons for the brevity of this notice are given in Ralph M. Wardle, *Oliver Goldsmith*, Lawrence, Kansas, 1957, pp. 168–9.

Through the whole course of our travels in the wild regions of romance, we never met with any thing more difficult to characterize, than the *Vicar of Wakefield*; a performance which contains beauties sufficient to entitle it to almost the highest applause, and defects enough to put the discerning reader out of all patience with an author capable of so strangely under-writing himself.——With marks of genius equal, in some respects, to those which distinguish our most celebrated novel-writers, there are in this work, such palpable indications of the want of a thorough acquaintance with mankind, as might go near to prove the Author totally unqualified for success in this species of composition, were it not that he finds such resources in his own extraordinary natural talents, as may, in the judgment of many readers, in a great measure, compensate for his limited knowledge of men, manners, and characters, as they really appear in the living world.—In brief, with all its faults, there is much rational entertainment to be met with in this very singular tale: but it deserves our warmer approbation, for its moral tendency; particularly for the exemplary manner in which it recommends and enforces the great obligations of universal BENEVOLENCE: the most amiable quality that can possibly distinguish and adorn the WORTHY MAN and the GOOD CHRISTIAN!

6. Unsigned review, *Critical Review*

June 1766, xxi, 439-41

THE following is the advertisement prefixed to this very singular novel;

'There are an hundred faults in this Thing, and an hundred things might be said to prove them beauties. But it is needless. A book may be amusing with numerous errors, or it may be very dull without a single absurdity. The hero of this piece unites in himself the three greatest characters upon earth; he is a priest, an husbandman, and the father of a family. He is drawn as ready to teach, and ready to obey; as simple in affluence, and majestic in adversity. In this age of opulence and refinement whom can such a character please? Such as are fond of high life, will turn with disdain from the simplicity of his country fire-side; such as mistake ribaldry for humour, will find no wit in his harmless conversation; and such as have been taught to deride religion, will laugh at one whose chief stores of comfort are drawn from futurity.

OLIVER GOLDSMITH.'

—But why, it will be asked, did the doctor break off so abruptly, and not proceed to give his reasons for publishing a thing to which he foreboded so unfavourable a reception?—That query he himself can best answer; and therefore to him we refer it. We are willing at the same time to believe, that whatever those reasons were, they had a much more solid foundation than his apprehensions; the early call for a second edition[1] being a pretty strong presumption that these last were but indifferently grounded.

This author seems to us to possess a manner peculiar to himself; it is what the French would term *naïveté*. Now and then, when he means to rise, he indulges a little to antithesis and ornament, of which he shews himself sufficiently capable: but simplicity is his characteristic excellence. He appears to tell his story with so much ease and artlessness, that one is almost tempted to think, one could have told it every bit

---

[1] Within ten weeks.

as well without the least study; yet so difficult is it to hit off this mode of composition with any degree of mastery, that he who should try would probably find himself deceived: *Imitabilis illa quidem videtur esse existimanti*, says an able judge, *sed nihil est experienti minus*.[1] That our novellist never falls into real negligence we dare not take upon us to affirm: it is certain, we have heard his best friends complain of his not doing justice to his own abilities by an adequate exertion of them. There is *something* about genius (we know not how to name it) that often occasions a particular propensity to remit its labours. Who can forbear to regret, that he who wrote the *Traveller* should not write much more, and in the same spirit?—Now that we mention our author as a poet, we cannot with-hold our warmest praise from the ballad which he has favoured us with, in the first volume of the work before us. It is an exquisite little piece, written in that measure which is perhaps the most pleasing of any in our language, versified with inimitable beauty, and breathing the very soul of love and sentiment.

We find nothing in this performance to turn the attention upon the writer, or to inflame the passions of the reader; as we see daily practised by the common herd of novelists. Genuine touches of nature, easy strokes of humour, pathetic pictures of domestic happiness and domestic distress, (a happiness proceeding from innocence and obscurity, and a distress supported with resignation and chearfulness) are some of the methods here made use of to interest and move us. If it be objected, that there is not a sufficient variety of character, or a larger display of what is called Knowledge of the world, it is to be remembered that the whole is supposed to be written by the Vicar himself; a man acquainted indeed with books, but in many particulars a stranger to men; of primitive manners, and an unsuspecting mind; living in the country, and confining his views to his family, his function, and his farm. As he is the principal figure, the scenery should be in proportion simple, unstudied, and unadorned. Piety and fortitude, a glowing benevolence, an uncommon share of parental fondness, with some vanity and more credulity, were to be represented in their natural workings, within a sphere which the *design* would not permit to be extensive; and the skill of the painter, we apprehend, was to appear by producing a strong effect from a piece in which simplicity must still predominate. Nor will it, we think, be denied, that the characters introduced are well marked and properly supported, and that there

---

[1] Cicero, *Orator*, xxiii, 76: 'For that [i.e. plainness of style] which seems easy to imitate at first thought, but when attempted nothing is more difficult.'

are occasionally interspersed many pertinent and useful observations, drawn from life, and directed to the heart.

Sir William Thornhill in disguise is a very original picture, and out of it a very amiable one. His worthless nephew we are prompted to detest and scorn throughout. Jenkinson too is a great rascal in his way, more extraordinary than the other, but less pernicious, and in the end susceptible of remorse; for which reason we are less offended with him, and at last pardon him. The affectation and folly of Mrs. Primrose divert us. As to the daughters and the boys, it is impossible not to be affected with the various play of their youthful passions. Sophia is a sweet girl. Poor Olivia! Honest Moses, and Dick, and Bill, cannot be forgotten. One passage in particular, where the two last are more immediately concerned, we must not pass unnoticed. When an unforeseen difficulty had started about lodging Mr. Burchell, all the beds of the house being already taken up by the family, and it being too late to send him to the next alehouse; little Dick offered the stranger his part of the bed, if his brother Moses would let him sleep with him; to which Bill instantly subjoined, that he would give Mr. Burchell his part of the bed, if his sisters would take him to theirs. 'Well done, my good children (cried the Vicar) hospitality is one of the first Christian duties. The beast retires to its shelter, and the bird flies to its nest; but hapless man can only find refuge from his fellow-creatures. The greatest stranger in this world, was he that came to save it. He never had an house, as if willing to see what hospitality was left remaining among us.—Deborah, my dear, give these boys a lump of sugar each; and let Dick's be the largest, because he spoke first.' We should be insensible not to pity George, and admire Miss Wilmott. But above all, who can help being delighted with the good Vicar for his sincerity, his hospitality, his fervent and overflowing affections, his divine propensity to forgiveness and reconciliation, his unaffected magnanimity in deep affliction, and his exemplary moderation when restored to affluence and joy?—But pray, Dr. Goldsmith, was it necessary to bring the concluding calamities so thick upon your old venerable friend; or in your impatience to get to the end of your task, was you not rather disposed to hurry the catastrophe?—Be this as it may, we cannot but wish you success, being of opinion, upon the whole, that your tale does no little honour to your head, and what is still better, that it does yet more to your heart.

7. Mme Riccoboni in a letter to David Garrick on the plot of *The Vicar of Wakefield*

11 September 1766

Richard Burke (1703–94), younger brother of Edmund, had sent the novelist Marie Jeanne Riccoboni (1714–92) a copy of *The Vicar* and praised it. Mme Riccoboni, then living in Paris and one of Garrick's admirers, disagreed with Richard Burke and wrote to Garrick giving her reasons. Burke's letter is found in *The Private Correspondence of David Garrick*, London, 1832, 2 vols, II, pp. 492–4. See also *The Correspondence of Edmund Burke*, ed. Thomas W. Copeland, Cambridge, England, 1958, I, p. 234.

Avez-vous un démon familier? un génie dirige-t'-il vos mouvemens? une fée expose-t'-elle à vos yeux les désirs de vos amis?—Le Vicaire de Wakefield! quoi, lui-même! en personne? vrai, en honneur, il est là! rien de plus étonnant, je vous le jure.

Jamais entêté Protestant n'eut plus d'horreur pour la terre papiste, et san enchantement il étoit impossible de l'engager à passer la mer. Un chien d'Écossois m'écrit au commencement de Mai, m'annonce un Mr. Jenkinson venant à Paris, m'apportant le Vicaire de Wakefield. Moi de me répandre en remerciemens! *Mon Dieu, Monsieur, vôtre souvenir, vôtre attention, vous êtes charmant*, et mille autres bêtises. Je fais des vœux pour l'heureux passage de Mr. Jenkinson. Je m'occupe de lui, je guette l'instant de son arrivée; je tourmente Mr. Changuion, Mr. Smith; point de nouvelle. Le gracieux Calédonien passe un mois à faire ses adieux à sa chère patrie, se donne les airs de prendre le plus long; se repose d'un côté, s'amuse de l'autre, se promène, s'instruit; je le maudis du fond du cœur. Enfin quand il plait au ciel l'indolent Mr. Jenkinson arrive. On m'avertit, me voilà bien contente. Un fort aimable philosophe va lui demander *le Vicaire*; un joli colonnel l'assiège pour avoir *le Vicaire*. Mr. Changuion a la bonté d'envoyer, d'écrire, d'aller lui-même:—O rage! o fureur! le tranquille Écossois n'a ni

48

curé, ni sacristain, ni vicaire; ne sçait ce que c'est, n'y comprend rien;
ne connoit ni moi, ni le vicaire, ni l'église, ni ses prêtres,—c'est un
grand hasard s'il connoit Dieu: Et moi de jurer comme un payen:
sang et furies!—Patience, disoit Mr. Changuion, eh, mon Dieu,
patience! Le vicaire viendra, je vous assure qu'il viendra.

Peu de jours après, voilà une lettre de Mr. Burke. Un style charmant,
des excuses de sa longue négligence, mille politesses, un badinage
léger, de l'esprit, de l'agrément, de la finesse; rien de plus joli. *Il
prend la liberté de m'envoyer*, il a *l'honneur de me présenter*,—qui, quoi?
devinez,—Le Vicaire de Wakefield. Un Irlandois doit me le remettre,
avec le livre de Mr. Burke l'ainé.

Je connois cet Irlandois, il est attaché à un de nos princes. On va
chez-lui: il est malade. On y retourne, il est absent, puis marié, puis
cocu, je crois. Je perds patience, je crie, je peste, je m'arrache les cheveux.
Là! doucement, disoit Mr. Changuion, d'un air posé, paisible à le faire
assommer: *il viendra, ce diable de Vicaire, croyez-m'en, il viendra.*

Un soir on me demande de la part de Mr. Wilkes[1]: moi, qui ne
suis point du parti de l'opposition, moi, l'amie des Écossois, je frémis
à ce nom. Un valet de chambre me remet un paquet adressé à Mr.
Colman, puis à moi: j'ouvre, c'est un billet de Mr. Garrick, une lettre
de Mr. Becket, et ce Vicaire si désiré, si long-tems attendu! je pousse
un cri de joie, charmée de le voir, plus charmée de le tenir de vous,
de vôtre amitié. À présent il en arrivera une douzaine, celui de Mr.
Changuion est venu, les autres le suivront, j'en leverai magazin.

Vous avez raison de dire qu'il ne m'apprendra rien. C'est un homme
qui va de malheurs en malheurs assez rapidement, et de bonheurs en
bonheurs tout aussi vîte. Cela ne ressemble guère à la vie du monde.
On devroit s'appliquer à peindre les situations les plus ordinaires,
celles où beaucoup de personnes peuvent se trouver. Alors les leçons
de conduite seroient utiles. Je ne suis pas un juge compétent du style,
mais le plan de l'ouvrage ne m'a pas intéressée; le pathétique annoncé
par Mr. Burke ne m'a point frappée: le plaidoyer en faveur des
vouleurs, des petits larrons, des gens de mauvaises mœurs, est fort
éloigné de me plaire. Il faut dire aux hommes: *soyez toujours honnêtes,
l'honneur perdu ne se recouvre jamais.* C'est les désespérer, dira-t'-on,
c'est leur ôter le désir de rentrer dans leur devoir. Mon ami, l'expérience
prouve, que celui dont la misère, dont le besoin a tourné les idées vers

[1] The men referred to in this paragraph are John Wilkes, George Colman, David Garrick,
Thomas Becket (the London publisher), and possibly Philip Changuion or a bookseller
named Francis Changuion.

la bassesse, vers le crime, qui a pu envisager la honte et s'exposer à la mériter, est un homme dont le cœur est corrompu. Le Vicaire prêche des coquins, les convertit; je ne voudrois pas rencontrer sa congrégation dans un bois, si j'avois mille louis dans ma poche.

Eh bien, Messieurs les Anglois, comment supportez-vous l'absence de Mr. de Lauraguais. Il est à la Bastille, et son beau cheval de course se promène comme si de rien n'étoit. C'est pourtant l'animal au pied léger qui tient son maître prisonnier.

On dit Mr. Hume et Jean-Jaques[1] raccommodés. Est-il vrai? Comment fait-on pour se raccommoder? de ma vie je n'ai compris cela. La mort de Mademoiselle de Malboissière a été imprévue, comme vous l'aurez sçu: le Colonnel Wedderburne en est désolé, confondu, désespéré, anéanti, et damné par-dessus le marché. Car il croit la défunte sainte, il l'invoque, il l'atteste, il la prie. Poor soul! c'est dommage qu'il perde l'esprit, car il a une jolie mine, une taille noble, et la conversation vive et très-séduisante. Ma foi, s'il n'avoit pas été s'enterrer chez Madame de Malboissière, il auroit fort réussi auprès de nos dames.

Recevez mes tendres remerciemens. Faites bien mes complimens à Madame Garrick; embrassez-la pour moi et pour ma compagne; nous l'aimons toujours. On m'imprime. Je vous enverrai le premier exemplaire qui sera sec. *Cela ne presse pas*, m'allez-vous dire, *je ne vous attends pas comme vous faisiez le Vicaire*. N'importe, vous aurez le premier exemplaire. Adieu, mon aimable ami.

[1] Rousseau.

8. Lady Sarah Pennington, *An Unfortunate Mother's Advice to Her Absent Daughters*

1767, 1773, 1790, 1794

Frank W. Bradbrook, *Jane Austen and Her Predecessors*, Cambridge, England, 1966, p. 9, has commented on this inclusion of *The Vicar* in a list of 'Books for Young Ladies': '[Lady Pennington] considers that very few novels and romances are worth the trouble of reading, but when Goldsmith's *The Vicar of Wakefield* appeared she made an exception to that in the later editions of her popular advice.'

In justice however to a late ingenious author, this letter must not be reprinted, without my acknowledging that, since the last edition was published, I have accidentally met with one exception to my general rule, namely, *The Vicar of Wakefield*; that novel is equally entertaining and instructive, without being liable to any of the objections that occasioned the above restriction. This possibly may not be the only unexceptionable piece of the kind, but, as I have not met with any other, amongst a number I have perused, a single instance does not alter my opinion of the sort of writing; and, I still think, the chance is perhaps a thousand to one against the probability of obtaining the smallest degree of advantage from the reading any of them, as well as that very few are to be found, from which much injury may not be received.

9. Fanny Burney compares *The Vicar of Wakefield* with other sentimental novels, in her early diary

1768

Fanny Burney (1752–1840) wrote numerous diaries and letters. In 1768 she was reading Goldsmith's novel, and Elizabeth and Richard Griffith's *Henry and Frances* (1766–80, 6 vols). Their points of similarity and difference prompted the comparison below, which is quoted from *The Early Diary of Frances Burney 1768–1778*, ed. Anne R. Ellis (1907, 2 vols), i. pp. 13–14. For further biographical material about Fanny Burney, see No. 48 below.

I have this very moment finish'd reading a novel call'd the *Vicar of Wakefield*. It was wrote by Dr. Goldsmith, author of the comedy of the *Good-Natured Man*, and several essays. His style is rational and sensible and I knew it again immediately. This book is of a very singular kind—I own I began it with distaste and disrelish, having just read the elegant *Letters of Henry*,[1]—the beginning of it, even disgusted me—he mentions his wife with such indifference—such contempt—the contrast of Henry's treatment of Frances struck me—the more so, as it is real—while this tale is fictitious—and then the style of the latter is so elegantly natural, so tenderly manly, so unassumingly rational!—I own I was tempted to thro' (*sic*) the book aside—but there was something in the situation of his family, which if it did not interest me, at least drew me on—and as I proceded, I was better pleased.—The description of his rural felicity, his simple, unaffected contentment—and family domestic happiness, gave me much pleasure—but still, I was not satisfied, a *something* was wanting to make the book satisfy me—to make me *feel* for the Vicar in every

1 Elizabeth and Richard Griffith, of Millicent, in the county of Kildare, had anonymously and jointly published *Henry and Frances*, which Fanny enjoyed. She was reading volumes one and two, according to her diary, at the same time she began to read *The Vicar*.

line he writes, nevertheless, before I was half thro' the first volume, I was, as I may truly express myself, *surprised into tears*—and in the second volume, I really sobb'd. It appears to me, to be impossible any person could read this book thro' with a dry eye at the same time the best part of it is that which turns one's grief out of doors, to open them to laughter. He advances many very bold and singular opinions— for example, he avers that murder is the sole crime for which death ought to be the punishment, he goes even farther, and ventures to affirm that our laws in regard to penalties and punishments are *all* too severe. This doctrine might be contradicted from the very essence of our religion—Scripture for . . . in the Bible—in Exodus particularly, death is commanded by God himself, for many crimes besides murder. But this author shews in all his works a love of peculiarity and of making originality of character in others; and therefore I am not surprised he possesses it himself. This Vicar is a very venerable old man—his distresses *must* move you. There is but very little story, the plot is thin, the incidents very rare, the sentiments uncommon, the vicar is contented, humble, pious, virtuous, [quite a darling charac-ter,][1] but upon the whole how far more was I pleased with the genuine productions of Mr. Griffith's pen—for that is the real name of Henry,— I hear that more volumes are lately published. I wish I could get them, I have read but two—the elegance and delicacy of the manner— expressions—style of that book are so superiour!—How much I should like to be acquainted with the writers of it!—Those Letters are doubly pleasing, charming to me, for being genuine—they have encreased my relish for *minute, heartfelt* writing, and encouraged me in my attempt to give an opinion of the books I read . . .

[1] Miss Ellis' note reads:

The *Vicar of Wakefield* had been published two years previously. Several sentences of faint praise, or blame, are erased—among these—'if it did not interest me at least,' 'I was not *satisfied*,' have been made out. On the other hand 'rational and sensible,' appears in her later writing, instead of some epithet which was, perhaps, less laudatory, and the whole sentence beginning with 'at the same time, the best part of it,' etc., appears to have been added to fill the place of five lines or more which were erased. 'Quite a darling character' also seems to be a later addition. 'The book is not all satisfactory' has been im-perfectly erased. If Goldsmith was, as has been said, a puzzle to his contemporaries, we can hardly wonder at a young girl who, at an age when she had 'few sorrows of her own,' and 'loved best the songs that made her grieve,' was perplexed by the *Vicar of Wakefield*, and not quite contented until she had been 'surprised into tears.' This passage has been to all appearance touched by the writer at a much later time, when she knew better how to estimate the *Vicar of Wakefield*.

10. Two brief estimates of Goldsmith's novel

1776, 1785

(a) Unsigned review in Hugh Kelly's *Babler*, 10 July 1776, no. lxxvii, pp. 55–9

It is a fine observation of the very learned and ingenious doctor Goldsmith, in the *Vicar of Wakefield*, an excellent Novel, with which he has lately obliged the public, that though the poorer part of mankind may in this world suffer more inconveniencies than the rich, still upon their entrance into another life, the joys of hereafter will be enhanced by contrast, in proportion to their afflictions here; and that consequently there can be no room to suppose the least partiality in providence, since sooner or later those who are entitled to it's benignity are certain of meeting with an equal degree of favour from it's hand.

This reflexion must undoubtedly be considered as a masterly vindication of that exterior disparity in the dispensations of providence, at which our modern infidels seem to triumph with so unceasing a satisfaction; and it must as undoubtedly yield a sublime consolation to the bosom of wretchedness to think, that if the opulent are blessed with a continual round of temporal felicity, they shall at least experience some moments of so superior a rapture in the immediate presence of their God, as will fully compensate for the seeming severity of their former situations.

Yet though there are a variety of calamitous circumstances in which this reflexion must administer the most lively consolation, nevertheles if we make a proper enquiry into the state of human nature we shall find, that in general the justice of providence can be fully vindicated without going to this remote and delicate consideration. It does not by any means follow, that because people are contracted in their fortunes, they should be wretched in their minds; nor does it by any means follow, that the greatness of their opulence should be put up as a criterion of their content.

THE principal number of those hydraheaded evils with which we perpetually torment ourselves, are the mere effect of a ridiculous pride, or a narrow understanding. Actuated by one or the other of these unfortunate causes, we are busy in creating an endless round of imaginary difficulties, as if the numberless accidents to which we are naturally exposed were not in themselves abundantly sufficient to imbitter the little span of our sublunary durations, and to dash the short-lived moments of satisfaction, with anxiety and distress.

THE generality of mankind when they take a survey of the world, are apt to estimate by the gradations of rank the gradations of happiness; hence next to a man with a coach and six, we think he must necessarily be the greatest object of envy who keeps a coach and four; after this we rank a chariot and pair, and think that person indeed possesses but a little share of felicity who cannot afford an hour or two's excursion in an humble hack, or take an eighteen-penny fare in occasional sedan.

LOOK on the other side the scene, and see how amazingly the picture is altered. The pride of coronetted pomp continually languishes for the peaceful cottage of rustic obscurity; and the man who has a hundred downy pillows at his command, imagines that repose is only to be met with in the peasant's solitary shed. Thus all of us discontented with the lot which we really possess, and languishing for the state with which we are utterly unacquainted, it is no wonder that many inconsiderate people endeavour by an act of suicide to throw off the severity of their own yoke, and to get free from a weight of oppressions which is constantly becoming more and more insupportable through the folly of themselves.

YET as in the extensive round of the most elaborate investigation, we generally find the rich as discontented with their lot as the poor; we must naturally conclude, that the great author of all things has even in this world designed a pretty equal degree of happiness for his creatures, notwithstanding the evident disparity of their situations. Indeed if we saw felicity in proportion to opulence, or could measure the real enjoyments of life by the standard of rank, we might reasonably imagine that the poor were not to receive their share of the divine benignity till they were going to possess it in a glorious eternity; but when we see that the meanest labourer in the street reaps as much pleasure over his underbred amusement as the first nobleman in the kingdom can possibly boast from the politest entertainment; and when we see the first make as hearty a dinner on a single shin of beef, as the latter ever enjoys at a table of fifty covers, we cannot but suppose that the common lot of mankind is nearly alike; and that all the impious accusations which have arisen from an imaginary partiality in providence, are the mere result of an ignorant pride, or the consequence of an affectation, no less destructive to our reputation in this world, than injurious to our felicity in the next.

UPON the whole, however, if we consider that let our lot in this life be never so severe, it is still infinitely better than what we are entitled to from our own deserts; if we reflect that every blessing which is showered upon us by the hand of heaven, is a blessing which proceeds from the excess of it's own goodness, and does not arise from any immediate merit in us: I say, if we consider these things with a proper degree of weight, and follow the dictates of that conviction which they must instantly strike upon our minds, we shall soon see that till we deserve the favour of existing at all, we cannot deserve to have our lives rendered comfortable in this probationary state; and that of course we ought to be thankful to the Deity for such instances of his benignity, as he may think proper to distinguish us with, instead of blasphemously murmuring that he does not honour us with more.

(b) Clara Reeve's estimate of *The Vicar of Wakefield* in *The Progress of Romance*, 1785, ii, p. 38

The *Vicar of Wakefield*, by Dr. *Goldsmith*, a work of great merit and great faults, but must ever afford both pleasure and benefit to a good heart.

11. Mrs Jane West commenting on 'criminal conversation' in *The Vicar of Wakefield*, in *Letters to a Young Lady: in which the duties and characters of women are considered . . .*

1806, 1811 (4th ed.), iii, Letter xi

In this letter on conversation, starting the third and final volume, Mrs West deals with the subject of the duty of mothers, duty to servants and inferiors, and duties of declining life and old age.

Petty contradictions are not the spur, but the quietus, of agreeable conversation. They proceed from a habit formed in early life, to which parents in the middle ranks of society are never sufficiently attentive. If half the pains that are taken in teaching young women accomplishments were bestowed on the regulation of their tempers, and the improvement of their manners, our social pleasures would receive most valuable improvements. It is to be lamented, that this most teasing habit often distinguishes very worthy people, who adopt it from a mistaken regard to truth and sincerity. As these are especially apt to suppose that a domestic party releases every body from all restraints, they frequently contrive to convert a family meeting into a battle royal; somewhat resembling the contest of a brood of turkey pouts in which everyone gets pecked, and none discover for what reason. The most miserable fate, however, awaits a stranger, who, supposing this engagement to proceed from secret enmity, unfortunately interferes to restore peace, and does not, till after he has received the rebuffs of *every* combatant, discover that they were all the while *cackling* in perfect friendship. This humour generally breaks out in the midst of some narrative, in which the repeater is interrupted with something quite as unessential as Miss Carolina Wilhelmina Amelia Skegg's elucidations of Lady Blarney's crim. con. story,[1] in the *Vicar*

[1] I.e. criminal conversation. See *The Vicar of Wakefield*, chaps xi-xii.

57

of Wakefield; and as both parties instantly quit the main point, to ascertain the verity of the appendage, all the spirit of the tale (if it ever had any) instantly evaporates, and leaves the combatants to fight over a dead body, like the heroic Greeks and magnanimous Trojans. A love of detailing wonders (another lamentable fault in conversation) is extremely apt to rouse this contradictious spirit, which really is a sort of wildfire very liable to agitation, irresistible in its progress, and incapable of extinction until it has consumed all the fuel within its reach. It is not always harmless, unless it is kindled among the weeds which overrun a rich but neglected soil. We may deduce family dissensions, breach of friendship, nay irreconciliable enmity, from this source, much oftener than we can ascribe these lamentable consequences to any great violations of the principles of morality.

Whenever, therefore, we feel inclined to deny what has just been advanced, let us previously reflect whether our motive for interference be such as will justify that interruption of general harmony which contradiction always endangers.

12. Edward Mangin compares Goldsmith and Richardson as novelists, in *An Essay on Light Reading*

1808, 117–29

If, notwithstanding, Richardson must be given up as antiquated, and that an author is to be found not liable to the same objection; I think one may be named, who, in the compass of a novel contained in two small volumes, has proved himself not only the friend and teacher of virtue, but a perfect master of all the powers requisite to accomplish his object: unequalled in humour, and irresistibly pathetic; writing in a nearly faultless style, and with such closeness of observation, that the characters in his work will be intelligible, and appear natural, as long as the English language is understood: and all this, without the slightest offence either to religion, virtue, or decorum. I allude to Oliver Goldsmith, and his novel, *The Vicar of Wakefield*.

That it should be universally admired, ought not to excite astonishment in any who are acquainted with this incomparable work; though they might be pardoned for wondering (as I must own I do) how a nation, capable of relishing some of the novels mentioned in the preceding part of these observations, can likewise possess a true taste for the merits of such a performance as this of Goldsmith.

From the advertisement prefixed to the work by its author, we have a view of the plan he has so ably executed. But every admirer of his will rejoice to perceive that he was mistaken in supposing his book would obtain but little celebrity; a conjecture in which, if he was sincere, he does injustice to his own talents, and to the discernment of mankind.

There are few to whom the *Vicar of Wakefield* is unknown; and I imagine that, amongst English readers, there does not exist an individual dull enough to refuse the tribute of unqualified praise to this novel.

'The hero of this piece,' says the author, 'unites in himself the three greatest characters upon earth: he is a priest, a husbandman, and a father of a family; he is drawn as ready to teach, and ready to obey; as simple in affluence, and majestic in adversity. In this age of opulence and refinement, whom can such a character hope to please? Such as are fond of high life, will turn with disdain from the simplicity of his country fire-side; such as mistake ribaldry for humour, will find no wit in his harmless conversation; and such as have been taught to deride religion, will laugh at one whose chief stores of comfort are drawn from futurity.'

The above passages are full of matter and meaning: with infinite modesty, and in the happiest expressions, the writer has delineated his work; and while he describes what novels should be, points the keenest satire at those which are composed upon other principles, and stamps a mark of opprobrium both on the authors of such and their admirers.

Goldsmith's declaration in his advertisement inclines me to say, that if there is a novel which should not be prohibited, and which should even be recommended to all, as pure, pleasing, and instructive, it is the *Vicar of Wakefield*. Every thing, indeed, which Goldsmith has written, deserves the same commendation as this charming tale.

According to the first couplet in Pope's fine prologue to Cato,[1] the aim of Goldsmith has constantly been,

> To wake the soul, by tender strokes of art;
> To raise the genius, and to mend the heart.

An encomium in which it is to be lamented so very few can share with him.

It would not be easy to find, within the compass of light literature, any thing more perfect in its kind than the scene unfolded in the opening chapters of the *Vicar of Wakefield*: it abounds in strokes of humour and tenderness; and fixes the attention by a most affecting picture of a happy *home*, enjoyed by persons in the middle rank of life, citizens of a free country, and possessing competent means and innocent minds. The group of characters, their circumstances, and local situation, are truly *English*, and could only belong to the enviable land within whose confines the scene is laid.

In England alone, amongst the nations of the earth, could such an individual as the vicar be supposed. Idolatry, Mahometanism, and superstition have indeed their priests; and the minister of religion exists alike under the fervour of Indian skies, and in the twilight of Lapland; in the cloisters of Madrid, and the conventicles of Philadelphia: but England only can exhibit the original from which the inimitable portrait of Dr. Primrose is taken.

He is drawn as pious, learned, charitable, hospitable; fearless in the cause of sanctity and rectitude; in affliction, at once magnanimous and resigned; in prosperity, grateful and humble; a kind and sympathizing neighbour; a most affectionate parent; and, as a pastor, almost worshipped for his virtues by the flock under his care.

As a shade, to counteract the dazzling effect of so much excellence, his learning is represented as not quite unmixed with inoffensive pedantry; and the awe inspired by his good natural understanding, is admirably tempered with a very endearing cast of simplicity; and the solemnity of his deportment relieved, by a well-managed introduction of comic traits.

If any thing can equal this portrait of the vicar, it is the delicacy with which his story is related; and the art shown by the author in conducting the personages of his fable through various vicissitudes, without the least appearance of exaggeration or force. The reader sheds tears at their sorrows, and exults in their restoration to felicity: but the depres-

---

[1] First acted on 14 April 1713.

sion of spirits created by the perusal has in it nothing shocking, nothing disgusting; it is rather the '*luxury of grief:*' and the most unsullied chastity may, without self-reproach, smile at all the pleasantries of Goldsmith.

This dexterity in the author of a novel cannot be too highly praised; particularly if we consider the period when Goldsmith wrote, the opportunities his own hard lot in life had afforded him of becoming acquainted with every phrase of vulgar humour, and how strongly (had he pleased to do so) he might have pourtrayed many of the incidents in his narrative.

His powers of description and command of language were nearly unlimited, and many of the events in the *Vicar of Wakefield* are such as would have tempted a writer of meaner talents and less true sensibility, to exceed those boundaries which he scorned to overleap; confident that the object in view might be otherwise attained, and that success would be purchased at too great a price by an outrage against the morals of his country.

Of a work so well known and so well executed, it is needless to quote what are usually esteemed the brilliant passages; and, in fact, to do this would be little else than to transcribe the entire. But, in general, it may be affirmed of it, that it includes examples of every variety of excellence required in a performance of the kind.

13. Byron comments on Friedrich von Schlegel's estimate of *The Vicar of Wakefield*

29 January 1821

This passage appears in *Byron: Letters and Diaries, 1798 to 1824*, ed. Peter Quennell, London, 1950, 2 vols, II, p. 579. Friedrich von Schlegel's (1772–1829) comment, too brief to be quoted, appeared in his *Geschichte der alten und neuen literature*, Vienna, 1815. Byron probably read the English translation *Lectures on the History of Literature, ancient and modern*, which had appeared in 1818 in 2 vols.

One o'clock

I have found out, however, where the German is right—it is about the *Vicar of Wakefield*. 'Of all romances in miniature (and, perhaps, this is the best shape in which Romance can appear) the *Vicar of Wakefield* is, I think, the most exquisite'. He *thinks*!—he might be sure. But it is very well for a Schlegel. I feel sleepy, and may as well get me to bed. To-morrow there will be fine weather.

14. George Eliot on story telling and narrative art in *The Vicar of Wakefield*, in *Essays and Leaves from a Notebook*

Edinburgh, 1884, 286–7

George Eliot seems to have known *The Vicar of Wakefield* well and may have been influenced by it in the opening sections of *Scenes of Clerical Life*. See W. J. Harvey, *The Art of George Eliot*, London, 1961, pp. 42–3.

The modes of telling a story founded on these processes of outward and inward life derive their effectiveness from the superior mastery of images and pictures in grasping the attention—or, one might say with more fundamental accuracy, from the fact that our earliest, strongest impressions, our most intimate convictions, are simply images added to more or less of sensation. These are the primitive instruments of thought. Hence it is not surprising that early poetry took this way—telling a daring deed, a glorious achievement, without caring for what went before. The desire for orderly narration is a later, more reflective birth. The presence of the Jack in the box affects every child: it is the more reflective lad, the miniature philosopher, who wants to know how he got there.

The only stories life presents to us in an orderly way are those of our autobiography, or the career of our companions from our childhood upwards, or perhaps of our own children. But it is a great art to make a connected strictly relevant narrative of such careers as we can recount from the beginning. In these cases the sequence of associations is almost sure to overmaster the sense of proportion. Such narratives *ab ovo*[1] are summer's-day stories for happy loungers; not the cup of self-forgetting excitement to the busy who can snatch an hour of entertainment.

[1] In origin.

But the simple opening of a story with a date and necessary account of places and people, passing on quietly towards the more rousing elements of narrative and dramatic presentation, without need of retrospect, has its advantages, which have to be measured by the nature of the story. Spirited narrative, without more than a touch of dialogue here and there, may be made eminently interesting, and is suited to the novelette. Examples of its charm are seen in the short tales in which the French have a mastery never reached by the English, who usually demand coarser flavors than are given by that delightful gayety which is well described by La Fontaine[1] as not anything that provokes fits of laughter, but a certain charm, an agreeable mode of handling, which lends attractiveness to all subjects, even the most serious. And it is this sort of gayety which plays around the best French novelettes. But the opening chapters of the *Vicar of Wakefield* are as fine as anything that can be done in this way.

Why should a story not be told in the most irregular fashion that an author's idiosyncrasy may prompt, provided that he gives us what we can enjoy?

[1] 'Je n'appelle pas gayeté ce qui excite le rire, mais un certain charme, un air agréable qu'on peut donner à toutes sortes de sujets, mesme les plus sérieux.'—Preface to Fables [George Eliot's note]. Jean de La Fontaine (1621-1695) had written his famed *Fables* in a familiar persuasive style and an almost inimitable naïveté.

15. Henry James's introduction to *The Vicar of Wakefield*

1900

At the request of publishers Henry James edited *The Vicar of Wakefield* in 1900. When, in 1902, his good friend Elizabeth Jessie Jane Allen made him a Christmas present of two large bearskin rugs, he wrote to his 'Dearest and worst Miss Allen,' steadfastly refusing to accept from her anying 'of value or even of *no* value.' He demonstrates his devotion to *The Vicar* when he adds (nearly two years after his introduction was written): 'See, too, what you compel me to sit up nights writing about, when I might be either reducing my oil-bill or at least writing about Shakespeare and the musical glasses . . . ' He did eventually relent and keep her gifts, but his condition for so doing was that from that time on he would address Miss Allen as 'Goody Two Shoes'—named after the heroine of the moral tale for the young attributed to Goldsmith. See Leon Edel, *Henry James*, 5 vols, New York, 1972, v, pp. 155–6.

IT is a sign of the wonderful fortune of *The Vicar of Wakefield* that the properest occasions for speaking of it continue to present themselves. Everything has been said about it, and said again and again, but the book has long since diffused an indulgence that extends even to commentators. In the degree of its fortune, indeed, it seems almost single of its kind. Stretch the indulgence as we may, Goldsmith's story still fails, somehow, on its face, to account for its great position and its remarkable career. Read as one of the masterpieces by a person not acquainted with our literature, it might easily give an impression that this literature is not immense. It has been reproduced, at all events, in a thousand editions, and the end is not yet. All the arts of book-making and of editing, all the graces of typography and of illustration, have been lavished upon its text. Painters, playwrights, and musicians have again and again drawn upon it, and there is not a happy turn in it, not a facetious figure nor a vivid image, that has not become familiar and famous. We point our phrases with its good things, and the fact that everybody knows them seems only to make them better.

If, therefore, I speak of something disproportionate in the case, between effect and cause, between so many honors and the object they are heaped upon, it is to couple the matter with an instant confession. If I have just re-read the book, I have re-read it after years, and the length of the interval has perhaps something to do with the force of the conviction brought freshly home to me—the idea that a literary production may have its luck as well as its merit, and an author his star as well as his genius. We are tempted to say of *The Vicar of Wakefield* that it has been happy in the manner in which a happy man is happy—a man, say, who has married an angel or been appointed to a sinecure. These various fates of books are to some extent a mystery and a riddle; but what is most striking in the fortune of Goldsmith's story is that, though we fail to explain it completely, we grudge it perhaps less than in any other case. The thing has succeeded by its incomparable amenity. That is a quality by itself, and *The Vicar* gives us the best chance we shall meet to catch this particular influence in the very fact. It has operated here as almost never—for it has operated almost singly—to produce a classic; and we say much in recognizing that under its charm we really resist the irritation of having to define that character. It makes us wonder once more what a classic consists of, and offers us abundant occasion for the study of the question, which it presents in conditions singularly simple and undisturbed.

What we most seem to gather, in the light of this truth, is that if a book have amenity it may, at a stretch, have scarcely anything else. It would not be difficult, on some such ground, I think, to go into the question of how little else, really, *The Vicar* has. I have felt its natural note, on this renewal, as much as ever, but, one by one and page after page, I have missed other matters. Nothing, perhaps, could be, critically, more interesting than to see them successively go and still leave the soft residuum that keeps the work green. It brings us back, of course, to the old, old miracle of style, and puts us in danger of relapsing again into the new, new heresy that style is everything; only to wake up, however, with the shock of the sense that that way madness lies, that *a priori* such a doctrine is fatal. And yet, as our masterpiece stands, we feel that, on other counts, it is really the infancy of art. A mature reader may well be stupefied at some of the claims that have been made for it in respect of skill of portraiture and liveliness of presentation. The first hundred pages—the first half of the first volume of the original edition—contain nearly all the happiest strokes. These, therefore, are comprised in but a quarter of the whole, and I suspect, moreover, that if we should reckon them up—I mean the felicities that have become familiar and famous—they would be found to consist of no great number: of the blue bed and the brown, of Moses and his spectacles, of the Flamboroughs and their oranges, of the family piece by the 'limner,'[1]—the prettiest page of all,—of Shakspere and the musical glasses, of Jernigan and the garters, of Mr. Burchell and his 'Fudge.'

Add to the above the few comparatively sharp little lights in the image of Mrs. Primrose, and what we are left to fall back upon is mere lovability. As a story, as we say nowadays, I am so unconscious of anything vivid in the several figures that I can only be astonished at the claim for difference and contrast in Olivia and Sophia. Such results are easily produced, surely, if the claim is just. The young rake, the base seducer, has so little dramatic substance that we almost resent, on behalf of the lovely Olivia, and indeed on behalf of the whole amiable family, that so much ravage should be represented as wrought by so immaterial a presence. The young man never sounds, never looks at us; and his kinsman, the virtuous Burchell, keeps him nebulous company. The thing goes to pieces—so far as it has been held together at all—from the moment little Dick comes in with the cry that his sister has gone. We are made, in a manner, to see the scene before the child's entrance—it gives us the climax of what is vivid in the first volume; but what immediately ensues illustrates the faintness of the author's touch in any business of emotion or action. His pathos and his tragedy fall, throughout, much below his humor, and the second half of the tale, dropping altogether, becomes almost infantine in its awkwardness, its funny coincidences, and big stitches of white thread.

No one would say as much as this, I hasten to add, and mean it as a reproach. Criticism, I think, does not get near the thing at all, for it only goes so far as to suggest that if it *were* to criticize—In fact, it never pretends to that, for it feels that we are never really troubled, and that to do so would spoil one of the most delicate of all artistic oddities. *The Vicar* throws itself upon our sensibility with a slenderness of means that suggests—for this very slimness—some angular, archaic

[1] See Johnson's definition in the *Dictionary*, 'a painter, a picture-maker.'

nudity. I spoke above of some passages as 'faint,' and the privilege of the whole thing is just to be delightfully so. This faintness, like the faded tone of an old sampler, an old spinet, the ink of an old letter, is of the positive essence of the charm and spell, so that here and there the least little lights gleam in it with effect: we just catch the white stocking of Moses and the brown of the hair that his sisters have tied with ribbon; we catch, in the pleasant paleness, the deep hue of the Flamborough oranges. In short, we make to our own mind, all the while, a plea for the peculiar grace, and feel that, in the particulars, it loses nothing through the want of art. One admits the particulars with the sense that, as regards the place the thing has taken, it remains, by a strange little law of its own, quite undamaged—simply stands there smiling with impunity.

It is the spoiled child of our literature. We cling to it as to our most precious example that we, too, in prose, have achieved the last amiability. Thus it is that the book converts everything it contains into a happy case of exemption and fascination—a case of imperturbable and inscrutable classicism. It is a question of tone. The tone is exquisite, and that's the end of it. It takes us through all the little gaps and slips, through all the artless looseness of the Vicar's disasters and rescues, through his confused and unconvincing captivity and his wonderful accidents and recognitions. It makes these things amusing, makes them most human even when—for there is no other way of putting it— they are most absurd. I will not say it makes them live, for I think it scarce does that at all, but leaves them to linger on as spiced, dead rose-leaves in a bowl, inanimate, fragrant, intensely present. There is not a small drollery at the end that does not work into the very texture that takes us: the punishment of the wicked seducer by being cut down to a single footman; the retinue of so many of these who attest, at the final hour, the real philanthropy of Sir William; the perpetual food that makes its appearance as the climax of everything; the supper of two well-dressed dishes that dissipates the gloom of the prison; the delightful forty pounds distributed among the captives, and the still more delightful 'coarser provisions' scattered among the populace.

If the tone is the great thing, this comes, doubtless, to saying that the Vicar himself is, and that the book has flourished through having so much of him. It is he who is the success of his story; he is always kept true, is what we call to-day 'sustained,' without becoming pompous or hollow. The especial beauty of this is surely that it contains something of the very soul of Goldsmith. It is the most natural imagination of the unspotted that any production, perhaps, offers, and the exhibition of the man himself—by which I mean of the author—combines with his instinctive taste to make the classicism for which we praise him. These two things, the frankness of his sweetness and the beautiful ease of his speech, melt together—with no other aid, as I have hinted, worth mentioning—to form his style. I am afraid I cannot go further than this in the way of speculation as to how a classic is grown. In the open air is perhaps the most we can say. Goldsmith's style is the flower of what I have called his amenity, and his amenity the making of that independence of almost everything by which *The Vicar* has triumphed. The books that live, apparently, are very personal, though there are many defunct, of course, even with that qualification.

The author of this one never, at any rate, lets go our hand; and we, on our side, keep hold with a kind of sense, which is one of the most touching things our literature gives us, of all that, by doing so, we make up to him for. It helps us to look with a certain steadiness on his battered and miserable life. It helps us even to evoke with a certain joy the free, incurable Irish play of fancy and of character that, in the most English of all English ages and circles, drew down on him so much ridicule. There was scarce a difficulty, a disappointment, an humiliation, or a bitterness of which he had not intimate and repeated knowledge; and yet the heavy heart that went through all this overflows in the little book as optimism of the purest water—as good humor, as good taste, and as a drollery that, after all, has oftener its point than its innocence. For these reasons, it would seem, fortune has singled him out, distinguished him with extraordinary favor, decreed that he should be forever known to us in an exceptionally human way. Never was such a revenge against the superior and the patronizing. The spirit still speaks to us of all that was taken to produce it, all the privation and pain and abasement, all the ugliness of circumstance and air; so we piously pluck it and keep it, press it between the leaves of the English prose that we show and boast of, treat it as a rare, fine flower that has sprouted in a rough, hard soil.

THE GOOD NATURED MAN

29 January 1768

16. Two early reviews of *The Good Natured Man*

1768, 1772

(a) Unsigned review, *Critical Review*, February 1768, xxv, 147–8

This play has much merit, and many faults. The chief merit, as well as principal aim of the author, seems to be the delineation of character: but surely he has fallen into an error by supposing, that, in the composition of a comedy, 'no more would be expected from him.' Much more may be, and always will be, expected from a comic writer; and if the author's prepossession in favour of our old poets had led him to a more studious imitation of them, he would have thought the fable as worthy his attention as the characters. Not that we would infer that this writer has wholly failed in the construction of his fable, or entirely succeeded in the delineation of character. Croker himself, whom the poet seems to have originally designed for a whimsical mixture of melancholy and humanity, is sometimes divested of the singularities which identify his character, and dwindles into the mere avaricious old curmudgeon, who appears in so many of our comedies. On the whole, his part is well sustained, and the circumstances of the fable naturally bring out the peculiarities of his mind. The scene on his first appearance, and that relative to the incendiary letter in the fourth act, are admirable. The *Good-natur'd Man* himself is not accurately drawn; nor is the part he sustains in the action made sufficiently capital, considering him as the hero of the piece. The weakness of super-abundant good-nature might be represented as carrying a virtue to a ridiculous excess, but should never appear to degenerate into absolute vice. Honeywood is in some instances a composition of vanity and injustice, which are by no means the ingredients of good-nature. A series of comic distresses, brought on by his easiness of temper, might have been imagined, and have been so conducted as to display his character to much more advantage, than as it stands in this comedy, wherein his difficulties are neither sufficiently varied nor multiplied. There are many happy *traits* in the draught of Lofty's character; but it is not made sufficiently clear what rank he really fills in society: nor is it probable that a family, like that of Croker, whose fortune is avowedly large, and whose connections are apparently creditable, should be so easily imposed on by an arrogant pretender, who knows neither persons of fashion, nor men in power. From the character of Mrs. Croker we are taught to expect entertainment; but expectation is raised without being gratified: from the other ladies we are led to expect but little, and but little is performed. 'The scene of the bailiffs, retrenched in the representation, and here restored by the author, in deference to the judgment of a few friends, who think in a particular way,' we neither wholly approve nor condemn. Coarse characters should be touched by a delicate pencil, and forcible situations should be rather softened than aggravated. 'Humour (it is true) will sometimes lead us into the recesses of the mean;' but in pursuing humour into those recesses, the author, like Jove under Philemon's roof, should not wholly abandon the dignity of his own character.

(b) Sir Nicholas Nipclose [pseudonym] commenting on Goldsmith and other theatrical delinquents in 1768, in *The Theatres. A Poetical Discussion*, published for Bell, 1772, pp. 33–5

[The anonymous notice of this work in the *Monthly Review*, December 1771, xlv, 508–9 begins: 'Now we have a fresh poetical discussion of theatrical delinquents, from—we know not who.—Nor is it material *who*.' The author has never been determined.]

Were all indeed like Hagley's(46) learned peer,
Taste would herself become their worshipper;
But Drury's lord,[1] on greatness only set,
Head or no head, admires a coronet.
    Why wilt thou, DAVY, harrass out thy pen?
Oh may it never judgement wound again;
No ear so dull, but what must surely tingle
To hear the jargon of thy dear Sir Dingle.[2]
    Bless'd be the sire, but hold—this starts a doubt—
'Tis a wise son can find his father out;
But what of this? legitimacy's fire
Equals not that catch'd from illegal sire;
Then blest be he, with warmth we speak the word,—
Should he perchance a footman be, or lord,
That gave us COLY(47)—oh luxurious grant!——
That pretty, peevish, pert annuitant:
Oh may he follow still parental path,
And, mother like, give all his love to BATH!(48)
    Here may he cry, let wounded withers wince,
I'm an invulnerable FAIRY PRINCE;
Such troops I pay, such management I claim,
As never grac'd before theatric name:
I've wrote enough; what needs there any more,
To gain fame's temple, and the public roar?
The LONDON PACKET(49), the St. JAMES's join
To vend the puffs which I and DAVY coin:
We, pleaders like, though at the public bar
We wrangle fiercely, wage no hostile war;
Behind the curtain we shake hands and smile,
United BUBBLE MASTERS of this isle.
    Why should I write? it costs a world of pains
To drag ev'n dialogue from hard-bound brains:

(46) LORD LYTTLETON [The following notes appear in the original edition of 1772].

(47) George Colman, Esq; the *ruling* pattentee of Covent-Garden.

(48) We don't mean by this, and the preceding lines, any ungenerous reflection; a man of merit we esteem, however born, but think arrogance sullies even bright abilities, and the noblest descent.

(49) Two evening papers, of which the managers are proprietors; therefore every defence of their impositions and absurdities, however vague, is greedily admitted: indeed we believe every thing favourable is written by *themselves*, for certainly no other person, save a fool or a flatterer, would undertake so impracticable a justification.

1 David Garrick.
2 Unidentified.

Then as for wit—my scull may be its tomb,
Upon my brows no laurel e'er can bloom,
They both forswore me in my mother's womb.   }
    GOLDSMITH, who teems with sentiments refin'd,
Speaks in his works a pregnant, lib'ral mind;
And shew'd, tho' we condemn his gen'ral plan,
Strong tints of life in his GOOD NATUR'D MAN;
Yet don't we wish to meet him on the stage,
'Twill spoil the foremost poet of our age;
Nor would we view him in historic path,
His politics may rouse up patriot wrath;
No writer can in many points excell;
We prize not writing much, but writing well;
Then, DOCTOR, stick to what we call thy own,
And sport in fields of poesy alone.

17. George Daniel on *The Good Natured Man*, in an edition of the *British Theatre* published by John Cumberland in 48 vols

1829

George Daniel (1789–1864) had contributed a critical preface to each play in Cumberland's series. As these remarks indicate, he considered Goldsmith a dramatic genius of the first order.

THIS Comedy was the first dramatic attempt of an author, dear to the lovers of English literature—Oliver Goldsmith. It was represented for the first time, on the 29th of January, 1768, at Covent Garden Theatre, with a Prologue written by Doctor Johnson. Compared with his later production, *She Stoops to Conquer*, it exhibits little incident and stage effect: yet its easy flow of humour, sprightliness of character, and elegance of language, place it in the first rank of Comedy; and in the absence of many requisites essential to a perfect drama, *The Good-Natured Man* will always be listened to with pleasure.

Mr. Honeywood is one of those characters, who partly from constitutional indifference, but more from the love of ease, are never out of temper. His benevolence is as ill-directed, as his mirth: he acquits the rogue, and laughs at the drunkard:—he approves folly, lest fools should disapprove:—and in his vanity to please *all*, forfeits the esteem of those whose good opinion is of any value.—His are not the weaknesses of an amiable mind, but the selfish compromises of an indolent spirit, that is resolved to let nothing ruffle its stagnant insensibility——Mr. Lofty is a well-drawn picture of a gratuitous gasconader, who having strutted his hour in borrowed plumes, is condemned to exchange them for the cap and bells for ever after. The lies of Falstaff are exquisitely amusing: his *'men in buckram'* are among the richest conceptions of the comic muse. Mr. Lofty's *'interest with the Secretary,'* though not so diverting, is equally in character: he is altogether a very ridiculous personage, to whom, however, an ample share of poetical justice is awarded: his falsehoods are punished by detection, and dismissed with contempt.

But the crown of the piece is Croaker—a character suggested by that of SUSPIRIOUS, in the *Rambler*;[1] yet so ingeniously amplified, as to give it all the force and value of an original conception. He is the Atlas upon whom the whole Comedy rests, every character being subordinate to this great masterpiece. His capital scene is in the fourth act, where he rushes in with the supposed incendiary letter. It is said, that the inimitable action of Shuter, in this scene, *saved* the piece on the first night of representation—for to the shame of that day be it recorded, that the public taste had become so vitiated by unmeaning sentimentality, that the Comedies of Goldsmith found difficult access to the stage, and, *when* fairly launched, narrowly escaped condemnation. So infected was even Garrick with this ridiculous mania, that he *rejected* the sterling humour of Goldsmith, for the mawkish insipidity

[1] Johnson, *Rambler* no. 59, 9 October 1750. Boswell, writing in the *Life of Johnson* for 1768, comments that Johnson 'praised Goldsmith's *Good-natured Man*; said it was the best comedy that had appeared since *The Provoked Husband*, and that there had not been of late any such character exhibited on the stage as that of Croaker. I observed it was the Suspirius of his Rambler. He said, Goldsmith had owned he had borrowed it from thence.' Johnson's remark, however succinct, is among the most praiseworthy of comments in 1768.

of Kelly,[1] to which the bard satirically alludes in his poem of 'Retaliation:'

> Ye Kenricks, ye *Kellys,* and Woodfalls so grave,
> What a commerce was yours, while you got and you gave?
> How did Grub Street re-echo the shouts that you rais'd,
> While *he* was be-Roscius'd, and *you* were be-prais'd

But the genius of Goldsmith ultimately triumphed over false taste; and when he made his second, and, unfortunately, his last dramatic attempt, in *She Stoops to Conquer,* Doctor Johnson declared, 'that he knew no comedy for many years that had so much exhilarated an audience that had answered so much the great end of comedy—making an audience merry . . .'

One amusing incident in the Comedy, that of Croaker prompting his son Leontine while he is addressing Miss Richland, has been borrowed by Mr. Sheridan in the scene between Captain Absolute, Sir Anthony, and Lydia Languish, in the *Rivals.*

[1] Hugh Kelly (1739-77), hack writer and friend of Goldsmith's. In the spring of 1768 Kelly and Goldsmith were dramatic rivals. While Goldsmith was preparing to bring out *The Good Natured Man,* Garrick took up with Kelly to produce *False Delicacy,* a comedy of the sentimental school. Its success was immediate and considerable and although Dr Johnson considered it 'totally void of character,' it was the talk of the season and made Kelly a fortune. Goldsmith, like Johnson, sneered at it.

THE DESERTED VILLAGE

26 May 1770

---

18. Unsigned review, *Critical Review*

June 1770, xxix, 435–43

IT would be doing great injustice to eminent poetical merit, not to give our particular attention to this poem.—It is evident, from the *Deserted Village*, and from the *Traveller*, that in descriptive poetry Dr. Goldsmith has few superiors. He *seems* to possess Thomson's amiable heart, and, in a great measure, his strain of poetical sentiment. But he has this advantage over the author of the *Seasons*, (for to those poems we refer when we compare Dr. Goldsmith with Thomson) that he writes excellent poetry in rhime. For that good rhime, where it can be properly used, is preferable to good blank verse, is now no longer questioned by critics of true taste.

The principle, or source, from which this poem flows, will be most clearly seen, by quoting the following lines towards the beginning of it.

> 'Ill fares the land, to hastening ills a prey,
> Where wealth accumulates, and men decay;
> Princes and lords may flourish, or may fade;
> A breath can make them, as a breath has made.
> But a bold peasantry, [*yeomanry*] their country's pride,
> When once destroyed, can never be supplied.

> 'A time there was, ere England's griefs began,
> When every rood of ground maintain'd its man; [*Quere.*]
> For him light labour spread her wholesome store,
> Just gave what life required, but gave no more.
> His best companions, innocence and health;
> And his best riches, ignorance of wealth.

'But times are altered; trade's unfeeling train
Usurp the land and dispossess the swain;
Along the lawn, where scattered hamlets rose,
Unwieldy wealth, and cumbrous pomp repose;
And every want to luxury allied,
And every pang that folly pays to pride.
These gentle hours that plenty bade to bloom,
Those calm desires that asked but little room,
Those healthful sports that graced the peaceful scene,
Lived in each look, and brightened all the green;
These far departing seek a kinder shore,
And rural mirth and manners are no more.'

Whether the argument of this piece, taken in all its latitude, is as just as the imagery is beautiful; whether he here shows himself as accurate a politician and philosopher, as he is a poet of a rich and elegant fancy, may, perhaps, be doubted by the most dispassionate and unprejudiced mind. To reject his theory at once, would be rash: for it brings to the mind a complication of objects; and tends to inculcate a regard for the general rights of man: it produces an affecting view of the sacred privileges, and the substantial blessings of nature. But simple truth seems to tell us, that every period of a state hath its peculiar advantages and defects; its peculiar publick happiness, and public misery. He who reads the *Deserted Village*, and is not acquainted with the face of our country, may imagine, that there are many deserted villages to be found in it, and many more tracts of uncultivated land than formerly. England wears now a more smiling aspect than she ever did; and few ruined villages are to be met with except on poetical ground.—Whatever is, must be ultimately right, and productive of universal good. When the author of nature formed us, he knew, that, by our constitution we must pass from barbarism to a more improved state; and that, in process of time, we should arrive at a state of opulence, luxury, and refinement; a state which, perhaps, is as productive of happiness as of misery, to mankind. If many individuals have been oppressed by wealth and power, to as many have those blessings flowed from wealth and power which, otherwise, they had wanted. Innocence, it is true, slumbers in the village; but virtue affords a nobler enjoyment; and it is in the great metropolis, that virtue and genius are most strenuously exerted, and most amply rewarded. If Dr. Goldsmith had hitherto passed his life at Auburn, he would not have been so conspicuous, nor, we hope, so happy a man as he is in

London. Fame, when it is a tribute paid to true desert, must greatly augment the felicity of man. If one unhappy female, who comes from the country to town, is, at length obliged, her friends, her virtue fled, to lay her head in the storm, near her betrayer's door—another rural maid, who repairs to London, more prudent, and more fortunate, leads a more agreeable life there by her honesty and industry than her native spot would ever have afforded her; and at length makes an advantageous and happy marriage, the reward of her diligence and virtue.

But we are rather departing from our present province, and entering into too minute a discussion.—A fine poem may be written upon a false hypothesis: as a poet is not confined to historical fact, neither is he bound by the strictness of political and philosophical truth. His leading object may be a chimera; but if he exhibits it uniformly and strongly; if he dignifies it with just, affecting, ardent images, and sentiments, and such as are its natural concomitants, the difficult, and noble task of the poet is discharged. It is needless to insist upon harmonious and vigorous versification; it is the spontaneous result of comprehensive and warm conception; it is as easy to a poet as the drapery of a picture is to a Reynolds.

We shall now quote some passages from this poem; by which the author's poetical talents will be full displayed. The few quotations we shall make will be sufficient to insure his reputation as a poet, however he may be attacked by ignorance and envy; or with whatever inaccuracies and faults he may be charged by just criticism, the friend at once to candour and to truth.

The objects of a village-evening, which affect the mind of a susceptible observer, are very warmly and beautifully described.—The character of the worthy parish priest of the village is a master-piece; it makes a sacred and most forcible appeal to the best feelings of the human heart. It would be unkind to our readers to give them so fine a part of the poem curtailed: we shall therefore print the venerable picture entire; first quoting, in the author's order, the description of the village-evening, and of the melancholy life of the sad historian of this rural desolation . . .

We rarely see a poem in which there are fewer instances of improper sentiment, or expression, than in this. Two lines, however, we must beg leave to animadvert upon.

'The sad historian of the *pensive* plain.'

Pensive is too bold an epithet, even in poetry; as it attributes too much of soul to inanimate matter.—Dryden, indeed, is guilty of a like impropriety in his noble imitation of the beginning of the first book of Lucretius: addressing himself to Venus, he says, of Mars,——

> 'Who oft retires from *fighting* fields, to prove
> The pleasing pains of thy eternal love.'

Dryden here ascribes too much action to the Fields, as Dr. Goldsmith has inspired his Plain with too reflecting a melancholy. Dryden has attributed to his Fields too strong a characteristic of the impetuous warriour; and Dr. Goldsmith has given to his Plain too much of the sensibility and contemplation of the poet: we should emulate the natural and great sublime of Dryden, but we should avoid his negligence and excess.

> 'His pity gave ere charity began.'

This line violates the perspicuity of poetry. And the thought it contains is but a quaint one; more worthy of Seneca, or of the worst poetry of Dr. Young, than of the author of the *Deserted Village*.

In giving the following lines to the sentimental reader, we need not desire him principally to mark the unhappy situation of the ruined country-girl: a home reproof to obdurate men; and a strong warning to unguarded innocence.

> 'Where then, ah, where shall poverty reside,
> To scape the pressure of contiguous pride;
> If to some common's fenceless limits strayed,
> He drives his flock to pick the scanty blade,
> Those fenceless fields the sons of wealth divide,
> And even the bare-worn common is denied.

> 'If to the city sped—What waits him there?
> To see profusion that he must not share;
> To see ten thousand baneful arts combined
> To pamper luxury, and thin mankind;
> To see each joy the sons of pleasure know,
> Extorted from his fellow-creature's woe.
> Here, while the courtier glitters in brocade,
> There the pale artist plies the sickly trade;
> Here, while the proud their long drawn pomps display,
> There the black gibbet glooms beside the way.
> The dome where pleasure holds her midnight reign,

79

Here richly deckt admits the gorgeous train,
Tumultuous grandeur crowds the blazing square,
The rattling chariots clash, the torches glare;
Sure scenes like these no troubles ere annoy!
Sure these denote one universal joy!
Are these thy serious thoughts—Ah, turn thine eyes
Where the poor houseless shivering female lies.
She once, perhaps, in village plenty blest,
Has wept at tales of innocence distrest;
Her modest looks the cottage might adorn,
Sweet as the primrose peeps beneath the thorn;
Now lost to all; her friends, her virtue fled,
Near her betrayer's door she lays her head,
And pinch'd with cold, and shrinking from the shower,
With heavy heart deplores that luckless hour,
When idly first, ambitious of the town,
She left her wheel and robes of country brown.'

The close of the poem is beautiful, but mere imagination and romance. In his enthusiastic vision, Commerce and Luxury drive the rural virtues from the land. Unfortunate Poetry too is transported; and the author takes a most pathetic leave of her.

'And thou sweet Poetry, thou loveliest maid,
Still first to fly where sensual joys invade;
Unfit in these degenerate times of shame,
To catch the heart, or strike for honest fame;
Dear charming nymph, neglected and decried,
My shame in crowds, my solitary pride.
Thou source of all my bliss, and all my woe,
That found'st me poor at first, and keep'st me so;
Thou guide by which the nobler arts excell,
Thou nurse of every virtue, fare thee well.
Farewell, and O where'er thy voice be tried,
On Torno's cliffs, or Pambamarca's side,
Whether where equinoctial fervours glow,
Or Winter wraps the polar world in snow,
Still let thy voice prevailing over time,
Redress the rigours of the inclement clime;
Aid slighted truth, with thy persuasive strain
Teach erring man to spurn the rage of gain;
Teach him that states of native strength possest;
Tho' very poor, may still be very blest;

That trade's proud empire hastes to swift decay,
As ocean sweeps the labour'd mole away;
While self-dependent power can time defy,
As rocks resist the billows and the sky.'

England is certainly not so inhospitable to poetry as the equinoctial fervour, or the polar cold would be. Poetry is of a delicate constitution; she would infallibly die, if she was banished either to Guinea, or to Greenland. Her powers would be dissolved in Guinea, and congealed in Greenland. She would want objects to enrich her genius, and her vigorous exertion would forsake her, in the one climate, or in the other. She would be employed on none of the noble themes, which the poet requests her to embellish in her exile, for the good of mankind. We differ so far from Dr. Goldsmith's theory, that we think the country distinguished from all others for its extensive commerce, its refined luxury, and its generous plan of freedom, the most favourable region to the muses. There the poet will find the amplest field for his imagination; the best judges, and the highest rewards of his merit. London, therefore, is the place to which a son of Apollo should direct his views; and by no means to the cliffs of Torno, or to the side of Pambamarca. In London, he will have the richest fund of thought, and the warmest incentives to write: and without these advantages in perfection, a great genius can never be *perfectly* displayed.—Here, it must be confessed, a poet often treads on dangerous ground; and the greater his talents are, his ruin is the more probable; for his sensibility is the more quick, and his virtuous conduct the more difficult. But if his abuse of external objects will lead him to destruction, his proper application of them will procure him, at least, a competent subsistence, and high reputation. Why do we excel the ancients in writing, (for that we do excel them, blind prejudice only and stupidity will deny) because the improvement of literature hath kept pace with all other improvements; because a justness, a delicacy of thinking, the true sublime, are the consequences of polished life; because genius is now furnished with the greatest variety of ideas, and stimulated by the most powerful incitements to excel. Do the ancients excel us in poetry? Certainly not, upon the whole. It is true, they preceded us; and therefore have transmitted many noble sentiments, which we can only repeat. They are likewise more fortunate than we are in another circumstance; they gave the fire of genius its immediate and full play; but we are apt to restrain and subdue it too much by art. They are often too negligent; we are sometimes too elaborate. But none of them are so sublime as our divine Shakespeare and Milton; in none of them is to be found so much vigour and correctness united as in Pope. Are the ancient historians preferable to our best historians as writers? By no means. They dwell upon trifles; they tell us a string of barbarous tales, which now would only be pardonable from the mouth of an old woman in a chimney-corner. Indeed they exhibit giants of virtue and patriotism to our view, of whom we have no living similitudes. Let us discriminate before we pronounce; and not mistake *old* characters, which we owe to the government, and manners of their country, for the excellence of *old* authors.

The reader, we hope, will not be displeased with this digression, which is not much out of the way, when we are animadverting upon Dr. Goldsmith's opinion that the complexion of the present times is unfavourable to literary merit.

The author, in his dedication to Sir Joshua Reynolds, makes a very singular confession, not much to the honour either of the painter, or the poet. He says 'I am ignorant of that art in which you are said to excel.'—If a poet, and a poet who chiefly excels in the picturesque, has no taste for fine painting, we must think him a phoenomenon.— 'I would not give a farthing,' says Voltaire, 'for those specimens of the fine arts, which only engage the attention of artists.'[1]

Dr. Goldsmith deserves the highest applause for employing his poetical talents in the support of humanity and virtue, in an age when sentimental instruction will have more powerful influence upon our conduct than any other; when abstruse systems of morality, and dry exhortations from the pulpit, if attended to for a while, make no durable impression.

1 Probably a bowdlerization; in any case, we are unable to identify the original quotation by Voltaire.

19. John Hawkesworth's review, *Monthly Review*

June 1770, xlii, 440-5

Hawkesworth, a miscellaneous writer in London, published another review in June 1770 which appeared in the *Gentleman's Magazine*, xl, pp. 271-3. Since it is almost identical with this review, it has not been included.

In a dedication of this poem to Sir Joshua Reynolds Dr. Goldsmith says, 'I know you will object (and indeed several of our best and wisest friends concur in the opinion) that the depopulation it deplores is no where to be seen, and the disorders it laments are only to be found in the poet's own imagination. To this I can scarce make any other answer than that I sincerely believe what I have written; that I have taken all possible pains, in my country excursions, for these four or five years past, to be certain of what I alledge, and that all my views and enquiries have led me to believe those miseries real, which I here attempt to display.'

He says also, 'in regretting the depopulation of the country, I inveigh against the increase of our luxuries; and here also I expect the shout of modern politicians against me. For twenty or thirty years past, it has been the fashion to consider luxury as one of the greatest national advantages; and all the wisdom of antiquity in that particular, as erroneous. Still however, I must remain a professed ancient on that head, and continue to think those luxuries prejudicial to states, by which so many vices are introduced, and so many kingdoms have been undone.'

There can be no doubt that luxury produces vice, and vice misery; but luxury is, notwithstanding, essentially necessary to national greatness, for of a great nation neither virtue nor happiness is a characteristic. It is indeed true that nations have been undone by luxury; but it is also true that no nation can subsist without it.

The word luxury, applied to nations, has perhaps never been defined. It seems to be, indefinitely, the pleasures arising from the gratification of artificial wants; and it will be found extremely difficult to draw a line between the artificial wants that should be admitted, and those that should be rejected. That they do not add to the happiness of life might perhaps be easily demonstrated, by comparing the state of those who supply them with that of those to whom they are supplied: it will appear that more is suffered by those who are employed in the gradual transmutation of ore into a service of plate, than is added to the enjoyment of a meal which is eaten from it. But no nation can be populous without employing more than agriculture can employ, and no nation that is not populous can be strong. Luxury, in a political view, is good when it provides employment for more than the inhabitants of a country; it is evil when it leaves part of the inhabitants unemployed. That luxury, at least in its consequences, may prevent employment in a particular country where is is carried farther than in other countries, might easily be proved: it might also easily be proved that it does not always produce population in the same degree that it produces employment: it produces a factitious necessity, which is not, like the necessities of nature, easily supplied. It therefore renders marriage inconvenient, and consequently prevents population. So far therefore we are ancients with Dr. Goldsmith, and cannot agree with modern politicians in their opinion, that national advantage is always in proportion to national luxury.

That luxury is at present depopulating our country, not only by preventing marriage, but driving our villagers over the Western Ocean, we may perhaps be disposed to deny with the best and wisest of Dr. Goldsmith's friends, but we do not therefore read his poem with the less pleasure. As a picture of fancy it has great beauty; and if we shall occasionally remark that it is nothing more, we shall very little derogate from its merit.

The Author writes in the character of a native of a country village, to which he gives the name of Auburn, and which he thus pathetically addresses: . . . [opening stanzas follow, lines 1–56].

In this extract there is a strain of poetry very different from the quaint phrase, and forced construction, into which our fashionable bards are distorting prose; yet it may be remarked, that our pity is here principally excited for what cannot suffer, for a brook that is choaked with sedges, a glade that is become the solitary haunt of the bittern, a walk deserted to the lapwing, and a wall that is half hidden by grass. We commiserate the village as a sailor does his ship, and perhaps we never contemplate the ruins of any thing magnificent or beautiful without enjoying a tender and mournful pleasure from this fanciful association of ideas.

He proceeds to contrast the innocence and happiness of a simple and natural state, with the miseries and vices that have been introduced by polished life: . . . [lines 57–74 follow].

This is fine painting and fine poetry, notwithstanding the absurdity of supposing that there was a time when England was equally divided among its inhabitants by a rood a man: if it was possible that such an equal division could take place, either in England or any other country, it could not continue ten years. Wherever there is property, there must of necessity be poverty and riches.

We come now to the following beautiful apostrophe to Retirement:

> 'O blest retirement, friend to life's decline,
> Retreats from care that never must be mine,
> How blest is he who crowns in shades like these,
> A youth of labour with an age of ease;
> Who quits a world where strong temptations try,
> And, since 'tis hard to combat, learns to fly.
> For him no wretches, born to work and weep,
> Explore the mine, or tempt the dangerous deep;
> No surly porter stands in guilty state
> To spurn imploring famine from his gate,
> But on he moves to meet his latter end,
> Angels around befriending virtue's friend;
> Sinks to the grave with unperceived decay,
> While resignation gently slopes the way;
> And all his prospects brightening to the last,
> His heaven commences ere the world be past!'[1]

But this passage, though it is fine, is fanciful. Does he who retires into the country to crown 'a youth of labour with an age of ease,' use no knife, eat no sugar, and wear neither shirt nor breeches? If he does, for him the mine must be explored, the deep tempted, and

> 'The pale artist ply the sickly trade.'

The following description of the parish priest would have done honour to any poet of any age: . . . [lines 137–92 follow].

The simile of the bird teaching her young to fly, and of the mountain

[1] Lines 97–112.

that rises above the storm, are not easily to be paralleled, and yet the construction of the last is not perfect. *As*, in the first verse, requires *so*, in the third, either expressed or implied: at present the construction is, 'As some cliff swells from the vale, sunshine settles upon its head, though clouds obscure its breast.' *So* cannot be admitted here, or, if it could, one part of the simile would be exemplified by another, and not the context by the simile, a very small alteration will remove the inaccuracy:

> So lifts some tow'ring cliff its awful form,
> Swells form the vale, and midway leaves the storm;
> Though round its breast the rolling clouds are spread,
> Eternal sunshine settles on its head.

The rest of the poem consists of the character of the village school-master, and a description of the village alehouse, both drawn with admirable propriety and force; a descant on the mischiefs of luxury and wealth, the variety of artificial pleasures, the miseries of those, who, for want of employment at home, are driven to settle new colonies abroad, and the following beautiful apostrophe to Poetry. Having enumerated the domestic virtues which are leaving the country with the inhabitants of his deserted village, he adds,

> 'And thou, sweet Poetry, thou loveliest maid,
> Still first to fly where sensual joys invade;
> Unfit in these degenerate times of shame,
> To catch the heart, or strike for honest fame;
> Dear charming nymph, neglected and decried,
> My shame in crowds, my solitary pride.
> Thou source of all my bliss, and all my woe,
> That found'st me poor at first, and keep'st me so;
> Thou guide by which the nobler arts excel,
> Thou nurse of every virtue, fare thee well.'[1]

We hope that, for the honour of the Art, and the pleasure of the Public, Dr. Goldsmith will retract his farewel to poetry, and give us other opportunities of doing justice to his merit.

---

[1] Lines 407-16.

20. An anonymous and 'impartial review,' *London Magazine*

June 1770, xxxix, 318

An extract without editorial commentary had appeared in the May issue.

This is a very elegant poem, written with great pains, yet bearing every possible mark of facility; in our last number we gave an extract from it containing the picture of a country curate. We shall now present the public with the description of a country school-master, and a village alehouse which we think particularly picturesque.

> Beside yon straggling fence that skirts the way,
> With blossomed furze uprofitably gay,
> There, in his noisy mansion, skill'd to rule,
> The village master taught his little school;
> A man severe he was, and stern to view,
> I knew him well, and every truant knew;
> Well had the boding tremblers learned to trace
> The day's disasters in his morning face;
> Full well they laugh'd with counterfeited glee,
> At all his jokes, for many a joke had he;
> Full well the busy whisper circling round,
> Conveyed the dismal tidings when he frown'd;
> Yet he was kind, or if severe in aught,
> The love he bore to learning was in fault;
> The village all declared how much he knew;
> 'Twas certain he could write and cypher too;
> Lands he could measure, terms and tides presage,
> And even the story ran that he could gauge . . . [1]

[1] The rest of *The Deserted Village* is quoted, almost in entirety.

21. Anthony King's poem 'The Frequented Village,' a poetic statement about *The Deserted Village*

Published by Godwin, 1771 [?], 18–19

The author of the anonymous review of King's poem in the *Monthly Review*, December 1771, p. 509–10, notes: 'This seems intended both as a companion and contrast to Goldsmith's *Deserted Village* . . . It may be thought somewhat cruel to damp the ardour of a young writer, by the severity of censure; but it would be greater cruelty to encourage a worthy youth, by fallacious complaisance, to an unavailing perseverance, in a pursuit, wherein the impossibility of his succeeding is but too obviously to be inferred from the imbecillity of his out-set.' Nothing of significance is known about Anthony King. A similar poem, not included here, is John Robinson's (1727–1802) *The Village Oppressed*.

Freedom, alas! thou much perverted name,
The sudden transport of a wanton flame,
Which oft to madness with the vulgar turns,
And with inconstant agitation burns,
The man who pleas'd how oft his premium scorn,
The evening hero, trampled on at morn;
Teach us, with true discerning minds, to know
The real fount whence patriot virtues flow,
Convinc'd that freedom properly we see,
When King and People's sentiments agree,
When due obedience to the laws is paid,
And just dependance in each order made;
And, Oh! if any courts the Patriot's name,
And, virtue-hurried, pants for deathless fame,
Warm'd with his country's zeal, undaunted stands,
And braves the fury of contending hands,

Oh! heap on him your envy'd gifts, nor spare
Your lavish honours on so bright a care,
Exalt him still, till nought remains to crown
Those labours which his country caus'd alone;
But if regardless of the common weal,
He wears an odious, hypocritic veil,
If nought but interest in his bosom glows,
And freedom there a cold reception knows;
Oh! speed your thunder on perdition's wings,
And crush the man who'd awe the best of Kings,
His people who'd in error's footsteps lead,
And point your vengeance at his rebel head!——

    Accept, dear GOLDSMITH, these ingenuous lines,
Whose generous breast no thought but truth confines,
Whose page, instructive as harmonious found,
A bright example, sheds its light around;
To thee, unfledg'd, my tender muse would soar,
Secur'd of thine, what praises wish I more?
Whose pensive ruins, sadly colour'd, tell
That, once, a people happily did dwell,
Whose desart waste, and unfrequented spot,
Proclaim a village, lost, forlorn, forgot,

    So some tall monument, of letter'd fame,
Records a brave commander's deathless name,
Warns us, how many battles he has won,
And regions travell'd with the journeying sun,
With grief, the speaking monument we leave,
And wish to snatch the hero from the grave.

22. Corbyn Morris's rhapsodic verses 'On Reading Dr. Goldsmith's Poem, the Deserted Village,' published in *The New Foundling Hospital for Wit*

new edition, 1784, vi, 95

Corbyn Morris (1710–79) was not strictly speaking a literary man but his set of verses combining personally held economic and artistic views appeared in a late edition of *The New Foundling Hospital for Wit*. They were probably composed around 1771–5. As Morris's own footnote indicates, the poem was occasioned by seeing Bowood in Wiltshire, the stately mansion, gardens, and park of the Earl of Shelburne. Biographical information about Morris is found in the *DNB* and in James L. Clifford's introduction to an edition of Morris's *An Essay towards Fixing the True Standards of Wit (1744)*, Los Angeles, California, Augustan Reprint Society, 1947.

Au Contraire.   The Reverse.

MARK the new scene*, how Wealth and Art unite
T' enrich the soil, and give the eye delight:
Here shady wastes and rushy bogs bore sway,
Now fields of corn the ploughman's toil obey,
And lowing pastures cheer the welcome day.
See roads new trac'd for universal good,
With stately bridges to surmount the flood.
The goddess Culture gains a new domain,
Enliv'ning all, and, with her busy train,
Spreads a rich mantle over hill and plain:
Whilst Nature views the happy changes made,
With pleasing wonder, like a country maid,
Who, drest in elegance, with rich array,
Scarce knows herself, blushing to look so gay.

* Bowood, in Wiltshire, the seat of the Right Honourable the Earl of Shelburne, &c. &c. [Morris's own note].

23. Edmund Burke on Goldsmith's pastoral images, in a letter to Richard Shackleton

6 May 1780

Printed in *The Correspondence of Edmund Burke*, ed. John A. Woods, Cambridge University Press, 1963, iv, p. 234.

Our Life is indeed a warfare. I keep up my Spirits as well as I can; and whilst I am in action they are well kept up; but my moments of rest are not always moments of quiet. I do not know any thing which would tend to make one forget all the disagreeable things which pass so much as a few calm moments with you at Beconsfield if I could get them; and though I should be happy in seeing any friend of yours, I think we should be rather more at home with yourself—but that shall be according to your pleasure.[1] When you were here last we were chained to the Town.[2] How that will be at your next coming I know not, for there is nothing with us altogether right. But you will see my Son who is a new accession to our Society and not the worst part of it. By the way I forgot, as indeed I forget many things which I ought to remember the pretty Poem you sent me about Ballitore.[3] It has that in it which I always consider as a mark of Genius—the turning to account the images and objects that one is familiar and conversant with—and not running all into repetition, or over improvement, (if that were possible) of the images which have struck others in other places and times. This latter shews, that people have little fire of their own, though they may be capable of kindling at the fire of others; and it does not mark them as good observers, though it may as retentive readers. What true and pretty Pastoral images has Goldsmith in his deserted Village—that

[1] Shackleton (1728–1792) visited Beaconsfield alone but brought friends to breakfast with Burke in London.
[2] Burke has been 'obliged to stay in London' when Shackleton had visited him in June 1776, but in any case Shackleton was reluctant to go to Beaconsfield.
[3] By Mary Shackleton. Written in 1778, the poem appeared in her *Poems* published in 1808.

beat all Pope and Philips[1] and Spenser too in my opinion, that is in the Pastoral—for I go no further—Our own manners afford food enough for Poetry if we knew how to dress it.

24. John Scott writes an early literary appraisal of *The Deserted Village*, in *Critical Essays on Some of the Poems of Several English Poets*

1785, 247–94

This estimate originally appeared as no. VIII of John Scott's (1730–83) *Critical Essays.* Entitled 'On Goldsmith's Deserted Village,' it was posthumously published. The other essays in the volume deal with illustrious poems by Denham, Milton, Pope, Dyer, Collins, and Thomson.

THE Temple of Fame, lately erected under the title of *The Works of the English Poets*,[2] affords a striking instance of caprice in the matter of admission to literary honours. Had Criticism, rational impartial criticism, kept the gate of this temple, several names which now appear within its walls, would certainly never have appeared there. But to drop the allegory, and change an imaginary edifice for a real book, it is difficult to guess the reason why that book admitted some authors, while others of similar character were rejected.

Poet is an appellation frequently used, without the annexion of its precise idea; which seems to be that of a person who combines pic-

---

[1] Ambrose Philips (*ca.* 1675–1749).
[2] See below p. 93, n. 3. This preamble is calculated to provide a context for Goldsmith's poetry.

turesque imagery, and interesting sentiment, and conveys them in melodious and regularly measured language. This is a definition, which will exclude the writer of Romances, and Prose Dramas, however sublime or pathetick, on the one hand; and the meer maker of Verses, however humorous or witty, on the other: were indeed the claim of either to be allowed, it must be that of the former; inasmuch as poetry must be nearer allied to the dignified and elegant, than to the mean and indelicate.

The title of Poet has been often bestowed on those who little deserved it. The name of English Classicks was surely ill merited, either by the Wits of Charles's days, that 'mob of gentlemen who wrote with ease,' or by the heroes of the Dunciad; their compositions were mostly trifling, and frequently immoral, and consequently unworthy of preservation. But in an Edition of poetry, where some of these are to be found, we rather wonder at not finding the others; where Rochester and Roscommon, Sprat, Hallifax, Stepney, and Duke, were received, why Carew, and Sedley, and Hopkins, were refused, one is puzzled to guess; and when Pomfret and Yalden are preferred to Eusden and Duck, it is not easy to account for the preference. The managers of this celebrated Edition,[1] as their work approached the present period, seem to have been more fastidious in their choice, and have omitted Writers who would have done their collection no discredit.[2] When the Publication was undertaken, Armstrong and Langhorne, poets of superior rank, were living; their works, consequently, could not be properly inserted; but Goldsmith was dead, and his certainly had a just claim to admission.[3]

Goldsmith's *Deserted Village*, the work now under consideration, is a performance of distinguished merit. The general idea it inculcates is this; that commerce, by an enormous introduction of wealth, has augmented the number of the rich, who by exhausting the provision

[1] See n. 3.
[2] Among such may be reckoned AARON HILL, who although in general a bombastick writer, produced some Pieces of merit, particularly the CAVEAT, an allegorical satire on Pope: ROBERT DODSLEY, author of Cleone, a Tragedy, and a Didactick Poem on Agriculture, intitled Publick Virtue: GRAINGER, translator of Tibullus, and author of another Didactick, called the Sugar Cane: CAWTHORN, author of Abelard to Eloisa, &c. &c. [Scott's own note].
[3] Johnson had not written a life of Goldsmith nor had Goldsmith's poetry appeared in the first edition of *The Works of the English Poets*, 68 vols, Printed for J. Nichols, 1779–81. Goldsmith's poetry did, however, appear in the new 1790 edition of *The Works* expanded to 75 vols. His poems are found in vol. 70. See also A. Tillotson, 'Dr. Johnson and the "Life of Goldsmith," ' *Modern Language Review*, xxviii, 1933.

of the poor, reduce them to the necessity of emigration. This principle is exemplified in the description of Auburn, a Country Village, once populous and flourishing, afterwards deserted and in ruins.

Modern poetry has, in general, one common defect, viz. the want of proper arrangement. There are many poems, whose component parts resemble a number of fine paintings, which have some connexion with each other, but are not placed in any regular series. *The Deserted Village* would have pleased me better, if all the circumstances relative to Auburn the inhabited, had been grouped in one picture; and all those relative to Auburn the deserted, in another. The Author's plan is more desultory; he gives us, alternately, contrasted sketches of the supposed place in its two different situations:

The Poem opens with an apostrophe to its subject:

> V. 1. Sweet Auburn, *loveliest* village of the plain,
>   Where health and plenty chear'd the *labouring*
>   swain;
>   Where smiling spring its earliest visit paid,
>   And parting summer's lingering blooms delay'd.
>   Dear *lovely bowers* of innocence and *ease*,
>   Seats of my youth, when ev'ry *sport* could please;
>   How often have I loiter'd on thy green,
>   Where humble happiness endear'd each scene.
>   How often have I paus'd on every charm,
>   The shelter'd cot, the cultivated farm;
>   The never-failing brook, the busy mill,
>   The decent church, that topt the neighb'ring
>   hill.
>   The hawthorn bush, with seats *beneath the shade*,
>   For talking age, and whispering lovers made!
>   How often have I blest the coming day,
>   When *toil remitting* lent its turn to play,
>   And all the village train from *labour free*,
>   *Led up their sports beneath the spreading tree;*
>   *While many a pastime circled in the shade,*
>   The young contending as the old survey'd;
>   *And many a gambol frolick'd o'er the ground,*
>   *And flights of art, and feats of strength went round.*
>   And still as each *repeated pleasure* tir'd,
>   *Succeeding sports* the mirthful band *inspir'd;*
>   The dancing pair, that simply sought renown
>   By holding out to tire each other down;
>   The swain mistrustless of his smutted face,

While secret laughter titter'd round the place;
The bashful virgin's side-long looks of love,
The matron's glance, that would those looks
    reprove;
These were thy charms *sweet* village; *sports* like
    these
With *sweet succession taught e'en toil to please*;
These round thy *bowers* thy chearful influence
    shed,
These were thy charms—But all these charms
    are fled.

This passage is one of that kind, with which the imagination may be pleased, but which will not fully satisfy the judgment. The four lines, '*Dear lovely bowers*,' &c. might perhaps have been spared. The village diversions are insisted on with too much prolixity. They are described first with a puerile generality, redundance, and confusion: they are *sports*, and *pastimes*, and *gambols*, and *flights of art*, and *feats of strength*; and they are represented sometimes as passive, the 'sports are *led up*;' sometimes as active, the 'pastimes *circle*,' and the gambols '*frolick*,' and the 'flights and feats go *round*.' But we are perhaps fully recompensed for this, by the classical and beautiful particularity and conciseness of the context, '*the dancing pair*,' '*the swain mistrustless of his smutted face*,' the '*bashful virgin's looks, &c.*' The paragraph in general has much inaccuracy, especially a disgusting identity of diction; the word '*bowers*,' occurs twice, the word '*sweet*,' thrice, and '*charms*,' and '*sport*,' singular or plural, four times. We have also '*toil remitting*,' and '*toil taught to please*,' '*succeeding sports*,' and '*sports with sweet succession*.'

  V. 35. *Sweet smiling* village, *loveliest of the lawn*,
    Thy *sports* are fled, and all thy *charms* with-
     drawn;
    Amidst thy *bow'rs* the *tyrant's hand* is seen,
    And *desolation saddens all thy green*:
    One only master grasps the whole domain,
    And half a tillage stints thy *smiling* plain;
    No more thy glassy brook reflects the day,
    But chok'd with sedges, works its weedy way.
    Along the glades a solitary guest,
    The hollow-sounding bittern guards its nest;
    Amidst thy desert walks the lapwing flies,

And tires their echoes with repeated cries.
Sunk are thy *bowers* in shapeless ruin all,
And the long grass o'er tops the mould'ring
    wall,
And trembling, shrinking, from the spoiler's
    hand,
Far, far away thy children leave the land.

The passage already examined, and this, have both the same character of verbosity. There is a repetition which indicates intention, and maintains regularity; and there is a repetition which discovers either carelessness, or poverty of language. Auburn had before, I. 1. been termed '*sweet*,' and '*the loveliest village of the plain*;' it is now termed '*sweet*,' and '*smiling*,' and '*the loveliest of the lawn*.' We had been told, l. 34. that '*all its charms were fled*;' and we are now told that '*its sports are fled, and its charms withdrawn*.' The '*tyrant's hand*,' seems mentioned rather too abruptly; and '*desolation saddening the green*,' is common place phraseology. The eight lines, '*No more the glassy brook, &c.*' are natural and beautiful; but the next two, '*And trembling, shrinking, &c.*' are ill-placed, for they prematurely introduce the subject of emigration.

    V. 51. *Ill* fares the land, to hastening *ills* a prey,
        Where wealth accumulates, and men decay;
        Princes and lords may flourish, or may fade;
        A breath can make them, as a breath has
            made;
        But a bold peasantry, their country's pride,
        When once destroy'd can never be supply'd.

        A time there was, e're England's griefs
           began,
        When every rood of ground maintain'd its man;
        For him light labour spread her wholesome store,
        Just gave what life requir'd but gave no more:
        His best companions innocence and health,
        And his best riches ignorance of wealth.

The first of these paragraphs, '*Ill fares the land, &c.*' with all its merit, which is great, for the sentiment is noble, and the expression little inferior, seems rather out of place; after the affair of depopulation had been more fully described, it might have appeared to advantage as a concluding reflection. The second asserts what has been repeatedly denied, that '*there was a time in England, when every rood of ground maintained its man.'* If however such a time ever was, it could not be so recent as when the Deserted Village was flourishing, a circumstance supposed to exist within the remembrance of the poet; consequently the idea had no business in the poem.

> V. 63. But times are alter'd; trade's unfeeling train,
> Usurp the land, and dispossess the swain;
> Along the lawn, where scatter'd hamlets rose,
> Unweildly wealth, and cumb'rous pomp re-
> pose;
> And every want to opulence allied,
> And every pang that folly pays to pride.
> Those *gentle hours* that plenty bade to *bloom,*
> Those calm desires that ask'd but little room,
> Those healthful *sports* that grac'd the peaceful
> scene,
> *Liv'd* in each *look,* and *brighten'd* all the
> green;
> *These far-departing, seek a kinder shore,*
> *And rural mirth and manners are no more.*

This passage is a mere superfluity. The first six lines, 'But times are alter'd,' might have been reserved for introduction in some other part of the piece. The next, 'These gentle hours, &c.' should have been totally suppressed: 'gentle hours that *are bade to bloom*,' and '*healthful sports* that *live* in *looks,* and *brighten a green*;' is certainly not vindicable language. The '*hours,*' and the '*sports,*' also, are said to '*seek a kinder shore,*' which '*kinder shore,*' is inconsistently described in the sequel of the poem, as fraught with every inconvenience and every danger. The mention of the '*sports,*' and of the emigration, '*These far-departing, &c.*' is here again unnecessarily repeated.

> V. 74. *Sweet* Auburn! parent of the blissful hour,
> Thy glades forlorn confess the *tyrant's* power.
> Here as I take my solitary rounds,
> Amidst thy tangling walks, and ruin'd grounds,
> And, many a year elaps'd, return to view,
> Where once the cottage stood the hawthorn
> grew,
> Here, as with doubtful, pensive steps I range,
> Trace every scene, and wonder at the change,[1]

[1] Here Scott quotes Virgil, *Eclogue,* I, lines 67–9:
> An unquam patrios longo post tempore fines,
> Pauperis et tuguri congestum cespite culmen,
> Post aliquot mea regna vibens mirabor aristas?

Remembrance wakes with all her busy train,
Swells at my breast, and turns the past to pain.

The adjective '*sweet*,' is frequently, and very properly, in use as a substitute for agreeable or pleasant, but it displeases in this work by perpetual repetition. The obscure and indefinite idea of a '*Tyrant*,' recurs also unnecessarily here again. There is pathos in the lines, '*And many a year, &c.*' but they are as evidently misplaced as some of their predecessors: we wish to hear more of the Village in its prosperity, before we hear so much of its desolation.

Subsequent to the above, we have an expatiation on the Author's fallacious hope of concluding his days at his favourite Auburn, and a paragraph in praise of retirement; both well written, but rather episodical.

> V. 115. *Sweet* was the sound, when oft at ev'ning's
> close,
> Up yonder hill the village murmur rose;
> There as I past with careless steps, and slow,
> The mingled notes came soften'd from below;
> The swain responsive as the milk-maid sung,
> The *sober* herd that low'd to meet their young;
> The noisy geese that gabbled o'er the pool,
> The playful children just *let loose* from school;
> The watch dog's voice, that bay'd the whisp-
> 'ring wind,
> And the loud laugh, that spoke the vacant mind;
> These all in soft confusion *sought the shade,*[1]
> And fill'd each pause the nightingale had made.
> But now the sounds of population fail,
> No chearful murmurs fluctuate in the gale,
> No busy steps the grass-grown footway tread,
> But all the *bloomy flush of life is fled.*
> *All but yon widow'd solitary thing,*
> That feebly bends beside the plashy spring;

'Ah, shall I ever, long years hence, look again on my country's bounds, on my humble cottage with its turf-clad roof - - shall I, long years hence, look amazed on a few ears of corn, once my kingdom?' (Loeb Library translation)

1 The village murmur, l. 116, is said '*to have risen up the hill*'; it is now said to have '*sought the shade.*' This seems at first sight an inconsistency, but perhaps the poet may be vindicated by supposing that the hill, like many other hills, was shaded with trees. Perhaps if a rhyme had not been wanted, we should not have met with the word '*shade,*' on this occasion [Scott's note].

> She wretched matron, forc'd, in age, for bread,
> To strip the brook with mantling cresses spread,
> To pick her wintry faggot from the thorn,
> To seek her nightly shade, and *weep till morn*;
> She only left of all the harmless train,
> The sad historian of the *pensive* plain.

This is indeed a passage of uncommon merit. The circumstances it describes are obvious in nature, but new in poetry; and they are described with great force and elegance. Milton, in a simile, which he thought capable of illustrating the idea of an Eden, among other objects of delight has introduced

> Each rural sight, each rural sound.—

The Epic Poet, however, only mentions sound in the general, but our Author descends to particulars, and those particulars are most happily selected; they bear one uniform consistent character, viz. that of a sober or serene chearfulness. The locality given by the intimation, that they were heard '*from below*,' has a fine effect. In *Paradise Lost*, b. v. l. 547. we have a beautiful instance of the same kind:

> Cherubic songs, by night from neighb'ring hills,
> Aerial music send.[1]——

The *Matron gathering water-cresses*, is a fine picture; but there is unnatural exaggeration in representing her as '*weeping*,' every night, '*till morning*;' sudden calamity occasions violent emotions, but habitual hardship will not produce incessant sorrow; time reconciles us to the most disagreeable situations. Our Author's language in this place, is also very defective in correctness. After mentioning the general privation of the '*bloomy flush of life*,' the exceptionary, '*all but*,' includes, as part of that '*bloomy flush*,' an '*aged decrepid matron*;' that is to say, in plain prose, '*the bloomy flush of life is all fled but one old woman*.'

The Poet now recurs again to the past. When Auburn is described as flourishing, its Clergyman as a principal inhabitant, is very properly introduced. This supposed Village Pastor, is characterized in a manner which seems almost unexceptionable, both for sentiment and expression. His contentment, hospitality, and piety, are pointed out with sufficient particularity, yet without confusion or redundance. Where indiscriminate approbation can be hazarded, quotation is the less

---

[1] The situation is here reversed, the songs proceed from above [Scott's note].

necessary; but probably few readers will think the following extracts
tedious.

> Near yonder copse, where once the garden
>   smil'd,
> And still where many a garden flower grows wild;
> There, where a few torn shrubs the place disclose,
> The village preacher's modest mansion rose.

This is a fine natural stroke—We see the '*copse*,' the '*torn shrubs*,' and
the '*scatter'd flowers*.' The last remaining vestige of what was once a
garden, is always the '*garden flower that grows wild*.'

> A man he was, to all the country dear,
> And passing rich with forty pounds a year;
> Remote from towns he ran his godly race,
> Nor o'er had chang'd, nor wish'd to change
>   his place . . .

The benevolent mind cannot but yield its hearty assent to this beautiful
oblique reprehension of that avarice which makes the crimes and errors
of the poor, a pretence to justify the indulgence of its own parsimony.

> —At church with meek and unaffected grace,
> His looks adorn'd the venerable place;
> Truth from his lips prevail'd with double sway,
> And fools who came to scoff, remain'd to pray . . .

Poetry attains its full purpose, when it sets its subjects strongly and
distinctly in our view. This is the case here: we behold the good old
man attended by his venerating parishioners, and with a kind of dignified complacence, even permiting the familiarities of their children.
The concluding simile has been much admired, and so far as immaterial
objects can be illustrated by material, it is indeed a happy illustration.

As every parish has its Clergyman, almost every parish has its
School-master. This secondary character is here described with great
force and precision. The Muse, in part of her description, has descended
to convey village ideas, in village language, but has contrived to give
just so much dignity to the familiar, as prevents it from disgusting.
The point is indeed so nice, that to say the lines in italicks are not
prosaick or mean, is perhaps to say all that can be said truly. We are
reconciled to them only, because we know that they are the effect of
choice, not of incapacity:

Beside yon straggling fence that skirts the way,
With blossom'd furze unprofitably gay,
There in his noisy mansion, skill'd to rule,
The village-master taught his little school;
A man severe he was, and stern to view,
I knew him well, and every truant knew. . .[1]

The description of the Village Alehouse, contains domestick minutiae, of a kind, which must necessarily have pleased in the original, but which the hand of a master alone, could have made to please in the copy. That learned and judicious Critick, Dr. Warton,[2] in his Essay on the Writings and Genius of Pope, justly observes, that 'The use, the force, and the excellence of language, consists in raising clear, complete, and circumstantial images, and in turning readers into spectators.' This theory he exemplifies, by quoting two passages from his author, in which, he says, that 'every epithet paints its object, and paints it distinctly.' The same may be said with equal justice of the following:

Near yonder thorn, that lifts its head on high,
Where once the sign-post caught the passing
    eye;
Low lies that house, where nut-brown draughts
    inspir'd,
Where grey-beard mirth, and smiling toil re-
    tir'd . . .

This fine poetical inventory of the furniture, is fully equalled by the character of the guests, and the detail of their amusements. The negative mode of expression, '*Thither no more, &c.*' by fixing the mind on the past, adds a kind of pleasing regretful pathos:

Vain transitory splendors! could not all
Reprieve the tottering mansion from its fall!
Obscure it sinks, nor shall it more impart
An hour's importance to the poor man's heart . . .

This is not poetical fiction, but historical truth. We have here no imaginary Arcadia, but the real country; no poetical swains, but the men who actually drive the plough, or wield the scythe, the sickle, the hammer, or the hedging bill. But though nothing is invented,

---

[1] The entire description of the schoolmaster is quoted.
[2] Joseph Warton (1722–1800), critic and schoolmaster, had criticized modern poetry for its emphasis on 'correct' tendencies.

something is suppressed. The rustick's hour of relaxation is too rarely so innocent; it is too often contaminated with extravagance, anger, and profanity: describing vice and folly, however, will not prevent their existing; and it is agreeable to forget for a moment, the reality of their existence.

The foregoing description not unnaturally introduces the following reflections:

> Yes! let the rich deride, the proud disdain,
> These simple blessings of the lowly train;
> To me more dear, congenial to my heart,
> One native charm, than all the gloss of art . . .

The sentiment here is better than the expression. The Poet is probably right in his supposition, that the pleasures of the rich are less genuine and lively than those of the poor; but his language is far from being simple or perspicuous. That intention and parade raise expectations which will be mostly disappointed; that the joys which are unanticipated, and unconstrained, or independent of the will of others, are the best; were undoubtedly the axioms intended to be conveyed in these lines, 'Spontaneous joys, &c.' By 'spontaneous joys,' we must understand, joys which without previous care or provision seem to offer themselves to our acceptance: to say that the soul readily accepts such, might be proper; but to say that the soul 'adopts' them, and at the same time 'owns their sway;' and to say that the 'sway,' is a 'first-born sway;' is to use thoughts and words not clear of confusion: but when these joys which the 'soul adopts,' and whose 'first-born sway it owns,' are said to 'frolick over the mind lightly, unenvied, unmolested, and unconfined;' we have surely a chaos, both of ideas and phraseology.[1] The lines have also an ambiguity: we know not whether it is meant, that 'the soul adopts spontaneous joys,' in which 'nature has her play;' or that 'where nature has her play, the soul adopts spontaneous joys:' be the sense what it may, it is superfluous, and superfluities always create obscurity. There is a most extraordinary confusion of ideas, in the 'long pomp' and 'midnight masquerade array'd' in the 'freaks of wanton wealth:' how pomp and a masquerade could be 'array'd' at all, is not

---

[1] To discover fully the nonsense of this passage, it is necessary to recur to the sense of the words metaphorically used. The joys, from the verb adopt, must be supposed to be children, something inferior, or dependent; from the substantive sway, they must be supposed to be kings, something superior, or governing; and from the verb frolick, one conceives an idea of a set of mischievous young rakes, or of a harlequin. The soul adopts the joys, and they rule it, and frolick over it [Scott's note].

easy to conceive; but certainly they could not be '*array'd*' with '*freaks.*'

The Poet now proceeds to the causes which produced the desertion of his village:

> Ye friends to truth, ye statesmen, who survey
> The rich man's joys increase, the poor's decay;
> Tis yours to judge, how wide the limits stand
> Between a splendid and a happy land. . .

Goldsmith undoubtedly was serious in the foregoing apostrophe, '*Ye friends to truth, &c.*' but his acquaintance with the world must be but superficial, who could think that statesmen in general merited the high character of friends of truth, or friends of the poor. He had said before,

> Along the lawn where scatter'd hamlets rose,
> Unweildy wealth and cumb'rous pomp repose:

He says now,

> ———The man of wealth and pride,
> Takes up a space that many poor supplied.

That the domain of the ancient Feudal Lord, or Rural Squire, was less extensive than that of the modern Peer, Placeman, or Nabob, may be doubted; but as many old mansions yet retain their surrounding parks, warrens, &c. and many new villas are erected, and adorned with spacious plantations; pleasure may be justly said to have encroached on cultivation, and the rich to have remotely abstracted from the provision of the poor. But the influx of foreign wealth has been mischievous in another point of view: the new or commercial gentry acquiring their money with ease, have, in verification of the proverb, '*light come, light go,*' wantonly raised the price of commodities: the old, or landed gentry, unwilling to descend from their state, and unable otherwise to support it, have been obliged to augment the size, and advance the rent of their farms:[1] the great farmer has not been injured by his increased payment, for the increased value of his corn and cattle has enabled him to pay it, and often to become opulent. But there has been one sufferer; the little farmer has been annihilated, or at least metamorphosed into a labourer; and the labourer has had less work, the same wages, and more expence for necessaries. The

[1] By augmenting the size of farms, repairs are saved, and rent is in general better paid. Whether the practice is so injurious to the community, as has been supposed, is a point not easy to determine [Scott's note].

Author of these remarks must confess, that when he has visited some of our capital seats, their seemingly interminable length of lawn, broken only by a few gloomy woods, has worn, to him, an air of melancholy solitude and idle waste, that was far from being agreeable. He has wished to exchange his situation for the vale of corn-clad inclosures, the winding lane, and shrub-hung brow, with their group of humble cottages, and chearful inhabitants. The possessors of these places are themselves sometimes not destitute of such feelings; the ingenious Mr. Potter, in his excellent Observations on the Poor laws,[1] has recorded a memorable instance of it: 'The late Earl of Leicester,' says he, 'being complimented upon the completion of his great design at Holkham, replied,' "It is a melancholy thing to stand alone in one's country. I look round; not a house is to be seen but mine. I am the giant of giant-castle, and have eat up all my neighbours." What then must be the case, when these fashionable decorations are acquired by immediate rapine, extortion, or oppression; by the plunder of Hindoos, and the slavery of Negroes? One is ready to ask if it be possible to enjoy them.

> —In their towers raz'd villages I see,
> And tears of orphans wat'ring every tree;
> Are these mock ruins that invade my view?
> They are the entrails of the poor Gentoo;
> That column's trophied base his bones supply,
> That lake the tears that swell'd his sable eye.
> LANGHORNE.[2]

Goldsmith's last quoted passage, 'Ye friends to truth, &c.' has been considered in a political view; some attention must now be given to its poetry. 'Folly hailing,' or welcoming, the ships to the shore, is a noble personification. The breaks in these lines, 'Yet count our gains,' 'Not so our loss, &c.' have rather a disagreeable effect. In blank verse, to continue the sense from one line to another, is always more or less necessary, but in rhyme it is seldom advantageous. The detached, or unconnected parts of a verse, unless very carefully managed, are always prosaisms. By this couplet,

1 Robert Potter (1721-1804), poet and politician, occupied much of his leisure time in translating the great Greek tragedians and was best known for his translations of Aeschylus (1777). His Observations on the Poor Laws appeared in 1785.
2 See his COUNTRY JUSTICE. A Poem in which a fine poetical fancy is united with just satire [Scott's note].

The robe that wraps his limbs in *silken sloth*,
Has robb'd the neighb'ring fields of half their
growth;

the poet undoubtedly meant to intimate, that a considerable tract of land would not produce more profit than was requisite to defray the expence of a rich man's clothing. Extravagance in dress, was perhaps more the foible of former ages than of the present; but be this as it may, the notion of a '*robe robbing fields of their growth*,' is hyperbolical, aukward, and far-fetched. It might have been more tolerable in a country of mulberry-trees. A juvenile writer would doubtless think the phrase of '*wrapping limbs in silken sloth*,' a grand stroke, conveying the combined ideas of finery and laziness. '*The seat spurning the cottage from the green*,' would have been a beautiful impersonation; but the effect of it is entirely destroyed by the context, '*where solitary sports are seen:*' the '*Seat*,' considered in itself, fancy might readily convert into a '*Person;*' but the '*seat where solitary sports are seen*,' must inevitably be '*a place*.' Our author uses the word '*sports*,' till it becomes almost insufferable; he mostly means by it the ale-house amusements of villagers: he here must mean the field-diversions of their superiors. The four lines, '*Around the world, &c.*' had better have been suppressed: the first two are introduced abruptly; the transition is not very natural or easy, from the great man's park, seat, and equipage, to the exportation of necessaries, and the importation of luxuries: the last two have little merit in themselves, '*A land all adorned for pleasure, in barren splendour feebly waiting a fall*,' is but an uncouth kind of language: . . . The predilection of criticks, and indeed of readers in general, in favour of the simile, as an essential constituent of poetry, is so strong, that whoever thinks lightly of it, will probably be deemed a sort of literary heretick. That similies are sometimes employed to great advantage, must be readily allowed; but that they are far from being always advantageous, is certain. In the above passage, nature and art are contrasted in two different subjects. Some distant kind of resemblance may be fancied, between a fine fashionable lady, and a country full of palaces and gardens; but the parallel, as Goldsmith has drawn it, is exceedingly defective. Ornament in the woman, is the effect of a deliberate systematical design to recommend herself, and please others; the country is incapable of such design; and even those who adorn it, scarcely think of rendering it pleasing to any but themselves. The emigration affair is 'here again hammered on the ear,' by repetition; it is indeed introduced like the burden of a song, at every opportunity.

There is however a noble picture, in '*Famine scourging the peasant from the land.*' Perhaps a writer has not a more difficult task than to know when he has said enough: '*Famine scourges the peasant from the land;*' so far the thought, however ill-placed, is proper; but while he is '*scourg'd away,*' he is very inconsistently represented as '*leading his humble band with him.*' We have then other new and unnecessary ideas; he is '*scourged away,*' and he '*leads his band;*' and now he '*sinks.*' We are not however to suppose, that he literally sinks into the ocean, or into the grave, but metaphorically,[1] into poverty or distress: and he sinks, '*without one arm to save;*' which is an aukward, and almost ludicrous substitute for saying, that there is no person able or willing to relieve him. The '*Country blooming a garden and a grave,*' is another absurdity: had the peasantry been described, as perishing at home, the expression would have been just; but the country could not be the '*grave of those who had left it.*' . .

The great fault of this Poem, is a disregard to consistency. The previous repeated hints of the emigration, had intirely superseded the above passage; for those whom '*Famine had scourged from the land,*' it surely need not have been asked, '*in what part of it they should reside.*' With similar impropriety Rural Poverty, which we were led to suppose had left its native land, is now introduced as retiring to the metropolis; but is shewn to derive no advantage from a retreat thither . . .

The Author now rather unskilfully returns to his subject, by the following inquiry:

> Do thine, *sweet* Auburn, thine the loveliest
> train . . . [lines 341–64 are quoted].

This piece is animated, and in general correctly drawn; the candid rational critick can have little objection to it. The general effect of the passage is indeed weakened by the two last couplets, '*Far different, &c.*' which are totally superfluous, and of dissimilar character. The compound '*grassy-vested,*' is a bad one; the adjective '*grassy,*' conveys the whole sense, consequently the participle, '*vested,*' is tautologous; grass-vested, or verdure-vested, would have been proper . . . [lines 367–86 follow].

An injudicious arrangement is obvious here again. This passage should have preceeded the passage last quoted, '*Ah no, to distant climes, &c.*' the people should have been introduced as going, before the place to

1 The metaphor is an *ignis fatuus*, that leads many a poet into the bog of nonsense . . . [Scott's note].

which they were to go, had been described. This disposition would have produced another advantage, a climax in character, from the pathetick to the sublime. This paragraph has many beauties: the heart must be insensible indeed, which does not feel the force of pathos, in the circumstances of the daughter relinquishing her lover, in order to attend her father; and the mother clasping her thoughtless babes, with additional tenderness. The *Labor limæ*, might however have been employed to advantage; the lines in italicks might have been spared; and the positive adjective, '*silent*,' in the 15th line, and the comparative, '*louder*,' in the 17th, do not agree: to say that some *accents* are *louder* than others, is proper; but to say that any *accents* are *louder* than *silence*, is absurd, because *silence* cannot be '*loud*' at all. The idea of habitations had been conveyed under the name of '*bowers*,' the mention of them again, under the name of '*the cot where every pleasure rose*,' was needless. The expression, '*where every pleasure rose*,' is unusual, and rather aukward.

This is succeeded by an apostrophe to Luxury, in which kingdoms inebriated by her potions, are not very elegantly compared to an hydropic human body. This apostrophe is ill placed, as it intercepts the connection between the last quotation, '*Good heaven*, &c.' and the following, which concludes the poem: . . . [lines 397–432 follow].
This is a fine passage, but it would admit of improvement: the first couplet, '*Even now*, &c.' is little better than an absurdity; the devastation is '*begun*,' and '*half done*,' at the same time. The connection with the preceeding quotation, would have been better, if those two lines had been omitted, and the third line had begun thus, '*With them*, &c.' '*The anchor'd vessel*,' with its '*flapping sail*,' is a natural and beautiful image. The address to Poetry has a noble enthusiasm, but wants correctness: the lines in italicks, '*Unfit in these degenerate*, &c.' might have been spared; '*Strike for honest fame*,' is an unmeaning phrase, nearly allied to nonsense; and what affinity the circumstance of the voice of Poetry '*prevailing over time*,' can have with the circumstance of its '*redressing the rigour of a climate*,' is not obvious. I am not one of those who discover even a casual imitation in every resemblance; but possibly the ideas of two former writers might have 'remurmured' in our poet's 'memorial cell,' when he wrote these lines. Prefixed to Pope's works are several complimentary copies of verses, in one of which, the author speaking of the story of Lodona, says,

The soft complaint shall over time prevail.

And Gray, in his progress of poetry, has the following:

> In climes beyond the solar road,
> Where shaggy forms o'er ice-built mountains
>   roam,
> The muse has broke the twilight gloom
>   To chear the shivering native's dull abode.

The *Deserted Village*, as has been hinted, is, on the whole, a performance of great merit; it has numerous excellencies, and numerous faults; and while we are charmed with the former, we cannot but regret that more pains was not taken to avoid the latter.

25. Edward Mangin on Goldsmith's greatness as a moral instructor, in *An Essay on Light Reading*

1808, 159–76

Edward Mangin (1772–1852), a miscellaneous writer who spent almost all his life at Bath, was best known in the nineteenth century for his *Essay on Light Reading*, which included fresh facts about Goldsmith's youth and an appreciative essay about his poetry. Much of the biographical material in Mangin's essay was included in the lives of Goldsmith by Prior (see No. 75) and Forster.

Amongst the most celebrated of these [great ornaments of English literature] may be mentioned Goldsmith, Cowper, and the too much neglected Langhorne, the author of *Owen of Carron;* . . . This delightful work, and the *Task* of Cowper, and the *Traveller* and *Deserted Village* of Goldsmith, do not, I admit, rank more properly under the denomination of LIGHT READING than hundreds which are stationed in private libraries, and which are read with avidity, and quoted with applause. But they possess certain attractive qualities, not easily described, though powerfully felt. They overflow with charms for every laudable variety of taste, and for each degree of understanding. To their matter, and the harmonious numbers in which it is conveyed, there exists something responsive in every bosom: no preparative erudition is required to make them intelligible, nor any comment wanting to indicate their beauties; and, to the reader of these pages, if not very fastidious, I should hope that an apology is unnecessary for introducing a few of the distinguished passages in each of these poems: and first, of the *Traveller* and *Deserted Village*.

Of these, Mr. Cumberland,[1] in his Memoirs of himself, has an observation which appears to me, and will, I believe, be thought by most other readers, exceedingly unjust. He says of Goldsmith, that the paucity of his verses does not allow us to rank him in that high poetical station to which his genius might have carried him; and adds, of the *Deserted Village, Traveller*, and *Hermit*, that they are only specimens— '*Birds*' eggs on a string, and eggs of small birds too.'

Mr. Cumberland's objection to the claims of Goldsmith, from the circumstances of his not having written more in verse than he did, is altogether so destitute of force, as to render a laboured refutation superfluous. He must know, as well as any one, that excellence in an author consists not in writing much but in writing well. When we read the ode addressed by Horace to Aristius (22nd ode, 1st book), the Pollio of Virgil,[2] or the Lycidas of Milton, we are satisfied that the minds, from which these inestimable productions emanated, were truly poetical, and of the highest class: and surely the dramatic reputation of the amiable and ingenious author[3] of the *West Indian* would not have suffered any diminution had he composed nothing more for the stage than that admired comedy . . .

If the *Traveller* and *Deserted Village* are examined, they will be found, in most respects, to bear the closest scrutiny of criticism, to abound with precepts of the soundest policy, the shrewdest remarks on human character, descriptions of local scenery as rich and as appropriate as any thing that ever came from the pen of Shakespeare or the pencil of Claude; and, for plaintive melody of versification, and pathetic appeals to the heart, they stand perhaps unrivalled.

[1] Richard Cumberland (1732–1811), dramatist who had known Goldsmith. See No. 61 below for the actual passages referred to here.
[2] I.e., Eclogue no. iii.
[3] Richard Cumberland (1732–1811); see Nos 34 and 61.

The exordium of the *Traveller, or a Prospect of Society*, is very happily conceived; and the reference to home and its delights, is an affecting instance of the poet's art in the commencement of a composition which depicts the wanderings over a foreign land of one, whose *'heart untravelled'* turns with fondness to the scenes of early life, and acknowledges so tenderly the ties of kindred. Though nothing can appear more easy or natural than this introduction of himself, yet thus completely to interest the reader in his private feelings is a proof of consummate skill.

The altitude which he makes choice of to take his purposed view of society, is selected with great judgment:

> 'Ev'n now, where Alpine solitudes ascend,
> I sit me down, a pensive hour to spend.'

Beneath him he sees, while *'above the storm's career,'* lakes, forests, cities, plains, the kingly palace, and the shepherd's cottage; and remembering that man, however destitute, should not cease to be benevolent, he exults in the visible prosperity of his fellow-beings, and exclaims, in the sublimest spirit of philanthropy and poetical fervour,

> 'Creation's heir, the world, the world is mine.'

Some of the landscapes which follow are executed with inimitable truth, and with surprising variety of expression; and his pictures of Italy and the United Provinces are drawn with great ability:

> 'Far to the right, where Appenine ascends,
> Bright as the summer Italy extends;
> The uplands sloping deck the mountain's side,
> Woods over woods, in gay, theatric pride;
> While oft some temple's mould'ring tops between,
> With venerable grandeur mark the scene.'

How few, but how masterly, the strokes used to produce this accurate and luxurious description!

Having sketched the *'churlish soil'* of Switzerland, and the sprightly region of France, with their inhabitants, he proceeds— . . . [to versify the Dutch].

His transition to England, *'the land of scholars, and the nurse of arms,'* is unquestionably one of the most majestic flights of poetry. The political observations, which adorn his view of Britain, are eminently just and spirited; and the versification of this concluding part of the poem is full of energy and grace.

Over this fine work there is spread an imposing air of philosophic dignity, which awes the reader; and, engaging his understanding rather than his sensibility, forces him to reflection.

The *Deserted Village*, written in the same measure, and with every mark of the same potent hand, has a distinct character; it applies more immediately to the softer feelings of our nature, than to our reasoning faculties; and evinces the fertility of Goldsmith's genius, by showing him equally capable of exciting emotions of tenderness and compassion. Here almost all the imagery is familiar to our eyes, and all the sentiments to our hearts. We seem rather to remember what the poet describes, than to receive information from his lines; we acknowledge without hesitation the fidelity of his outline; we instantaneously grow acquainted with every interesting object; each 'rural sight and sound;' the hamlet, its humble children, and their saintly pastor; their joys and their sorrows. We share their sufferings, and shed tears over the downfal of their happiness, when, at the poet's bidding, this lovely pageant vanishes; and for the mansion of festivity, and the fields which industry had taught to smile, we behold only a ruin and a desert.

Whether or not this, and other poems of Goldsmith, would bear the test of a critical inquisition, is a question that does not belong to my present purpose; which is to exhibit him in a far higher capacity than that of a versifier: as A MORAL INSTRUCTOR, WHOSE TALENTS WERE UNIFORMLY DIRECTED TO THE GREAT AND PRAISE WORTHY END OF COMMUNICATING TO HIS COUNTRYMEN A PARTIALITY FOR THE DICTATES OF VIRTUE. And this he has done so effectually, that, in reading his lines, we are more apt to weigh the thoughts they contain, than the powers that produced them; and, overlooking the graces and sweetness by which his verse is distinguished, to dwell with intense admiration on the substance.

In support of this remark, I shall extract only a few passages from the *Deserted Village*; the construction of which, however beautiful, is scarcely ever adverted to by the multitudes who are enraptured with the images which they present to the mind.

Nothing of its kind can be more finished than the picture of the village-clergyman: but the simile employed to illustrate the poet's account of his strict performance of the pastoral office, the affection he feels for his people, and the persevering piety by which he wins them to paths of holiness and peace, if not matchless, has never been excelled:

'And as a bird each fond endearment tries
To tempt its new-fledg'd offspring to the skies,

He try'd each art, reprov'd each dull delay,
Allur'd to brighter worlds, and led the way.'

If this idea can be equalled by another, in any language, ancient or modern, it is by that with which the portrait concludes:

'To them his heart, his love, his griefs were giv'n;
But all his serious thoughts had rest in heav'n.
As some tall cliff, that lifts its awful form,
Swells from the vale, and mid-way leaves the storm,
Tho' round its breast the rolling clouds are spread,
Eternal sunshine settles on its head.'

His heart and his taste must be alike vitiated, who unmoved could contemplate the subject of the following lines, or be insensible to the melody with which they flow: . . . [lines 327–38 follow].

The *Deserted Village* ends with an address to Poetry, not only affecting for the solemnity of its *personal* allusion, and pleasing to the reader for the smooth current of its versification, but remarkable as displaying the virtuous enthusiasm of Goldsmith, and a generous declaration of what was *his* notion concerning a poet's duty, and the influence of his art on mankind: . . .

26. Johann Wilhelm von Goethe on the pictures evoked by *The Deserted Village* in *Dichtung und Wahrheit* (*Truth and Poetry*)

1821

Goethe (see Nos 71 and 79 below for biographical information) throughout his life continued to believe in the greatness of Goldsmith as a thinker and writer. 'It is not the *mass* of creations,' he told his confidant Johann Peter Eckermann in 1828, 'that counts. We have in literature, poets considered very productive because volume after volume of their poems has appeared. But in my opinion,' Goethe continued to explain, 'these people ought to be called thoroughly *unproductive*; for what they have written is without life and durability. Goldsmith, on the contrary, has written so few poems that their number is not worth mentioning; nevertheless, I must pronounce him a thoroughly productive poet—indeed, even on that account; because the little he has written has an inherent life which can sustain itself' (*Conversations of Goethe with Eckermann*, ed. Havelock Ellis, 1930, p. 247). If Goldsmith *had* written more poetry, one wonders if Goethe could have paid such close attention to each of his poems. In the passage below, Goethe describes the impression made on him and his friends by *The Deserted Village*; it is quoted from *The Autobiography of Goethe: Truth and Poetry: From My Own Life*, trans. by John Oxenford (1848, 2 vols), Bk xii, i. p. 474.

. . . a little poem, which we passionately received into our circle, allowed us from henceforward to think of nothing else. Goldsmith's *Deserted Village* necessarily delighted every one at that grade of cultivation, in that sphere of thought. Not as living and active, but as a departed, vanished existence was described, all that one so readily looked upon, that one loved, prized, sought passionately in the present, to take part in it with the cheerfulness of youth. Highdays and holidays in the country, church consecrations and fairs, the solemn assemblage of the elders under the village linden-tree, supplanted in its turn by the lively delight of youth in dancing, while the more educated classes show their sympathy. How seemly did these pleasures appear, moderated as they were by an excellent country pastor, who understood how to smooth down and remove all that went too far,—that gave occasion to quarrel and dispute. Here again we found an honest Wakefield, in his well-known circle, yet no longer in his living bodily form, but as a shadow recalled by the soft mournful tones of the elegiac poet. The very thought of this picture is one of the happiest possible, when once the design is formed to evoke once more an innocent past with a graceful melancholy. And in this kindly endeavour, how well has the Englishman succeeded in every sense of the word! I shared the enthusiasm for this charming poem with Gotter, who was more felicitous than myself with the translation undertaken by us both; for I had too painfully tried to imitate in our language the delicate significance of the original, and thus had well agreed with single passages, but not with the whole.

SHE STOOPS TO CONQUER

March 1773

---

27. Two unfavorable notices

1773

(a) William Woodfall's review, *Monthly Review*, March 1773, xlviii, 309–14

A WRITER so much, and so justly, in favour with the Public, as the Author of this play, is entitled to more than mere candor for his imperfections. When, therefore, we meet with any thing to disapprove in his compositions, it is really with some degree of concern, and we are under a difficulty in discharging our duty to the Public.

Comedy has been defined by all theatrical Critics, from Aristotle down to the correspondents of a News-paper. We do not, however, remember a definition exactly in the following terms: Comedy is a dramatic representation of the prevailing manners of people not in very high or very low life. It must therefore vary, as those manners vary; and be wholly regulated by them. Hence the difference between Plautus and Menander; (as Menander is represented by Terence) and between all those original writers, who at different periods of time have written immediately from the manners passing in review before them. Few of our English writers of Comedy have aimed at being originals. Some exception may be made in favour of Vanbrugh, Congreve, and Farquhar; the great merit of whose Comedies is, that they represent the manners of the times. Sir Richard Steel, Mr. Cibber, & c. did little more than translate; they were happy, however, in the choice of their plays, and in accommodating them to the customs which it was the business of the stage to regulate or correct.—Our customs and manners have undergone a gradual alteration. A general correspondence arising from trade, and the progress of the arts, has brought the nation, as it were, together, and worn off those prepossessions and habits which made every little neighbourhood a separate community, and marked every community with its peculiar character. The business of comedy is therefore changed; and a man who would now exhibit a Lady Bountiful, a Lord Foppington, or an Abel Drugger, would be considered as copying from history or from old comedies. Such characters do not now exist; at least not in the general walks of men. Some of our late writers have therefore very judiciously had recourse to what is called *Sentimental Comedy*, as better suited to the principles and manners of the age. A general politeness has given a sameness to our external appearances; and great degrees of knowledge are every where diffused. An author, therefore, has not that variety of character, and that simplicity and ignorance to describe, which were the capital ingredients in the old Comedy. Modern writers may indeed have carried the matter too far, and perhaps kept their eyes too much on French models. They may have neglected some remains of English oddities which are still left, and would have very much enlivened their writings. They have erred however only in the execution: they are right in their general principle. The business of the old Comedy, and that of the present, are as different as the people they represent; and persons who have renounced the manners and religion of their fathers, and who would laugh at that wit which was their terror or delight, are affected and influenced by what is called sentiment. Some of our late plays might be mentioned, on this occasion, with great honour.

But Dr. Goldsmith does not seem to have been of this opinion. Having read more about even his own countrymen[1] than he had ever seen of them,[2] and recollecting that the comedies he had perused were very different from those which now prevailed, he imagined the Comic Muse had fled the land. He determined to call her back, and employ her first in introducing the *Good-natured Man*, and afterwards the present Comedy.

The fable of *She Stoops to Conquer* is a series of blunders, which the Author calls the *Mistakes of a Night*; but they are such mistakes as never were made, and, we believe, never could have been committed.

---

1 All the subjects of the British government are countrymen [Woodfall's own note].
2 The point here is confusing and certainly doesn't correspond to any factual truth in Goldsmith's life.

Two young men are going to the seat of a country gentleman, as lovers. They call at an alehouse, where the hopeful heir of the family which they intend to visit is drinking with his pot-companions. It comes into the head of this *genius* to put a trick on the travellers, to say, they were yet a great way from the place they were bound to, and to send them to his father's house as to an inn. Almost all the incidents at this pretended inn; the discovery of the young 'squire's plot to one of the gentlemen, and his readiness as well as that of his mistress to continue the deception of it for their own purposes; Miss Hardcastle's being a fine lady in the morning to pay country visits, and to dress in the evening so as to be mistaken for a bar-maid; Mr. Hardcastle's taking a walk at night, when his house was full of company, and himself in the highest bustle about them; Mrs. Hardcastle's thinking she was forty miles from home when at the bottom of her own garden; and Tony's[1] being of age when it was convenient he should be so;—these and several other circumstances are the most improbable, and lugged in, the most violently, of any things we ever remember to have either read or seen.

Some modern wits have endeavoured to render this kind of offence venial. They have said, that the fable is of no consequence; and that it is immaterial how the incidents are introduced, provided they are pleasing.

To support this strange opinion, they refer to several of our plays, in which the finest circumstances have been *forced in* against probability. We could give instances, in moral life, where the happiest consequences have attended a falsehood; and yet lying is a crime; and a man would be laughed at, if not detested, who would plead, from any accidental advantage, against the general principles of truth. All the general principles of nature are sacred; and we offend against them, in all cases, at our peril. When the temptation is great, and the advantages such as could not be obtained in any other way, we pardon the offender, and perhaps applaud the offence; but still we retain our attachment to the principles of nature. Hence the *virtuous lie* of Tasso; and hence the applauded licences of some fine writers. This, however, does not excuse a man who gives into a *habit* of immorality, or an author who writes a *series* of improbabilities.

In this light we are obliged to consider Dr. Goldsmith's play, as most of its incidents are offences against nature and probability. We are sorry for it, because he certainly has a great share of the *vis*

[1] The booby-heir, before-mentioned [Woodfall's note].

comica;[1] and when he has thrust his people into a situation, he makes them talk very *funnily*. His merit is in that sort of dialogue which lies on a level with the most common understandings; and in that low mischief and mirth which we laugh at, while we are ready to despise ourselves for so doing. This is the reason why the Reader must peruse the present Comedy without pleasure, while the representation of it may make him laugh.

We apprehend the following dialogue to be the best in the whole play, and the most proper to select as a specimen, where we cannot bestow our commendation . . .

The whole of this conversation is very laughable on the stage: so is the interview between Marlow and Miss Hardcastle; and the droll distress of Mrs. Hardcastle, when she thinks herself on Crackskull Common, forty miles from home. Shuter, Quick, and indeed all the performers, top their parts in these scenes, and make the house, the upper regions especially, very merry. We wish, however, that the ingenious Author could employ his talents, so as to divert the galleries, without offending others who have a right to his attention. This he might do, by taking some story of a distant date, when the manners were generally such as he chuses to represent. He would then find characters and circumstances to his hand; and his language and dialogue would have all their effect: we should put ourselves back in imagination, and have the same kind of pleasure which is now given us by the best of our old comedies.

(b) Horace Walpole to William Mason on Goldsmith's opposition to sentimental comedy in *She Stoops to Conquer*, 27 March 1773

Dr. Goldsmith has written a comedy—no, it is the lowest of all farces; it is not the subject I condemn, though very vulgar, but the execution. The drift tends to no moral, no edification of any kind—

[1] The comic force.

the situations however are well imagined, and make one laugh in spite of the grossness of the dialogue, the forced witticisms, and total improbability of the whole plan and conduct. But what disgusts me most, is that though the characters are very low, and aim at low humour, not one of them says a sentence that is natural or marks any character at all. It is set up in opposition to sentimental comedy, and is as bad as the worst of them. Garrick would not act it, but bought himself off by a poor prologue.

28. Unsigned review, *London Magazine*

March 1773, xlii, 144–6

On Monday the 15th of this month [i.e. March] was first performed at this theatre a new comedy, called *She Stoops to Conquer, or The Mistakes of a Night*, written by Dr. Goldsmith. The characters are,

Hardcastle – – – – –	*Mr. Shuter.*
Young Marlow – – – –	*Mr. Lewes.*
Hastings – – – – –	*Mr. Dubellamy.*
Squire Lumpkin – – – –	*Mr. Quick.*
Sir Cha. Marlow – – – –	*Mr. Gardner.*
Alehouse-keeper, Countrymen, and Servants – – – –	*Mess. Thompson, Saunders, Davis, &c.*
Mrs. Hardcastle – – – –	*Mrs. Green.*
Miss Hardcastle – – – –	*Mrs. Bulkley.*
Miss Neville – – – – –	*Mrs. Kniveton.*

Mr. Hardcastle is a plain honest country gentleman. His wife is well-meaning, but foolish and positive, and so indulgent to her son, Squire Lumpkin, that she has given him no education for fear of hurting his health. This Squire is quite a spoiled child, regardless of his mother, fond of low company, and full of mischievous humour. Miss Hardcastle is a lively and amiable young lady, whom her father is desirous of marrying to young Marlow the son of Sir Charles. This Marlow is a fashionable young fellow, who has constantly lived in the pleasures of the town; and by being accustomed to the company of courtesans only, is in great dread of modest women, and behaves in their presence with a very aukward bashfulness. Miss Neville is a niece of Mrs. Hardcastle's, has a good fortune, and lives in the family. It is the purpose of the relations to have this young lady married to Squire Lumpkin; but this couple have not the least regard for each other. On the contrary, the Squire is enamoured with a vulgar country-beauty; and Miss Neville has a strong *penchant* for Mr. Hastings, the friend of Young Marlow. These two gentlemen had never been at Hardcastle's, but the former is expected every moment from London; and Hastings, by an agreement with Marlow, was to accompany him thither as his friend, but in fact to have an opportunity of seeing and conversing with his mistress, Miss Neville.

Thus the whole story is situated at the beginning of the play; near which time the young Squire is discovered in an ale-house, revelling with his pot companions. At this time the landlord enters to inform him, that two gentlemen were at the door enquiring their way to Mr. Hardcastle's. He, on seeing them, guessed Marlow to be one of them, because he was expected. The Squire, after cracking many of his coarse jokes upon the travellers, mischievously informs them that as it was late, and they cannot be accommodated that night at the ale-house, if they will walk on for about a mile, they will come to a very good inn, which they might know by seeing a pair of stag's horns over the gate. This, in truth, was Hardcastle's; but the Squire wanted fun, and he got it; for when the gentlemen arrived there, thinking themselves in an inn, they used very great freedom, to the utter astonishment of Hardcastle; for he accidentally heard Marlow named, and knew him; but he resolved to hold his tongue.

Soon after their arrival here, Hastings meets with Miss Neville, who undeceives him with respect to their mistake; but he begs her to conceal it yet from Marlow, whose natural diffidence would force him to quit the family immediately, which he had so freely, though unwittingly used. Miss Neville informs her cousin Miss Hardcastle of the whole; and this lady (being obliged to dress herself very plainly every evening to please a whim of her father's) agrees to pass herself upon Marlow as the bar-maid of the inn, in order to carry on the plot. From these different dispositions arise all the Mistakes of the Night.

After many laughable scenes which arise from the mutual misunderstanding of the several parties, Hardcastle at length flies into a violent passion, and accidentally mentions some circumstances to Marlow which alarm him. Marlow, in short, discovers his error, and consequently undergoes much confusion and agitation; but the arrival of his father adjusts every difference, and he receives with joy the hand of Miss Hardcastle, who, in her character of bar-maid, had greatly charmed him, and who, in consequence, might be said to have Stooped to Conquer.

While these things are transacting, the counter-plot goes on successfully. Hastings gains over the Squire to his interest, and this hopeful son contrives to steal Miss Neville's jewels out of his mother's bureau, and gives them to Hastings, who was preparing to run away with his mistress. But the jewels being very valuable, he is unwilling to carry them with him on so hasty a journey, and gives them to Marlow to keep for him: Marlow, from the same laudable motives of security, consigns them to the keeping of Mrs. Hardcastle, whom he at this time supposed to be the landlady of the inn. Thus the old lady recovers the jewels; by which, and by means of a letter from Hastings to the Squire, which she read, she discovers the plot laid by the lovers for an elopement.

This plot known, Mrs. Hardcastle is greatly alarmed, as it threatened the destruction of her favourite scheme of marriage between her son and Miss Neville. She therefore determines to carry her that very night to her aunt's, about forty miles off. She soon hurries the young lady into the coach, and sets off under the guidance of the Squire on the horseback. Before their departure, however, the Squire whispers to Hastings not to despair yet, for he was still his friend, and would meet him behind the garden at a certain time which he named. Having set off, he leads his mother through danks, bogs, and quagmires, in a dirty condition, round through lanes and by-roads, till he landed her just at the back of her own garden, and then told her she was at least 40 miles from home, and upon a heath. Here, after a variety of roguish tricks with which he alarmed her, Hardcastle advances, and, after some misunderstanding, the parties recognize each other. In the mean time Hastings fled to his mistress, who was left in the coach; but they agree, instead of running away, to return to the family, and throw themselves upon the generosity of the Hardcastles. Mrs. Hardcastle will by no means consent to their union, insisting that Miss Neville cannot be married till her son is of age, who by articles was either to accept or refuse her hand—articles upon which her fortune depended. Hardcastle, however, obviates this, by informing the Squire that he has been already of age three months, and that he may do what he pleases. Lumpkin willingly refuses her, and her hand is consequently given to Hastings: with which the play concludes.

This comedy is not ill calculated to give pleasure in the representation; but when we regard it with a critical eye, we find it to abound with numerous inaccuracies. The fable (a fault too peculiar to the hasty productions of the modern Comic Muse) is twisted into incidents not naturally arising from the subject, in order *to make things meet*; and consistency is repeatedly violated for the sake of humour. But perhaps we ought to sign a general pardon to the author, for taking the field against that monster called Sentimental Comedy, to oppose which his comedy was avowedly written. Indeed, the attempt was bold, considering the strength of the enemy; and we are glad to observe that our author still keeps the field with flying colours.—But, (metaphor apart) it appears that the Doctor was too ardent. Well considering that the public were long accustomed to cry, he resolved to make them laugh at any rate. In aiming at this point, he seems to have stepped too far; and in lieu of comedy he has sometimes presented us with farce.

These redundancies are certainly the chief blots in his play. A stricter consistency in the fable, and a better attention to the unity of time in particular, would have exalted the comedy to a good and just reputation.

29. Unsigned review, *Critical Review*

March 1773, xxxv. 229–30

The public have for some years submitted to be imposed on by a species of comedy very different from what the ancients conceived, or the moderns, upon the revival of literature, adopted. Aristotle, who defined comedy to be an exhibition of human manner in low life, gave the law to every comic writer, and the *Dramatis Personae* never rose above the private gentleman or the respectable merchant. The Italians, upon the restoration of letters, sunk beneath the ancients in the lowness of their personages; and tired of the difficulty of studying individual life, applied themselves only to national character. A Neapolitan, a Bergamasco, or a Florentine, their local peculiarities and language, produce all the mirth of the scene; and thus variety of character is entirely banished from their stage.

The French followed a better track, and brought comedy to very great perfection. It was still sufficiently distinguished from tragedy, as all the incidents were humorous, and sufficiently discriminated from farce, as provincial peculiarities and blunders by no means made the prominent parts of the exhibition.

The English seem to us to have excelled other nations in the strength of their characters, the warmth and bustle of their plots, and the variety of their incidents. An English comedy upon the great stile of the ancients, is a very difficult undertaking. Being twice as long as that of either the ancients or the French, it requires the utmost exertion of skill, to vary the humour in such a manner as to keep up the spectator's pleasure, and still never lose sight of the plot. This end, however, Vanbrugh, Farquhar, and Steele have very happily attained.

After such excellent examples, comedy, both in France and England, has been seen entirely to languish. La Chaussé first set the fashion of the *Comédie Larmoyant*, or the *Tradesman's Tragedy*, as Voltaire expresses it;[1] and it has since prevailed in France to the utter extinction of all other comic representation. As we often imitate not only the dress of that people, but also their manner of thinking, we have followed them in their dramatic declension; and it was supposed, by the lovers of the old comedy, that she was extinct among us. The present play is an attempt to revive the dying art; and the author's well-deserved and unprecedented success, has shewn how ready mankind are to welcome back a favourite mistress, even after she had been guilty of a long elopement.

What Dr. Johnson, to whom this piece is dedicated, has observed of Shakespeare, is equally applicable to the present writer, 'whose excellence cannot be ascertained by the splendor of particular passages, but by the progress of his fable and the tenour of his dialogue; and should we try to recommend him by select quotations, we should

---

[1] Pierre Claude Nivelle de la Chaussée (1692–1754) had invented 'comédie larmoyant.' See David Williams, *Voltaire: Literary Critic* (1966), p. 255ff. and G. Lanson, *Les Origines du drame contemporain . . . Chaussée et la comédie larmoyante* (Paris, 1903).

succeed like the pedant in Hierocles, who, when he offered his house to sale, carried a brick in his pocket as a specimen.'[1]

To conclude; the utmost severity of criticism could detract but little from the uncommon merit of this performance; and the most laboured encomiums could add as little to the general and judicious applause with which it still continues to be received.

30. Unsigned letter about Goldsmith's brand of sentiment sent 'To the Printer of the *St. James's Chronicle*, March 1773,' and reprinted in the *London Chronicle*

March 1773

Similar letters appeared in other daily and weekly newspapers in March 1773.

SIR,

IN this Letter, according to my Promise, I shall throw out some observations upon Dr. Goldsmith's new Comedy.

I have declaimed very warmly, Mr. Baldwin,[2] against Sentimental Comedy, and I do not now wish to retract. The Goddess of Dullness has almost entirely buried the livelier Passions under her leaden Wing:

---

[1] See *Johnson on Shakespeare*, in *The Yale Edition of the Works of Samuel Johnson*, ed. Arthur Sherbo (New Haven, 1968), VII, p. 62. The story about Hierocles is found in *Hieroclis Commentarius in Aurea Carmina*, ed. Peter Needham (1709), p. 462. Boswell attributed to Samuel Johnson 'A free translation of the Jests of Hierocles, with an Introduction,' which appeared in the *Gentleman's Magazine* in 1741. G. B. Hill rejected the attribution (*Life*, 1934, I, p. 150 and note), but D. J. Greene (*PMLA*, 1959, 75–84) argues for its reception into the Johnson canon.

[2] Henry Baldwin (dates unknown), London printer of the *Daily London Chronicle* and *Read's Weekly Journal*.

Her soporific Poppies (frequent as Sentiments in a modern Comedy) have spread their Influence every where; and even the Actor who repeats, yawns as widely as the Audience who sit on the Benches. Immortality to every Pen that opposes the pestiferous Infection! In this Regard, Dr. Goldsmith merits the Bosom of the Publick; and those few who seem to remember, that Nature once gave Laws upon our Theatre, felicitate themselves in seeing one Man of Genius made a Proselyte, and forsaking that dull Herd of comic Writers, who have turned the Holy Bible into Scenes and Acts.

Allowing them the Doctor's Intention to have been in the highest Degree Praise-worthy, let us examine how he has executed it. It is of the Scenes between the Gentleman and the Master of the Family, or one Expression to alarm him: all this, I say, exceeds even English Credulity. We could admit this in a Farce, but in a Comedy we cannot. But there is one Circumstance which completes the Improbability of this: Marlow on his Arrival calls for a *Bill of Fare*! Is it then usual to call for a *Bill of Fare* in a Gentleman's Family? Is it possible that Hardcastle should not put this very Question to his impudent Guest? It is at least the only natural Reply that could be made to so extraordinary a Demand.

The Doctor, aware perhaps of these Improprieties, has called in the Assistance of several Circumstances to their Support, and even wrested them to his Purpose. Among these I place the Incident of Miss Hardcastle's changing her Dress. In the Morning she is allowed to dress in a gay Stile, to make her Visits, and to please herself; in the Evening she puts on a humbler Garb, to please her Father. Now, let us be informed what the Visits are, which a young Lady living in a remote and retired Country has to repeat every Day. When I heard her talk of paying her Morning-Visits, my Mind recurred to the Streets and the Inhabitants at the West End of the Town; but when I compared the Idea with the Circumstances of a young Lady's Life, whom we cannot suppose (from what we are told) to be situated in the Neighbourhood of any People of Fortune or Fashion, and who, at any Rate, could not have Visits to repeat every Day. When I reflected upon this, I conceived the Affair in its true Light, and was convinced that the Circumstance of the Change of Dress was dragged in, on purpose to give the Lady a more plausible Pretext of passing upon her Lover as a Bar-Maid. But another Reflection greatly heightened the Inconsistency of the Thing. Allowing the Motives of the Change of Dress to be as they are stated; allowing that the Lady visited in the Morning, and pleased her Father in the Evening—is it probable that she would assume a mean Dress *this* Evening, when she was formally to meet a Lover, and when the House had Strangers in it, and another was still expected? This is a whimsical Idea, which, I think, is not accounted for.

I have observed that Faults of this Nature are too common in the Practice of our Dramatic Writers. Instead of tracing Nature Step by Step, and following her by the Line of their Fable, till the last Period, they convert it from its natural Channel, on Purpose to cover their Errors, or to surprize us with something which we do not, and which we ought not, to expect. This is trifling with our Judgment, in order to dazzle our Imagination.

It is to such Inclinations as these we must attribute the following Inconsistency among several others:—Hardcastle, in order no Doubt to heighten the Extravagance of Marlow's Behaviour, informs us, that he had not only taken Possession of his great Chair, but *taken off his Boots* in the Parlour. Now this sounds very well to the Ear; but when we appeal to the Eye, and find that Marlow had no Boots *on* him to be *taken off*, how can we excuse the old Man for telling *Lyes*?

The Characters in this Piece have but little of Originality to boast of. With respect to these, the Author's chief Merit consists in having carried the Humour of them farther than his Predecessors. This is more particularly applicable to the 'Squire and to Marlow. And yet the Character of the latter is extremely similar to that of Young Philpot, in the Farce of the *Citizen*;[1] I mean only in regard to his Bashfulness in the Company of modest Women. The first Scene between Marlow and Miss Hardcastle is almost a Transcript of a Scene of the same Nature between Young Philpot and Maria. Marlow faithfully copies the Words and Behaviour of Philpot, and Miss Hardcastle displays to us not a few of the Features of the lively and agreeable Maria.

In this Comedy the Unity of Time is repeatedly violated in the second or third Act (I do not remember which). Half an Hour is mentioned for the Time of an Appointment which takes Place in very few Minutes after; and Tony desires Hastings to meet him "two Hours Hence" at the Back of the Garden, tho' they both take Care to meet there very punctually at the End of a short Half Hour. In these *thirty Minutes*, however, we are desired to suppose that a Chaise has been got ready, the Horses harnessed, and a Company prepared themselves for a Journey, and that they actually did travel so much Road as appeared to Mrs. Hardcastle to be *forty Miles*. All this Business is supposed to be

1 *The Citizen* by Arthur Murphy, first performed in 1761.

finished in the *Half Hour*; for a Half Hour it actually was, though Tony, on his Return, informs us, that he had been absent *three Hours*. To believe this, our *Conscience* must move in as wide a Latitude as the Author's who wrote it.

I do not mention, to aggravate these Lapses of the Judgement, the utter Improbability of a timid old Lady setting off with a young one, at Midnight, upon a journey of forty Miles, through imperious Roads, impassable Ditches, and Heaths frequented by Robbers; though the Journey could have been with greater Convenience performed the next Day, and all Danger removed in the mean Time, by securing the Lady from the Reach of the Lover.

I regard these Incongruities in Comedy as the Errors of a Man who is either too hasty, or too unequal to the Task of writing one. It appears not well, when the Poet, instead of bending his Fancy to the Fable, bends the Fable to his Fancy. I honour Dr. Goldsmith when he writes a *Poem*; but when he writes a *Comedy*, I lose Sight of the Man of Genius.

BOSSU

RETALIATION

19 April 1774, posthumously published

---

31. Unsigned notice, *Monthly Review*

April 1774, 1, 313–14

'Dr. Goldsmith,' says the Editor, 'belonged to a club of *Beaux Esprits*, where wit sparkled sometimes at the expence of good-nature. It was proposed to write epitaphs on the Doctor. His country, dialect, and person, furnished subjects of witticism. The Doctor was called on for *Retaliation*, and at their next meeting produced the following poem.'—

The persons who figure principally in this poetical group are Edmund Burke; his brother, Richard Burke; his cousin, William Burke; David Garrick; Dr. Cumberland, author of the West Indian; Dr. Douglas, the detector of Lauder;[1] Sir Joshua Reynolds; and a few others. We are informed that the Author intended to enlarge his list; which seems very probable, as the piece appears to be imperfect: a circumstance which its admirers (in which number we may venture to include all its readers) will certainly lament. The poem abounds with wit, free from even the slightest tincture of ill nature; and the characteristics of all the parties, as far as they are known to us, are equally pointed and just. As a specimen, we shall give the epitaph on the celebrated orator, Mr. Burke:

'Here lies our good Edmund, whose genius was such,
We scarely can praise it or blame it too much;
Who, born for the universe, narrow'd his mind,
And to party gave up what was meant for mankind.
Though fraught with all learning, kept straining his throat
To persuade Tommy Townsend to lend him a vote;

---

[1] Referring to Dr John Douglas (1721–1807), who had exposed William Lauder's claim that Milton had plagiarized from certain modern Latin poets in *Paradise Lost*.

Who, too deep for his hearers, still went on refining,
And thought of Convincing, while they thought of Dining;
Though equal to all things, for all things unfit,
Too nice for a statesman, too proud for a wit.
For a patriot too cool; for a drudge disobedient,
And too fond of the *right* to pursue the *expedient*.
In short 'twas his fate, unemploy'd, or in play, Sir,
To eat mutton cold, and cut blocks with a razor.'

The lines on Mr. Garrick are perhaps the most masterly part of this very agreeable fragment; but they have been sufficiently retailed in the news-papers.

32. Unsigned notice, *Critical Review*

May 1774, xxxvii, 392

This poem, we are told, was produced in consequence of the ingenious author being called on to retaliate for some raillery thrown out against him, at a club of beaux esprits[1] to which he belonged. It begins with the following exordium:

'Of old, when Scarron his companions invited,
Each guest brought his dish, and the feast was united:
If our landlord supplies us with beef, and with fish,
Let each guest bring himself, and he brings the best dish:
Our Dean shall be venison, just fresh from the plains;
Our Burke shall be tongue, with a garnish of brains;
Our Will, shall be wild fowl, of excellent flavour,
And Dick with his pepper, shall heighten their savour:
Our Cumberland's sweet-bread, its place shall obtain,
And Douglas's pudding, substantial and plain:
Our Garrick's a sallad, for in him we see
Oil, vinegar, sugar, and saltness agree:
To make out the dinner, full certain I am,

[1] Dr Johnson's Club.

That Ridge is anchovy, and Reynolds is lamb;
That Hickey's a capon, and, by the same rule,
Magnanimous Goldsmith, a goosberry fool:
At a dinner so various, at such a repast,
Who'd not be a glutton, and stick to the last:
Here, waiter, more wine, let me sit while I'm able,
'Till all my companions sink under the table;
Then with chaos and blunders encircling my head,
Let me ponder, and tell what I think of the dead.'

The members of the club are characterised in a poetical strain of panegyric or delicate satire, in which good humour, and a facetious turn of thought are equally conspicuous. However frivolous the occasion and nature of this jeu d'esprit may be, it is a production which will reflect no discredit on the genius of the author.

33. Unsigned notice in the *London Chronicle* containing an epitaph on Goldsmith

7–9 July 1774

In addition to such epitaphs as the anonymous one printed here, there were many others including epitaphs by David Garrick, Richard Cumberland (see No. 34), and Dean Thomas Barnard (see No. 53). That printed here remains anonymous.

An Impartial Character *of the late Dr.* Goldsmith; *with a Word to his Encomiasts.* A Poem.
The Author's motive for writing this piece he informs the Reader was this:— 'When Dr. Goldsmith undertook his last Poem, since called *Retaliation*, he designed, in the course of his characters, to wind up the whole with his own; for which, he had declared to some of

his friends, he was determined to sit (as far as self could possibly be divested) to the most general opinion conceived of him by his acquaintance; the death of the Doctor, unhappily for the Public, crossing this design induced the Author of this Poem to undertake it.'

The following is the character of Dr. Goldsmith as drawn by this Writer:

'HERE rests from the cares of the world, and his pen,
A Poet whose like we shall scarce meet again,
Who though form'd in an age when corruptions ran high,
And folly alone seem'd with folly to vie,
When Genius, with traffic too commonly train'd,
Recounted her merits by what she had gain'd,
Yet spurn'd at those walks of debasement and pelf,
And, in poverty's spite, dare think for himself.
Thus free from those letters the Muses oft bind,
He wrote from the heart to the hearts of mankind;
And such was the prevalent force of his song,
Sex-ages, and parties, he drew in a throng.
 The lovers, 'twas theirs to esteem and commend,
For his *Hermit* had prov'd him their tutor and friend;
The Statesman, his politic passions on fire,
Acknowledg'd repose from the charms of his lyre;
The Moralist too had a feel for his rhymes,
For his *Essays* were curbs on the rage of the times;
Nay the Critic, all school'd in grammatical sense,
Who look'd in the glow of description for *tense;*
Reform'd as he read, fell a dupe to his art,
And confess'd by his eyes what he felt at his heart.
Yet, blest with original powers like these,
His principal *forte* was on *paper* to please;
Like a fleet-footed hunter, tho' first in the chace,
On the road of *plain sense* he deserted his pace,
Whilst dullness and cunning, by whipping and goring
Their hard-footed hackneys *paraded* before him;
Compounded likewise of such primitive parts,
That his manners alone would have gain'd him our hearts;
So simple from truth—so ingenuously kind,
So ready to feel for the wants of mankind:
If an Author once held but a popular quill,
This flux of Philanthropy quickly stood still;
Transform'd from himself he grew meanly severe,
And rail'd at those talents he ought not to fear.

Such then were his foibles—but though they were such
As shadow'd the picture a little too much,
The style was all graceful, expressive and grand,
And the whole the result of a masterly hand.

34. Richard Cumberland's imitation of *Retaliation* entitled 'A Poetical Epistle, from Mr. Cumberland to Dr. Goldsmith, or Supplement to his *Retaliation*, a Poem,' printed in *The New Foundling Hospital for Wit*

new edition, 1784, vi, 255–7

Richard Cumberland (1732–1811), the dramatist, had been
interested in Goldsmith's writings throughout his life and wrote
at length about them in his memoirs (see No. 62).

DOCTOR! according to our wishes,
You've character'd us all in dishes,
Serv'd up a sentimental treat
Of various emblematic meat:
And now it's time, I trust, you'll think
Your company should have some drink;
Else, take my word for it, at least
Your Irish friends won't like your feast.
Ring then, and see that there is plac'd
To each according to his taste.

To Douglas,[1] fraught with learned stock
Of critic lore, give antient Hock;[2]
Let it be genuine, bright, and fine,
Pure unadulterated wine;
For if there's fault in taste, or odour,
He'll search it, as he search'd out Lauder.

To Johnson, philosophic sage,
The moral Mentor of the age,
Religion's friend, with soul sincere,
With melting heart, but look austere,
Give liquor of an honest sort,
And crown his cup with priestly Port!

Now fill the glass with gay Champaigne,
And frisk it in a livelier strain;
Quick! quick! the sparkling nectar quaff,
Drink it, dear Garrick!——drink, and laugh!

Pour forth to Reynolds, without stint,
Rich Burgundy, of ruby tint;
If e'er his colours chance to fade,
This brilliant hue shall come in aid,
With ruddy lights refresh the faces,
And warm the bosoms of the Graces.

To Burke a pure libation bring,
Fresh drawn from clear Castalian spring;
With civic oak the goblet blind,
Fit emblem of his patriot mind;
Let Clio as his taster, sip,
And Hermes hand it to his lip.

Fill out, my friend, the D★★★ of D★★★y,[3]
A bumper of conventual Sherry!

Give Ridge and Hi——ky, generous souls!
Of whisky punch convivial bowls;
But let the kindred Burkes regale
With potent draughts of Wicklow Ale;
To C★★★★k next, in order turn you,
And grace him with the vines of Furney!

[1] See No. 31, p. 128, n. 1.
[2] Could this be a reference to Sir John Hawkins (1719–89), a member of Johnson's Club and old enough in 1774 to be called 'antient'?
[3] Thomas Barnard (1728–1806), see No. 52; the other blank names refer to Thomas Hickey(*fl.* 1760–90), a portrait painter and acquaintance of Goldsmith's; Joseph Cradock (1742–1826), see No. 69.

Now, DOCTOR, thou'rt an honest sticker,
So take your glass, and chuse your liquor:
Wilt have it steep'd in Alpine snows,
Or damask'd at Silenus' nose?
Will Wakefield's Vicar sip your tea,
Or to Thalia drink with me?
And, DOCTOR, I wou'd have you know it,
An honest, I, tho' humble poet:
I scorn the sneaker like a toad,
Who drives his cart the Dover road;
There, traitor to his country's trade,
Smuggles vile scraps of French brocade;
Hence, with all such! for you and I,
By English wares will live, and die.
Come, draw your chair and stir the fire:
Here, boy!—a pot of Thrale's Entire!

HISTORY OF THE EARTH, AND ANIMATED NATURE

1 July 1774, posthumously published

---

35. Descriptive and analytic review, *Critical Review*

August–November 1774, xxxviii, 97–105, 220–7, 258–66, 329–40

By the mere length of this review, one of the longest ever published in the *Critical Review*, the editors indicate their high estimate of this work, sometimes called Goldsmith's 'most substantial literary legacy' (see Ralph Wardle, *Oliver Goldsmith*, 1957, p. 283). Samuel Johnson and Edmund Burke were also impressed although they had reservations. Johnson, when told that Goldsmith was writing a natural history, is known to have commented: 'Goldsmith, Sir, will give us a very fine book upon the subject; but if he can distinguish a cow from a horse, that, I believe, may be the extent of his knowledge of natural history.' Burke was less skeptical and observed in the *Annual Register* for 1774 that it would be received 'with partiality and indulgence.' Because it is the earliest review as well as the lengthiest, we quote it almost in entirety, excluding long quotations only.

A judicious system of natural history, blending entertainment with information, has hitherto never appeared in the English language, nor indeed been accomplished in any other. The several works of this kind that have been published originally in our own tongue, are universally defective with respect to the essential quality which alone can render the study of natural knowledge both useful and agreeable. The only book on this subject, in which the author has endeavoured to unite philosophy with description, is la Pluche's *Nature Displayed*. But even this justly admired work is far from being void of imperfections. Though it presents us with a pleasing idea of natural history, it is too superficial, and it receives an air of puerility from being written in the form of dialogue. To these objections we may add, that it contains many dissertations entirely foreign to natural history, gives no account of the later improvements that have been made in the science, and is raised upon the foundation of the exploded systems of the Cartesian and Ramistic philosophy.

Many of the defects of *Nature Displayed* are carefully obviated in the work now under our consideration, in which Dr. Goldsmith appears to have exerted great application, and to have consulted the whole accumulated tribe of the writers on natural history; particularly Buffon, Linnaeus, Duhamel, Hale, &c.

In the beginning of this work, we are presented with a Sketch of the Universe, or the Solar System; to which succeeds a Short Survey of the Globe, from the Light of Astronomy and Geography; with a View of the Surface of the Earth. The author then delivers a concise account of the different theories of the earth, the most conspicuous of which are those of Burnet, Whiston, Woodward, and Buffon. Though these systems be merely imaginary, we agree with the author, that it is incumbent on the natural historian to be acquainted at least with the out-lines of them; as such a knowledge may prevent his indulging himself in similar speculations, from the idea of their being his own invention. For this reason we shall lay before our readers a part of each of these systems.

'The first who formed this amusement of earth making into system was the celebrated Thomas Burnet, a man of polite learning and rapid imagination. His Sacred Theory, as he calls it, describing the changes which the earth has undergone, or shall hereafter undergo, is well known for the warmth with which it is imagined, and the weakness with which it is reasoned, for the elegance of its style, and the meanness of its philosophy. The earth, says he, before the deluge, was very differently formed from what it is at present: it was at first a fluid mass; a chaos composed of various substances, differing both in density and figure: those which were most heavy sunk to the center, and formed in the middle of our globe an hard solid body; those of a lighter nature remained next; and the waters, which were lighter still, swam upon its surface, and covered the earth on every side. The air, and all those fluids which were lighter than water, floated upon this also; and in the same manner encompassed the globe; so that between the surrounding body of waters, and the circumambient air, there was formed a coat of oil, and other unctuous substances, lighter than water. However, as the air was still extremely impure, and must have carried up with it many of those earthly particles with which it once was intimately blended, it soon began to defecate, and to depose these particles upon the only surface already mentioned, which soon uniting together, the earth and oil formed that crust, which soon became an habitable surface, giving life to vegetation, and dwelling to animals.

'This imaginary antediluvian abode was very different from what we see it at present. The earth was light and rich; and formed of a substance entirely adapted to the feeble state of incipient vegetation: it was an uniform plain, every where covered with verdure; without mountains, without seas, or the smallest inequalities. It had no difference of seasons, for its equator was in the plain of the ecliptic, or, in other words, it turned directly opposite to the sun, so that it enjoyed one perpetual and luxuriant spring. However, this delightful face of nature did not long continue the same, for, after a time, it began to crack and open in fissures; a circumstance which always succeeds when the sun dries away the moisture from rich or marshy situations. The crimes of mankind had been for some time preparing to draw down the wrath of heaven; and they, at length, induced the Deity to defer repairing these breaches in nature. Thus the chasms of the earth every day became wider, and, at length, they penetrated to the great abyss of waters; and the whole earth, in a manner, fell in. Then ensued a total disorder in the uniform beauty of the first creation, the terrene surface of the globe being broken down: as it sunk the waters gushed out into its place; the deluge became universal; all mankind except eight persons were punished with destruction, and their posterity condemned to toil upon the ruins of desolated nature.'

—' The next theorist was Woodward, who, in his Essay towards a Natural History of the Earth, which . . .'.[1]

After exhibiting the above mentioned theories, which, as being an history of opinions rather than things, the author has related succinctly, he proceeds to give a short account of those animal productions that are found either on the surface of the earth, or at different depths below it. These are shells, and other extraneous fossils, the existence of which

[1] Several pages of quotations follow in which Goldsmith discusses the theories of William Whiston and Buffon.

within the bowels of the earth, has afforded ample subject of speculation to natural historians. The philosophers of this class have for a long time considered these marine substances as productions, not of the sea, but of the earth; though, upon closer examination this opinion has at length been exploded; it being found that such shells have, in every respect, the properties of animal and not of mineral nature. In consequence of this discovery, some extraordinary conjectures have been formed, respecting the means by which those fossils have been deposited in the earth. Our author observes, that an Italian supposes this deposition to have been made at the time of the crusades, by the pilgrims who returned from Jerusalem.

'But, says he, this conjecturer seems to have but a very inadequate idea of their numbers. At Touraine, in France, more than an hundred miles from the sea, there is a plain of about nine leagues long, and as many broad, from whence the peasants of the country supply themselves with marle for manuring their lands. They seldom dig deeper than twenty feet, and the whole plain is composed of the same materials, which are shells of various kinds, without the smallest portion of earth between them. Here, then, is a large space, in which are deposited millions of tons of shells, which pilgrims could not have collected though their whole employment had been nothing else. England is furnished with its beds, which though not quite so extensive, yet are equally wonderful.' . . . [further extracts follow].

The deposition of these extraneous fossils is now generally ascribed to the sea by the writers on natural history; and undoubtedly this conjecture appears to be the best supported. The author of the work before us, however, makes one remark which tends to invalidate this opinion. It is, that we find fossil trees, which no doubt once grew upon the earth, as deep and as much in the body of solid rocks, as these shells are found to be; and that some of the former have lain at least as long, if not longer, in the earth than the latter; being found sunk deep in a marly substance, composed of decayed shells, and other marine productions. Mr. Buffon, he observes, has proved that fossil shells could not have been deposited in such quantities all at once by the flood; and, from the above instance, the author of the History thinks it is plain, that, in whatever way they were deposited, the earth was covered with trees before their deposition: consequently, that the sea could not have made a very permanent stay; as he supposes, for the same reason, that the earth was habitable, if not inhabited, before these substances were deposited.

'How then shall we account, says he, for these extraordinary appearances in nature? A suspension of all assent is certainly the first, although the mortifying conduct. For my own part, were I to offer a conjecture, and all that has been said upon this subject is but conjecture, instead of supposing them to be the remains of animals belonging to the sea, I would consider them rather as bred in the numerous fresh water lakes that, in primaeval times, covered the face of uncultivated nature. Some of these shells we know to belong to fresh waters: some can be assimilated to none of the marine shells now known; why, therefore, may we not as well ascribe the production of all to fresh waters, where we do not find them, as we do that of the latter to the sea only, where we never find them? We know that lakes, and lands also, have produced animals that are now no longer existing, why, therefore, might not these fossil productions be among the number? I grant that this is making a very harsh supposition; but I cannot avoid thinking, that it is not attended with so many embarassments as some of the former, and that it is much easier to believe that these shells were bred in fresh water, than that the sea had for a long time covered the tops of the highest mountains.'

After conjectural subject, the author advances to the internal structure of the earth, which is described in the subsequent chapter.

The first layer that is commonly found at the surface where it has not been washed off by rains, or removed by some other external violence, is a light coat of blackish mould, which seems to have been formed from animal and vegetable substances. Under this mould there generally lies gravel or sand, then clay or marle, next chalk or coal, marbles, ores, sands, gravels, and thus an alternation of these substances, each growing more dense as its situation is deeper. Such in general is observed to be the disposition of the different materials where the earth seems to have remained unmolested; but this order is frequently inverted, whether in consequence of original formation, or from accidental causes. In our next Review we shall finish the entertaining account which the author has delivered of the earth.

After delivering an account of the internal structure of the earth, the author proceeds to the caves and subterraneous passages. Many of these, he observes, are not the production of nature, but of human industry; such as the famous labyrinth of Candia, and the stone-quarry of Maestricht; the latter of which is so large that forty thousand people may be contained in it. Among the artificial caverns, are likewise to be ranked the catacombs in Egypt and Italy. Few countries, if any, are destitute of natural caverns. In England those of Oakey-hole, the Devil's hole, and Penpark-hole, are the most conspicuous; but the grotto of Antiparos, a small island in the Archipelago, is admitted to be the most extraordinary production yet discovered of this kind, both for beauty and extent. Dr. Goldsmith has translated the account delivered of it by Magni, an Italian traveller, about an hundred years ago, in a letter to Kircher, which we extract for the amusement of our readers . . .[1]

By what means those immense caverns have been formed, is a subject of disquisition to the writer of natural history. The author, therefore, adopts the opinion that this effect has been produced by waters, which finding subterraneous passages, and gradually hollowing the beds in which they flowed, the ground immediately above them has sunk down closer to their surface, leaving the upper strata still suspended.

The next chapter treats of mines, damps, and mineral vapours. Here the author observes, that upon our descent into mines of considerable depth, the cold seems to increase for some time; till having descended further, the air becomes gradually warmer, so that at last the labourers can scarce bear any covering while they work. This phenomenon, the historian observes, was supposed by Boyle to proceed from magazines of fire lying nearer the centre of the earth, and diffusing their heat around them.

Our author afterwards delivers a distinct account of the several species of vapours that are found in mines; to the qualities of which he imputes in a great measure the salubrity or unwholsomeness of different climates and soils. As an instance of noxious exhalations being confined to a spot, we are presented with an account of the famous grotto del Cane, near Naples, the effects of which are thus related . . . [further extracts of the letter follow].

The ninth chapter comprises the subject of volcanoes, or burning mountains. There is no quarter of the world where some of these perpetual conflagrations are not to be found. In Europe, Aetna, Vesuvius, and Hecla, are universally well known. In Asia, particularly in the islands of the Indian ocean, volcanoes are more numerous. The most famous on the continent is that of Albouras, near mount Taurus. In the island of Ternato, there is a volcano, which is said to burn most furiously at the equinoxes, on account of the winds which then agitate the flames. In Africa, there is a burning cavern near Fez,

[1] The letter is omitted.

with the volcanoes of the island del Fuogo, and the Peak of Teneriffe. In America, however, these tremendous scenes are most frequent and remarkable. Vesuvius and Aetna itself, we are told, are but mere fire works, when compared to the burning mountains of the Andes. Arequipa, Carassa, and Malahallo are each of great consideration; but that of Cotopaxi, in the province of Quito, is described as superlatively wonderful. This mountain is said to be more than three miles of perpendicular height from the sea, and became a volcano at the time when the Spaniards first arrived in that country.

The author of this work dissents, with good reason, from the opinion of M. Buffon, who imagines that a volcano extends only a very little way below the base of the mountain.

'We can never suppose, says the great naturalist last mentioned, that these substances are ejected from any great distance below, if we only consider the great force already required to fling them up to such vast heights above the mouth of the mountain; if we consider the substances thrown up, which we shall find upon inspection to be the same with those of the mountain below; if we take into our consideration, that air is always necessary to keep up the flame; but, most of all, if we attend to one circumstance, which is, that if these substances were exploded from a vast depth below, the same force required to shoot them up so high, would act against the sides of the volcano, and tear the whole mountain in pieces . . .'

From treating of volcanoes, the author proceeds, by a natural transition, to consider the phenomenon of earthquakes, which are so much of the same nature with the former, that they both seem to originate from one common cause; there being no other perceptible difference between them but that the rage of the volcano is spent in the eruption, while that of the earthquake, by being confined, produces more violent convulsions. He justly rejects the distinctions which philosophers have made of earthquakes into the tremulous, the pulsative, the perpendicular, and the inclined kind; observing, that these are mere accidental differences arising either from the situation of the country that is agitated, or the cause of the concussion. He no less philosophically disapproves of the distinction introduced by M. Buffon, who supposes one species of earthquake to be occasioned by fire, and another by the expansion of confined air.

'For how, says our author, do these two causes differ? Fire is an agent of no power whatsoever without air. It is the air, which being at first comprest, and then dilated in a cannon, that drives the ball with such force. It is the air struggling for vent in a volcano, that throws up its contents to such vast heights. In short, it is the air confined in the bowels of the earth, and acquiring elasticity by heat, that produces all those appearances which are generally ascribed to the operation of fire. When, therefore, we are told that there are two causes of earthquakes, we only learn, that a greater or smaller quantity of heat produces those terrible effects; for air is the only active operator in either.'

In the eleventh chapter our attention is fixed on the appearance of new islands, and tracts of land, and the disappearing of others. These extraordinary phenomena are the consequence of the great operations of nature which have afforded subject for the two preceding divisions of the work. New islands, our author observes, are formed in two ways; either suddenly by the action of subterraneous fires, or more slowly, by the deposition of mud, carried down by rivers, and stopped by some accident; of both which kinds, as also of the disappearing of land, he produces several instances.

In the subsequent chapter, the author proceeds to take a view of the mountains, those immense piles of nature's erecting, as he styles them, that seem to mock the minuteness of human magnificence. He observes, that in flat countries, the smallest elevation is regarded as a remarkable eminence; and that in Holland, they shew a little ridge of hills, near the sea side, which Boerhaave[1] was used to point out to his pupils as being mountains of no small consideration. Though such an anecdote may seem very extraordinary to an English reader, the historian remarks, that even in this country we have no adequate ideas of a mountain-prospect; our hills being generally of easy ascent, and covered to the top with verdure.

Various are the conjectures which have been formed by philosophers, respecting the origin and use of mountains. Some suppose them to have been formed at the time of the deluge; others imagine, that they existed from the creation; while a different class of enquirers maintain they were produced by earthquakes; and a fourth ascribes them entirely to the fluctuations of the deep, with which they suppose in the beginning the whole globe was surrounded. Our author confesses his surprize to find the question agitated among philosophers, who might with equal reason have enquired concerning the final cause of plains.

'The most rational answer, therefore, says he, why either mountains or plains were formed, seems to be, that they were thus fashioned by the hand of

---

1 Hermann Boerhaave (1668-1738), the celebrated Dutch scientist and professor at the University of Leyden. Although Goldsmith himself had studied medicine in Leyden, he could not have studied under Boerhaave.

Wisdom, in order that pain and pleasure should be so contiguous as that morality might be exercised either in bearing the one, or communicating the other.'

The historian observes that, whatever may be the cause, the greatest and highest mountains are found under the equator; whereas towards the poles, though the earth be craggy and uneven, the height of the mountains is very inconsiderable. Among the most remarkable mountains mentioned by the author, a particular description of the Andes, which he has translated from Ulloa, conveys a lively idea of those wonderful objects of nature; but which our limits will not afford room for inserting.

The succeeding chapter contains an account of the element of water, where we are presented with the various observations and opinions of philosophers respecting this fluid. Water, the author remarks, is proved by many experiments to be the most penetrating body, next to fire, and the most difficult to be confined. It enters into the composition of all bodies, vegetable, animal, and fossil; and was imagined by Thales, and other ancient philosophers, to be the substance of which the universe is made. It would swell this article to too great a length were we to give a particular account of the curious experiments that have been made for elucidating the nature of this fluid; for which reason we shall refer our readers to the work itself, where the author has omitted no fact that is interesting to an inquisitive mind, and has been ascertained by those who have most attentively enquired into the properties of this part of nature.

The subject next treated is, Of the Origin of Rivers, a point which has been variously agitated in the philosophical world. Our author classes the several champions in this controversy under two leaders, M. de la Hire,[1] and Dr. Halley; the former of whom contends that rivers must be supplied from the sea, and the latter from the clouds alone. It is sufficient to observe of this dispute, that the arguments advanced, and the mathematical demonstrations produced, in support of either hypothesis leave the subject still undetermined. In this department, the author gives a description of the four quarters of the globe, their rise and course; after which he mentions the several remarkable cataracts which are found in those rivers. His description of that of Niagara, in the river St. Laurence, in Canada, which is admitted

[1] Philippe de la Hire (1640–1719), geometrician and astronomer, member of the French Academy of Sciences, and author of a celebrated work on rivers entitled *Mémoires de Mathematique* . . . (Paris, 1694).

to be the most astonishing and magnificent of any thing of the kind that is known in the whole compass of nature, we shall insert for the gratification of our readers.

'This amazing fall of water is made by the river St. Lawrence, in its passage from the lake Erie into the lake Ontario. We have already said that St. Lawrence was one of the largest rivers in the world; and yet the whole of its waters are here poured down, by a fall of an hundred and fifty feet perpendicular. It is not easy to bring the imagination to correspond with the greatness of the scene; a river, extremely deep and rapid, and that serves to drain the waters of almost all North America into the Atlantic ocean, is here poured precipitately down a ledge of rocks, that rise, like a wall, across the whole bed of its stream. The width of the river, a little above, is near three quarters of a mile broad; and the rocks, where it grows narrower, are four hundred yards over. Their direction is not streight across, but hollowing inwards like an horse-shoe; so that the cataract, which bends to the shape of the obstacle, rounding inwards, presents a kind of theatre the most tremendous in nature. Just in the middle of this circular wall of waters, a little island, that has braved the fury of the current, presents one of its points, and divides the stream at top into two; but it unites again long before it has got to the bottom. The noise of the fall is heard at several leagues distance; and the fury of the waters at the bottom of their fall, is inconceivable. The dashing produces a mist that rises to the very clouds; and that produces a most beautiful rainbow, when the sun shines. It may easily be conceived, that such a cataract quite destroys the navigation of the stream; and yet some Indian canoes, as it is said, have been known to venture down it with safety.'

The historian afterwards treats at large of the ocean in general, and of its saltness; of the tides, motion, and currents of the sea, with their effects; and of the changes produced by the sea upon the earth. On these several subjects he presents us with the opinions of the most approved philosophers, to which he adds many judicious observations. He proceeds in the same manner through the remaining part of the first volume, which contains, A summary account of the mechanical properties of air; an ingenious essay towards a natural history of the air; the theory of winds, irregular and regular; with that of meteors, and such appearances as result from a combination of the elements. To the whole is subjoined a pertinent, beautiful, and sentimental Conclusion.[1]

So far as we have already advanced in the examination of this work,

[1] The reviewer, although he does not say so, obviously appreciated Goldsmith's prose style and historical mode, as this sentence and the next indicate.

we may safely pronounce it to be the most copious and entertaining system of natural history, that has hitherto been published in the English language.

Having delivered a distinct and entertaining account of the earth in general, the author has proceeded, in the second volume of the work, to the consideration of the animal kingdom; beginning by a comparison of animals with the inferior ranks of creation. The precise boundaries of animal and vegetable life have hitherto not been ascertained by the most intelligent naturalists. For whether the signs of sensibility, or the power of motion be considered as the discriminating criterion, the terraqueous globe affords some productions, the peculiarity of which invalidates every established rule of determination.

'The sensitive plant, says our author, that moves at the touch, seems to have as much perception as the fresh water polypus, that is possessed of a still slower share of motion. Besides, the sensitive plant will not re-produce upon cutting in pieces, which the polypus is known to do; so that the vegetable production seems to have the superiority. But, notwithstanding this, the polypus hunts for its food, as most other animals do. It changes its situation; and therefore possesses a power of chusing its food, or retreating from danger. Still, therefore, the animal kingdom is far removed above the vegetable; and its lowest denizen is possessed of very great privileges, when compared with the plants with which it is often surrounded.'

The historian remarks, that there is a strong similitude between vegetables and animals, with respect to the places where they are found; those of each tribe, which grow in a dry and sunny soil, being vigorous, though not luxuriant; while, on the contrary, such as are produced conjunctly by heat and moisture, are luxuriant and tender. To confirm this observation, he instances the interior parts of South America, and Africa, where the higher grounds are usually scorched, while the lower are covered with inundations. There, the insects, reptiles, and other animals, are said to grow to a prodigious size. 'The earth-worm of America, says the naturalist, is often a yard in length, and as thick as a walking cane; the boiguatu, which is the largest of the serpent kind, is sometimes forty feet in length; the bats, in those countries, are as big as a rabbit; the toads are bigger than a duck, and their spiders are as large as a sparrow.' While such is the law of animal growth in the torrid and humid regions, where nature is luxuriant in all her productions, it is observed, that in the high northern latitudes, both animals and vegetables are proportioned to the ungenial state of the climate. All the wild animals, the bear excepted, are much smaller than in milder countries; and such of the domestic kinds as are carried thither quickly degenerate, and grow less. But the similitude between animals and vegetables, is no where observed to be more obvious than in those that belong to the ocean, where the nature of the one is likewise admirably adapted to the necessities of the other.

Of all the races of animated nature, the historian proceeds to observe, man is the least affected by the soil where he resides, or influenced by the variations of vegetable food. He can exist in climates of the most opposite temperature, and suffers but very gradual alterations from the nature of any situation. That we may not prevent, by a detail of the subjects, the satisfaction which may be reaped from perusing this part of the work, we shall lay before our readers the following passage . . . [the passage follows].

In the beginning of the second chapter, which treats of the generation of animals, we meet with a few philosophical reflections on human fragility, of so striking a nature, that we cannot with-hold from citing them.

'Before we survey animals in their state of maturity, and performing the functions adapted to their respective natures, method requires that we should consider them in the more early periods of their existence. There was a time when the proudest and the noblest animal was a partaker of the same imbecility with the meanest reptile; and, while yet a candidate for existence, was equally helpless and contemptible. In their incipient state all are upon a footing; the insect and the philosopher being equally insensible, clogged with matter, and unconscious of existence. Where then are we to begin with the history of those beings, that make such a distinguished figure in the creation? Or, where lie those peculiar characters in the parts that go to make up animated nature, that mark one animal as destined to creep in the dust, and another to glitter on the throne?'

After relating the several opinions that have been entertained with respect to the share contributed by the sexes towards generation, the author traces the progress of animal nature from its earliest rudiments. But first he remarks, that the general distinction of animals into viviparous and oviparous has been questioned by some naturalists, who have thought it not improbable that certain animals are produced merely from putrefaction. In our opinion, however, this hypothesis is not sufficiently supported: for it cannot be affirmed with any degree of certainty, that the animals supposed to be thus produced, had not really been contained in ova deposited in the putrefying matter; and it seems more reasonable to admit this conjecture, than acquiesce in the supposition of a law of nature so directly repugnant to her general analogy. But whatever may be determined on this subject, it is certain that there obtains in the animal world a mode of generation yet more incontestable and extraordinary, which is merely by cuttings . . .

The third chapter contains an Account of the Infancy of Man, which is rendered interesting by a variety of pertinent observations . . .

The subsequent chapter treats of Puberty, a period which the author observes is variable in different countries, and always more late in the male than the female sex. A swelling of the breasts in the one, and a roughness of the voice in the other, are the usual symptoms with which this stage of life is accompanied. The author here enters into a detail of the customs which the passion that is excited in the heart at the time of puberty, has produced in different countries, animadverting particularly on those which have subjected the women to a life of slavery, secluded from the free enjoyment of social pleasures. Our readers may not be displeased to see the instances that are produced for confirming the various ideas of personal beauty, entertained by different nations.

'Female beauty, is always seen to improve about the age of puberty: but, if we should attempt to define in what this beauty consists or what constitutes its perfection, we should find nothing more difficult to determine. Every country has its peculiar way of thinking, in this respect; and even the same country thinks differently, at different times. The ancients had a very different taste from what prevails at present. The eye-brows joining in the middle was considered as a very peculiar grace, by Tibullus, in the enumeration of the charms of his mistress. Narrow foreheads were approved of, and scarce any of the Roman ladies that are celebrated for their other perfections, but are also praised for the redness of their hair. The nose also of the Grecian Venus, was such as would appear at present an actual deformity; as it fell in a straight line from the forehead, without the smallest sinking between the eyes; without which we never see a face at present . . .' [several more paragraphs are quoted].

The fifth chapter is employed on the Age of Manhood, and is chiefly a translation from M. Buffon, who has written on the subject with great abilities. Wherever Dr. Goldsmith dissented from the opinion of his author, he has informed his readers either in the text, or by a note at the bottom of the page. The observations contained in this chapter are so various, that it would be tedious to enumerate them, and we must therefore refer our readers to the work itself, in which we may assure them that they will meet with a multitude of entertaining disquisitions.

The five succeeding chapters treat respectively of the following subjects, viz. Of Sleep and Hunger; Of Seeing; Of Hearing; Of Smelling, Feeling, and Tasting; Of Old Age and Death. This part of the work abounds not only with speculations properly physical, but with many observations of a political and moral nature, and includes much entertainment on a multiplicity of curious subjects in natural history.

In the eleventh chapter, the author treats of the Varieties in the Human Race. A diversity in the form of the body, and the tincture of the skin, is observable in the natives of the different quarters of the globe, proceeding, it is probable, from the difference of climate, their food, and customs. These varieties have been divided into six distinct classes; the first comprehending the race of men who are found towards the polar regions; the second, the Tartars, including the greater part of the inhabitants of Asia; the third is the southern Asiatics; the fourth, the negroes of Africa; the fifth, the natives of America; and the sixth great variety, the Europeans. These various species of mankind are here accurately described, and their difference is yet more fully delineated by plates . . .

In the subsequent divisions of the work, the naturalist presents us with an account of monsters, mummies, wax-works, &c. His observations, in these several disquisitions, are equally entertaining and instructive, and he has frequently enlivened them with historical anecdotes. On the whole, we may justly pronounce, with respect to the part of the work which we have at present surveyed, the same eulogium that was bestowed in our former Review.[1]

After treating of man, the historian proceeds to the other parts of the animated creation, which he introduces with philosophical remarks on animals in general, and an account of the various methods of classification which the writers of natural history have devised. This division of the work begins with a survey of the several species of quadrupeds, the first in the order of the detail being the horse, the ass, and the zebra.

The animals next treated of are those of the ruminating kind, or such as chew the cud; a class which the author observes is the most harmless, and the most easily tamed. Living entirely on vegetables,

[1] In the August issue. The review was divided into four parts which appeared in the August, September, October, and November issues of the *Critical Review*. Each of the four parts was longer than the average review in this periodical, and the editors apparently felt it to be necessary to quote at great length from each chapter and section of Goldsmith's *History*.

they have no inducement to make war upon the rest of the brute creation; and having nothing to fear from the rapaciousness of each other, they usually go in herds for their mutual security. This tribe of animals is remarkable for a peculiar formation of the bowels, adapted by nature to their exigences. The food on which they live being of the least nourishing kind, it became necessary that they should receive it in greater quantity; and for this purpose they are provided with four stomachs. For the gratification of such of our readers as are unacquainted with comparative anatomy, we shall lay before them the account here delivered of this subject.

But nature has not been less careful in another respect, in fitting the intestines of these animals for their food. In the carnivorous kinds they are thin and lean; but in ruminating animals they are strong, fleshy, and well covered with fat. Every precaution seems taken that can help their digestion: their stomach is strong and muscular, the more readily to act upon its contents; their intestines are lined with fat, the better to preserve their warmth; and they are extended to a much greater length, so as to extract every part of that nourishment which their vegetable food so scantily supplies.

The author then treats largely of the quadrupeds of the cow-kind, and the buffalo. The animals of the sheep and goat-kind, with the numerous varieties of the latter; and the gazelles. The musk animal; animals of the deer-kind, comprehending the fallow-deer, the roebuck, the elk, the rein-deer. Quadrupeds of the hog kind, viz. the peccary, or ta-jacu, the capibara, or cabiai, the babyrouessa, or Indian hog. Animals of the cat kind; namely, the lion, tyger, panther, and leopard. Animals of the dog-kind, the wolf, fox, jackall, isatis, hyaena. Animals of the weasel kind; as the ermine, or stoat, the ferret, polecat, martin, sable, ichneumon, stinkards, genett, civet, and glutton.

The fourth volume begins with an account of the animals of the hare kind. These are, the rabbit, squirrel, flying squirrel, marmout, agouti, paca, guinea pig. Next follow animals of the rat kind, the mouse, dormouse, musk-rat . . .

In the author's account of the foregoing animals, which is no less instructive than entertaining, he has judiciously avoided the tedious uniformity of system, and thereby presented his readers with a pleasing variety. He has minutely described each animal, its way of living, its peculiarities and dispositions. Through the whole, the authority of the best naturalists is followed, and we frequently meet with observations which had not hitherto found a place in any work of the kind.

The fifth volume is entirely employed on birds. This class being extremely numerous, the author has strictly followed the systematic arrangement, beginning with the most general distinction of birds into those that live by land, and those that live by water; or as they are usually denominated, land-birds, and water-fowl. In this part of the work, we are also presented with a curious and philosophical account of the anatomical structure of birds, with that of their generation, nestling and incubation . . . [This section has been considerably abbreviated].

The sixth volume begins with a continuation of the preceding part, containing the history of the bittern or mire-drum; the spoon-bill or shoveler, flamingo, avosetta, or scooper, corrira or runner; small birds of the crane kind, with the thighs partly bare of feathers, the water-hen and the coot. The sixth part treats of water-fowl in general; of the pelican, albatross, cormorant, gannet, or soland goose, smaller gulls and petrals, the penguin kind, the goose kind, the swan, the duck and its varieties, the king fisher.

After the system of ornithology, which is much more entertaining than any we have perused, the author enters on the account of fishes, and he introduces this subject with general observations of such a nature as will afford pleasure to philosophical readers . . .

The naturalist next enquires into the state of the organs of sensation in fishes, giving also an account of the peculiar structure of this tribe of animals, that fits them for the element in which they live. Having discussed these subjects in a manner equally instructive and agreeable, he proceeds to deliver a particular account of fishes; first distinguishing them into three grand divisions, the cetaceous, the cartilaginous, and the spinous. He then treats of cetaceous fishes in general, the whale and its varieties; the narwhal, the cachalot and its varieties; the dolphin, grampus, porpus, and their varieties. The second part contains an account of cartilaginous fishes in general, the shark kind, the ray kind, the lamprey, and its affinities; the sturgeon and its varieties; with anomalous cartilaginous fishes. The third part presents us with a division of spinous fishes; the apodal fish, jugular, thoracic, and abdominal fishes. Soft finned fishes of various kinds, and observations on spinous fishes in general. The fourth part treats of the crustaceous or shell-fish. The lobster kind, the tortoise and its kinds, turbinated shell-fish of the snail kind, bivalved shell-fish, or the oyster kind, and multivalve shell-fish.

Our knowledge of fishes is the most imperfect of any part of the natural history of animals, and it requires all the address of a writer to preserve the account of them from becoming insipid. The author of the work before us, however, has proved more successful in the description of these tribes than could well be expected; having enlivened his narrative with a great variety of pertinent, and we may add, entertaining observations.

After this entertaining department, in which many curious observations are made, and ancient prejudices exposed, we are presented with the account of insects; a subject, perhaps, the most extensive and pleasing of any in natural history. The author first treats of insects in general, then of insects without wings, the spider and its varieties; the flea; the louse, and its varieties; the bug, and its varieties; the wood-louse, and its varieties; monoculous, or arborescent water-flea; scorpion and its varieties; scolopendra, gally-worm, and the leech. Next follows the second order of insects; viz. the libella, or dragon fly, formica leo, or lion-ant, grashopper, locust, cicada, cricket, and the mole cricket; the earwig, the froth-insect, and ephemera.

The eighth volume opens with an account of caterpillars in general, after which the author treats of the transformation of the caterpillar into its corresponding butterfly, or moth; of butterflies and moths; of the enemies of the caterpillar, and of the silk-worm. To these succeeds the history of the fourth order of insects, viz. the bee, wasp, and hornet, ichneumon-fly, ant, beetle, and its varieties; the gnat and the tipula. In the last part of the work is contained an account of zoo-phytes in general, worms, the star-fish, polypus, lithophytes, and sponges.

The bare enumeration of the multiplicity of subjects comprehended in this work, is sufficient to establish its superiority over every other system of natural history in the English language; but its title to pre-eminence is founded on considerations of a more unquestionable and convincing kind. The various subjects, while exceedingly numerous, are copiously and distinctly treated; and the author has not only enriched his narrative with an account of the latest discoveries in the several departments of natural knowledge, but greatly embellished it with pertinent and judicious observations.

The reader is here taught to view the wonderful works of nature, through the pleasing medium of philosophy, in a detail which is not only rendered agreeable by a variety of just and apposite observations, but which is also divested of the dry, uninteresting manner of some preceding writers on the subject, and the frivolous minuteness of others. On the whole, though this work, (no more than any other on

Natural History,) cannot be considered as a perfect system of a science which the accumulated enquiries of all succeeding ages will, probably, never be able to accomplish; yet as it contains the latest discoveries on the subject, it deserves the preference to former systems, and is un-questionably the most entertaining. The plates with which it is illus-trated, are numerous and beautifully engraved.

As many of our readers may be pleased to see an author's first conceptions of an intended work, we shall lay before them the original plan of this system of Natural History, drawn up by Dr. Goldsmith himself, with which we have lately been favoured. It evidently appears, that the author had thought maturely of his subject; the work is, for the most part, conducted according to the idea here delineated, except that the authorities are not cited at the bottom of the page, as had been proposed.

36. Edward Bancroft attacks Goldsmith's *History of the Earth, Monthly Review*

April 1775, lii, 310–14

Edward Bancroft (1744–1821), M.D., F.R.S., naturalist and chemist, had already published *An Essay on the Natural History of [Dutch] Guiana* (1769). By 1770 he had become a freethinker, as evidenced by his novel, *The History of Charles Wentworth*, and his religious beliefs in the 1770s clearly color the following appraisal of Goldsmith's *History*.

THE reputation which our Author had acquired by his former pro-ductions, and particularly by those of the poetical class, will acquire no addition from the performance under consideration; for however well qualified he was to excel in works of *imagination*, his talents appear to have been ill suited to those of *Science*—Natural history, especially, from the number and variety of its objects, requires a much more extensive knowledge than appears to have been possessed by this Writer.

Several of the most eminent modern naturalists, particularly Linnaeus, Klein, Brisson, Artedi, Willoughby and Ray,[1] have employed themselves chiefly in naming and arranging the various animal, vegetable, and fossil productions, and in describing concisely those characteristic peculiarities of structure which distinguish each of them, respectively, from all others, disregarding, in a great degree, their manners, habits, instincts, properties, and uses, which constitute the most pleasing, and perhaps the most important, part of natural knowledge.

From an accurate systematic arrangement of natural objects, we acquire *general conceptions* of all the individuals composing the system, and of their relations and diversities in those particulars on which such arrangement is made to depend. But these conceptions must necessarily be, in many respects, factitious and imperfect; for the connexions and variations of the several productions of Nature, are, if we may be allowed the expression, so *reticulated*, that by whatever peculiarities a natural historian may chuse to distinguish and arrange them, yet the artificial separations and combinations which constitute his classes, &c. will necessarily break through many of the relations naturally subsisting between different objects, and change their original positions with respect to each other.—Such disadvantages are indeed sufficiently compensated, by the readiness with which these distributions enable us to ascertain the particular species of every known object, and the greater facility with which the imagination will contain and the memory call forth *ideas, systematically arranged*, and *connected* to each other.—Our Author has however adopted no methodical arrangement worthy of notice; and his descriptions, negligent of those distinguishing peculiarities of structure, which enable us to discover the name and species of each individual, are almost wholly employed upon their more amusing properties and relations.—His work indeed, collectively, is to be considered as a *compilation* of but very indifferent though unequal merit; for being almost wholly unacquainted with his subject, and consequently unable to discriminate between the merits and defects of his authorities, he frequently adopts and repeats errors that have been exploded by later discoveries; of which indeed he appears to have been surprisingly ignorant, considering the accessions of

---

[1] Identification of these writers and all the topics mentioned in this review are found in J. H. Pitman, *Goldsmith's Animated Nature* (New Haven, 1924). See also W. Lynskey, 'The Scientific Sources of Goldsmith's Animated Nature,' *Studies in Philology*, xl, 1943.

GOLDSMITH

knowledge that must obtrude themselves upon every man of literary character, residing in this metropolis,[1] and engaged in the ordinary intercourses of society. Of this we could produce numerous instances: a few, however, selected only from the first volume (which is confined to the inanimated parts of Nature) will be sufficient to justify a censure that has been some time delayed, and is now delivered, only from a sense of our duty to the Public.

1st, In Chap. VIII. treating 'Of Mines, *Damps*, and *Mineral Vapours*,' he appears wholly ignorant of the late discoveries respecting the different kinds of air, and especially of those made by Drs. Hales, Priestley, Brownrigg, and Black, Mr. Cavendish, &c. and therefore in considering the effects of the *Grotto di Cani* near Naples, and of what is called the *Stith* or Choak Damp in mines, (and which we now certainly know to result only from the action of *mephitic* or *fixable air*) and also in considering the explosions and other phenomena in mines, (which we also know are produced from the *inflammable air*) he repeats many *vague*, *erroneous*, and exploded opinions, explanations, and conjectures.

2dly, In Chap. XV. treating 'Of the Ocean in general, and its saltness,' he says (p. 237) . . . [the whole passage is quoted]. The preceding passage will prove our Author to have been ignorant even of a discovery which has been attended with circumstances of uncommon notoriety; for after all that had been believed of a bituminous substance and a spirit of sea-salt rising in the distillation of sea-water, Dr. *James Lind*, Physician to the hospital at *Haslar*, so long ago as the year 1761, publickly demonstrated by several trials and experiments made at the Royal Academy at Portsmouth, in the presence of Mr. Hughes, resident Commissioner of the Navy there, and others, '*that a simple distillation, rendered sea-water* perfectly fresh, pure, and wholesome:' and in the month of May 1762, an account of this discovery was read to a numerous audience of the Royal Society; and soon after a book containing the same was published by the authority of the Lords Commissioners of the Admiralty; and early in the year 1772, a parliamentary reward of £5000 was granted to Mr. Irvine, for a *supposed* improvement in the apparatus for executing Dr. Lind's discovery.—After all which, it is not a little surprising that our Author should mislead himself or the Public with an opinion that salt of tartar, or *calcined bones*, are necessary to render sea-water fresh by distillation.

3dly. In the same chapter, at page 247, he says, 'I will conclude this chapter with one effect more, produced by the saltness of the sea;

[1] London, of course.

154

. . .' [the whole paragraph is quoted]. It had been long observed that vegetables were rendered *luminous* by putrefaction, as in the well-known instance of *rotten wood*: later experiments had also proved that animal matters, left to putrify in water, gave it a luminous fiery appearance; and this discovery has been some years publickly applied to explain the phenomena under consideration, nor have we ever heard that any person has disputed the justice of this explanation.

4thly, Chap. XIX. is styled 'An Essay on the Natural History of the Air,' which, from what we observed on the subject of *Mines*, our Readers will justly expect to find very imperfect. Indeed our Author appears to have had no knowledge of any difference in the kinds of air, except what was known in the time of Mr. Boyle, who had observed that what he calls *factitious air*, extracted from apples, cherries, amber, hartshorn, &c. proved noxious when inspired by animals, and our Author, not understanding this to be a distinct species of air, concludes that *wholesome respirable air* consists only of the *effluvia* of different kinds of matter, and that noxious effects happen from inspiring the effluvium of *one* substance *only*. 'In order (says he, page 320) that air should be wholesome, it is necessary, as we have seen, that it should *not be of one kind, but the compound of several substances*; and the more various the composition, to all appearance, the more salubrious.'

5thly, In the same chapter, at page 333, observing that 'a candle quickly goes out in an exhausted receiver,' he adds, 'wood also set on fire immediately goes out, and its flame ceases upon removing the air, for something is then wanting to *press the body of the fire against that of the fuel*, and to prevent the too speedy diffusion of the flame.'— By this explanation our Author discovers a total ignorance of the *nature of fire*, or rather of the *process of burning*, which takes place with inflammable substances, and which is no more than a *chemical combination of respirable air*, and the principle of inflammability or phlogiston, which, like many other mixtures and solutions, produces heat.—This process, however, necessarily ceases whenever the air, applied to the burning substance, is fully *saturated*, and incapable of uniting with any more of the inflammable principle: and an extinction of fire will then happen, not from any want of *pressure*, but because the *combination* from which *it results*, can no longer take place when one of the combining substances becomes wanting.—We could, without quitting our Author's first volume, cite many instances of the like nature, which however we shall overlook, only observing that he is not always satisfied with repeating the opinions of others; for we occasionally find him attempting to reason with an unbecoming temerity, even in opposition to what is apparently the truth: of this an instance occurs in page 370, where, after noticing and rejecting Dr. Hamilton's opinion that *evaporation* is produced from a solution of water by the atmospherical air, he delivers a theory of his own on that subject, viz. 'We know that a repelling power prevails in Nature, not less than an attractive one. This repulsion prevails strongly between the body of fire and that of water. If I plunge the end of a red hot bar of iron into a vessel of water, the fluid rises, and large drops of it fly up in all manner of directions, every part bubbling and steaming until the iron be cold. Why may we not, for a moment, compare the rays of the sun, darted directly upon the surface of the water, to so many bars of red hot iron; each bar, indeed, infinitely small, but not the less powerful? . . .'

We are however persuaded that every man who is qualified to reason properly on this subject, and who considers the facts and arguments that have been advanced, particularly by Lord Kaims, to prove that evaporation is the effect of a solution of water by air, will conclude that our Author might have spared himself the trouble of converting *the rays of the sun into red hot bars of iron*, thereby to explain the process in question.

The second, third, and fourth volumes comprehend the natural history of *mankind* and of quadrupeds; and these, as well as the first volume, are chiefly borrowed from Buffon's diffused writings, from which he transcribes many errors; even that which (as a Brother Critic has justly remarked) was long the jest of naturalists,—we mean the assertion that *cows*, when three years old, shed their horns, and that new ones rise in their stead.

His descriptions of birds are extremely loose and superficial, and they do not extend to one-fifth of the species which have been described by Linnaeus. Neither are his accounts of fishes, insects, &c. much less faulty: indeed the four last volumes are particularly defective, probably because in composing them, he no longer derived any assistance from the writings of Buffon, whose volumes on birds he does not appear to have seen. It is however but justice to observe, that notwithstanding the faults of our Author's performance, the manner and style in which it is written are generally pleasing, and the entertainment which it affords is occasionally increased by the interposition of pertinent speculative reflections.

ON GOLDSMITH'S LIFE AND WORKS

---

37. William Rider on Goldsmith's prose style, in *An Historical and Critical Account of the Lives and Writings of the Living Authors of Great Britain*

1762, 13–14

This work published in 1762 has been doubtfully attributed to William Rider (1723–85), a miscellaneous writer who had translated Voltaire's *Candide* in 1759. His high appraisal of Goldsmith's prose style reflects an attitude popular in 1761–3. In December 1761, for example, the *Court Magazine*, a miscellaneous magazine edited by Hugh Kelly, singled out Goldsmith, along with Johnson, Young, Gray, and a few others, from a list of fifty-six living authors and hailed him as a writer accomplished in 'taste and understanding.' Rider's article, largely biographical, proceeds with brief eulogies of Goldsmith's *Enquiry into the Present State of Polite Learning*, his *Bee*, and his *Citizen of the World*, and ends with an appreciation of his prose style. Since it is the earliest known printed statement about Goldsmith, I have not abbreviated it.

THIS Gentleman was born in *Ireland*. He studied Physic at *Leyden*, and took the Degree of Doctor at *Edinburgh*. He has wrote many Treatises, which have met with universal Approbation. His *Essay on the present State of polite Learning in all Parts of* Europe, at once does Honour to his Taste and Genius. His miscellaneous Collection of

Essays, published under the Title of the *Bee*, was greatly admired, both on Account of the Elegance of the Stile, in which it is wrote, and the Variety of entertaining Articles which it contains. But the *Chinese Letters*, first published in the *Ledger*, in Numbers, and since republished in Volumes, under the Title of the *Citizen of the World*, are, of all the Productions of this Author, those that do the highest Honour to his Genius, as they must be acknowledged by every Reader free from the Influence of Prepossession, to be but little inferior to the *Persian Letters* of the celebrated *Montesquieu*. To conclude Dr. *Goldsmith's* Character as an Author, it must be acknowledged, that whilst he is surpassed by few of his Contemporaries with Regard to the Matter which his Writings contain, he is superior to most of them in Style, having happily found out the Secret to unite Elevation with Ease, a Perfection in Language, which few Writers of our Nation have attained to, as most of those who aim at Sublimity swell their Expressions with Fustian and Bombast, whilst those who affect Ease, degenerate into Familiarity and Flatness.

38. James Beattie on Goldsmith's envy of other authors, in *A London Diary*

14 June 1773

Dr James Beattie (1735–1803), the Scottish professor, poet and author of the *Minstrel* (Book I, 1771; Book II, 1774), had recently gained fame and adulation by the publication of his *Essay on Truth* (1770), a defence of Christianity. The London literary world was sufficiently impressed by the worth of this essay to award him a pension of £200 per annum. Goldsmith was enraged when he heard about the pension and told Dr Johnson, 'here's such a stir about a fellow that has written one book, and I have written many.' 'Ah, Doctor!' retorted Johnson, to his indigent, unpensioned friend, 'there go two-and-forty sixpences, you know, to one guinea,' whereupon the lively Mrs Thrale apparently clasped her hands and Goldsmith withdrew to a corner to sulk. See *Thraliana*, June 1777. The following extract is quoted from the edition of *James Beattie's London Diary* by Ralph S. Walker, Aberdeen University Press, 1946, p. 55.

—Miss Reynolds[1] told me to day some particulars of Goldsmith. He, it seems, not only is, but even acknowledges himself to be, envious of all contemporary authors whose works are succesful, and has several times spoken wt. some peevishness of the attention that has been shown to me in England. 'Why should he have a pension?' (he said one day in a company where I happened to be mentioned)—'For writing the minstrel? Then surely I have a better claim.' One of the company told him, that my claim was founded on the Essay on Truth, a work of public utility, and which had been attended wt. danger or at least no small inconvenience to the Author. Here Foote[2] the player

---

[1] Sir Joshua Reynolds' sister, Frances who knew many of the members of Johnson's Club.
[2] Samuel Foote (1720–77), though by this time past the height of his powers as a satirical actor and mimic, was still popular on the London stage. In July of 1773 he produced a

interposed: 'I have read (said he) the Minstrel and think it an excellent poem; but the Author of the Essay on Truth is peculiarly entitled to publick encouragement for writing one of the best and most ingenious books which have appeared this age.'—We came not away from Richmond till it was dark and by the way met wt. more than one adventure, owing to the drunkenness of the coachman; however we got safely into town about 11 o'clock: Sir Joshua, Mess. Ed. & Wm. Burke's, Goldsmith and I in one coach; & Mrs. Burke Miss Reynolds Mrs. Beattie and Dick Burke in another. Rainy and dark evening.

---

play of his own called *The Bankrupt*, and in the same season a puppet-show which he named *The Primitive Puppet-Show*.

39. Courtney Melmoth writing about Goldsmith's greatness on the day of his funeral, 9 April 1774, *The Tears of Genius, Occasioned by the Death of Dr. Goldsmith*

Printed for T. Becket, April 1774, 1–13

Courtney Melmoth (1749–1814), pseudonym for Samuel Jackson Pratt, had abandoned the clergy and by 1774 appeared as a miscellaneous writer. His poem occasioned by the death of Goldsmith and the tradition of *momento mori* verse, is subtitled 'An Elegy on the favourite English Poets lately deceased, imitative of the stile of each.' The poem is dedicated to Sir Joshua Reynolds.

SIR,

THE veneration I bear to the memory of Doctor Goldsmith, has drawn me into the present publication; and the sentiments of affection to be found in his Dedication of the *Deserted Village*, have induced me to inscribe *this* Elegy to Sir Joshua Reynolds; who will naturally receive with kindness whatever is designed, as a testimony of justice, to a Friend that is no more.

In contemplating the death of this excellent man, and admirable poet, I have been led to contemplate likewise the fate of others; for within a very few years our literary losses have been fatally multiplied, and many of the most valuable members have been suddenly lopped off from science and society. In pursuit of this undertaking, where the same pathetic subject was to be considered to the end, I resolved to set out upon an irregular principle, that without enchaining myself to any critical uniformity, I might have scope and latitude for whatever varieties of versification should fall in my way.

As I was to deplore the loss of different writers, each of which possessed very strongly a marking originality, I thought it best to write a sort of Epitaph upon each: accordingly, the following Verses are intended as so many separate Imitations of the style and manner of the Authors which they commemorate.

That the occasion which produced the Elegy, might not lose the strength of the impression, by delay—for alas, the traces of sorrow for the loss of the learned, are soon worn out by the tumults of life—I hurried the composition to the press, the moment I could withdraw my hand from the manuscript; the whole of which was begun and finished within a few hours after the news reached me, that Dr. Goldsmith was dead . . .

THE

TEARS OF GENIUS.

THE village-bell tolls out the note of death,
And thro' the echoing air, the length'ning sound,
With dreadful pause, reverberating deep;
Spreads the sad tydings, o'er fair Auburn's vale.
There, to enjoy the scenes her bard had prais'd
In all the sweet simplicity of song,
GENIUS, in pilgrim garb, sequester'd sat,
And herded jocund with the harmless swains:
But when she heard the fate-foreboding knell,
With startled step, precipitate and swift,
And look pathetic, full of dire presage,
The church-way walk, beside the neighb'ring green,
Sorrowing she sought; and there, in black array,
Borne on the shoulders of the swains he lov'd,
She saw the boast of Auburn mov'd along.
Touch'd at the view, her pensive breast she struck,
And to the cypress, which incumbent hangs
With leaning slope, and branch irregular,
O'er the moss'd pillars of the sacred fane,
The briar-bound graves shadowing with funeral gloom,
Forlorn she hied; And there the crowding woe
(Swell'd by the parent) press'd on bleeding thought.
Big ran the drops from her maternal eye,
Fast broke the bosom-sorrow from her heart,
And pale Distress, sat sickly on her cheek,
As thus her plaintive Elegy began.

And must my children all expire?

Shall none be left to strike the lyre?
Courts Death alone a learned prize?
Falls his shafts only on the wise?
Can no fit marks on earth be found,
From useless thousands swarming round?
What crowding cyphers cram the land!
What hosts of victims, at command!
Yet shall th' Ingenious drop alone?
Shall Science grace the tyrant's throne?
Thou murd'rer of the tuneful train!
I charge thee, with my children slain!

Scarce has the Sun thrice urg'd his annual tour,
Since half my race have felt thy barbarous power;

    Sore hast thou thinn'd each pleasing art,
    And struck a muse with every dart:

Bard, after bard, obey'd thy slaughtering call,
Till scarce a poet lives to sing a brother's fall.

    Then let a widow'd mother pay
    The tribute of a parting lay.

Tearful, inscribe the monumental strain,
And speak aloud, her feelings, and her pain!

And first, farewel to thee, my son, she cried,
Thou pride of Auburn's Dale—sweet bard, farewel.

Long for thy sake, the peasants tear shall flow,
And many a virgin-bosom heave with woe,
For thee shall sorrow sadden all the scene,
And every pastime, perish on the green;
The sturdy farmer shall suspend his tale,
The woodman's ballad shall no more regale,
No more shall Mirth, each rustic sport inspire,
But every frolic, every feat, shall tire.
No more the evening gambol shall delight,
Nor moonshine revels crown the vacant night,
But groupes of villagers (each joy forgot)
Shall form, a sad assembly round the cot.
Sweet bard, farewel—and farewel, Auburn's bliss,

The bashful lover, and the yielded kiss;
The evening warble Philomela made,
The echoing forest, and the whispering shade,
The winding brook, the bleat of brute content,
And the blithe voice that 'whistled as it went.'
These shall no longer charm the plowman's care,
But sighs shall fill, the pauses of despair.

GOLDSMITH adieu! the 'book-learn'd priest' for thee
Shall now in vain possess his festive glee,
The oft-heard jest in vain he shall reveal,
For now alas, the jest he cannot feel.
But ruddy damsels o'er thy tomb shall bend,
And conscious weep for their and virtue's friend:
The milkmaid shall reject the shepherd's song,
And cease to carol as she toils along:
All Auburn shall bewail the fatal day,
When from her fields, their pride was snatch'd away;
And even the matron of the cressy lake
In piteous plight, her palsied head shall shake,
While all adown the furrows of her face
Slow shall the lingering tears each other trace.

And, Oh my child! severer woes remain,
To all the houseless, and unshelter'd train:
Thy fate shall sadden many an humble guest,
And heap fresh anguish on the beggar's breast.
For dear wert thou to all the sons of pain;
To all that wander, sorrow, or complain.
Dear to the learned, to the simple dear,
For daily blessings mark'd thy virtuous year;
The rich receiv'd a moral from thy head,
And from thy heart the stranger found a bed.
Distress came always smiling from thy door;
For God had made thee agent to the poor;
Had form'd thy feelings on the noblest plan,
To grace at once, the Poet, and the Man.
Here GENIUS paus'd to dry the gathering tear,
Which Nature started in her matron eye.
She paus'd an instant, then the strain renew'd.

THEE too, thou favourite of the moral strain,
  Pathetic GRAY; for thee does GENIUS mourn:
Science and Taste, thy early fate shall plain,
  And Virtue drop a tear into thy urn . . .

40. A tribute to Goldsmith as a poet by John Tait, author of *The Druid's Monument*

Printed for T. Davies, 1774

John Tait (dates unknown) was a minor writer who flourished during 1774–6 and had written the *Cave of Morar*. His poem shows that Goldsmith's verse appealed to writers especially interested in Celtic primitivism.

THE moon shone bright—I stray'd along,
  Where Thames so sweetly flows,
And oft I rais'd the rustic song,
  Impell'd by fancied woes.

I sung of love, and all its charms,
  Of love with scorn repaid,
I sung of jealousy's alarms,
  And blam'd th' inconstant maid.

'Farewell, I cried, ye giddy train,
  'So fickle and untrue,
'And heav'n protect that hapless swain,
  'Who builds his hopes on you.

'These hopes, alas! will quickly fly,
  'Nor leave a shade behind,

'And cold disdain shall arm that eye,
 'Which lately beam'd so kind.

'Tho' now the Spring, so blythe and gay,
 'Adorns the fields with flow'rs,
'Tho' now the Linnet pours her lay
 'Amid yon sylvan bow'rs:

'Yet to that slighted youth, the Spring
 'Smiles chearfully in vain,
'And tho' the Linnets sweetly sing,
 'They cannot ease his pain.'—

Thus flow'd my strain, as fancy bade,
 I thought no mortal nigh—
I turn'd me to the sylvan shade,
 A stranger caught my eye.

Grief mark'd his face, his locks were grey,
 An ancient harp he bore,
And plain and rude was his array,
 As that which Druids wore.

'Mortal, he said, thy cares are vain,
 'Such cares thou must forego;
'It ill becomes thee to complain,
 'Or grieve at fancied woe.

'If grief you love, come follow me,
 'And where yon elms appear,
'A mournful monument you'll see
 'That justly claims a tear.

'That monument the DRUIDS rais'd,
 'It bears a Poet's name,
'Whom Britain's children long have prais'd,
 'A fav'rite son of fame.

'Oft have we seen him on these plains,
 '(He lov'd the calm retreat)
'Oft have we heard his polish'd strains,
 'And every note was sweet.

'Say, *Nature* say, for thou canst tell,
 'Are not the words thy own,

'When to the *hermit's*[1] peaceful cell—
   'The poet leads us on.

'Do not thy thoughts appear,
   'Does not thy voice adorn,
'When these sweet sounds salute the ear,
   '*Turn, gentle hermit, turn.*

'O! say what beauties grace the song,
   'What heavenly Ardor warms,
'When ANGELINA, lost so long,
   'Is lock'd in EDWIN's arms.

'This strain the *Druids* oft repeat
   'In some sequester'd grove,
'Where with the *Fairy* train they meet,
   'To hear the tales of love.

'For still the Druids haunt this isle,
   'And fairies oft are seen,
'When sleep rewards the plowman's toil,
   'And shepherds leave the green.

'Oft hand in hand, in mirthful mood,
   'At night we tread the lawn,
'And hide us in this lonely wood,
   'When day begins to dawn.

'And here with some bewitching strain,
   'We cheat the ling'ring hours,
'Till the pale moon returns again,
   'And makes all nature ours.

'And oft in hearing GOLDSMITH's lays,
   'These lays that touch the soul,
'We've pass'd the longest Summer days,
   'And wonder'd how they stole.

'But ah! these strains we'll hear no more,
   'For to yon darksome dell,
'This morn the weeping shepherds bore,
   'The bard we lov'd so well:

[1] This alludes to Dr Goldsmith's well known *Ballad of the Hermit* [Tait's own note]. The poem is 'Edwin and Angelina.'

'With decent grace we saw them bend,
  'And lay in yonder grave,
'The friend of man, the muse's friend,
  'Whom virtue could not save.

'And can we stay when he is gone?
  'Can we enjoy these plains?
'Ah! no, their sweetest charms are flown,
  'They've lost their poet's strains.—

'*Auburn* farewell[1]—no more we'll stray
  ''Mid thy *deserted* bow'rs,
'T'applaud thy poet's plaintive lay,
  'And pluck thy withering flow'rs.

'No more the Druids shall appear,
  'But like thy hapless train,
'Drop, as they pass, a silent tear,
  'And seek some happier plain.

'Yet on that plain, where'er it is,
  'We'll oft together join,
'And fondly tell the scenes of bliss
  'The joys that once were thine.

'Ev'n there we'll crown thy bard with bays,
  'And give him just applause,
'When we recall his pleasing lays,
  'And think what *Auburn* was.

'Perhaps where *Alpine* hills[2] ascend,
  'We'll sit us down at last,
'And see fair ITALY extend,
  'And think of pleasures past;

'Then turning, trace the various scenes
  'Which GOLDSMITH's pencil drew,
'And own, with tears, that all his strains
  'Are just, are strictly true.

'Yet ere we left our native land,
  'We rais'd this sacred stone,

---

[1] *The deserted Village* [Tait's note].
[2] *The Traveller* [Tait's note].

'Where SCULPTURE, with an artful hand,
  'The poet's worth hath shown.

'Then turn and read—nor rail at love,
  'Nor drop that useless tear,
'Nor let *unreal* sorrow move,
  'But pay a tribute *here*.'

I turned, I read, I heav'd a sigh,
  My conduct who can blame,
For every bard that passes by
  Will always do the same.

The INSCRIPTION[1]

'Adieu, sweet bard, to each fine feeling true,
'Thy virtues many, and thy foibles few,
'Those form'd to charm, ev'n vicious minds, and these
'With harmless mirth the social soul to please,
'Another's woe thy heart could always melt,
'None gave more free, for none more deeply felt.
'Sweet bard adieu, thy own harmonious lays
'Have sculptur'd out thy monument of praise.
'Yes—these survive to time's remotest day,
'While drops the bust, and boastful tombs decay.—
'Reader, if number'd in the muse's train,
'Go tune the lyre, and imitate his strain;
'But, if no poet thou, reverse the plan,
'Depart in peace, and imitate the man.'

[1] The inscription is by William Woty (1731–91).

41. Edmund Burke writes a fitting monument to Goldsmith, in a letter to Thomas Davies

28 June 1776

Burke is known to have burst into tears when he heard on 5 April 1774 of Goldsmith's death. After *Retaliation* appeared on 19 April 1774, with its memorable portrait of Burke, everyone expected that Burke might reply to the accusation that he 'to party gave up what was meant for mankind' (*Retaliation*, line 32). But Burke never did. Instead he continued to think of Goldsmith as one of England's greatest writers, as the following letter indicates.

Sir,

I have received a poem on the death of Dr Goldsmith[1] which the author has done me the honour to inscribe to me. I am very much flattered by a compliment on so distinguished a subject and from so very ingenious a writer. I shall take it as an additional favour (if I do not intrude too much into his secret) if the gentleman will let me know to whom I owe the obligation of this great politeness and the satisfaction I have had in the perusal of the fine poem in which he has been pleased to give me a particular interest.

I am, Sir,

Your most obedient and humble servant,

EDM. BURKE.

[1] Possibly John Tait's *The Druid's Monument* (see above, No. 40) or *A Monody on the Death of Dr Oliver Goldsmith*, T. Davies, 1774, which was dedicated to Burke. On or around 5 May 1774 Burke had received a set of verses from Caleb Whitefoord, which were intended to be an addition to *Retaliation*. It is not clear, however, whether Whitefoord himself or Goldsmith wrote the lines. See *The Correspondence of Edmund Burke*, ed. Dame Lucy S. Sutherland, Cambridge, 1960, II, 535–6 for a statement about the problem of attribution of these verses.

42. Francis Spilsbury esteems Goldsmith as a poet in a medical pamphlet, *Free Thoughts on Quacks and their Medicines, Occasioned by the Death of Dr. Goldsmith* . . .

1776, xxii

Because the circumstances surrounding Goldsmith's death had been mysterious, Dr William Hawes immediately prepared *An Account of the Late Dr. Goldsmith's Illness* (1774), describing his handling of the case and Goldsmith's use of Dr James's famed fever powders. Hawes's account stirred a controversy and impelled many authors to reply. One reply was by Spilsbury, who, like Goldsmith, was medically trained.

. . . Dr. GOLDSMITH who, a bad physician enough because he had only been bred to it, had distinguished himself among us by some tolerable good poetical productions, because he was born to poetry, was not altogether unworthy an honourable notice being taken of the loss we had sustained by his death, and of the accident to which this had been owing.—But, as, from the context of the same *account*, it is more than evident this was but the least object of the pamphlet,[1] and served only as a basis, on which a much dearer one was to be established, we shall quit it without further animadversions, to pass to a more scrupulous examen of the second *query*.

[1] Hawes's.

43. Sir Joshua Reynolds on the total genius of Goldsmith in a sketch of his character

1776[?]

This sketch was found among Boswell's papers and has been printed in *Portraits by Sir Joshua Reynolds*, ed. Frederick W. Hilles, New York, 1952, pp. 44–59. As Hilles writes (p. 29), 'no one knew Goldsmith better than Sir Joshua.' The two men had met in 1762 and later became important members of Dr Johnson's Club. Reynolds (1723–92), the painter and drawing master, here attempts to write a somewhat dispassionate account, free from anecdotes and legends, of the real achievement of his friend.

If anyone thinks that Dr. Goldsmith was a man not worth the investigation, we must refer him to the public advertisements, where he will find the booksellers have lived upon his reputation, as his friends have lived upon his character, ever since his death.[1]

The literary world seemed to deplore his death more than could be expected, when it is considered how small a part of his works were wrote for fame; yet epigrams, epitaphs and monodies to his memory were without end. And what is still a greater proof of his popularity, the booksellers still continue to live upon his name, which they shamefully prostitute by prefixing it to works which he never saw, and which were probably written since his death.

Dr. Goldsmith's genius is universally acknowledged. All that we shall endeavour to do is to show what indeed is self-apparent, that such a genius could not be a fool or such a weak man as many people thought him.

Dr. Goldsmith was, in the truest as the most common sense of the word, a man of genius. But if we take the popular opinion of genius—that it is a gift, or supernatural power, entirely distinct from wisdom,

---

[1] An assertion established as fact by twentieth-century historians of publishing and students of printing history.

knowledge, learning, and judgment, and that all these acquisitions contribute to destroy, rather than increase, the operations of genius—the Doctor must be acknowledged to have in this sense greater claim to the name of genius than any other man whatever, not excepting M. La Fontaine.[1] I do not mean that the Doctor entirely wanted all these qualities, but he appeared to want them in conversation.

Among those, therefore, who knew him but superficially, many suspected he was not the author of his own works, whilst others pronounced him an idiot inspired.[2] The supposition that he did not write his own works had a great appearance of probability to those who knew him but superficially, but whoever knew him intimately and still continued of that opinion, it would reflect no great compliment to his sagacity. His more intimate acquaintances easily perceived his absurdities proceeded from other causes than from a feebleness of intellect, and that his follies were not those of a fool.

A great part of Dr. Goldsmith's folly and absurdity proceeded from principle, and partly from a want of early acquaintance with that life to which his reputation afterwards introduced him.

The author was intimately acquainted with Dr. Goldsmith. They unbosomed their minds freely to each other, not only in regard to the characters of their friends, but what contributed to make men's company desired or avoided. It was agreed that it was not superior parts, or wisdom, or knowledge that made men beloved—that men do not go into company with a desire of receiving instruction, but to be amused—that people naturally avoid that society where their minds are to be kept on the stretch.

He was of a sociable disposition. He had a very strong desire, which I believe nobody will think very peculiar or culpable, to be liked, to have his company sought after by his friends. To this end, for it was a system, he abandoned his respectable character as a writer or a man of observation to that of a character which nobody was afraid of being humiliated in his presence. This was his general principle, but at times, observing the attention paid to the conversation of others who spoke with more premeditation, and the neglect of himself though greedy and impatient to speak, he then resolved to be more formal and to carry his character about with him. But as he found he could not unite both, he naturally relaxed into his old manner, and

[1] Legend had it that he had been one of the greatest literary geniuses of all times.
[2] Referring to a comment Horace Walpole (see No. 27b) is said to have made but which cannot be proved to have been said by him.

which manner, it must be acknowledged, met with all success for the purposes he intended it.

The Doctor came late into the great world. He had lived a great part of his life with mean people. All his old habits were against him. It was too late to learn new ones, or at least for the new to sit easy on him. However, he set furiously about it. For one week he took one for a model and for another week [another]. This disadvantage, joined to an anxious desire and impatience to distinguish himself, brought him often into ridiculous situations. As he thought, and not without reason, that he had distinguished himself by his writings, he imagined therefore he ought at all times and in all places to be equally distinguished from the rest of the company, which, if neglected, he thought it incumbent on him to do that little service for himself. Without therefore waiting for a fit opportunity, he always took care to stand forward and draw the attention of the company upon himself. He talked without knowledge, not so much for the sake of shining as [from] an impatience of neglect by being left out of the conversation. He would therefore, to draw the attention of the company upon [himself], sing, stand upon his head, [or] dance about the room.

His *Traveller* produced an eagerness unparalleled to see the author. He was sought after with greediness. He knew much was expected from him. He had not that kind of prudence to take refuge in silence. He would speak on subjects [of] which he had not thought, and of which he was ignorant; he was impatient of being overlooked; he wished to be the principal figure in every group. Goldsmith having adopted this mode of conduct forgot that he must with the advantages accept of all the disadvantages that belonged to it. But he envied Johnson. It may easily be conceived what absurdity of conduct he must fall into in whom this restless desire predominates.

No man's company was ever more greedily sought after, for in his company the ignorant and illiterate were not only easy and free from any mortifying restraint, but even their vanity was gratified to find so admirable a writer so much upon a level, or inferior to themselves, in the arts of conversation. The ingenious and the learned, who wished to display their knowledge, were sure to find an opportunity of gratifying their desire by the triumph of refuting his paradoxes. And it must be acknowledged that he often fought like a tiger, and like the tiger he fought when turned on his back. He risked every opinion which that moment came into his head.

He was impatient when praises were bestowed on any person,

however remote these might be from interfering with his own department. It was enough for him if they filled the mouths of men, to
oppose their pretensions.

With this fighting, absurdity, and ridiculous kind of envy, he made
always a sort of bustle, and wherever he was there was no yawning.
The conversation never stagnated or languished. The same company
[that], the moment he had turned his back, were in open cry on his
absurdity and folly, were still desirous of meeting him again the next
day.

He considered him as a friend indeed who would ask him to tell a
story or sing a song, either of which requests he was always very ready
to comply with, and very often without being asked, and without
any preparation, to the great amazement of the company. His favourite
songs were *Johnny Armstrong*, *Barbara Allen*, and *Death and the Lady*.
In singing the last he endeavoured to humour the dialogue by looking
very fierce and speaking in a very rough voice for Death, which he
suddenly changed when he came to the lady's part, putting on what
he fancied to be a lady-like sweetness of countenance with a thin,
shrill voice. His skill in singing those ballads was no ways superior to
the professors of this art which are heard every day in the streets, but
whilst he was thus employed he was a conspicuous figure at least and
was relieved from that horror which he entertained of being overlooked
by the company.

It must be confessed that whoever excelled in any art or science,
however different from his own, was sure to be considered by him as
a rival. It was sufficient that he was an object of praise, as if he thought
that the world had but a certain quantity of that commodity to give
away, and what was bestowed upon others made less come to his
share. This odious quality, however, was not so disagreeable in him as
it generally is in other people. It was so far from being of that black
malignant kind which excites hatred and disgust, that it was, from its
being so artless and obvious, only ridiculous.

The following happened once in a large company, which may
serve as an instance to characterize the Doctor's manner. Somebody
said that one of Mr. Garrick's excellencies, amongst many others,
was his powers in telling of a story. This being universally agreed to,
excited the Doctor's envy.

'I do not see what difficulty there can be in telling a story well.
I would undertake to tell a story as well as Mr. Garrick, and I will
tell you one now, and I will do my best. There lived a cobbler—some

people do laugh at this story and some do not; however, the story is this—there lived a cobbler in a stall. This stall was opposite our house, so I knew him very well. This cobbler a bailie came after, for I must tell you he was a very low fellow.'

('But you was acquainted with him, you say. He used to be often at your house.')

'Ay, he used to come over to fetch our shoes when they wanted mending, but not as an acquaintance, I always kept the best company.'

('Go on with your story, Doctor.')

'This cobbler was afraid of being arrested.——Why, the very best company used to come in our house. Squire Thomson used to dine with us, who was one of the first men in the country. I remember his coach and six, which we used to see come galloping down the hill, and then my mother, who was a little woman, was quite hid at the head of the table behind a great sirloin of beef. You could but just see the top of her head.'

('Well, but go on, Doctor Goldsmith, with your story.')

'When the bailie came to, and knocked at, the door of the cobbler's stall in order to have it opened, the cobbler, being aware, answered in the voice of a child (here the Doctor changes his voice), "Put in your finger into the hole and lift up the latch," which as soon as he had done, the cobbler with his knife cut the finger off, and still speaking in the child's voice, "Put in the other finger, Sir, if you please." '

The Doctor's folly, freaks, and nonsense, though there was seldom anything in it which marked it to be the nonsense of a man of genius, yet neither had it any of those marks of feebleness by which weakness and ignorance is immediately discovered. If he was sometimes foolish out of season, he never was what is worse, wise out of season. For instance, Dr. Goldsmith never made common observations with the air and as if he had spoke oracles, or even acquiesced in what others advanced, in order to conceal his own ignorance. On the contrary, he delighted in advancing paradoxes, and opposed others with false authorities, by which he often indeed discovered his ignorance, but not weakness. (The sterlings.)[1]

Goldsmith had no wit in conversation, but to do him justice, he did not much attempt it. When in company with ladies he was always endeavouring after humour, and as continually failed; but his ill success was equally diverting to the company as if he had succeeded.

[1] The words in round brackets are Sir Joshua's note to himself to include at this point an example of what he has just said.

If they laughed, he was happy and did not seem to care whether it was with him or at him. But when he was in company with the philosophers, he was grave, wise, and very inclinable to dispute established opinions. This immediately produced a general cry. Every man had arguments of confutation ready, and he himself was at once placed in the situation he so much loved, of being the object of attention of the whole company. However this disposition to paradoxes might be sometimes troublesome, it often called out the rest of the company into conversation, and as has been often observed, wherever the Doctor was, the conversation was never known to languish.

What Goldsmith intended for humour was purposely repeated as serious. However, to do justice to the world, a man seldom acquires the character of absurd without deserving it. As the *bons mots* of other wits are handed about the town, the Doctor's blunders and absurdities, circulated with equal success, helped to increase his fame and give everybody a desire of seeing the man, and this perhaps not without some mixture of self-congratulation to find a person whom they were obliged to look up to for superior talent sink below their own level when in conversation.

Goldsmith's mind was entirely unfurnished. When he was engaged in a work, he had all his knowledge to find, which when he found, he knew how to use, but forgot it immediately after he had used it.

He was so far from exciting envy in others by any exhibition of his own superior powers in extempore thinking that he would in a shorter time write the poem in his closet than give a satisfactory account in company of the plan or conduct of the work, or give any satisfactory explanation of a passage. This reminds me of a story of two sculptors who were rival candidates for a great work which was to be given to the most able artist. They were desired, by those who were appointed to be the judges of their respective merit, to speak upon their art with regard to their intention. After one of them had finished his speech with all the ostentation of eloquence, when it came to his rival's turn to speak, who had not the same gift of elocution, though a better sculptor, he only said, 'What this man *says* I can *do*.'

Perhaps one of the reasons why the Doctor was so very inexpert in explaining even the principles of his own art was his ignorance of the scholastic or technical terms by which similar things are distinguished. He professed himself an enemy to all those investigations which he said did not at all increase the powers of doing, but only enabled a person to talk about it, of those researches of which you receive the full result and advantage without study or attention equal to those who have spent their life in the pursuit. He considered this as superfluous and needless a science as that which was taught the *bourgeois gentilhomme*, who was persuaded he had made a great proficiency in rhetoric when he knew the operation of the organs of speech, or, as he himself says, what he did when he said *u*.

No man ever wrote so much from his feelings as Dr. Goldsmith. I do not mean here the vulgar opinion of being possessed himself with the passion which he wished to excite. I mean only that he governed himself by an internal feeling of the right rather than by any written rules of art. He judged, for instance, by his ear, whether the verse was musical, without caring or perhaps knowing whether it would bear examination by the rules of the *prosodia*.

He felt with great exactness, far above what words can teach, the propriety in composition, how one sentiment breeds another in the mind, preferring this as naturally to grow out of the preceding and rejecting another, though more brilliant, as breaking the chain of ideas. In short, he felt by a kind of instinct or intuition all those nice discriminations which to grosser minds appear to have no difference. This instinct is real genius if anything can be so called. But little of this judgment, as was before observed, appeared in conversation. It came when he took up the pen and quitted him when he laid it down.[1] Even his friends did not think him capable of marking with so much sagacity and precision the predominant and striking features of their characters as he did in the epitaphs.

These were the excellencies and the defects of the author of *The Traveller* and *The Deserted Village*, two of the most excellent works in the English language.

His name as a poet must depend upon the quality, not the quantity, of his works. *The Traveller*, *The Deserted Village*, the ballad in *The Vicar of Wakefield*, his two comedies (*The Good-Natured Man* and *She Stoops to Conquer*), and if to these we add his epitaphs on his friends, they make all his works in poetry which he owned.

His *Traveller* alone would have entitled him to a place in the Poets' Corner. It is a small, well-polished gem, the work of many years. It was begun when he was abroad and retouched at different periods since, and is more completely finished than any of his other works. There is a

---

[1] 'No man,' remarked Johnson, 'was more foolish when he had not a pen in his hand, or more wise when he had.' As usual, Johnson seems to utter the aptest comments about Goldsmith.

general commanding air of grandeur that pervades the whole, that never sinks into languor. The general and popular character of each nation is strongly marked.

He is very sparing of epithets, which though they give a richness destroy simplicity, which I think is the peculiar characteristic of his poetry.

His works in prose were *The History of England in Letters from a Father to his Son*, which the booksellers endeavour to pass upon the world as the work of the late Lord Lyttelton, *The State of Polite Literature in Europe, Chinese Tales*, a periodical paper called *The Bee, The Life of Mr. Beau Nash of Bath, The Life of Dr. Parnell, The Vicar of Wakefield*, a novel, *The Roman History* in [two] volumes, *The English History* in [four] volumes, and *The History of Animated Nature* in [eight] volumes.

Of his style in prose we may venture to say he was never languid, tedious, or insipid. It is always sprightly and animated. He very well knew the art of captivating the attention of the reader, both by his choice of matter and the lively narration with which it is accompanied.

44. Samuel Foote on Goldsmith as a dramatist and a person, in *Memoirs of Samuel Foote, Esq.*

1777

Samuel Foote (1720–77), actor and dramatist, was an acquaintance of Goldsmith's, especially in 1772–3, when both men frequently congregated, together with Richard Cumberland (see No. 61) and Caleb Whitefoord, at the St James's Coffeehouse. The selections below appear in *Foote's Memoirs . . . In Three Volumes*, by William Cooke, 3 vols, London, Richard Phillips, 1805, i, pp. 184–6; iii, pp. 77–8.

Dr. Goldsmith was the first to attack this illegitimate species of writing [sentimentalism], by his successive productions of *The Good Natured Man*, and *She Stoops to Conquer*. Our hero followed,[1] with his *Piety in Pattens*; in which he introduces, in the true ballad style, 'How *a maiden of low degree*, by the mere effects of morality and virtue, raised herself to riches and honours.' These two being supported by other writers, soon laid the ghost of *sentimental comedy*; and John Bull was once more restored to his usual laugh and good humour.

But it sometimes unfortunately happens in mental, as well as in corporeal diseases, that in curing one species of complaint, unskilful physicians induce another equally dangerous. This was the case in the cure of sentimental comedy. Those writers who succeeded Goldsmith and Foote in their design, but who could not follow them in their talents, perceiving the success of the ridicule against gravity, thought that by making comedy *still more laughable*, it would accommodate more the taste of the public. They, therefore, to banish the style of *The Whole Duty of Man*, and *The Economy of Human Life*,[2] took their

1 Samuel Foote brought out *Piety in Pattens* in 1773.
2 Devotion books respectively by Richard Allestree (1619–81) and Robert Dodsley (1703–64).

model from Joe Miller; whence it resulted, that by a profusion of stale jests clumsily fitted to modern circumstances, and pantomimic tricks which were called *dramatic situations*, the stage, in general, is even at present so contaminated, that not only our best poets on the stock list are out of fashion, but many men of real dramatic knowledge feel the shame, as well as the risk, of writing under such a degrading and discouraging patronage . . .

Every body who knew Goldsmith intimately, must have known that he was no less distinguished as a poet, than for the eccentricities and varieties of his character; being by turns vain and humble, coarse and refined, judicious and credulous. In one of his humiliating moments, he accidentally met with an old acquaintance at a chop-house, soon after he had finished his comedy of *She Stoops to Conquer*; and, talking to him upon the subject, requested of him as a friend, and as a critic whose judgment he relied on, that he would give him an opinion of it.

The Doctor then began to tell the particulars of his plot, in his strange, uncouth, deranged manner; which the other could only make out to be, 'that the principal part of the business turned upon one gentleman mistaking the house of another for an inn:'—at which he shook his head, observing at the same time, that he was afraid the audience, under their then *sentimental impressions*, would think it too broad and farcical for comedy.

Goldsmith looked very serious at this, and paused for some time. At last, taking him by the hand, he piteously exclaimed: 'I am much obliged to you, my dear friend, for the candour of your opinion: but it is all I can do; for, alas! I find that my genius (if ever I had any) has of late totally deserted me.' One of the performers of the Haymarket Theatre was observing to Foote, 'what a *hum-drum* kind of man Dr. Goldsmith appeared to be in the green-room, compared with the figure he made in his poetry.'—'The reason of that,' said he, 'is, because the *muses* are better companions than the *players*.'

45. John Watkinson relates the circumstances of Goldsmith's early life and his struggle to write, in *A Philosophical Survey of the South of Ireland*

Printed by W. Strahan, 1777, 286–8, 437

But this county [Co. Wesmeath] boasts of a still greater honour, the birth of the much lamented Oliver Goldsmith. I have learned a very curious anecdote of this extraordinary man, from the widow of a Doctor Radcliffe, who had been his Tutor in Trinity College Dublin. She mentioned to me a very long letter from him, which she had often heard her husband read to his friends, upon the commencement of Goldsmith's celebrity. But this, with other things of more value, was unfortunately lost by accidental fire, since her husband's death.

It appears, that the beginning of his career was one continued struggle against the waves of adversity. Upon his first going to England he was in such distress, that he would have gladly become an usher to a country school; but so destitute was he of friends to recommend him, that he could not, without difficulty, obtain even this low department. The master of the school scrupled to employ him, without some testimonial of his past life. Goldsmith referred him to his tutor, at college, for a character; but, all this while, he went under a feigned name. From this resource, therefore, one would think, that little in his favour could be even hoped for. But he only wanted to serve a present exigency—an ushership was not his object.

In this streight, he writes a letter to Dr. Radcliffe, imploring him, as he tendered the welfare of an old pupil, not to answer a letter which he would probably receive, the same post with his own, from the schoolmaster, He added, that he had good reasons for concealing, both from him and the rest of the world, his name, and the real state of his case: every circumstance of which he promised to communicate upon some future occasion. His tutor, embarrassed enough before to know what answer he should give, resolved at last to give none. And thus was poor Goldsmith snatched from between the horns of his present dilemma, and suffered to drag on a miserable life for a few probationary months.

It was not till after his return to London, from his rambles over great part of the world, and after having got some sure footing on this slippery globe, that he at length wrote to Dr. Radcliffe, to thank him for not answering the schoolmaster's letter, and to fulfil his promise of giving the history of the whole transaction. It contained a comical narrative of his adventures from his leaving Ireland to that time: His musical talents having procured him a welcome reception wherever he went . . .

It would perhaps be injurious to the memory of Dr. Goldsmith, to draw his poetical character from his theatrical pieces, though they are replete with the true *vis comica*.[1] His fame must be founded upon his *Traveller*, *Deserted Village*, and *Vicar of Wakefield*.

[1] Comic force.

46. Words on Goldsmith's writing career and poetic achievement by Edmond Malone, in the preface to *Poems and Plays by Oliver Goldsmith*

1777, 1780, v–viii

Edmond Malone (1741–1812), a critic and author, had in 1782 joined Dr Johnson's Club. When a group of publishers decided to bring out a new edition of Goldsmith's works, he contributed a short biography of Goldsmith, his friend, based on Glover's *Anecdotes* which had originally appeared in May 1774 in the *Universal Magazine*. A London edition in two volumes appeared in 1780 with Malone's biography slightly altered.

His finances were so low on his return to England, that he with difficulty got to this metropolis, his whole stock of cash amounting to no more than a few halfpence! An entire stranger in London, his mind was filled with the most gloomy reflections in consequence of his embarrassed situation! He applied to several apothecaries in hopes of being received in the capacity of a journeyman, but his broad Irish accent, and the uncouthness of his appearance, occasioned him to meet with insult from most of the medicinal tribe. The next day, however, a chymist near Fish-street, struck with his forlorn condition, and the simplicity of his manner, took him into his laboratory, where he continued 'till he discovered his old friend Doctor Sleigh was in London. This gentleman received him with the warmest affection, and liberally invited him to share his purse till some establishment could be procured for him. Goldsmith, unwilling to be a burden to his friend, a short time after eagerly embraced an offer which was made him to assist the late Rev. Dr. Milner, in instructing the young gentlemen at the Academy at Peckham; and acquitted himself greatly to the Doctor's satisfaction for a short time; but, having obtained some reputation by the criticisms he had written in the *Monthly Review*, Mr. Griffiths, the principal proprietor, engaged him in the compilation of it; and, resolving to pursue the profession of writing, he returned to London, as the mart where abilities of every kind were sure of meeting distinction and reward. Here he determined to adopt a plan of the strictest oeconomy, and took lodgings in Green Arbour-court in the Old Bailey, where he wrote several ingenious pieces. The late Mr. Newbery,[1] who at that time gave great encouragement to men of literary abilities, became a kind of patron to our young Author, and introduced him as one of the writers in the Public Ledger, in which his *Citizen of the World* originally appeared, under the title of 'Chinese Letters.'

Fortune now seemed to take some notice of a man she had long neglected. The simplicity of his character, the integrity of his heart, and the merit of his productions, made his company very acceptable to a number of respectable persons, and he emerged from his shabby apartments near the Old Bailey to the politer air of the Temple, where he took handsome chambers, and lived in a genteel style. The publication of his *Traveller*, his *Vicar of Wakefield*, and his *Letters on the History of England*, was followed by the performance of his comedy of *The Good-natured Man* at Covent-Garden Theatre, and placed him in the first rank of the poets of the present age.

Our Doctor, as he was now universally called, had a constant levee of his distrest countrymen; whose wants, as far as he was able, he always relieved, and he has been often known to leave himself even without a guinea, in order to supply the necessities of others!

Another feature in his character we cannot help laying before the reader. Previous to the publication of his *Deserted Village*, the Bookseller had given him a note for one hundred guineas for the copy, which the Doctor mentioned, a few hours after, to one of his friends, who observed it was a very great sum for so short a performance. 'In truth,' replied Goldsmith, 'I think so too, it is much more than the honest man can afford, or the piece is worth, I have not been easy since I received it; therefore I will go back and return him his note;' which he absolutely did, and left it entirely to the Bookseller, to pay him according to the profits produced by the sale of the poem, which turned out very considerable.

During the last rehearsal of his comedy, intitled, *She Stoops to Conquer*,

[1] John Newbery (1713–67), who was a London publisher and patent manufacturer of medicines.

which Mr. Colman had no opinion would succeed, on the Doctor's objecting to the repetition of one of Tony Lumpkin's speeches, being apprehensive it might injure the play, the Manager, with great keenness replied, 'Psha, my dear Doctor, do not be fearful of *squibs*, when we have been sitting almost these two hours upon a *barrel of gunpowder.*' The piece, however, contrary to Mr. Colman's expectation, was received with uncommon applause by the audience; and Goldsmith's pride was so hurt by the severity of the above observation, that it entirely put an end to his friendship for the gentleman who made it.

Notwithstanding the great success of his pieces, by some of which, it is asserted, upon good authority, he cleared £1800 in one year, his circumstances were by no means in a prosperous situation! partly owing to the liberality of his disposition, and partly to an unfortunate habit he had contracted of gaming, the arts of which he knew very little of, and consequently became the prey of those who were unprincipled enough to take advantage of his ignorance.

Just before his death he had formed a design for executing an Universal Dictionary of Arts and Sciences, the prospectus of which he actually printed and distributed among his acquaintance. In this work several of his literary friends (particularly Sir Joshua Reynolds, Dr. Johnson, Mr. Beauclerc, and Mr. Garrick) had engaged to furnish him with articles upon different subjects. He had entertained the most sanguine expectations from the success of it. The undertaking, however, did not meet with that encouragement from the Booksellers which he had imagined it would undoubtedly receive; and he used to lament this circumstance almost to the last hour of his existence.

He had been for some years afflicted, at different times, with a violent strangury, which contributed not a little to imbitter the latter part of his life; and which, united with the vexations he suffered upon other occasions, brought on a kind of habitual despondency. In this unhappy condition he was attacked by a nervous fever,[1] which, being improperly treated, terminated in his dissolution on the 4th day of April, 1774, in the forty-third year of his age. His friends, who were very numerous and respectable, had determined to bury him in Westminster-abbey, where a tablet was to have been erected to his memory. His pall was to have been supported by Lord Shelburne, Lord Louth, Sir Joshua Reynolds, the Hon. Mr. Beauclerc, Mr. Edmund Burke, and Mr. Garrick; but from some unaccountable circumstances this design was

[1] Referring to the mysterious circumstances of Goldsmith's death.

dropped, and his remains were privately deposited in the Temple burial-ground.

As to his character, it is strongly illustrated by Mr. Pope's line;

'In wit a man, simplicity a child.'[1]

The learned leisure he loved to enjoy was too often interrupted by distresses which arose from the openness of his temper, and which sometimes threw him into loud fits of passion; but this impetuosity was corrected upon a moment's reflection, and his servants have been known, upon these occasions, purposely to throw themselves in his way, that they might profit by it immediately after; for he who had the good fortune to be reproved was certain of being rewarded for it. His disappointments at other times made him peevish and sullen, and he has often left a party of convivial friends abruptly in the evening, in order to go home and brood over his misfortunes. A circumstance which contributed not a little to the encrease of his malady.

The universal esteem in which his poems are held, and the repeated pleasure they give in the perusal, is a striking test of their merit. He was a studious and correct observer of nature, happy in the selection of his images, in the choice of his subjects, and in the harmony of his versification; and, though his embarrassed situation prevented him from putting the last hand to many of his productions, his *Hermit*, his *Traveller*, and his *Deserted Village*, bid fair to claim a place among the most finished pieces in the English language.

The writer of these Anecdotes cannot conclude without declaring, that as different accounts have been given of this ingenious man, these are all founded upon facts, and collected by one who lived with him upon the most friendly footing for a great number of years, and who never felt any sorrow more sensibly than that which was occasioned by his death.

[1] Pope, 'Epitaph on John Gay,' l. 2.

47. Boswell reports Johnson's account of Goldsmith's work, in Boswell's *Life of Johnson*

25 April 1778

Boswell's *Life of Johnson* is the source of much biographical material about Goldsmith and his works. This episode is quoted from the edition of the *Life of Johnson* edited by G. B. Hill and revised by L. F. Powell, Oxford, 1934–50, rev. 1964, iii, pp. 320–1.

BOSWELL. 'A man often shews his writings to people of eminence, to obtain from them, either from their good-nature, or from their not being able to tell the truth firmly, a commendation, of which he may afterwards avail himself.' JOHNSON. 'Very true, Sir. Therefore a man, who is asked by an authour, what he thinks of his work, is put to the torture, and is not obliged to speak the truth; so that what he says is not [to] be considered as his opinion; yet he has said it, and cannot retract it; and this authour, when mankind are hunting him with a cannister at his tail, can say, "I would not have published, had not Johnson, or Reynolds, or Musgrave, or some other good judge commended the work." Yet I consider it as a very difficult question in conscience, whether one should advise a man not to publish a work, if profit be his object; for the man may say, "Had it not been for you, I should have had the money." Now you cannot be sure; for you have only your own opinion, and the publick may think very differently.' SIR JOSHUA REYNOLDS. 'You must upon such an occasion have two judgements; one as to the real value of the work, the other as to what may please the general taste at the time.' JOHNSON. 'But you can be *sure* of neither; and therefore I should scruple much to give a suppressive vote. Both Goldsmith's comedies were once refused; his first by Garrick, his second by Colman, who was prevailed on at last by much solicitation, nay, a kind of force, to bring it on. His

Vicar of Wakefield I myself did not think would have had much success. It was written and sold to a bookseller before his *Traveller*; but published after; so little expectation had the bookseller from it. Had it been sold after *The Traveller*, he might have had twice as much money for it, though sixty guineas was no mean price. The bookseller had the advantage of Goldsmith's reputation from *The Traveller* in the sale, though Goldsmith had it not in selling the copy.'

48. Madame D'Arblay's (Fanny Burney) high opinion of *The Vicar of Wakefield* in her *Diary*

August 1778

Fanny Burney (1752–1840) had recorded her feelings about *The Vicar of Wakefield* ten years before this (see No. 9 and the biographical information there). Now in 1778, the year she anonymously published *Evelina, or a Young Lady's Entrance into the World*, she recorded this estimate, an opinion almost the same as her early one; in any case, she seems never to have vacillated. For further background to her appraisal of Goldsmith's novel, see Joyce Hemlow, *The History of Fanny Burney* (Oxford, 1958), pp. 19–20. The passage here appears in the *Diary and Letters of Madame D'Arblay*, ed. Charlotte Barrett (Philadelphia, 1842), pp. 38–9.

She [Mrs. Thrale] gave me a long and very entertaining account of Dr. Goldsmith, who was intimately known here; but in speaking of *The Good-natured Man*, when I [Fanny Burney] extolled my favourite Croaker, I found that admirable character was a downright theft from Dr. Johnson. Look at the *Rambler* and you will find Suspirius is the man, and that not merely the idea, but the particulars of the character, are all stolen thence![1]

While we were yet reading this *Rambler* Dr. Johnson came in: we told him what we were about.

'Ah, madam!' cried he, 'Goldsmith was not scrupulous; but he would have been a great man had he known the real value of his own internal resources.'

'Miss Burney,' said Mrs. Thrale, 'is fond of his *Vicar of Wakefield*: and so am I;—don't you like it, sir?'

'No, madam, it is very faulty; there is nothing of real life in it, and very little of nature. It is a mere fanciful performance.'

He then seated himself upon a sofa, and calling to me, said 'Come,— Evelina,—come and sit by me.'

I obeyed; and he took me almost in his arms . . .

[1] The point had been made earlier; see No. p. 74.

49. Thomas Davies on Goldsmith's life and art, in *Memoirs of the Life of David Garrick, Esq. . . . in Two Volumes*

1780, 1808, ii, 141–62

Thomas Davies (1712?–85), bookseller, had entertained Goldsmith, quarreled with him, published his books, and finally decided that he was 'an inexplicable existence in creation.' In his important *Memoirs of Garrick* he intersperses many chapters with comments about Goldsmith.

DR. Goldsmith having tried his genius in several modes of writing, in essays, descriptive poetry, and history, was advised to apply himself to that species of composition which is said to have been long the most fruitful in the courts of Parnassus. The writer of plays has been ever supposed to pursue the quickest road to the temple of Plutus.

The Doctor was a perfect heteroclite, an inexplicable existence in creation; such a compound of absurdity, envy, and malice, contrasted with the opposite virtues of kindness, generosity, and benevolence, that he might be said to consist of two distinct souls, and to be influenced by the agency of a good and bad spirit.

The first knowledge Mr. Garrick had of his abilities, was from an attack upon him by Goldsmith, when he was but a very young author, in a book called *The Present State of Learning*. Amongst other abuses (for the Doctor loved to dwell upon grievances) he took notice of the behaviour of managers to authors: this must surely have proceeded from the most generous principles of reforming what was amiss for the benefit of others, for the Doctor at that time had not the most distant view of commencing dramatic author.

Little did Goldsmith imagine he should one day be obliged to ask a favour from the director of a playhouse: however, when the office of secretary to the Society of Arts and Sciences[1] became vacant, the

---

[1] Known since 1909 as the Royal Society of Arts. See Sir Henry Trueman Wood's comment on this matter in *The History of the Royal Society of Arts* (London, 1913), p. 24.

Doctor was persuaded to offer himself as a candidate. He was told that Mr. Garrick was a leading member of that learned body, and his interest and recommendation would be of consequence to enforce his pretensions.

He waited upon the manager, and, in few words, requested his vote and interest. Mr. Garrick could not avoid observing to him, that it was impossible he could lay claim to any recommendation from him, as he had taken pains to deprive himself of his assistance by an unprovoked attack upon his management of the theatre, in his State of Learning. Goldsmith, instead of making an apology for his conduct, either from misinformation or misconception, bluntly replied, in truth he had spoken his mind, and believed what he said was very right. The manager dismissed him with civility; and Goldsmith lost the office by a very great majority...

The Doctor's reputation, which was daily increasing from a variety of successful labours, was at length lifted so high, that he escaped from indigence and obscurity to competence and fame.

The first man of the age, one who, from the extensiveness of his genius and benevolence of his mind, is superior to the little envy and mean jealousy which adhere so closely to most authors, and especially to those of equivocal merit, took pleasure in introducing Dr. Goldsmith to his intimate friends, persons of eminent rank and distinguished abilities. The Doctor's conversation by no means corresponded with the idea formed of him from his writings.

The Dutchess of Rambouillet, who was charmed with the tragedies of Corneille, wished to have so great an author among her constant visitors, expecting infinite entertainment from the writer of the Cid, the Horace, and Cinna. But the poet lost himself in society; he held no rank with the beaux esprits who met at the hotel of this celebrated lady; his conversation was dry, unpleasant, and what the French call *distrait*. So Dr. Goldsmith appeared in company to have no spark of that genius which shone forth so brightly in his writings; his address was awkward, his manner uncouth, his language unpolished, his elocution was continually interrupted by disagreeable hesitation, and he was always unhappy if the conversation did not turn upon himself.

To manifest his intrepidity in argument, he would generously espouse the worst side of the question, and almost always left it weaker than he found it. His jealousy fixed a perpetual ridicule on his character, for he was emulous of every thing and every body. He went with some friends to see the entertainment of the Fantoccini, whose uncommon agility and quick evolutions were much celebrated. The Doctor was asked how he liked these automatons. He replied, he was surprised at the applause bestowed on the little insignificant creatures, for he could have performed their exercises much better himself. When his great literary friend was commended in his hearing, he could not restrain his uneasiness, but exclaimed, in a kind of agony, 'No more, I desire you; you harrow up my soul!' More absurd stories may be recorded of Goldsmith than of any man: his absence of mind would not permit him to attend to time, place, or company. When at the table of a nobleman of high rank and great accomplishments . . . to this great man Goldsmith observed, that he was called by the name of Malagrida; 'but I protest and vow to your Lordship, I can't conceive for what reason, *for Malagrida was an honest man!*'

When the Doctor had finished his comedy of *The Good-natured Man*, he was advised to offer it to Mr. Garrick. The manager was fully conscious of his merit, and perhaps more ostentatious of his abilities to serve a dramatic author, than became a man of his prudence: Goldsmith was, on his side, as fully persuaded of his own importance and independent greatness. Mr. Garrick, who had been so long treated with the complimentary language paid to a successful patentee and admired actor, expected that the writer would esteem the patronage of his play as a favour: Goldsmith rejected all ideas of kindness in a bargain that was intended to be of mutual advantage to both; and in this he was certainly justifiable. Mr. Garrick could reasonably expect no thanks for the acting a new play, which he would have rejected, if he had not been convinced it would have amply rewarded his pains and expense. I believe the manager was willing to accept the play, but he wished to be courted to it; and the Doctor was not disposed to purchase his friendship by the resignation of his sincerity. He then applied to Mr. Colman, who accepted his comedy without any hesitation.

The Good-natured Man bears strong marks of that happy originality which distinguishes the writings of Dr. Goldsmith. Two characters in this comedy were absolutely unknown before to the English stage; a man who boasts an intimacy with persons of high rank whom he never saw, and another who is almost always lamenting misfortunes he never knew. Croaker is as strongly designed, and as highly finished a portrait of a discontented man, of one who disturbs every happiness he possesses, from apprehension of distant evil, as any character of

Congreve, or any other of our English dramatists . . . The great applause and profit which attended the acting of this comedy, contributed to render the author more important in his own eyes, and in the opinion of the public. But no good fortune could make Goldsmith discreet, nor any increase of fame diminish his envy, or cure the intractability of his temper. John Home[1] was taught by experience, that his connexions with the great were of no avail with the public; and that courtly approbation was no protection from popular dislike; he therefore veiled himself in obscurity, and prevailed upon a young gentleman, his friend, to adopt his play of *The Fatal Discovery*; but the foster-father performed his assumed character so awkwardly at the rehearsal of this tragedy, that it was soon discovered that the child was not his own; for he submitted to have the piece altered, lopped, and corrected, with such tranquillity of temper, as the real parent could not have assumed. Of the true author Goldsmith by chance found out the knowledge; and when the play was announced to the public, it will hardly be credited, that this man of benevolence, for such he really was, endeavoured to muster a party to condemn it; alleging this cogent reason for the proceeding, that such fellows ought not to be encouraged.

'No author ever spar'd a brother:
'Wits are game-cocks to one another.'[2]

The tragedy of *The Countess of Salisbury* [by Hall Hartson] was in a good degree of favour with the town. This was a crime sufficient to rouse the indignation of Goldsmith, who issued forth to see it, with a determined resolution to consign the play to perdition. He sat out four acts of *The Countess of Salisbury* with great calmness and seeming temper; but as the plot thickened, and his apprehension began to be terrified with the ideas of blood and slaughter, he got up in a great hurry, saying, loud enough to be heard, *Brownrig! Brownrig! by G—.*[3]

Goldsmith never wanted literary employment; the booksellers understood the value of his name, and did all they could to excite his industry; and it cannot be denied that they rewarded his labours generously: in a few years he wrote three *Histories of England*; the first in two pocket volumes in letters, and another in four volumes

[1] John Home (1722–1808), minor dramatist and author.
[2] John Gay, Fable X, 'The Elephant and the Bookseller,' lines 75–6.
[3] William Brownrigg (1711–1800), a well-known chemist who did research into fire-damp, an explosive gas formed in coal mines. He became known as the famous 'apprenti-cide.'

octavo; the first, an elegant summary of British transactions; and the other, an excellent abridgment of Hume, and other copious historians. These books are in every body's hands. The last is a short contraction of the four volumes in one duodecimo. For writing these books he obtained £750 or £800.

His squabbles with booksellers and publishers were innumerable; his appetites and passions were craving and violent; he loved variety of pleasures, but could not devote himself to industry long enough to purchase them by his writings: upon every emergency half a dozen projects would present themselves to his mind; these he communicated to the men who were to advance money on the reputation of the author; but the money was generally spent long before the new work was half finished, or perhaps before it was commenced. This circumstance naturally produced reproach from one side, which was often returned with anger and vehemence on the other. After much and disagreeable altercation, one bookseller desired to refer the matter in dispute to the Doctor's learned friend, a man of known integrity, and one who would favour no cause but that of justice and truth. Goldsmith consented, and was enraged to find that one author should have so little feeling for another, as to determine a dispute to his disadvantage, in favour of a tradesman.

His love of play involved him in many perplexing difficulties, and a thousand anxieties; and yet he had not the resolution to abandon a practice for which his impatience of temper and great unskilfulness rendered him totally unqualified.

Though Mr. Garrick did not act his comedy of *She Stoops to Conquer*; yet, as he was then upon very friendly terms with the author, he presented him with a very humorous prologue, well accommodated to the occasion, of reviving fancy, wit, gaiety, humour, incident, and character, in the place of sentiment and moral preachment.

Woodward[1] spoke this whimsical address in mourning, and lamented pathetically over poor dying Comedy. To her he says,

> ——A mawkish drab of spurious breed,
> Who deals in *sentimentals*, will succeed.[2]

In the close of the Prologue, the Doctor is recommended as a fit person to revive poor drooping Thalia; with a compliment which hinted, I imagine, at some public transaction, of not dealing in poisonous drugs.

[1] Henry Woodward (1714–77), an actor at Covent Garden.
[2] Lines from David Garrick's Prologue.

She Stoops to Conquer, notwithstanding many improbabilities in the economy of the plot, several farcical situations, and some characters which are rather exaggerated, is a lively and faithful representation of nature; genius presides over every scene of this play; the characters are either new, or varied improvements from other plays.

Marlow has a slight resemblance of Charles in *The Fop's Fortune*, and something more of Lord Hardy in Steele's *Funeral*; and yet, with a few shades of these parts, he is discriminated from both. Tony Lumpkin is a vigorous improvement of Humphry Gubbins, and a more diverting picture of ignorance, rusticity, and obstinacy; Hardcastle, his wife, and daughter, I think, are absolutely new; the language is easy and characteristical; the manners of the times are slightly, but faithfully, represented; the satire is not ostentatiously displayed, but incidentally involved in the business of the play; and the suspense of the audience is artfully kept up to the last. This comedy was very well acted . . .

Though the money gained by this play amounted to a considerable sum, more especially so to a man who had been educated in straits and trained in adversity; yet his necessities soon became as craving as ever: to relieve them, he undertook a new *History of Greece*; and a book of animals, called, *The History of Animated Nature*. The first was to him an easy task; but as he was entirely unacquainted with the world of animals, his friends were anxious for the success of his latter undertaking. Notwithstanding his utter ignorance of the subject, he has compiled one of the pleasantest and most instructive books in our language; I mean, that it is not only useful to young minds, but entertaining to those who understand the animal creation.

Every thing of Goldsmith seems to bear the magical touch of an enchanter; no man took less pains, and yet produced so powerful an effect: the great beauty of his composition consists in a clear, copious, and expressive style.

Goldsmith's last work was his poem called *Retaliation*, which the historian of his life[1] says was written for his own amusement, and that of his friends, who were the subjects of it. That he did not live to finish it, is to be lamented, for it is supposed he would have introduced more characters. What he has left is so perfect in its kind, that it stands not in need of revisal.

In no part of his works has this author discovered a more nice and critical discernment, or a more perfect knowledge of human nature,

[1] Thomas Percy, see No. 59.

196

than in this poem; with wonderful art he has traced all the leading features of his several portraits, and given with truth the characteristical peculiarities of each; no man is lampooned, and no man is flattered . . .

Not long before his death, he had formed a design of publishing an Encyclopaedia, or an *Universal Dictionary of Arts and Sciences*; a prospectus of which he printed and sent to his friends, many of whom had promised to furnish him with articles on different subjects; and, among the rest, Sir Joshua Reynolds, Dr. Johnson, and Mr. Garrick. His expectations from any new-conceived projects were generally very sanguine; but from so extensive a plan his hopes of gain had lifted up his thoughts to an extraordinary height.

The booksellers, notwithstanding they had a high opinion of his abilities, yet were startled at the bulk, importance, and expense of so great an undertaking, the fate of which was to depend upon the industry of a man with whose indolence of temper and method of procrastination they had long been acquainted: the coldness with which they met his proposal was lamented by the Doctor to the hour of his death, which seems to have been accelerated by a neglect of his health, occasioned by continual vexation of mind, arising from his involved circumstances. Death, I really believe, was welcome to a man of his great sensibility.

The chief materials which compose Goldsmith's character are before the reader; but, as I have with great freedom exposed his faults, I should not have dwelt so minutely upon them, if I had not been conscious, that, upon a just balance of his good and bad qualities, the former would far outweigh the latter.

Goldsmith was so sincere a man, that he could not conceal what was uppermost in his mind: so far from desiring to appear in the eye of the world to the best advantage, he took more pains to be esteemed worse than he was, than others do to appear better than they are. His envy was so childish, and so absurd, that it may be very easily pardoned, for every body laughed at it; and no man was ever very mischievous whose errors excited mirth: he never formed any scheme, or joined in any combination, to hurt any man living . . . It cannot be controverted, that he was but a bad economist, nor in the least acquainted with that punctuality which regular people exact. He was more generous than just; like honest Charles, in *The School for Scandal*, he could not, for the soul of him, make justice keep pace with generosity. His disposition of mind was tender and compassionate; no unhappy person ever sued to him for relief, without obtaining it, if he had any thing to give; and, rather than not relieve the distressed, he would borrow. The poor woman, with whom he had lodged during his obscurity several years in Green Arbour Court, by his death lost an excellent friend; for the Doctor often supplied her with food from his table, and visited her frequently with the sole purpose to be kind to her.

50. Unsigned notice on Goldsmith's pride, in *European Magazine*

January 1784, p. 15

The anecdote was advertised in January 1784 as 'never published' before.

One of the great points in the Doctor's pride was to be liberal to his poor countrymen, who applied to him in distress. The expression *pride* is not improper, because he did it with some degree of ostentation: one that was artful never failed to apply to him as soon as he published any new work, and while it was likely the Doctor would be in cash. He succeeded twice, but very often found that all the copy money was gone before his works saw light. The Doctor, tired of his applications, told him he should write himself, and ordered him to draw up a description of China, interspersed with political reflections, a work which a book-seller had applied to Goldsmith for at a price he despised, but had not rejected. The idle carelessness of his temper may be collected from this, that he never gave himself the trouble to read the manuscript, but sent to press an account which made the Emperor of China a Mahometan, and which supposed India to be between China and Japan. Two sheets were cancelled at Goldsmith's expence, who kicked his newly created author down stairs. While this ingenious man was in the pay of Newbury, and lived in Green Arbour-Court, he was a tolerable oeconomist, and lived happily; but when he emerged from obscurity, and enjoyed a great income, he had no principle or idea of saving or any degree of care; was dreadfully necessitous ten months of every year, and never at that period was quiet and free from demands, he could not pay. When the excess of evil aroused him, he retired at times into the country to a farm-house in Hampshire, where he lived for little or nothing, letting nobody know where he was, and employing almost the whole day in writing, did not return to London till he was so well stocked with finished manuscripts, as to be able to clear himself. These intervals of labour and retirement, he has declared were among the happiest periods of his life. Some years before his death, he was much embittered by disappointed expectation. Lord L[yttelton] had promised him a place; the expectation contributed to involve him, and he often spoke with great asperity of his dependance on what he called moonshine. He enjoyed brilliant moments of wit, festivity, and conversation, but the bulk of all his latter days were poisoned with want and anxiety.

51. Two poems on Goldsmith by David Garrick, in *The Poetical Works of David Garrick*

Printed by George Kearsley, 1785, ii, 532–3

These ironic poems are among the many originally written as replies to Goldsmith's *Retaliation*.

A JEU D'ESPRIT.

ARE these the choice dishes the Doctor has sent us?
Is this the great Poet whose works so content us?
This Goldsmith's fine feast, who has written fine books?
Heaven sends us good *meat*, but the *Devil sends cooks*.

JUPITER and MERCURY.

A FABLE.

HERE Hermes, says Jove who with nectar was mellow,
Go fetch me some clay——I will make an odd fellow:
Right and wrong shall be jumbled—much gold and some dross;
Without cause be he pleas'd, without cause be he cross;
Be sure as I work to throw in contradictions,
A great love of truth; yet a mind turn'd to fictions;
Now mix these ingredients, which warm'd in the baking,
Turn to learning, and gaming, religion and raking.
With the love of a wench, let his writings be chaste;
Tip his tongue with strange matter, his pen with fine taste;
That the rake and the poet o'er all may prevail,
Set fire to the head, and set fire to the tail:
For the joy of each sex, on the world I'll bestow it:
This Scholar, Rake, Christian, Dupe, Gamester and Poet,
Thro' a mixture so odd, he shall merit great fame,
And among brother mortals—be GOLDSMITH his name!
When on earth this strange meteor no more shall appear,
You, Hermes, shall fetch him—to make us sport here!

52. Thomas Barnard, Dean of Derry, on Goldsmith's rivalry with Garrick, in *The New Foundling Hospital for Wit*

Printed for J. Debrett, 1786, ii, 254

Goldsmith's poem *Retaliation*, published on 19 April 1774, two weeks after his death, established a vogue of ironic burlesque and lapidary verse. Richard Cumberland and David Garrick (see No. 51) also wrote replies. Thomas Barnard (1728–1806) is not known to have been a close friend of Goldsmith's but both were members of Dr Johnson's Literary Club.

> GOLDSMITH I yield: restrain thy rage,
>   And spare a hapless stranger,
> Who ne'er had ventur'd to engage,
>   Had he but known his danger.
>
> Draw not thy angel's quill for shame,
>   On one who cries peccavi![1]
> But rather seek for nobler game,
>   Go set thy wit at DAVY!
>
> On him let all thy vengeance fall,
>   On me you but misplace it;
> Remember how he call'd thee POLL,
>   But ah! he dares not face it.[2]
>
> That wily loon has too much art
>   To shew his guilty head,
> But Parthian like, he drew his dart,
>   Has wounded thee,—and fled!

[1] I have sinned.
[2] David Garrick, Esq. was absent when these were first read [Barnard's own note].

201

53. Hester Lynch Piozzi on Goldsmith's relations with Johnson in the 'Literary Club,' printed in *Anecdotes of the Late Samuel Johnson, LL.D.*

T. Cadell, 1786, 119–22, 178–81, 245

It has never been made perfectly clear precisely why Dr Johnson so direly wanted Goldsmith to become and remain a member of his Club. Hester Lynch Piozzi (1741–1821), later Mrs Thrale and a friend of both Johnson and Goldsmith, provides a few clues in these anecdotes published shortly after Johnson's death.

I have forgotten the year, but it could scarcely I think be later than 1765 or 1766, that he [Johnson] was called abruptly from our house after dinner, and returning in about three hours, said, he had been with an enraged author [Goldsmith], whose landlady pressed him for payment within doors, while the bailiffs beset him without; that he was drinking himself drunk with Madeira to drown care, and fretting over a novel which when finished was to be his whole fortune; but he could not get it done for distraction, nor could he step out of doors to offer it to sale. Mr. Johnson therefore set away the bottle, and went to the bookseller, recommending the performance, and desiring some immediate relief; which when he brought back to the writer, he called the woman of the house directly to partake of punch, and pass their time in merriment.

It was not till ten years after, I dare say, that something in Dr. Goldsmith's behaviour struck me with an idea that he was the very man, and then Johnson confessed that he was so; the novel was the charming *Vicar of Wakefield* . . .

Of that respectable society [the Literary Club] I have heard him speak in the highest terms, and with a magnificent panegyric on each member, when it consisted only of a dozen or fourteen friends; but as soon as the necessity of enlarging it brought in new faces, and took off from his confidence in the company, he grew less fond of the meeting, and loudly proclaimed his carelessness *who* might be admitted, when it was become a mere dinner club. I *think* the original names, when I first heard him talk with fervor of every member's peculiar powers of instructing or delighting mankind, were Sir John Hawkins, Mr. Burke, Mr. Langton, Mr. Beauclerc, Dr. Percy, Dr. Nugent, Dr. Goldsmith, Sir Robert Chambers, Mr. Dyer, and Sir Joshua Reynolds, whom he called their Romulus, or said somebody else, of the company called him so, which was more likely: but this was, I believe, in the year 1775 or 1776 . . .

. . . Dr. Goldsmith said once to him [Johnson], we should change companions oftener, we exhaust one another, and shall soon be both of us worn out. Poor Goldsmith was to him indeed like the earthen pot to the iron one in Fontaine's fables;[1] it had been better for *him* perhaps, that they had changed companions oftener; yet no experience of his antagonist's strength hindered him from continuing the contest. He used to remind me always of that verse in Berni,[2]

> *Il pover uomo che non sen' èra accorto,*
> *Andava combattendo—ed era morto.*

Mr. Johnson made him a comical answer one day, when seeming to repine at the success of Beattie's Essay on Truth—'Here's such a stir (said he) about a fellow that has written one book, and I have written many.' Ah, Doctor (says his friend), there go two-and-forty sixpences you know to one guinea.

They had spent an evening with Eaton Graham[3] too, I remember hearing it was at some tavern; his heart was open, and he began inviting away; told what he could do to make his college agreeable, and begged the visit might not be delayed. Goldsmith thanked him, and proposed setting out with Mr. Johnson for Buckinghamshire in a fortnight; 'Nay hold, Dr. *Minor*[4] (says the other), I did not invite you.'

---

[1] Jean de la Fontaine's (1621–95) fable of the pot of iron and the pot of clay.
[2] Francesco Berni (1497–1535), sixteenth-century poet who had written a modern adaptation of Ariosto's *Orlando Innamorato*. Miss Piozzi probably used the Venice edition of 1785, 5 vols, iv, p. 279, canto liii, 60: 'the poor man who had not realized it was still fighting—and was already dead.'
[3] The Rev. George Graham (d. 1767), an assistant master at Eton who had written several plays.
[4] A name given to Goldsmith to contrast him with Johnson, Dr 'Major.' See Boswell's *Journal of a Tour to the Hebrides* for the full story and his *Life of Johnson*, ed. G. B. Hill, rev. L. F. Powell (1950), v, p. 97.

Many such mortifications arose in the course of their intimacy to be sure, but few more laughable than when the newspapers had tacked them together as the pedant and his flatterer in *Love's Labour lost*. Dr. Goldsmith came to his friend, fretting and foaming, and vowing vengeance against the printer, &c. till Mr. Johnson, tired of the bustle, and desirous to think of something else, cried out at last, 'Why, what would'st thou have, dear Doctor! who the plague is hurt with all this nonsense? and how is a man the worse I wonder in his health, purse, or character, for being called *Holofernes*?'[1] I do not know (replies the other) how you may relish being called Holofernes, but I do not like at least to play *Goodman Dull* . . .

Returning home one day from dining at the chaplain's table, he told me, that Dr. Goldsmith had given a very comical and unnecessarily exact recital there, of his own feelings when his play was hissed; telling the company how he went indeed to the Literary Club at night, and chatted gaily among his friends, as if nothing had happened amiss; that to impress them still more forcibly with an idea of his magnanimity, he even sung his favourite song about an old woman tossed in a blanket seventeen times as high as the moon; but all this while I was suffering horrid tortures (said he), and verily believe that if I had put a bit into my mouth it would have strangled me on the spot, I was so excessively ill . . .

1 An anagram of 'Joh'nes Florio,' the first and last letters being omitted. Shakespeare, in *Love's Labour's Lost*, ridicules the lexicographer John Florio (d. 1625) as well as the general pedantry of the age. 'Goodman Dull' refers to Constable Dull in Shakespeare's play, a pompous official who reasons everything to absurdity via the syllogism.

54. Further remarks on Goldsmith as a writer and member of Dr Johnson's Club, in *The Life of Samuel Johnson, LL.D.* by *Sir John Hawkins, Knt.*

[1760–4], 1787

Sir John Hawkins (1719–89), author and a charter member of Johnson's Club, wrote an early and important biography of Johnson in which he also passed judgment on the members of the Club. His appraisal of Goldsmith's greatness as a writer, written during 1760–4, is more dispassionate than most and balances strengths and weaknesses. He also views Goldsmith's inordinate vanity and pride, his envy and jealousy, more objectively than many other early writers. For further discussion of Hawkins's estimate of Goldsmith, see Bertram H. Davis, *Sir John Hawkins, A Biography*, Bloomington, Indiana, 1972. The selection quoted below is from Davis's edition of Hawkins's *Life of Johnson*, New York, Macmillan, 1961, pp. 179–83.

Johnson had now considerably extended the circle of his acquaintance, and added to the number of his friends sundry persons of distinguished eminence: among them were, Sir Joshua Reynolds, Mr. Edmund Burke, Mr. Beauclerk, and Mr. Langton. With these he passed much of his time, and was desirous of being still closer connected. How much he delighted in convivial meetings, how he loved conversation, and how sensibly he felt the attractions of a tavern, has already been mentioned; and it was but a natural consequence of these dispositions, that he should wish for frequent opportunities of indulging them in a way that would free him from domestic restraints, from the observance of hours, and a conformity to the regimen of families. A tavern was the place for these enjoyments, and a weekly club was instituted for his gratification and the mutual entertainment and delight of its several

members. The first movers in this association were Johnson and Sir
Joshua Reynolds: the number of persons included in it was nine:
the place of meeting was the Turk's Head in Gerard Street: the day
Monday in every week, and the hour of assembling seven in the evening. To this association I had the honour of being invited. The members
were,

Johnson,

Sir Joshua Reynolds,

Mr. Edmund Burke,

Christ. Nugent, M.D.,

Oliver Goldsmith, M.B.

Mr. Topham Beauclerk,

Mr. Bennet Langton,

Mr. Anthony Chamier, and

Myself.

As some of the persons above-mentioned are happily yet living,
and are too eminently known to receive honour from anything
I am able to say of them, I shall content myself with giving the characters of such of them as are now no more . . .

Goldsmith is well known by his writings to have been a man of
genius and of very fine parts; but of his character and general deportment, it is the hardest task anyone can undertake to give a description.
I will, however, attempt it, trusting to be excused if, in the spirit of a
faithful historian, I record as well his singularities as his merits.

There are certain memoirs of him extant, from which we learn,
that his inclination, co-operating with his fortunes, which were but
scanty, led him into a course of life little differing from vagrancy,
that deprived him of the benefits of regular study: it however gratified
his humour, stored his mind with ideas and some knowledge, which,
when he became settled, he improved by various reading; yet, to all
the graces of urbanity he was a stranger. With the greatest pretensions
to polished manners he was rude, and, when he most meant the
contrary, absurd. He affected Johnson's style and manner of conversation, and, when he had uttered, as he often would, a laboured sentence,
so tumid as to be scarce intelligible, would ask, if that was not truly
Johnsonian;[1] yet he loved not Johnson, but rather envied him for his
parts; and once entreated a friend to desist from praising him, 'for in
doing so,' said he, 'you harrow up my very soul.'

He had some wit, but no humour, and never told a story but he

[1] Dr Joseph Warton told the same story to his brother on 22 January 1766. See John
Wooll, *Biographical Memoirs of Joseph Warton, D.D.* (1806), p. 312: 'Of all solemn cox-
combs, Goldsmith is the first; yet sensible—but affects to use Johnson's hard words in
conversation.' See also Boswell's *Life of Johnson*, ed. G. B. Hill, rev. L. F. Powell (1950),
i, pp. 411–12.

spoiled it. The following anecdotes will convey some idea of the style and manner of his conversation:

He was used to say he could play on the German flute as well as most men;—at other times, as well as any man living. But, in truth, he understood not the character in which music is written, and played on that instrument, as many of the vulgar do, merely by ear. Roubiliac the sculptor, a merry fellow, once heard him play, and minding to put a trick on him, pretended to be charmed with his performance, as also, that himself was skilled in the art, and entreated him to repeat the air, that he might write it down. Goldsmith readily consenting, Roubiliac called for paper, and scored thereon a few five-lined staves, which having done, Goldsmith proceeded to play, and Roubiliac to write; but his writing was only such random notes on the lines and spaces as anyone might set down who had ever inspected a page of music. When they had both done, Roubiliac showed the paper to Goldsmith, who looking it over with seeming great attention, said, it was very correct, and that if he had not seen him do it, he never could have believed his friend capable of writing music after him.

He would frequently preface a story thus:—'I'll now tell you a story of myself, which some people laugh at, and some do not.'—

At the breaking up of an evening at a tavern, he entreated the company to sit down, and told them if they would call for another bottle they should hear one of his *bons mots*:—they agreed, and he began thus:—'I was once told that Sheridan the player, in order to improve himself in stage gestures, had looking glasses, to the number of ten, hung about his room, and that he practised before them; upon which I said, then there were ten ugly fellows together.'—The company were all silent: he asked why they did not laugh, which they not doing, he, without tasting the wine, left the room in anger.

In a large company he once said, 'Yesterday I heard an excellent story, and I would relate it now if I thought any of you able to understand it.' The company laughed, and one of them said, 'Doctor, you are very rude'; but he made no apology.

He once complained to a friend in these words:—'Mr. Martinelli is a rude man: I said in his hearing, that there were no good writers among the Italians, and he said to one that sat near him, that I was very ignorant.'

'People,' said he, 'are greatly mistaken in me: a notion goes about, that when I am silent I mean to be impudent; but I assure you, gentlemen, my silence arises from bashfulness.'

Having one day a call to wait on the late Duke, then Earl of Northumberland, I found Goldsmith waiting for an audience in an outer room; I asked him what had brought him there: he told me an invitation from his lordship. I made my business as short as I could, and, as a reason, mentioned, that Dr. Goldsmith was waiting without. The earl asked me if I was acquainted with him: I told him I was, adding what I thought likely to recommend him. I retired, and stayed in the outer room to take him home. Upon his coming out, I asked him the result of his conversation:—'His lordship,' says he, 'told me he had read my poem,' meaning *The Traveller*, 'and was much delighted with it; that he was going Lord Lieutenant of Ireland, and that, hearing that I was a native of that country, he should be glad to do me any kindness.' —And what did you answer, asked I, to this gracious offer? 'Why,' said he, 'I could say nothing but that I had a brother there, a clergyman, that stood in need of help: as for myself, I have no dependence on the promises of great men: I look to the booksellers for support; they are my best friends, and I am not inclined to forsake them for others.'

Thus did this idiot in the affairs of the world, trifle with his fortunes, and put back the hand that was held out to assist him! Other offers of a like kind he either rejected or failed to improve, contenting himself with the patronage of one nobleman, whose mansion afforded him the delights of a splendid table, and a retreat for a few days from the metropolis.

While I was writing the *History of Music*, he, at the club, communicated to me some curious matter: I desired he would reduce it to writing; he promised me he would, and desired to see me at his chambers: I called on him there; he stepped into a closet, and tore out of a printed book six leaves that contained what he had mentioned to me.

As he wrote for the booksellers, we, at the club, looked on him as a mere literary drudge, equal to the task of compiling and translating, but little capable of original, and still less of poetical composition: he had, nevertheless, unknown to us, written and addressed to the Countess, afterwards Duchess, of Northumberland, one of the finest poems of the lyric kind that our language has to boast of, the ballad 'Turn Gentle Hermit of the Dale';[1] and suprised us with *The Traveller*, a poem that contains some particulars of his own history. Johnson was supposed to have assisted him in it; but he contributed to the perfection of it only four lines: his opinion of it was, that it was the best written poem since the time of Pope.

[1] 'Edwin and Angelina' [1765].

Of the booksellers whom he styled his friends, Mr. Newbery was one. This person had apartments in Canonbury House, where Goldsmith often lay concealed from his creditors. Under a pressing necessity he there wrote his *Vicar of Wakefield*, and for it received of Newbery forty pounds.

Of a man named Griffin, a bookseller in Catherine Street in the Strand, he had borrowed by two and three guineas at a time, money to the amount of two hundred pounds; to discharge this debt, he wrote the *Deserted Village*, but was two years about it. Soon after its publication, Griffin declared, that it had discharged the whole of his debt.

His poems are replete with fine moral sentiments, and bespeak a great dignity of mind; yet he had no sense of the shame, nor dread of the evils, of poverty. In the latter he was at one time so involved, that for the clamours of a woman, to whom he was indebted for lodging, and for bailiffs that waited to arrest him, he was equally unable, till he had made himself drunk, to stay within doors, or go abroad to hawk among the booksellers a piece of his writing, the title whereof my author does not remember.[1] In this distress he sent for Johnson, who immediately went to one of them, and brought back money for his relief.

In his dealings with the booksellers, he is said to have acted very dishonestly, never fulfilling his engagements. In one year he got of them, and by his plays, the sum of £1800, which he dissipated by gaming and extravagance, and died poor in 1774.

He that can account for the inconsistencies of character above-noted, otherwise than by showing, that wit and wisdom are seldom found to meet in the same mind, will do more than any of Goldsmith's friends were ever able to do. He was buried in the Temple Church yard. A monument was erected for him in the poets' corner in Westminster Abbey, by a subscription of his friends, and is placed over the entrance into St. Blase's Chapel. The inscription thereon was written by Johnson. This I am able to say with certainty, for he showed it to me in manuscript.

The members of our club that remain to be spoken of, were persons of less celebrity than him above-mentioned, but were better acquainted with the world, and qualified for social intercourse.

---

[1] *The Vicar of Wakefield.*

55. Goldsmith given credit for having predicted the French Revolution, in an unsigned article in *European Magazine*

February 1792, xxi, 88

The August-October issues of *European Magazine* for 1793 contained some further notices about Goldsmith but they repeat earlier statements and have been omitted here.

This ingenious writer, in his 'Chinese Letters' (first published in 'The *Ledger*' about the year 1760) seems to have predicted the present Revolution in France. 'As the Swedes,' says he, 'are making concealed approaches to despotism, the *French*, on the other hand, are imperceptibly vindicating themselves into freedom. When I consider that these Parliaments (the Members of which were all created by the Court, the Presidents of which can act only by immediate direction) presume even to mention privileges and freedom, who till of late, received directions from the Throne with implicit humility:—when this is considered, I cannot help fancying, that the Genius of *freedom* has entered that kingdom in disguise. If they have but three *weak* Monarchs more successively on the Throne, the mark will be laid aside, and the country will certainly *once more be free.*'

The Doctor had not the same love of something new that prevails at present so much in our writings and in our opinions.

'Whatever is new,' said he, 'is in general false.' The Doctor was a great admirer of Rowley's Poems, and wished much to purchase the MS. copy of them, then in the possession of Mr. George Catcott, of Bristol. The Doctor had, however, nothing but his note of hand to offer for them. 'Alas, Sir,' replied Mr. Catcott, 'I fear a Poet's note of hand is not very current upon our exchange of Bristol.' Of the Doctor's poetry the late Dr. Johnson thought so highly, that when a friend of his was, rather coldly perhaps, commending *The Traveller*, 'So, Sir,

you call it only a fine poem, do you? it is the finest poem since Mr.
Pope's time, I assure you.' In his manner and conversation Dr. Goldsmith exhibited very little of that knowledge of the world and of
life which his Essays universally displayed. Many of them were printed
in the periodical and ephemerical publications of his time, and deserved,
most assuredly, more durable vehicles. This, however, very kindly for
the public, has been afforded to them by the care of an Anonymous
Editor, who has collected them, together with some Essays of Dr.
Smollett, Dr. Kenrick, and the late ingenious Mr. Bradcock, in three
volumes, 12 mo.; and which we hear will soon be ready for publication.

56. Further comments on the relation between Goldsmith and Johnson as writers and in the Club, from Arthur Murphy's *Essay on the Life and Genius of Samuel Johnson, LL.D.*

1792, 96–7

Arthur Murphy (1727–1805) was one of the leading playwrights
and actors of the age. Like Sir John Hawkins (see No. 54) he wrote
an early life of Johnson in which he explicated Johnson's beliefs
about Goldsmith.

Johnson felt not only kindness, but zeal and ardour for his friends.
He did every thing in his power to advance the reputation of Dr.
Goldsmith. He loved him, though he knew his failings, and particularly
the leaven of envy which corroded the mind of that elegant writer,
and made him impatient, without disguise, of the praises bestowed on

any person whatever. Of this infirmity, which marked Goldsmith's character, Johnson gave a remarkable instance. It happened that he went with Sir Joshua Reynolds and Goldsmith to see the Fantoccini, which were exhibited some years ago in or near the Haymarket. They admired the curious mechanism by which the puppets were made to walk the stage, draw a chair to the table, sit down, write a letter, and perform a variety of other actions with such dexterity, that *though Nature's journeymen made the men, they imitated humanity*[1] to the astonishment of the spectator. The entertainment being over, the three friends retired to a tavern. Johnson and Sir Joshua talked with pleasure of what they had seen; and says Johnson, in a tone of admiration, 'How the little fellow brandished his spontoon!' 'There is nothing in it,' replied Goldsmith, starting up with impatience; 'give me a spontoon; I can do it as well myself.'

1 Alluding to Hamlet's instructions to the players in *Hamlet*, III, ii, lines 31–2.

57. Goldsmith's life viewed at the turn of the eighteenth and nineteenth centuries by Robert Anderson, in *The Works of the British Poets . . . In Ten Volumes*

1795, x, 809–14

Robert Anderson, M.D. (1750–1830), a physician with literary interests, had written 'Biographical and Critical Prefaces' to all ten volumes of *British Poets*. The last volume (x) of his edition containing the works of the eighteenth-century poets from Young and Gray to Churchill and Goldsmith, was especially popular and sold thousands of copies.

OLIVER GOLDSMITH was the third son of the Rev. Charles Goldsmith, and was born at Elphin, in the county of Roscommon, (according to his epitaph in Westminster-Abbey, at Pallas, in the county of Longford) in Ireland, in 1729. He was instructed in classical learning at the school of Mr. Hughes, from whence he was removed to Trinity-College, Dublin, where he was admitted an usher the 11th of June 1744. At the University, he exhibited no specimen of that genius which distinguished him in his maturer years. On the 27th of February 1749, O. S.[1] two years after the regular time, he obtained the degree of Bachelor of Arts. Intending to devote himself to the study of physic, he left Dublin, and proceeded to Edinburgh, in 1751, where he continued till the beginning of the 1754, when, having imprudently engaged to pay a considerable sum of money for a fellow student, he was obliged precipitately to quit the place. He made his escape as far as Sunderland; but there was overtaken by the emissaries of the law, and arrested. From this situation, he was released by the friendship of Mr. Laughlin Maclane and Dr. Sleigh, who were then in the College. On his being set at liberty, he took his passage on board a Dutch ship for Rotterdam; from whence, after a short stay, he proceeded to Brussels. He then

[1] I.e., old style.

visited great part of Flanders; and, after passing some time at Strasbourg and Louvain, where he obtained the degree of Bachelor in Physic, he accompanied an English gentleman to Geneva.

This tour was made for the most part on foot. He had left England with little money, and being of a thoughtless disposition, and at that time possessing a body capable of sustaining any fatigue, he proceeded resolutely in gratifying his curiosity, by the sight of different countries.

He had some knowledge of the French language and of music; he played tolerably well on the German flute, which now at times became the means of his subsistence. His learning procured him an hospitable reception at most of the religous houses that he visited, and his music made him welcome to the peasants of Flanders and Germany . . .

On his return he found himself so poor, that it was with difficulty he was enabled to reach London with a few halfpence only in his pocket. He was an entire stranger, and without any recommendation. He offered himself to several apothecaries, in the character of a journeyman, but had the mortification to find every application without success.

At length he was admitted into the house of a chemist near Fish-Street-Hill, and was employed in his laboratory, until he discovered the residence of his friend Dr. Sleigh, who patronised and supported him.

'It was Sunday,' said Goldsmith, 'when I paid him a visit, and it is to be supposed, in my best clothes. Sleigh scarcely knew me.—*Such is the tax the unfortunate pay to poverty*. However, when he did recollect me, I found his heart as warm as ever; and he shared his purse and his friendship with me, during his continuance in London.'

By the recommendation of the chemist, who saw in Goldsmith talents above his condition, he soon after became an assistant to Dr. Milner, who kept an academy at Peckham. He remained not long in this situation; but being introduced to some booksellers, he returned to London, took a lodging in Green-Arbour-Court, near the Old Bailey, and commenced author.

Mr. Griffiths, the proprietor of the *Monthly Review*, gave him a department in his Journal, and Mr. Newbery, the philanthropic bookseller in St. Paul's Church-Yard, gave him a department in the *Public Ledger*, where he wrote those periodical papers, called *Chinese Letters*, which now appear in his works, under the title of the *Citizen of the World*.

His first works were *The Bee*, a weekly pamphlet, and *An Inquiry into the Present State of Polite Learning in Europe*, published before the close of the year 1759.

Soon after his acquaintance with Mr. Newbery, for whom he held the 'pen of a ready writer,' he removed to lodgings in Wine-Office-Court, Fleetstreet, where he finished the *Vicar of Wakefield*, which by the friendly interference of Dr. Johnson, was sold for sixty pounds, to discharge his rent. 'A sufficient price when it was sold,' as he informed Mr. Boswell; for then the fame of Goldsmith had not been elevated, as it afterwards was by his *Traveller*; and the bookseller had so faint hopes of profit by his bargain, that he kept the manuscript by him a long time, and did not publish it till after *The Traveller* had appeared. Then to be sure, it was accidentally worth more money.

In 1765, he published *The Traveller; or, a Prospect of Society*, 4to, of which Dr. Johnson said, 'There has not been so fine a poem since Pope's time.' Part of his poem, as he says in his dedication to his brother, the Rev. Henry Goldsmith, was formerly written to him from Switzer-land, and contained about two hundred lines. The manuscript lay by him some years without any determined idea of publishing, till persuaded to it by Dr. Johnson, who gave him some general hints towards enlarging it; and in particular, as Mr. Boswell informs us, furnished line 240,

To stop too fearful, and too faint to go.

and the concluding ten lines, except the last couplet but one.

The lifted ax, the agonizing wheel,
Luke's iron crown, and Damien's bed of steel.

Luke, in the last line, is mentioned by mistake for *George*. In the *Respublica Hungarica*, there is an account of a desperate rebellion in 1514, headed by two brothers of the name of *Zeck*, George and Luke. When it was quelled, *George*, not *Luke* was punished, by his head being encircled with a red hot iron . . .

This poem established his reputation among the booksellers, and introduced him to the acquaintance of several men of rank and abilities, Lord Nugent, Mr. Burke, Sir Joshua Reynolds, Dr. Nugent, Topham Beauclerc, Mr. Dyer, &c. who took pleasure in his conversation, and by turns laughed at his blunders, and admired the simplicity of the man, and the elegance of his poetical talents.

215

The same year he published a collection of *Essays*, which had been printed in the newspapers, magazines, and other periodical publications.

He now made his appearance in a professional manner, in a scarlet great coat, buttoned close under the chin, a physical wig and cane, as was the fashion of the times, and declined visiting many of those public places, which formerly were so convenient to him in point of expence, and which contributed so much to his amusement. 'In truth,' said he, 'one sacrifices something for the sake of good company; for here I am shut out of several places where I used to play the fool very agreeably.'

In 1766, the *Vicar of Wakefield* appeared, and completely established his literary reputation.

Soon after the publication of *The Traveller*, he removed from Wine-Office-Court to the Library Staircase, Inner-Temple, and at the same time took a country house, in conjunction with Mr. Bot, an intimate literary friend, on the Edgware Road, at the back of Cannons. This place he jocularly called the Shoemaker's Paradise, being originally built, in a fantastic taste, by one of the craft.

Here he wrote his *History of England, in a series of letters from a nobleman to his son*, 2 vols. 12mo, a work generally attributed to Lyttleton, and, which is rather singular, never contradicted either directly or indirectly by that nobleman or any of his friends. This book had a very rapid sale, and continues to be esteemed one of the most useful introductions of that sort to the study of our history.

His manner of compiling this history is thus described by an intelligent writer, who lived in the closest habits of intimacy with him for the last ten years of his life, in the *European Magazine for 1793* . . .

In 1768, he brought on the stage at Covent Garden his *Good-natured Man*, a comedy; which, though evidently written by a scholar and a man of observation, did not please equal to its merits. Many parts of it exhibit the strongest indications of his comic talents. There is, perhaps, no character on the stage more happily imagined and more highly finished than *Croaker's*. His reading of the *incendiary letter* in the fourth act,[1] was received with a roar of approbation. Goldsmith himself was so charmed with the performance of Shuter in that character, that he thanked him before all the performers, telling him, 'he had exceeded his own idea of the character, and that the fine comic richness of his colouring made it almost appear as new to him as to any other person in the house.' The prologue was furnished by Dr. Johnson.

[1] See *The Good Natured Man*, IV, lines 210–36.

The injustifiable severity with which this play was treated by the town, irritated his feelings much, and what added to the irritation, was the very great success of Kelly's *False Delicacy*, which appeared at the other house, just at the same time.

Such was the taste of the town for sentimental writing, in which this comedy abounds, that it was played every night to crowded audiences; ten thousand copies of the play were sold that season, and the book-sellers concerned in the profits of it, not only presented Kelly with a piece of plate, value £20, but gave him a public breakfast at the Chapter coffeehouse.

The success of *False Delicacy* dissolved the intimacy between Kelly and Goldsmith; who, though the type of his own *Good-natured Man*, in every other respect, yet in point of authorship, and particularly in poetry,

Could bear no rival near his throne.

Had Kelly been content to keep in the back ground, Goldsmith would have shared his last guinea with him, and in doing it would have felt all the fine influences of his good-nature; but to contend for the bow of Ulysses, 'this was a fault; that way envy lay.'

Goldsmith cannot be acquitted of all manner of blame in his enmity to Kelly, who was a very deserving man, and, by the publication of his *Thespis, Babbler*, some novels, and *False Delicacy*, had raised himself much into public notice; and what justly increased it, was the considera-tion of his doing all this from an humble beginning, and a very narrow education. He had a growing family too, which he supported with decency and reputation.

Though the fame of his *Good-natured Man* did not bear him triumph-antly through; yet, by the profits of his nine nights, and the sale of the copy, he cleared five hundred pounds. With this, and the savings made by his compilations of a *Roman History*, in 2 vols. 8vo, and a *History of England*, in 4 vols. 8vo. which he used to call 'building a book' he descended from his attic story in the Staircase, Inner-Temple, and purchased chambers in Brooke-Court, Middle-Temple, for which he gave four hundred pounds. These he furnished rather in an elegant manner, fitted up and enlarged his library, and commenced quite a man of 'lettered ease' and consequence.

About this time he was concerned in a fortnightly publication, called *The Gentleman's Journal*, in conjunction with Dr. Kenrick, Bickerstaff, &c. which was soon discontinued. When a friend was observing what an extraordinary sudden death it had, 'Not at all, Sir,' says Goldsmith, 'a very common case, it died of too many doctors.'

His next original publication was *The Deserted Village*, which came out in the spring of 1770, and had a very rapid sale. He received a hundred pounds for the copy from Mr. Griffin his bookseller, which he returned, under an idea of its being too much; and his way of computation was this: 'That it was near five shillings a couplet, which was more than any bookseller could afford, or indeed more than any modern poetry was worth.' He, however, lost nothing by his generosity, as the bookseller paid him the hundred pounds, which the rapid sale of the poem soon enabled him to do. He was, by his own confession, four or five years collecting materials in all his country excursions for this poem, and was actually engaged in the construction of it above two years. Dr. Johnson furnished the four last lines.

The year following, he prefixed *a Life of Parnell*, to a new edition of his *Poems on Several Occasions*, by T. Davies, 8vo.; a performance worthy of Parnell's genius and amiable disposition.

His next original work was his comedy of *She Stoops to Conquer, or, the Mistakes of a Night*, which was acted at Covent Garden, in 1772; and, notwithstanding the opinion of Mr. Colman and some others, that there were parts in it too farcical, it met with great success, and restored the public taste to his good opinion. One of the most ludicrous circumstances it contains, that of the robbery, is borrowed from *Albumazar*.[1] The first night of its performance, instead of being at the theatre, he was found sauntering between seven and eight o'clock in St. James's Park; and it was on the remonstrance of a friend, who told him how 'useful his presence might be in making some sudden alterations which might be found necessary in the piece,' that he was prevailed upon to go to the theatre. He entered the stage-door, just in the middle of the 5th act, when there was a hiss at the improbability of *Mrs. Hardcastle* supposing herself fifty miles off, though in her own ground, and near her own house. 'What's that?' says he, terrified at the sound. 'Pshaw, Doctor,' says Colman, who was standing by the side of the scene, 'don't be fearful of *squibs*, when we have been sitting almost these two hours upon a barrel of gun-powder.' He never forgave Colman this reply to the last hour of his life.

He cleared eight hundred pounds by this comedy: but though this

---

1 *Albumazar* by Thomas Tomkis (*fl.* 1604-15). The reference is to lines 84-220 of *She Stoops to Conquer*, III, supposedly adapted from Act III of Tomkis's play.

year was very successful to him, by the *History of Greece*, 2 vols, the *Life of Bolingbroke*, prefixed to a new edition of the *Patriot King*, and other publications; what with his liberality to poor authors . . . and a ridiculous habit of gaming, he found himself, at the end of it, considerably in debt. This he lamented in secret, but took no effectual means for the cure of it.

This period is farther remarkable for his dismissing the title of *Doctor* from his address, and calling himself *Mr.* Goldsmith. Whether he had only then decided never to practise the profession he was bred to, or that he thought *Mr.* a more familiar manner of launching himself into the fashionable world, which he was then vain enough to affect to be fond of, is not ascertained; this, however, was the fact, that the world would not *let him lose his degree*, but called him *Doctor* (though he was only Bachelor of Physic) to the end of his life.

Besides his *Histories of England*, *of Greece*, and *of Rome*, he submitted to the drudgery of compiling *An History of the Earth and Animated Nature*, 8 vols. 8vo, 1774, which procured for him more money than fame. Just before his death, he had formed a design for executing *An Universal Dictionary of Arts and Sciences*; a plan which met with no encouragement.

The poem of *Retaliation* was his last performance, which he did not live to finish. It was written in answer to certain illiberal attacks, which had been made on his person, writings, and dialect, in a club of literary friends, where wit is said to have sometimes sparkled at the expence of good-nature. When he had gone as far as the character of Sir Joshua Reynolds, he read it in full club, where, though *some* praised it, and others *seemed* highly delighted with it, they still thought the publication of it not altogether so proper. He now found that a little sparkling of *fear* was not altogether an unnecessary ingredient in the friendship of the world, and though he meant not immediately, at least, to publish *Retaliation*, he kept it, as he expressed himself to a friend, 'as a rod in pickle upon any future occasion;' but this occasion never presented itself: A more awful period was now approaching, 'when kings as well as poets cease from their labours.'

He had been for some years afflicted with a strangury, which, with the derangement of his worldly affairs, brought on a kind of habitual despondency, in which he used to express 'his great indifference about life.' At length, in March 1774, being seized with a nervous fever, he, against the advice of his physician, took so large a portion of James's powder, that it was supposed to have contributed to his dissolution, on the 4th of April 1774, after an illness of ten days, in the 45th year of his age. He was buried in the Temple Church-yard, the 9th of the same month. A pompous funeral was intended; but most of his friends sent excuses, and a few coffeehouse acquaintances, rather suddenly collected together, attended his remains to the grave. A monument has since been erected to his memory, in Westminster Abbey, at the expence of the literary club to which he belonged . . .

His *Miscellaneous Essays* in prose and verse were collected into one volume, 8vo, 1775. His *Poetical* and *Dramatic Works* were collected, and printed in 2 vols. 8vo, 1780. An edition of his *Miscellaneous Works* was printed at Perth, 3 vols, 8vo, 1793. His *Traveller* and *Deserted Village* have been frequently reprinted, and with his *Retaliation* and other pieces, were received into the edition of the 'English Poets,' 1790.

With some awkward impediments and peculiarities in his address, person, and temper, Goldsmith attained a share of literary eminence and emolument, which, with common prudence, might have protected the remainder of his life from the irritating uncertainties of want. In the course of fourteen years, the produce of his pen is said to have amounted to more than eight thousand pounds. But all this was rendered useless by an improvident liberality, which prevented him from distinguishing properly the objects of his generosity, and an unhappy attachment to gaming, with the arts of which he was very little acquainted. He was so humane in his disposition, that his last guinea was the general boundary of his munificence. He had two or three poor authors always as pensioners, besides several widows and poor housekeepers; and when he had no money to give the latter, he always sent them away with shirts or old clothes, and sometimes with the whole contents of his breakfast-table, saying, with a smile of satisfaction, after they were gone, 'Now let me suppose, I have ate a heartier breakfast than usual, and am nothing out of pocket.' He was always very ready to do service to his friends and acquaintance, by recommendations, &c.; and as he lived latterly much with the great world, and was much respected, he very often succeeded, and felt his best reward, in the gratification of doing good. Dr. Johnson knew him early, and always spoke as respectfully of his heart as of his talents. Goldsmith, in some respect, conciliated his good opinion, by almost never contradicting him; and Dr. Johnson, in return, laughed at his oddities, which only served as little foils to his talents and moral character.

'His person,' says Mr. Boswell, in his *Life of Dr. Johnson,* 'was short, his countenance coarse and vulgar, his deportment that of a scholar, awkwardly affecting the complete gentleman. No man had the art of displaying with more advantage as a writer, whatever literary acquisitions he made. His mind resembled a fertile but thin soil; there was a quick, but not a strong vegetation of whatever chanced to be thrown upon it. No deep root could be struck. The oak of the forest did not grow there; but the elegant shrubbery, and the fragrant parterre appeared in gay succession. It has been generally circulated and believed, that he was a mere fool in conversation. In allusion to this, Mr. Horace Walpole, who admired his writings, said, he was 'an inspired idiot;' and Garrick described him as one

———for shortness call'd *Noll*,
Who wrote like an angel, and talk'd like poor *Poll*.[1]

But in truth this has been greatly exaggerated. He had, no doubt, a more than common share of that hurry of ideas, which we often find in his countrymen, and which sometimes produces a laughable confusion in expressing them. He was very much what the French call *un etourdie*;[2] and from vanity, and an eager desire of being conspicuous wherever he was, he frequently talked carelessly, without any knowledge of the subject, or even without thought. Those who were in any way distinguished, excited envy in him to so ridiculous an excess, that the instances of it are hardly credible. He, I am told, had no settled system of any sort, so that his conduct must not be too strictly criticised; but his affections were social and generous, and when he had money, he gave it away liberally. His desire of imaginary consequence predominated over his attention to truth.'

As a prose writer, Goldsmith must be allowed to have rivalled, and even exceeded Dr. Johnson, and his imitator, Dr. Hawkesworth, the most celebrated professional prose writer of his time. His prose may be regarded as the model of perfection, and the standard of our language; to equal which, the efforts of most would be vain, and to exceed it, every expectation, folly.

'Goldsmith,' says Dr. Johnson, 'was a man of such variety of powers, and such felicity of performance, that he always seemed to do best what he was doing; a man who had the art of being minute without

---

[1] From David Garrick's imaginary epitaph on Goldsmith which, along with several others, inspired *Retaliation*.
[2] A giddy type of fool.

tediousness, and general without confusion; whose language was copious without exuberance, exact without constraint, and easy without weakness.'[1]

Of his prose writings, his *Vicar of Wakefield, Essays, History of England, Letters from a Nobleman to his Son, Life of Parnell*, and *Natural History*, have obtained most distinction. His *Vicar of Wakefield* ranks in the first class of English novels. The language which 'angels might have heard, and virgins told,'[2] deserves the highest praise. If we do not always admire his knowledge or extensive philosophy, we feel the benevolence of his heart, and are charmed with the purity of its principles. If we do not follow with awful reverence the majesty of his reason, or the dignity of the long-extended period, we at least catch a pleasing sentiment, in a natural and unaffected style.

His *Essays*, originally written for newspapers, cannot be read without lamenting his fate (the fate of hapless genius!) while some venal and ignorant Procrustes of the house of literature, stood over him to extend or contract his elegance, till it just filled the destined space.

'It is the great excellence of a writer,' says Dr. Johnson, 'to put into his book as much as it will hold. Goldsmith has done this in his *History*. Goldsmith tells you shortly all you wish to know. His plain narrative will please again and again. He has the art of compiling, and saying every thing he has to say in a plain manner. He is now writing a *Natural History*, and will make it as entertaining as a "Persian tale."'

His *Natural History* is a compilation of unequal merit. He has adopted no methodical arrangement worthy of notice; and his descriptions, negligent of those distinguishing pecularities of structure which enables us to discover the name and species of each individual, are almost wholly employed upon their more amusing properties and relations. The second, third, and fourth volumes, comprehending the natural history of *mankind* and of *quadrupeds*, are chiefly borrowed from Buffon's diffusive writings, from which he has transcribed many errors. The four last volumes, comprehending the history of *birds, fishes, insects*, &c. are particularly defective, probably because in composing them, he no longer derived any assistance from Buffon, whose volumes on birds he does not appear to have seen. The manner and style in which it is written, are generally pleasing, and the entertainment which it affords, is occasionally increased by the interposition of pertinent speculative reflections.

1 See Dr Johnson's *Life of Parnell*, opening paragraph.
2 Unidentified.

As a poet, he is characterised by elegance, tenderness, and simplicity. He is of the school of Dryden and Pope, rather than that of Spenser or Milton. In sweetness and harmony, he rivals every writer of verse since the death of Pope. It is to be regretted, that his poetical performances are not more numerous. Though he wrote prose with great facility, he was rather slow in his poetry, not from the tardiness of fancy, but the time he took in pointing the sentiment, and polishing the versification. His manner of writing poetry, it is said, was this: he first sketched a part of his design in prose, in which he threw out his ideas as they occurred to him; he then sat carefully down to versify them, correct them, and add such other ideas as he thought better fitted to the subject. He sometimes would exceed his prose design, by writing several verses impromptu; but these he would take uncommon pains afterwards to revise, lest they should be unconnected with his main design.

His *Traveller, Deserted Village, Hermit*,[1] and *Retaliation*, are the chief foundation of his fame. *The Traveller* is one of those delightful poems, that allure by the beauty of their scenery, a refined elegance of sentiment, and a correspondent happiness of expression. In the address to his brother, to whom the poem is inscribed, it is impossible not to be pleased with the *untravelled heart*, and the happy image of the *lengthening chain*. The simile of the rainbow, is equally just and magnificent; and is one of those real beauties in imagery, which have the power of pleasing universally, by being at once obvious to the mind, and at the same time possessing native dignity enough to secure them from that indifference, with which things frequently contemplated are beheld.

The Traveller *sits him down* (as he expresses it) on an eminence of the Alps, and from thence takes a view of the several kingdoms that lie around him, not with the contracted eye of a recluse, but with the liberal spirit of a man who rightly considers and embraces the general blessings of Providence.

> For me your tributary stores combine,
> Creation's tenant, all the world is mine.

He then inquires, whether superior happiness be the lot of any particular country, but concludes, that, though every man thinks most favourably of his own, nature has, in general, observed an equality in the distribution of her bounties. The description of the people of Italy is not less just, than that of their country is picturesque and harmonious:

[1] 'Edwin and Angelina'.

but the moralist may object to the conclusion, as unfavourable to the interests of virtue.

> Each nobler aim represt by long controul,
> Now sinks at last, or feebly mans the soul;
> While low delights succeeding fast behind,
> In happier meanness occupies the mind.

The beauties of the description of the *Swiss* are so natural and obvious, that no eye can overlook them. Whether the severity of a Helvetian winter *chills the lap of May, when no zephyr sooths the breast of the mountain*; whether the hardy Swiss *sees his little lot, the lot of all*; *breasts the keen air, and carols as he goes, drives his ploughshares to the sleep, or drags the struggling savage into day*; the whole is beautiful. Whether he *sits down the monarch of a shed, and surveys his children's looks, that brighten at the blaze*, or entertains the *pilgrim*, whose *tale repays the nightly bed*, the whole is still beautiful; but the simile of the *babe* is something more; there is a grandeur as well as beauty in the application of it.

But having found that the rural life of a *Swiss* has its evils as well as comforts, he turns to *France*, and describes a people almost of a different species. He next makes a transition to *Holland*, and from thence proceeds to *Britain*. The characteristics of the different nations, are just and ingenious; but the descriptions are neither full nor perfect. He has contented himself with exhibiting them in those points of view in which they are generally beheld; but the lights are much strengthened by the powers of poetic genius.

The *Deserted Village*, is a performance of distinguished merit. The general idea it inculcates is this, that commerce, by an enormous introduction of wealth, has augmented the number of the rich, who, by exhausting the provision of the poor, reduce them to the necessity of emigration. The poem opens with an apostrophe to its subject, with which the imagination may be pleased, but which will not fully satisfy the judgment. The village diversions are perhaps insisted on with too much prolixity and amplification. But we are recompensed for this generality and redundance, by the classical and beautiful particularity and conciseness of the context, *the dancing pair, the swain mistrustless of his smutted face, the bashful virgin, &c.* The paragraph in general has much inaccuracy, especially a disgusting identity of diction; the word *bowers* occurs twice, the word *sweet* thrice, and *charms* and *sport*, singular or plural, four times. We have also *toil remitting*, and *toil taught to please, succeeding sports,* and *sports with sweet succession.* The paragraph beginning, *Ill fares the land, &c.* has great merit; the sentiment is noble, and the expression little inferior. The following one asserts what has been repeatedly denied, that *there was a time in England, when every rood of ground maintained its man.* Wherever there is property, there must of necessity be poverty and riches. The apostrophe to *Retirement* is beautiful, but fanciful; for him who retires into the country to *crown a youth of labour with an age of ease, the mine must be explored, the deep tempted, and*

> The pale artist ply the sickly trade.

The paragraph beginning, *Sweet was the sound, &c.* has uncommon merit. The circumstances it describes are obvious in nature, but never in poetry; and they are described with great force and elegance. The particulars are most happily selected; and they bear one uniform consistent character, that of a sober or serene cheerfulness. The *Matron gathering water cresses,* is a fine picture. When *Auburn* is described as flourishing, the *village preacher* is very properly introduced, and characterised in a manner which seems almost unexceptionable, both for sentiment and expression. His contentment, hospitality and piety, are pointed out with sufficient particularity, yet without confusion or redundance. The *copse,* the *torn shrubs,* and the garden flower that *grows wild,* are fine natural strokes. The *good man,* attended by his venerating parishioners, and with a kind of dignified complacence, even permitting the familiarities of their children, is strongly and distinctly represented. The similes of a bird teaching her young to fly, and the mountain that rises above the storm, are not easily to be paralleled. The last has been much admired; and is indeed a happy illustration, so far as immaterial objects can be illustrated by material . . .

58. A scientist appraises Goldsmith as a writer, in 'A Critical Dissertation' describing Goldsmith's poetic achievement in relation to his contemporaries', in *The Poetical Works of Oliver Goldsmith, M.B.*

1796, i–29

During 1799–1815 Dr John Aikin (1747–1822), a naturalist and chemist of considerable distinction, wrote brief lives of Englishmen of note. His own interests were scientific, yet he moved comfortably in his sister's (Mrs Anna Barbauld) non-scientific circle as well as in Dr Joseph Priestley's medical circle. Aikin had been interested in Goldsmith's writing from the early 1770s. In *An Essay on the Application of Natural History to Poetry* (Warrington, 1777, p. 54), he commented in the most favorable terms on Goldsmith's description of the skylark in his *History of Animated Nature,* calling him 'a poet of nature's creation.' 'Pliny has nothing more rich, delicate, and expressive,' Aikin concluded of this description. Two decades later, Aikin again turned to Goldsmith in writing short lives of great men; his biographical sketch, hastily tossed off and repetitive of earlier biographies, says little that is new, but his critical essay makes some bold assertions and is more adventuresome than one would expect from a fairly conservative thinker like Aikin. For this reason, Aikin's brief life of Goldsmith in *Lives of the Most Eminent Persons of All Ages* (1796) is omitted and his critical essay is here printed.

AMONG those false opinions which, having once obtained currency, have been adopted without examination, may be reckoned the prevalent notion, that notwithstanding the improvement of this country in many species of literary composition, its poetical character has been on the decline ever since the supposed Augustan age of the beginning

226

of this century. No one poet, it is true, has fully succeeded to the laurel of Dryden or Pope; but if without prejudice we compare the minor poets of the present age, (*minor*, I mean, with respect to the *quantity*, not the *quality*, of their productions) with those of any former period, we shall, I am convinced, find them greatly superior not only in taste and correctness, but in every other point of poetical excellence. The works of many late and present writers might be confidently appealed to in proof of this assertion; but it will suffice to instance the author who is the subject of the present Essay; and I cannot for a moment hesitate to place the name of GOLDSMITH, as a poet, above that of *Addison, Parnel, Tickel, Congreve, Lansdown*, or any of those who fill the greater part of the voluminous collection of the *English Poets*. Of these, the main body has obtained a prescriptive right to the honour of classical writers, while their works, ranged on the shelves as necessary appendages to a modern library, are rarely taken down, and contribute very little to the stock of literary amusement. Whereas the pieces of GOLDSMITH are our familiar companions; and supply passages for recollection, when our minds are either composed to moral reflection, or warmed by strong emotions and elevated conceptions. There is, I acknowledge, much of habit and accident in the attachments we form to particular writers; yet I have little doubt, that if the lovers of English poetry were confined to a small selection of authors, GOLDSMITH would find a place in the favourite list of a great majority. And it is, I think, with much justice that a great modern critic[1] has ever regarded this concurrence of public favour, as one of the least equivocal tests of uncommon merit. Some kinds of excellence, it is true, will more readily be recognized than others; and this will not always be in proportion to the degree of mental power employed in the respective productions: but he who obtains general and lasting applause in any work of art, must have happily executed a design judiciously formed. This remark is of fundamental consequence in estimating the poetry of GOLDSMITH; because it will enable us to hold the balance steady, when it might be disposed to incline to the superior claims of a style of loftier pretension, and more brilliant reputation.

Compared with many poets of deserved eminence, GOLDSMITH will appear characterised by his *simplicity*. In his language will be found few of those figures which are supposed *of themselves* to constitute poetry;—no violent transpositions; no uncommon meanings and constructions; no epithets drawn from abstract and remote ideas; no

[1] Dr Johnson.

coinage of new words by the ready mode of turning nouns into verbs; no bold prosopopoeia, or audacious metaphor:—it scarcely contains an expression which might not be used in eloquent and descriptive prose. It is replete with imagery; but that imagery is drawn from obvious sources, and rather enforces the simple idea, than dazzles by new and unexpected ones. It rejects not common words and phrases; and, like the language of Dryden and Otway, is thereby rendered the more forcible and pathetic. It is eminently nervous and concise; and hence affords numerous passages which dwell on the memory. With respect to his matter, it is taken from human life, and the objects of nature. It does not body forth things unknown, and create new beings. Its humbler purpose is to represent manners and characters as they really exist; to impress strongly on the heart moral and political sentiments; and to fill the imagination with a variety of pleasing or affecting objects selected from the stores of nature. If this be not the highest department of poetry, it has the advantage of being the most universally agreeable. To receive delight from the sublime fictions of Milton, the allegories of Spencer, the learning of Gray, and the fancy of Collins, the mind must have been prepared by a course of particular study; and perhaps, at a certain period of life, when the judgment exercises a severer scrutiny over the sallies of the imagination, the relish for artificial beauties will always abate, if not entirely desert us. But at every age, and with every degree of culture, correct and well-chosen representations of nature must please. We admire them when young; we recur to them when old; and they charm us till nothing longer can charm. Further, in forming a scale of excellence for artists, we are not only to consider who works upon the noblest design, but who fills his design best. It is, in reality, but a poor excuse for a slovenly performer to say 'magnis tamen excidit ausis;' and the addition of one master-piece of any kind to the stock of art, is a greater benefit, than that of a thousand abortive and mishapen wonders.

If GOLDSMITH then be referred to the class of *descriptive poets*, including the description of moral as well as of physical nature, it will next be important to enquire by what means he has attained the rank of a master in his class. Let us then observe how he has selected, combined, and contrasted his objects, with what truth and strength of colouring he has expressed them, and to what end and purpose.

As poetry and eloquence do not describe by an exact enumeration of every circumstance, it is necessary to *select* certain particulars which may excite a sufficiently distinct image of the thing to be represented.

In this *selection*, the great art is to give *characteristic marks*, whereby the object may at once be recognized, without being obscured in a mass of common properties, which belong equally to many others. Hence the great superiority of *particular* images to *general* ones in description: the former identify, while the latter disguise. Thus, all the hackneyed representations of the country, in the works of ordinary versifiers, in which groves, and rills, and flowery meads are introduced just as the rhyme and measure require, present nothing to the fancy but an indistinct daub of colouring, in which all the diversity of nature is lost and confounded. To catch the discriminating features, and present them bold and prominent, by few, but decisive strokes, is the talent of a master; and it will not be easy to produce a superior to GOLDSMITH in this respect. The mind is never in doubt as to the meaning of his figures, nor does it languish over the survey of trivial and unappropriated circumstances. All is alive—all is filled—yet all is clear.

The proper *combination* of objects refers to the impression they are calculated to make on the mind; and requires that they should harmonize, and reciprocally enforce and sustain each other's effect. They should unite in giving one leading tone to the imagination; and without a sameness of form, they should blend in an uniformity of hue. This, too, has very successfully been attended to by GOLDSMITH, who has not only sketched his single figures with truth and spirit, but has combined them into the most harmonious and impressive groups. Nor has any descriptive poet better understood the great force of *contrast*, in setting off his scenes, and preventing any approach to wearisomeness by repetition of kindred objects. And with great skill, he has contrived that both parts of his contrast should conspire in producing one intended moral effect. Of all these excellencies, examples will be pointed out as we take a cursory view of the particular pieces.

In addition to the circumstances already noted, the *force* and *clearness* of representation depend also on the diction. It has already been observed that GOLDSMITH's language is remarkable for it's general simplicity, and the direct and proper use of words. It has ornaments, but these are not far-fetched. The epithets employed are usually qualities strictly belonging to the subject, and the true colouring of the simple figure. They are frequently contrived to express a necessary circumstance in the description, and thus avoid the usual imputation of being expletive. Of this kind are, 'the *rattling* terrors of the *vengeful* snake'; '*indurated* heart'; 'shed *intolerable* day'; '*matted* woods'; '*ventrous* ploughshare'; '*equinoctial* fervours'. The examples are not few of that indisputable mark of true poetic language, where a single word conveys an image; as in these instances: 'resignation gently *slopes* the way'; '*scoops out* an empire'; 'the vessel idly waiting *flaps* with every gale'; 'to *winnow* fragrance'; 'murmurs *fluctuate* in the gale'. All metaphor, indeed, does this in some degree; but where the accessory idea is either indistinct or incongruous, as frequently happens when it is introduced as an artifice to force language up to poetry, the effect is only a gaudy obscurity.

The *end* and *purpose* to which description is directed is what distinguishes a well-planned piece from a loose effusion; for though a vivid representation of striking objects will ever afford some pleasure, yet if aim and design be wanting, to give it a basis, and stamp it with the dignity of meaning, it will in a long performance prove flat and tiresome. But this is a want which cannot be charged on GOLDSMITH; for both the *Traveller* and the *Deserted Village* have a great moral in view, to which the whole of the description is made to tend. I do not now enquire into the legitimacy of the conclusions he has drawn from his premises; it is enough to justify his plans, that such a purpose is included in them.

The *versification* of GOLDSMITH is formed on the general model that has been adopted since the refinement of English poetry, and especially since the time of Pope. To manage rhyme couplets so as to produce a pleasing effect on the ear, has since that period been so common an attainment, that it merits no particular admiration. GOLDSMITH may, I think, be said to have come up to the usual standard of proficiency in this respect, without having much surpassed it. A musical ear, and a familiarity with the best examples, have enabled him, without much apparent study, almost always to avoid defect, and very often to produce excellence. It is no censure of this poet to say that his versification presses less on the attention than his matter. In fact, he has none of those peculiarities of versifying, whether improvements or not, that some who aim at distinction in this point have adopted. He generally suspends or closes the sense at the end of the line or of the couplet; and therefore does not often give examples of that greater compass and variety of melody which is obtained by longer clauses, or by breaking the coincidences of the cadence of sound and meaning. He also studiously rejects triplets and alexandrines. But allowing for the want of these sources of variety, he has sufficiently avoided monotony; and in the usual flow of his measure, he has gratified the ear with as much change, as judiciously shifting the line-pauses can produce.

Having made these general observations on the nature of GOLDSMITH's poetry, I proceed to a survey of his principal pieces.

The *Traveller*, or *Prospect of Society*, was first sketched out by the author during a tour in Europe, great part of which he performed on foot, and in circumstances which afforded him the fullest means of becoming acquainted with the most numerous class in society, peculiarly termed *the people*. The date of the first edition is 1765. It begins in the gloomy mood natural to genius in distress, when wandering alone

Remote, unfriended, melancholy, slow.

After an affectionate and regretful glance to the peaceful seat of fraternal kindness, and some expressions of self-pity, the Poet sits down amid Alpine solitudes to spend a pensive hour in meditating on the state of mankind. He finds that the natives of every land regard their own with preference; whence he is led to this proposition,— that if we impartially compare the advantages belonging to different countries, we shall conclude that an equal portion of good is dealt to all the human race. He further supposes, that every nation, having in view one peculiar species of happiness, models life to that alone; whence this favourite kind, pushed to an extreme, becomes a source of peculiar evils. To exemplify this by instances, is the business of the subsequent descriptive part of the piece.

Italy is the first country that comes under review. Its general landscape is painted by a few characteristic strokes, and the felicity of its climate is displayed in appropriate imagery. The revival of arts and commerce in Italy, and their subsequent decline, are next touched upon; and hence is derived the present disposition of the people—easily pleased with splendid trifles, the wrecks of their former grandeur; and sunk into an enfeebled moral and intellectual character, reducing them to the level of children.

From these he turns with a sort of disdain, to view a nobler race, hardened by a rigorous climate, and by the necessity of unabating toil. These are the *Swiss*, who find, in the equality of their condition, and their ignorance of other modes of life, a source of content which remedies the natural evils of their lot. There cannot be a more delightful picture than the Poet has drawn of the Swiss peasant, going forth to his morning's labour, and returning at night to the bosom of domestic happiness. It sufficiently accounts for that *patriot passion* for which they have ever been so celebrated, and which is here described in lines that reach the heart, and is illustrated by a beautiful simile. But this state of life has also its disadvantages. The sources of enjoyment being few, a vacant listlessness is apt to creep upon the breast; and if nature urges to throw this off by occasional bursts of pleasure, no stimulus can reach the purpose but gross sensual debauch. Their morals, too, like their enjoyments, are of a coarse texture. Some sterner virtues hold high dominion in their breasts, but all the gentler and more refined qualities of the heart, which soften and sweeten life, are exiled to milder climates.

To the more genial climate of *France* the Traveller next repairs, and in a very pleasing rural picture he introduces himself in the capacity of musician to a village party of dancers beside the murmuring Loire. The leading feature of this nation he represents as being the love of praise; which passion, while it inspires sentiments of honour, and a desire of pleasing, also affords a free course to folly, and nourishes vanity and ostentation. The soul, accustomed to depend for its happiness on foreign applause, shifts its principles with the change of fashion, and is a stranger to the value of self-approbation.

The strong contrast to this national character is sought in *Holland*; a most graphical description of the scenery presented by that singular country, introduces the moral portrait of the people. From the necessity of unceasing labour, induced by their peculiar circumstances, a habit of industry has been formed, of which the natural consequence is a love of gain. The possession of exuberant wealth has given rise to the arts and conveniences of life; but at the same time has introduced a crafty, cold and mercenary temper, which sets every thing, even liberty itself, at a price. How different, exclaims the poet, from their Belgian ancestors! how different from the present race of Britain!

To Britain, then, he turns, and begins with a slight sketch of the country, in which, he says, the mildest charms of creation are combined,

Extremes are only in the master's mind.

He then draws a very striking picture of a stern, thoughtful, independent freeman, a creature of reason, unfashioned by the common forms of life, and loose from all its ties;—and this he gives as the representative of the English character. A society formed by such unyielding self-dependent beings, will naturally be a scene of violent political contests, and ever in a ferment with party. And a still worse fate awaits it; for the ties of nature, duty and love failing, the fictitious bonds of wealth and law must be employed to hold together such a reluctant association; whence the time may come, that valour, learning, and patriotism may all lie levelled in one sink of avarice. These are the ills of freedom; but the Poet, who would only repress to secure, goes on to deliver his ideas of the cause of such mischiefs, which he seems to place in the usurpations of aristocratical upon regal authority; and with great energy he expresses his indignation at the oppressions the poor suffer from their petty tyrants. This leads him to a kind of anticipation of the subject of his *Deserted Village*, where, laying aside the politician, and resuming the poet, he describes by a few highly pathetic touches, the depopulated fields, the ruined village, and the poor forlorn inhabitants driven from their beloved home, and exposed to all the perils of the trans-atlantic wilderness. It is by no means my intention to enter into a discussion of GOLDSMITH's political opinions, which bear evident marks of confused notions and a heated imagination. I shall confine myself to a remark upon the English national character, which will apply to him in common with various other writers, native and foreign.

This country has long been in the possession of more unrestrained freedom of thinking and acting than any other perhaps that ever existed; a consequence of which has been, that all those peculiarities of character, which in other nations remain concealed in the general mass, have here stood forth prominent and conspicuous; and these being from their nature calculated to draw attention, have by superficial observers been mistaken for the general character of the people. This has been particularly the case with political distinction. From the publicity of all proceedings in the legislative part of our constitution, and the independence with which many act, all party differences are strongly marked, and public men take their side with openness and confidence. Public topics, too, are discussed by all ranks; and whatever seeds there are in any part of the society of spirit and activity, have full opportunity of germinating. But to imagine that these busy and high-spirited characters compose a majority of the community, or perhaps a much greater proportion than in other countries, is a delusion. This nation, as a body, is, like all others, characterised by circumstances of its situation; and a rich commercial people, long trained to society, inhabiting a climate where many things are necessary to the comfort of life, and under a government abounding with splendid distinctions, cannot possibly be a knot of philosophers and patriots.

To return from this digression. Though it is probable that few of GOLDSMITH's readers will be convinced, even from the instances he has himself produced, that the happiness of mankind is every where equal; yet all will feel the force of the truly philosophical sentiment which concludes the piece,—that man's chief bliss is ever seated in his mind; and that a small part of real felicity consists in what human governments can either bestow or withhold.

The *Deserted Village*, first printed in 1769,[1] is the companion-piece of the *Traveller*, formed, like it, upon a plan which unites description with sentiment, and employs both in inculcating a political moral. It is a view of the prosperous and ruined state of a country village, with reflections on the causes of both. Such it may be defined in prose; but the disposition, management and colouring of the piece, are all calculated for poetical effect. It begins with a delightful picture of *Auburn* when inhabited by a happy people. The view of the village itself, and the rural occupations and pastimes of it's simple natives, is in the best style of painting by a selection of characteristic circumstances. It is immediately contrasted by a similar bold sketch of its ruined and desolated condition. Then succeeds an imaginary state of England, in a kind of golden age of equality; with its contrast likewise. The apostrophe that follows, the personal complaint of the poet, and the portrait of a sage in retirement, are sweetly sentimental touches, that break the continuity of description.

He returns to *Auburn*, and having premised another masterly sketch of its two states, in which the images are chiefly drawn from sounds, he proceeds to what may be called the interior history of the village. In his first figure he has tried his strength with Dryden. The *parish-priest* of that great poet, improved from Chaucer, is a portrait full of beauty, but drawn in a loose unequal manner, with the flowing vein of digressive thought and imagery that stamps his style. The subject of the draught, too, is considerably different from that of GOLDSMITH, having more of the ascetic and mortified cast, in conformity to the saintly model of the Roman Catholic priesthood. The pastor of *Auburn* is more *human*, but is not on that account a less venerable and interesting figure; though I know not whether all will be pleased with his familiarity with vicious characters, which goes beyond the purpose of mere reformation. The description of him in his professional character is truly admirable; and the similes of the bird instructing his young to fly, and the tall cliff rising above the storm, have been universally applauded. The first, I believe, is original;—the second is not so, though it has probably never been so well drawn and applied. The subsequent sketches of the village school-master and alehouse are close imitations of nature in low life, like the pictures of Teniers and Hogarth. Yet

[1] An error; it was printed in 1770.

even these humorous scenes slide imperceptibly into sentiment and pathos; and the comparison of the simple pleasures of the poor, with the splendid festivities of the opulent, rises to the highest style of moral poetry. Who has not felt the force of that reflection,

> The heart distrusting asks, if this be joy?

The writer then falls into a strain of reasoning against luxury and superfluous wealth, in which the sober enquirer will find much serious truth, though mixed with poetical exaggeration. The description of the contrasted scenes of magnificence and misery in a great metropolis, closed by the pathetic figure of the forlorn ruined female, is not to be surpassed.

Were not the subjects of GOLDSMITH's description so skilfully varied, the uniformity of manner, consisting in an enumeration of single circumstances, generally depicted in single lines, might tire; but where is the reader who can avoid being hurried along by the swift current of imagery, when to such a passage as the last, succeeds a landscape fraught with all the sublime terrors of the torrid zone;—and then, an exquisitely tender history-piece of the departure of the villagers; concluded with a groupe (slightly touched, indeed) of allegorical personages? A noble address to the genius of poetry, in which is compressed the moral of the whole, gives a dignified finishing to the work.

If we compare these two principal poems of GOLDSMITH, we may say, that the *Traveller* is formed upon a more regular plan, has a higher purpose in view, more abounds in thought, and in the expression of moral and philosophical ideas; the *Deserted Village* has more imagery, more variety, more pathos, more of the peculiar character of poetry. In the first, the moral and natural descriptions are more general and elevated; in the second, they are more particular and interesting. Both are truly original productions; but the *Deserted Village* has less peculiarity, and indeed has given rise to imitations which may stand in some parallel with it; while the *Traveller* remains an *unique*.

With regard to GOLDSMITH's other poems, a few remarks will suffice. The *Hermit*, printed in the same year with the Traveller, has been a very popular piece, as might be expected of a tender tale prettily told. It is called a *Ballad*, but I think with no correct application of that term, which properly means a story related in language either naturally or affectedly rude and simple. It has been a sort of fashion to admire these productions; yet in the really ancient ballads, for one stroke of beauty, there are pages of insipidity and vulgarity; and the imitations have been pleasing in proportion as they approached more finished compositions. In GOLDSMITH's *Hermit*, the language is always polished, and often ornamented. The best things in it are some neat turns of moral and pathetic sentiment, given with a simple conciseness that fits them for being retained in the memory. As to the story, it has little fancy or contrivance to recommend it.

We have already seen that GOLDSMITH possessed humour; and, exclusively of his comedies, pieces professedly humorous form a part of his poetical remains. His imitations of Swift are happy, but they *are* imitations. His tale of the *Double Transformation* may vie with those of Prior. His own natural vein of easy humour flows freely in his *Haunch of Venison* and *Retaliation*; the first, an admirable specimen of a very ludicrous story made out of a common incident by the help of conversation and character; the other, an original thought, in which his talent at drawing portraits, with a mixture of the serious and the comic, is most happily displayed.

59. Thomas Percy's memoir of Goldsmith, in an introduction to *The Miscellaneous Works of Goldsmith, M.B.... in Four Volumes*

1801, 1806, i, 102–18

Goldsmith had named his friend the Rev. Thomas Percy (1729–1811), Bishop of Dromore, to be his official biographer and provided him with materials to accomplish this task. For various complicated personal and printing reasons (see Katherine C. Balderston, *History and Sources of Percy's Memoir of Goldsmith*, Cambridge, 1926; T. Shearer and A. Tillotson, *The Library*, 3rd s., xv, 1934, pp. 224–36) Percy's life was delayed from actual publication until 1801. But by this time it was too late to set the record straight. Goldsmith's image had already settled and hardened in the public mind. He was an idiot and fool, consumed by envy and vanity, and nothing could change the record. Now, after almost two centuries, it is clear that Percy's memoir was published in vain. Because so much in Percy's memoir had been stated earlier, brief selections only are printed here.

This comedy [*She Stoops to Conquer*] was very successful, and afterwards kept possession of the stage as a stock play. It added very much to the author's reputation, and, as was usual with Dr. Goldsmith, brought down upon him a torrent of congratulatory addresses and petitions from less fortunate bards, whose indigence compelled them to solicit his bounty, and of scurrilous abuse from such of them, as being less reduced, only envied his success. We shall produce an instance of each.

ON DR. GOLDSMITH's COMEDY

'SHE STOOPS TO CONQUER.'

Quite sick in her bed Thalia was laid,
A sentiment puke had quite kill'd the sweet maid,

Her bright eyes lost all of their fire:
When a regular Doctor, one Goldsmith by name,
Found out her disorder as soon as he came,
And has made her (for ever 'twill crown all his fame)
    As lively as one can desire.

Oh! Doctor, assist a poor bard who lies ill,
Without e'er a nurse, e'er a potion or pill;
    From your kindness he hopes for some ease.
You're a GOOD-NATUR'D MAN all the world does allow,
O would your good-nature but shine forth just now,
In a manner—I'm sure your good sense will tell how,
    Your servant most humbly 'twould please.

The bearer is the author's wife, and an answer from Dr. Goldsmith
by her, will be ever gratefully acknowledged by his

Humble Servant,

JOHN OAKMAM.

Orange Court; Swallow street,
Carnaby Market.

Saturday, March 27, 1773.

The other was an attempt to check our Author's triumph, on the
ninth night of the representation, and was inserted in the London
Packet of Wednesday evening, March 24th, 1773, printed for T. Evans,
in Paternoster Row* . . .

* Unwilling to defile our text with this scurrilous production, we have
introduced it in a note.

FROM THE LONDON PACKET.

TO DR. GOLDSMITH.

Vous vous noyez par vanitè.

SIR,

THE happy knack which you have learnt of puffing your own compositions
provokes me to come forth. You have not been the editor of newspapers and
magazines, not to discover the trick of literary *humbug*. But the gauze is so thin,
that the very foolish part of the world see through it, and discover the doctor's
monkey face and cloven foot. Your poetic vanity, is as unpardonable as your

personal; would man believe it, and will woman bear it, to be told, that for hours the *great* Goldsmith will stand surveying his grotesque Oranhotan's figure in a pier glass: Was but the lovely H——k[1] as much enamoured, you would not sigh, my gentle swain, in vain. But your vanity is preposterous. How will this same bard of Bedlam ring the changes in the praise of Goldy!

. . . .

Dr. Johnson took every opportunity that presented itself of praising the talents and genius of our author . . .

. . . .

One of his last publications was, *An History of the Earth and animated Nature*, . . . published in 1774, and which for two or three years before he had been preparing. The elegance and purity of the style, the interesting and striking reflections with which it abounds, and the powers of description which so frequently appear, must atone for the want of original information on the subjects introduced, and for the occasional mistakes, which were impossible to be avoided by a writer who took all his materials on trust; and, as far as they could be supplied, chiefly from Buffon. For this work he is said to have been paid by the bookseller, £850, and during the time he was engaged in this undertaking he had received the copy money for his comedy, and the profits of his third nights: so that his receipts amounted at this time to a considerable sum. He was, however, so liberal in his donations, and profuse in his disbursements; he was unfortunately so attached to the pernicious practice of gaming; and from his unsettled habits of life, his supplies being precarious and uncertain, he had been so little accustomed to regulate his expenses by any system of economy, that his debts far exceeded his resources; and he was obliged to take up money in advance from the managers of the two theatres, for comedies, which he engaged to furnish to each; and from the booksellers, for publications which he was to finish for the press. All these engagements he fully intended, and doubtless would have been able to fulfil with the strictest honour, as he had done on former occasions in similar exigencies; but his premature death unhappily prevented the execution of his plans, and gave occasion to malignity to impute those failures to deliberate intention, which were merely the result of inevitable mortality.

Dr. Goldsmith, however, wrote by intervals about this time, his poems entitled, *The Haunch of Venison*, *Retaliation*, and some other

[1] Probably Mary Horneck (*ca.* 1750–1840), with whom Goldsmith is said to have then been in love.

little sportive sallies, which were not printed till after his death . . .
He had engaged all his literary friends, and the members of the club,
to contribute articles, each on the subject in which he excelled; so that
it could not but have contained a great assemblage of excellent disquisitions. He accordingly had prepared a *Prospectus*, in which, as usual,
he gave a luminous view of his design; but his death unfortunately
prevented the execution of the work.

He was subject to severe fits of the stranguary, owing probably to
the intemperate manner in which he confined himself to the desk,
when he was employed in his compilations, often indeed for several
weeks successively without taking exercise. On such occasions he
usually hired lodgings in some farm house a few miles from London,
and wrote without cessation till he had finished his task. He then
carried his copy to the bookseller, received his compensation, and
gave himself up perhaps for months without interruption, to the
gayeties, amusements, and societies of London.

And here it may be observed, once for all, that his elegant and enchanting style in prose flowed from him with such facility, that in
whole quires of his histories, *Animated Nature*, &c. he had seldom
occasion to correct or alter a single word; but in his verses, especially
his two great ethic poems,[1] nothing could exceed the patient and
incessant revisal which he bestowed upon them. To save himself the
trouble of transcription, he wrote the lines in his first copy very wide,
and would so fill up the intermediate space with reiterated corrections,
that scarcely a word of his first effusions was left unaltered.

In the Spring of 1774, being embarrassed in his circumstances, and
attacked with his usual malady, his indisposition, aggravated too by
mental distress, terminated in a fever; which, on 25th March, had
become exceedingly violent, when he called in medical assistance . . .

. . . . .

The general traits of Dr. Goldsmith's character have been in a
great measure delineated in the preceding pages. He was generous in
the extreme, and so strongly affected by compassion, that he has been
known at midnight to abandon his rest, in order to procure relief
and an asylum for a poor dying object who was left destitute in the
streets. Nor was there ever a mind whose general feelings were more
benevolent and friendly. He is, however, supposed to have been often
soured by jealousy or envy; and many little instances are mentioned
of this tendency in his character: but whatever appeared of this kind

[1] *The Traveller* and *The Deserted Village*.

was a mere momentary sensation, which he knew not how like other men to conceal. It was never the result of principle, or the suggestion of reflection; it never embittered his heart, nor influenced his conduct. Nothing could be more amiable than the general features of his mind: those of his person were not perhaps so engaging.

His stature was under the middle size, his body strongly built, and his limbs more sturdy than elegant: his complexion was pale, his forehead low, his face almost round, and pitted with the small-pox; but marked with strong lines of thinking. His first appearance was not captivating; but when he grew easy and cheerful in company, he relaxed into such a display of good humour, as soon removed every unfavourable impression . . .

60. William Mudford on Goldsmith's achievement in poetry, in a preface to Mudford's *Essays*

4 June 1804

Mudford (1782–1848), a miscellaneous writer who had published in 1802–3 a critical volume on the *Moral Writings of Samuel Johnson*, was persuaded that Goldsmith's real greatness lay in his poetry, not in his prose—a critical precept not uncommon at the turn of the nineteenth century. The selection printed here appeared as a preface to his *Essays on Men and Manners . . . with a life and critique on the writings and genius of the author* (London, 1804), a rare work of which the British Museum has a copy.

In considering the merits of Goldsmith as a writer, the mind first reverts to his poetical productions, which, though few, certainly were what principally contributed to give him that eminence he at present enjoys.

His versification has found many admirers; and it has been asserted, that his numbers are the most harmonious of any writer since the days of Pope. This is probably true; but let it be remembered he had Pope for a model. All excellence is great in proportion to its originality; and I do not know that any man deserves extravagant praise for having imitated another. Had the poetry of Goldsmith been the production of a century earlier, there would have been room for encomiums; but as it succeeded the comparative polish of Waller and Denham, the strength, ease, and variety of Dryden, and the almost cloying regularity, terseness, and harmony of Pope, there is little to praise, except his skill in imitating correct models.

But this can be said only of his versification, or that mechanical part of poetry which consists in the regular cadence of syllables, so as to produce the sensation of harmony in the reading. His thoughts and his expressions are his own; and it cannot be denied, that he generally thinks correctly, and expresses himself elegantly. He never composed

242

rapidly, but laboured each line as it arose in his mind; and he very patiently submitted to the drudgery of scrupulously correcting his poetical writings, until there was no farther room for amendment. It may be said in his praise, that he has dextrously united the harmony of Pope to the variety of Dryden; for in reading his *Deserted Village*, or his *Traveller*, the mind is agreeably relieved by a skilful intertexture of different measures. Yet this sometimes led him into harshness, and forced inversion, frequent instances of both of which, an attentive reader will easily discover.

The *Traveller*, is not so happy a production as his *Deserted Village*. It is hardly possible to conceive any thing more rugged, harsh, and unpleasing, than the initial paragraph. The poem teaches nothing but what we knew before,—that every man thinks his own country the happiest spot upon the globe; and it contains much about philosophic retirement, contented dignity, &c. and at last confesses that such things are *vox et preterea nihil*![1] It is probable he had formed juster views of things, and cultivated a more extensive range of contemplation when he wrote his *Deserted Village*, which contains much to admire, and little to condemn. The microscopic eye of criticism might perhaps detect some things that were better away, and some faults that vigilance might have corrected: but where is the performance of man that has not its errors?

I never read this poem but with increased delight; its sentiments speak to the heart; and I know no author more capable of seizing upon the feelings of his reader than Goldsmith. It is in this that he excels, if he excel in any thing; for in his poetry we can admire neither the plaintive sublimity of Gray; the concise elegance, apothegmatical morality, or caustic severity of Pope; the diffuse variety of Dryden; or the compact energy of Johnson; the characteristics of his muse are simplicity, pathos, and sentiment; an exquisite delicacy of delineation; and a happy felicity in adorning with the appearance of novelty reflections that are natural to every bosom. It will, I believe, readily be confessed, that he could not have chosen a more fit subject on which to exercise his peculiar powers, and that he appears with unrivalled excellence, as

'The sad historian of the pensive plain.'

This poem appears to have occupied his attention a long time, and to have been sent into the world at last, finished with all the accuracy

[1] 'A voice and nothing more.'

he was capable of. Every line is laboured with uncommon exactness, and every expression weighed with nice precision; such exactness and such precision, as perhaps Goldsmith alone could have given.

There is nothing in our language which can surpass his descriptions of the *parish priest*, of the *country school-master*, and of the *village alehouse*. They are full without exaggeration, correct without minuteness, and animated without extravagance. They are drawn from the sacred fountain of truth, without any of the ordinary embellishments of poetry, or hyperboles of fiction. The reader, as he peruses them, feels the throbbing of assent beat in his bosom; and he recognises, with a mixture of wonder and delight, the scenes of reality moulded into the cadences of poetry. Goldsmith shews most of his genius in these delineations; for, he does not avail himself of the bold and invariable characteristics which are alike open to the observation of the careless and the attentive; but with the true discrimination of the poet, he seizes on those minute, yet distinctive circumstances which appear least susceptible of poetical dignity . . .

It was the object of Goldsmith, in this poem, to speak to the judgment, through the medium of the affections. He perceived, or thought he perceived, a national calamity; a calamity which he would willingly have been instrumental in redressing; and in order to rouse the energies of those who were capable of acting decisively, he probably thought he could not adopt a better plan to engage their moral feelings in the task, by painting, in strong colours, the prevalent misery. But two objections may be urged against the availability of this plan: first, poetry is not the proper vehicle for producing extensive reformation; poetry may shame a man out of a petty fault, or it may ridicule a woman into virtue; but it never yet redressed a public grievance. Men in general read poetry for amusement; they do not expect serious argumentation; and if they find it, they regard it only as the sportive sallies of imagination, or the fictitious embellishments of an ardent fancy.

Secondly it may be said, that a poem does not admit of that which is necessary in a serious attempt toward convincing mankind. Force of reasoning, accuracy of deduction, and strength of application, can rarely, if ever, be attained within the magic circle of poetry; or if any pedagogue were to succeed in it, its inevitable repulsive rigidity would deter those from reading for whom it was intended, and thus defeat its own purpose. But it may justly be doubted whether Goldsmith seriously believed what he wished to inculcate; or if he believed, whether he cared that his poem should be regarded as a stimulus to the dormant energies of men in power; he probably excogitated the subject in the usual course of reflection; found it suitable to his powers, and capable of that kind of embellishment he was best able to bestow.

Considered, however, without any reference to its ultimate object, it certainly stands without a rival, though it has engendered a host of imitations. It has some weak lines, and some lax expressions; but they bear so small a proportion to the blaze of excellence that is every where visible, that I should pity that man who was pedantic, or malignant enough to point them out as objects of censure.

It contains one simile; that appears to be at once grand, awful, and sublime: yet I must dispute Goldsmith's claim to it as his own, upon the authority of the late learned Gilbert Wakefield, who in his life, written by himself,[1] (p. 360) has, I think, pretty clearly pointed out its origin.

> 'As some tall cliff, that lifts its awful form,
> 'Swells from the waves and midway leaves the storm,
> 'Tho' round its breast the rolling clouds are spread,
> 'Eternal sunshine settles on its head.'

> ———'Ut altus Olympi
> 'Vertex, qui spatio ventos hiemesque relinquit,
> 'Perpetuum nulla temeratus nube serenum,
> 'Celsior, exsurgit pluviis auditque ruentes
> 'Sub pedibus nimbos et ranca tonitrua calcat.'

Of his smaller poetical pieces little need be said. They are sometimes spritely and sometimes elegant; suitable to the subject, and never carelessly written. His Retaliation, as a sportive sally of humour, shews him to have been capable of satire . . . It would be idle to characterize all his petty productions, for they are beneath serious animadversion or praise.

Goldsmith's merits as a novelist are of a doubtful nature. It is impossible to say, with confidence, what he would have been, had he cultivated that species of writing. What he has done that way, he has done well.

His prose partakes neither of the dignity of Johnson's, nor of the easy levity of Addison's. He never rises with his subject, but is always

[1] Gilbert Wakefield (1756–1801), scholar and radical thinker, had written Memoirs of [his] Life (1792). The Latin passage is from a poem by Claudian, but many other parallel passages exist.

even and alike. It has great purity, great elegance, and great harmony; and I would sooner propose it as a 'model for imitation than the prose of Addison, which has generally been much admired, but is so loaded with expletives, so tame and diffuse, and sometimes so disgraced with colloquial barbarisms, that I wonder any can yet be found who are willing to consider it as a model. Goldsmith's appears to flow naturally from him, and he neither seeks for recondite words, to express simple ideas, nor for harmonious periods to conceal common maxims. Yet I prefer the style of Johnson, with all his onerose [sic] pedantry; it is more calculated to impress the mind, than that equable prose, which is for ever the same . . .

Goldsmith is not very conspicuous as a dramatic writer; his comedies are now seldom performed, though they are far superior to the trash of the present day. His characters, his incidents, and his dialogue, have something of farcical vulgarity about them, which probably procured them the short lived celebrity they enjoyed. He draws coarsely, but correctly; and, satisfied with the general resemblance of his delineations, he neglected, or perhaps, could not attain that minute shading, and characteristic colouring, which secures perpetuity to dramatic writings. His expedients are sometimes good, and they seldom fail to excite merriment, which is one of the ends of comedy; but we must not look for the other more important ones in the dramas of Goldsmith.

Considered as an historian, he has little merit, unless it be the merit of compilation. He was content to retail again, sometimes in a new dress, what had already been told to the public; it cannot, however, be denied, that he does this so well, as to make the reader regret he did not venture farther into the depths of historical knowledge. Goldsmith's histories are little more than a perspicuous and lucid arrangement of facts, such as he already found them; he does not attempt to clear up difficulties, to remove obstructions, or to disentangle contradictions. He may be read for his elegance, but I fear cannot be trusted for his accuracy, or admired for his penetration. After we allow him force, spirit, and precision, it may be said, that he is often too concise, and more so than even the contracted limits of his plan necessarily required; he does not inform on those points which ought to be known; points, that are requisite in order to obtain a thorough acquaintance even with the mere outline of history; and he aspires to nothing further. He is seldom attentive to the dates of particular events; and never explanatory in the geographical and topographical parts.

His *Citizen of the World* has no equal in our language. It is one of the most delicate, the most refined, and the most correct satires, upon the English nation and its manners, that can be pened. It shews, that he viewed the conduct of man with the eye of a philosopher; for it requires no common penetration to detect the absurdities and inconsistencies of those customs, with which from our infancy we have been familiar; which are engrafted upon our bosoms with a degree of reverential authority; and which arise in the ordinary course of common things, almost without our knowledge. A stranger going into a foreign country is continually wondering at something he never saw before; the impressions of novelty are mistaken for inherent singularity; and he tells the world on his return, with unfeigned astonishment, of things which are no more singular or surprising than others which he daily commits himself, or beholds his fellow-countrymen commit. But the whole of life is an illusion!

Goldsmith had probably learnt to form a juster estimate of men and things from his pedestrian tour, in which he mingled with various classes of society, and noted, at his leisure, their foibles and peculiarities. He was able to overcome the bias of habit, and strip events of all extrinsic qualities, by which he attained to view them without disguise. The effects of this acquisition are admirably displayed in his *Chinese Letters*.

His *Essays* are such as the man of taste will read with pleasure, and the unlearned with advantage. They are evidently the offspring of much and acute reflection, and contain many solid maxims, and some excellent argument. His portraits are sketched with the hand of a master, and display a considerable force of ridicule . . .

In his smaller productions there is enough to make them interesting, and worthy of their author. It is a folly to expect that a man shall be always the same. He, who in the outset of his life commences author as a means of subsistence, must hold a ready pen for his employer, and sometimes write that which he cordially dislikes, and, not unfrequently, that which he knows little about. When a man chooses his own studies, we have a right to expect from him all the excellence he possesses, and, perhaps, all that the subject is capable of; but when he writes, not what he wishes, but what is wanted, we must be content with such perfection as in those cases can be attained. Of Goldsmith it may be said, that whatever he does, he does pleasingly; and no one, perhaps, ever yet closed a work of his without confessing, that he eminently possessed the art of rendering interesting whatever he wrote; that he was never trifling or absurd; and that what he left undone was, perhaps, rather from indolence, than from want of intellectual power.

As a poet, he probably stands in the first class; but in the other departments of literature, he has many equals, and many superiors.

61. Richard Cumberland on Goldsmith's dramatic difficulties, in *Memoirs of Richard Cumberland*

1806–7, 366–9

Dramatist Richard Cumberland (1732–1811) had known Goldsmith well during the last years of his life and frequently met with him and other members of their circle at the St James's Coffeehouse.

'You and I,' said he [Goldsmith], 'have very different motives for resorting to the stage. I write for money, and care little about fame—' I [Cumberland] was touched by this melancholy confession, and from that moment busied myself assiduously amongst all my connexions in his cause. The whole company pledged themselves to the support of the ingenuous poet, and faithfully kept their promise to him. In fact he needed all that could be done for him, as Mr. Colman, then manager of Covent-Garden theatre, protested against the comedy, when as yet he had not struck upon a name for it. Johnson at length stood forth in all his terrors as champion for the piece, and backed by us his clients and retainers demanded a fair trial. Colman again protested, but, with that salvo for his own reputation, liberally lent his stage to one of the most eccentric productions that ever found its way to it, and *She Stoops to Conquer* was put into rehearsal.

We were not over-sanguine of success, but perfectly determined to struggle hard for our author: we accordingly assembled our strength at the Shakespear Tavern in a considerable body for an early dinner, where Samuel Johnson took the chair at the head of a long table, and was the life and soul of the corps: the poet took post silently by his side with the Burkes, Sir Joshua Reynolds, Fitzherbert, Caleb Whitefoord and a phalanx of North-British pre-determined applauders, under the banner of Major Mills, all good men and true. Our illustrious president was in inimitable glee, and poor Goldsmith that day took all his raillery as patiently and complacently as my friend Boswell would have done any day, or every day of his life. In the mean time we did not forget our duty, and though we had a better comedy going, in which Johnson was chief actor, we betook ourselves in good time to our separate and allotted posts, and waited the awful drawing up of the curtain. As our stations were pre-concerted, so were our signals for plaudits arranged and determined upon in a manner, that gave every one his cue where to look for them, and how to follow them up.

We had amongst us a very worthy and efficient member, long since lost to his friends and the world at large, Adam Drummond, of amiable memory, who was gifted by nature with the most sonorous, and at the same time the most contagious, laugh, that ever echoed from the human lungs. The neighing of the horse of the son of Hystaspes[1] was a whisper to it; the whole thunder of the theatre could not drown it. This kind and ingenuous friend fairly fore-warned us that he knew no more when to give his fire than the cannon did, that was planted on a battery. He desired therefore to have a flapper at his elbow, and I had the honour to be deputed to that office. I planted him in an upper box, pretty nearly over the stage, in full view of the pit and galleries, and perfectly well situated to give the echo all its play through the hollows and recesses of the theatre. The success of our manoeuvres was complete. All eyes were upon Johnson, who sate in a front row of a side box, and when he laughed every body thought themselves warranted to roar. In the mean time my friend followed signals with a rattle so irresistibly comic, that, when he had repeated it several times, the attention of the spectators was so engrossed by his person and performances, that the progress of the play seemed likely to become a secondary object, and I found it prudent to insinuate to him that he might halt his music without any prejudice to the author; but alas, it was now too late to rein him in; he had laughed upon my signal

---

[1] The Persian King Darius I. He was a member of a conspiracy that hoped to usurp power by meeting at early dawn; the conspirator whose horse should neigh first at the rising of the sun would possess the kingdom.

where he found no joke, and now unluckily he fancied that he found a joke in almost every thing that was said; so that nothing in nature could be more mal-a-propos than some of his bursts every now and then were. These were dangerous moments, for the pit began to take umbrage; but we carried our play through, and triumphed not only over Colman's judgment, but our own.

As the life of poor Oliver Goldsmith was now fast approaching to its period . . .

62. Goldsmith contrasted with George Crabbe by Robert Southey in a letter to J. Neville White

30 September 1808

By the end of the first decade of the nineteenth century critics such as Southey were turning away from anecdotal gossip about Goldsmith, and attempting to view him in relation to other authors. Southey (1774–1843), for a long time interested in George Crabbe's (1754–1832) poems, here compares and contrasts the two poets.

With Crabbe's poems I have been acquainted for about twenty years, having read them when a schoolboy on their first publication, and, by the help of the Elegant Extracts, remembered from that time what was best worth remembering. You rightly compare him to Goldsmith.[1] He is an imitator, or rather an *antithesizer*, of Goldsmith, if such a word may be coined for the occasion. His merit is precisely the same as Goldsmith's,—that of describing actual things clearly and

1 Neville White's letter does not survive.

strikingly; but there is a wide difference between the colouring of the two poets. Goldsmith threw a sunshine over all his pictures, like that of one of our water-colour artists when he paints for ladies,—a light and a beauty not to be found in Nature, though not more brilliant or beautiful than what Nature really affords. Crabbe's have a gloom, which is also not in Nature,—not the shade of a heavy day, of mist, or of clouds, but the dark and overcharged shadows of one who paints by lamp-light,—whose very lights have a gloominess . . .

63. Unsigned preface to an early American edition of Goldsmith's works

Boston, 1809, i, 82–9

This anonymous life, based almost exclusively on Percy's *Memoir of Goldsmith* (see No. 59 for a brief selection), repeats many details of earlier lives. The two volumes to which it was attached were printed in 1809 for Hastings, Etheridge and Bliss, a firm located at No. 8 on State Street in Boston. A copy is in the Harvard University Library and is titled *The Miscellaneous Works of Oliver Goldsmith, M.B.*

In another of his undertakings for the trade, he [Goldsmith] was not so successful; for, being desired by Griffin the bookseller to make a selection of elegant poems from our best English classics, for the use of boarding schools, and to prefix to it one of his captivating prefaces; he carelessly, without reading it, marked for the printer one of the most indecent tales of Prior. This, as might be supposed, prevented the sale of the book, which had been printed in two vols. Of this production the late ingenious Mr. Headley says, 'Dr. Goldsmith, who was only unhappy amidst all the works he undertook in his

Beauties of English Poetry, disgraced himself by a very superficial and hasty publication of this kind.'[1]

Our author wrote also the life of Lord Bolingbroke, which he prefixed to the Dissertations on Parties, which was printed for T. Davies, in 1771, and again in the year 1775, with Goldsmith's name affixed to it;—it is also inserted in the large edition of Bolingbroke's works, which appeared in the year 1777.

We are not sure that we have mentioned the preceding publications in their regular order, and have doubtless omitted many similar pieces, as well as occasional contributions to periodical works.

But his admirable poem, *The Deserted Village*, published in 1769, atoned for every defect or mistake of the author: who frequently looked back with regret on those sacrifices to necessity. It has been said by former biographers, that, having received for the copy of his poem a note for one hundred guineas from the bookseller, and one of his acquaintances observing to him, that it was a great sum for so short a performance, he went and returned the note. But although this would have been perfectly in character, the doctor was not quite so ignorant of the value of his own time and labour; and it is well known from the severe corrections and high finishing which he bestowed on that and his former ethic poem, that each of them had cost him more time than many of his compilations, for which he demanded a larger price than the sum above-mentioned.

At the establishment of the Royal Academy of Painting, his friend Sir Joshua Reynolds had procured for him the appointment of Professor of Ancient History; a mere complimentary distinction, attended neither with emolument nor trouble, but which gave him a respectable seat at their occasional meetings . . .

[1] Henry Headley's (1765–88) *Select Beauties of Ancient English Poetry*, 2 vols (1787), vol. I, p. ix.

64. An artist writing memoirs of Sir Joshua Reynolds comments on Goldsmith, in *Memoirs of Sir Joshua Reynolds ... by James Northcote, Esq., R.A.*

1813, 1818

Reynolds and Goldsmith, despite constant disagreement, remained good friends and Reynolds seemed to understand Goldsmith better than most (see No. 43). When James Northcote (1746–1831), a painter and author, wrote memoirs of Reynolds it seemed impossible to leave out Goldsmith—so intimate were the literary relations of the two men. Northcote later told William Hazlitt (see *Conversations of James Northcote, Esq., R.A.* in Hazlitt, *The Collected Works*, 12 vols, 1903, vi, p. 421) in an interview that Goldsmith and Johnson had undergone a radical reappraisal since the last quarter of the eighteenth century: 'These men were not looked upon in their age as they are at present [i.e. in 1826]: Johnson had his "Lexiphanes," and Goldsmith was laughed at—their merits were to the full as much called in question, nay, more so, than those of the Author of *Waverly* have ever been, who has been singularly fortunate in himself or in lighting upon a barren age: but because their names have since been established, and as it were sacred, we think they were always so . . .' Goldsmith appears in *Memoirs of Sir Joshua Reynolds* on pp. 84–5, 100–1, 106–9, 126–9, 136–7, 146–7, 166–7, 170–5, and 240–1, but for the purposes of this volume these selections have been greatly abbreviated.

Much of the attention which even Goldsmith personally met with was undoubtedly owing to the patronage of his admired friend; yet Sir Joshua used to say, that Goldsmith looked at, or considered, public notoriety, or fame, as one great parcel, to the whole of which he laid

253

claim, and whoever partook of any part of it, whether dancer, singer, slight of hand man, or tumbler, deprived him of his right, and drew off the attention of the world from himself and which he was striving to gain. Notwithstanding this, he lamented that whenever he entered into a mixed company, he struck a kind of awe on them, which deprived him of the enjoyment and freedom of society, and which he then made it his endeavour to dispel by playing wanton and childish pranks in order to bring himself to the wished-for level.

It was very soon after my first arrival in London, where every thing appeared new and wonderful to me, that I expressed to Sir Joshua my impatient curiosity to see Dr. Goldsmith, and he promised I should do so on the first opportunity. Soon afterwards Goldsmith came to dine with him, and immediately on my entering the room, Sir Joshua, with a designed abruptness, said to me, 'This is Dr. Goldsmith; pray why did you wish to see him?' I was much confused by the suddenness of the question, and answered, in my hurry, 'Because he is a notable man.' This, in one sense of the word, was so very contrary to the character and conduct of Goldsmith, that Sir Joshua burst into a hearty laugh, and said, that Goldsmith should, in future, always be called the notable man.

What I meant, however, to say was, that he was a man of note, or eminence.

He appeared to me to be very unaffected and good-natured; but he was totally ignorant of the art of painting, and this he often confessed with much gaiety . . .

When Goldsmith's comedy of She Stoops to Conquer, was to be brought out on the stage, on the 15th of March in this year, he was at a loss what name to give it, till the very last moment, and then, in great haste, called it She Stoops to Conquer, or the Mistakes of a Night. Sir Joshua, who disliked this name for a play, offered a much better to him, saying, 'You ought to call it the Belle's Stratagem, and if you do not I will damn it.' However, Goldsmith chose to name it himself, as above; and Mrs. Cowley has since given that name to one of her comedies.

Goldsmith was in great anxiety about its success, he was much distressed in his finances at the time, and all his hopes hung on the event . . .

Sir Joshua was much affected by the death of Goldsmith, to whom he had been a very sincere friend. He did not touch the pencil for that day, a circumstance most extraordinary for him, who passed no day *without a line.* He acted as executor, and managed in the best manner, the confused state of the Doctor's affairs. At first he intended, as I have already stated, to have made a grand funeral for him . . . but, on second thoughts, he resolved to have him buried in the plainest and most private manner possible, observing, that the most pompous funerals are soon past and forgotten; and that it would be much more prudent to apply what money could be procured, to the purpose of a more substantial and more lasting memorial of his departed friend, by a monument; and he was, accordingly, privately interred in the Temple burying ground.

Sir Joshua went himself to Westminster Abbey, and fixed upon the place where Goldsmith's monument now stands, over a door in the Poets' Corner. He thought himself lucky in being able to find so conspicuous a situation for it, as there scarcely remained another so good . . .

In the course of the year 1768, Goldsmith's comedy, called the *Good-Natured Man*, came out at Covent Garden theatre. In this play, the bailiff scene was thought to be vulgar by the company in the galleries, who violently testified their disapprobation at dialogue so low; and when the speech in that scene was uttered, containing the words 'That's all my eye,' their delicacy was so much hurt, that it was apprehended the comedy (which in other respects was approved of) would have been driven from the stage for ever. However, by expunging the objectionable parts, that composition became a stock play, as it is called, to the theatre, and put five hundred pounds into Goldsmith's pocket . . .

Speaking to Sir Joshua concerning Goldsmith, I asked his opinion of him as a poet, and if he did not consider him as very excellent: his answer was, that Goldsmith, as a poet, he believed, was about the degree of Addison.

Goldsmith, it is well known, was of an imprudent and careless disposition, insomuch, that I have heard Sir Joshua remark of him, in times of his greatest distress, he was often obliged to supplicate a friend for the loan of ten pounds for his immediate relief; yet, if by accident a distressed petitioner told him a piteous tale, nay if a subscription for any folly was proposed to him, he, without any thought of his own poverty, would, with an air of generosity, freely bestow on the person, who solicited for it, the very loan he had himself but just before obtained. . .

Goldsmith, indeed, may serve as an instance to shew how capriciously nature deals out her gifts to mankind; thus frequently bestowing, on the same individual, qualities which the wisest must admire, accompanied by those which the weakest may despise.

65. John Keats to Fanny Keats in a letter

11 February 1819

It is perhaps difficult to imagine John Keats (1795–1826) liking Goldsmith, but he enjoyed that poet's works enough to give his sister Fanny (1803–90) an inscribed copy of Goldsmith's *Poems and Essays* (1817), now in the Houghton Library of Harvard University. The letter below is quoted from *The Letters of John Keats: 1814–1821*, ed. Hyder E. Rollins, 2 vols, Cambridge, Mass., 1958, ii, p. 39.

. . . I am in hopes Mr Abbey will not object any more to your receiving a letter now and then from me—How unreasonable!—I want a few more lines from you for George—there are some young Men, acquaintances of a School-fellow of mine, going out to Birkbeck's at the latter end of this Month—I am in expectation every day of hearing from George—I begin to fear his last letters Miscarried. I shall be in town tomorrow—if you should not be in town, I shall send this little parcel by the Walthamstow Coach. I think you will like Goldsmith. Write me soon—

66. William Hazlitt on Goldsmith's writings and quality of mind

1819–24

(a) On *Citizen of the World* in 'On the Periodical Essayists,' from *Lectures on Comic Writers* (1819), included in *The Collected Works*, 12 vols, London, 1903, viii, p. 104

(b) On *The Vicar of Wakefield* in 'On the English Novelists,' from *Lectures on Comic Writers* (1819), included in *The Collected Works*, ibid., viii, p. 115

(c) On *The Good Natured Man* and *She Stoops to Conquer* in 'The Comic Writers of the Last Century,' from *Lectures on Comic Writers* (1819), included in *The Collected Works*, ibid., viii, p. 164

(d) On Goldsmith's genius in 'On Genius and Common Sense,' from *Table-Talk* (1821), included in *The Collected Works*, ibid., vi, p. 47

(e) Hazlitt's estimate of Goldsmith in *A Critical List of Authors from Select British Poets* (1824), included in *The Collected Works*, ibid., v, p. 375

Hazlitt (1778–1830), unlike many of his contemporaries, maintained an exalted opinion of Goldsmith as a writer and continued to revere him throughout his life.

(a)

Goldsmith's *Citizen of the World*, like all his works, bears the stamp of the author's mind. It does not 'go about to cozen reputation without the stamp of merit.' He is more observing, more natural and picturesque than Johnson. His work is written on the model of the Persian Letters; and contrives to give an abstracted and somewhat perplexing view of things, by opposing foreign prepossessions to our own, and thus stripping objects of their customary disguises.

(b)

Fielding did not often repeat himself; but Dr. Harrison, in America, may be considered as a variation of Adams: so also is Goldsmith's *Vicar of Wakefield*; and the latter part of that work, which sets out so delightfully, an almost entire plagiarism from Wilson's account of himself, and Adams's domestic history.[1]

(c)

Goldsmith's *Good-Natured Man* is inferior to *She Stoops to Conquer*; and even this last play, with all its shifting vivacity, is rather a sportive and whimsical effusion of the author's fancy, a delightful and delicately managed caricature, than a genuine comedy.

(d)

If Goldsmith had never written any thing but the two or three first chapters of the *Vicar of Wakefield*, or the *Character of a Village-School-master*, they would have stamped him a genius.

(e)

Goldsmith, both in verse and prose, was one of the most delightful writers in the language. His verse flows like a limpid stream. His ease is quite unconscious. Everything in him is spontaneous, unstudied, yet elegant, harmonious, graceful, nearly faultless. Without the point of refinement of Pope, he has more natural tenderness, a greater suavity of manner, a more genial spirit. Goldsmith never rises into sublimity, and seldom sinks into insipidity, or stumbles upon coarseness. His *Traveller* contains masterly national sketches. The *Deserted Village* is sometimes spun out into mawkish sentimentality; but the characters of the *Village Schoolmaster*, and the *Village Clergyman*, redeem a hundred faults. His *Retaliation* is a poem of exquisite spirit, humour, and freedom of style.

1 See *Joseph Andrews*, Bk III, iii.

67. Wilhelm Adolf Lindau, German critic and author, introduces *The Vicar of Wakefield* in a new edition

Dresden 1825, v–xx

In no other country in Europe was *The Vicar of Wakefield* so enthusiastically received as in Germany. Critics have ascribed this hearty reception partly to the simplicity of Goldsmith's prose style and partly to the appeal of the vicar to a Protestant reading audience (see Hertha Sollas, *Goldsmiths Einfluss in Deutschland*, Heidelberg, 1903). Goethe went further in his autobiography *Dichtung und Wahrheit* (see No. 79) and claimed that all contemporary German literature derived from Goldsmith and Fielding, an overstatement to be sure but nevertheless uttered. In this early German edition introduced by Wilhelm Lindau (1774–1849) facts and fictions about the English author's life and works are presented. Very little is known about Lindau except that he was a miscellaneous writer who had written a history of Ireland in 1829 and translated various English prose works. Lindau's appraisal is ultimately more interesting for the critical heritage of Goldsmith than J. J. C. Bode's (1776), C. M. Winterling's (1833), or von der Oelsnitz's (1851). A rare work, it is not in the British Museum but appears by kind permission of the Heidelberg University Library which has a copy. The somewhat literal translation below is a collaborative effort between myself and several scholars, including Miss Elizabeth Weinruth who is writing a doctoral dissertation on German prose of the early nineteenth century.

. . . Goethe's words in his autobiography serve superbly to renew the memory of the brave vicar; and because they are so eloquent I plan to use them in introducing this novel into my series of translated English novels.

Almost sixty years have passed since these pastoral pictures were exhibited; and although the customs they represent—customs that are only partly familiar to Englishmen by virtue of a long tradition—still speak out in lively vividness, they continue to appeal to humanity everywhere because of their human expressiveness. 'There are few authors,' says Washington Irving, 'with whom the reader feels so intimately acquainted as with Oliver Goldsmith.' The magical ease and simplicity of his style must capture every reader and capture him thoroughly . . .

The circumstances of his life, especially his youthful adventures, his early struggles and poverty, the short course of his brilliant, almost unparalleled, fame; all have been adequately studied and related by his countrymen . . .[1]

In this unhappy condition, almost destitute, he took his walking stick in his hand and a shirt in his pack. And with the almost incredible trust of a child to be clothed by lilies of the field, he expected to be, and was, fed by the ravens. Originally, only a walking tour through Belgium and France was projected, but his love of travel understandably awakened through the force of his early experiences and drove him much further. Into the heart of Europe he now wandered on foot, and it was a great part of Europe, too. In Chapter 20 of *The Vicar of Wakefield* he has doubtlessly drawn upon these autobiographical experiences, drawing, as it were, portions out of his own adventures. Here, also, he describes how he undertook, in Geneva, to guide the prospectively rich nephew of a London pawnbroker who separated away from him (Goldsmith) after a short while. Goldsmith, like George Primrose, whistled and argued his way through Flanders, Germany, and Italy; it is even likely that he went elsewhere and that for some unknown reason he does not communicate this to us in his *Vicar*. How regrettable, indeed, is it that he did not write an account of these travels; had he done so, they would certainly have provided the stuff of a most entertaining book. One wonders if, in his later years, Goldsmith did not reluctantly recollect all these youthful adventures. For he spent almost a full twelve months on these wanderings, until early 1756 when he returned to England.

From this time forward he was cut off from every source of income and financial support, and in this city he saw the most incredible poverty before his eyes—poverty in all its bitterness and grotesque

[1] Several pages containing biographical material have been deleted, and the rest of the selection is also abbreviated.

horror; poverty so sordid and squalid that Goldsmith is almost without peer in this regard. His indulgent uncle had died in the interim and the remainder of his friends, mostly in Ireland, had either given him up or forgotten him altogether. In these dire circumstances he assumed different names in order not to starve—especially the position of assistant master in a boarding school which has been so horribly, although vividly, described by his fictional figure George Primrose. Later on, as a chemist's assistant for whom the young man's knowledge of medicine—he had been trained in medicine—was a welcome asset, he still fared no better in the world . . .

His acquaintance with Johnson, which commenced around the year 1761, was significant for all his future literary endeavours. Both viewed each other in a thoroughly reciprocal manner, and despite the inevitable seizures of jealousy which gripped poor Goldsmith and provoked in him such tempestuous but nevertheless passing disturbances, the two men still remained constant in their friendship. It has been said that this relationship had drawbacks for Goldsmith because he would always appear in literary circles as the 'Fool of the Giant of Words.' But this has been said without cause. After all it was not long after the beginning of this friendship, that Goldsmith wrote his great novel.[1] He brought it to a close when he saw himself inextricably caught up in debt. In the last distress he turned to Johnson, who went to him at once, bought the manuscript for £60, and immediately relieved his friend. Newbery the publisher, a man as well disposed and eager to help as he himself was well-to-do, and to whom Goldsmith dedicated a memorial in the eighteenth printing of his novel, had little hopes for a good sale. So much so, that he did not allow the first printing of the novel until shortly after the appearance of Goldsmith's poem *The Traveller* in 1765.[2]

By this time Goldsmith's fame was established and Newbery could rest confident. It is true that Goldsmith had finished the draft of this poem during his visit to Switzerland; the execution and prosecution of it blessed the happiest hours which he could steal from his daily tasks. The novel, *The Vicar of Wakefield*, first appeared in 1766, and brought the publisher as much profit as it brought the author new fame. As a result Goldsmith's household furnishings now became more splendid than they previously were; he appeared in the traditional apparel of doctors: scarlet coat, fancy wig, golden cane, walking

[1] The logic and drift of thought here are unclear.
[2] Wrong date, 1764; in this and other passages Lindau's facts are often inaccurate.

stick, and he became a respected member of Johnson's literary club, which was founded about 1764 and still stands in London, where Johnson, Burke, Reynolds, and shortly thereafter Garrick and Jones shone . . .

The fame newly gained paved the way—indeed smoothed it—to the stage. Goldsmith's first piece, *The Good Natured Man*, was produced in 1768 at Covent Garden with tremendous applause and a warm reception, even though Garrick had promptly and unflinchingly rejected it. Much to Garrick's surprise, and others, it brought Goldsmith £500 sterling after only nine performances. One year later, 1769, he brought out his descriptive poem *The Deserted Village*, which in spirit and tone was similar to his earlier poetry, but was more widely read and appreciated than any of his previous poems. The village Lishoy near Ballymahon in Ireland, where Goldsmith had lived in his youth and where his brother Henry preached, is the source of his recollections in these descriptive landscapes.[1] It is the desolation and tragedy of this village which Goldsmith transformed into Auburn. Moreover, the current owner, even after he had restored all those deserted places with tender sensitivity, prevailed upon Goldsmith to celebrate his town.

The landslide reception of Goldsmith's first dramatic work did not scare him away from new dramatic endeavours. His second comedy, *She Stoops to Conquer*, was performed at Covent Garden in 1773 through the efforts of various of his friends who concerted their efforts to talk up the play. All this is adequately described by Cumberland in his memoirs. And it won a shining and everlasting victory: this cheerful piece based on a real adventure that the author experienced during his youth as he was inspecting a possible country seat for an inn, still lives on the stage and is much performed . . .

Whoever contemplates the rich and splendid union of unusual attributes formed by his characters, must overlook some of Goldsmith's personal traits. One cannot of course blot out these personal traits, but they have been exaggerated. True, no one can truncate his admittedly eccentric abuses nor ought one to cut him into the mold of austere virtue. 'Let us not think of his weaknesses,' said Johnson, 'he was a very great man.' But we would rather say: *let us indeed think about them*, since we believe that he himself would have liked to hear that his readers had considered him in his totality. That they had con-

---

[1] No evidence exists to assert that Goldsmith had a particular village in mind; moreover, the next point about the owner of Auburn is equally untenable.

sidered all the evidence for his greatness and closed his book with the good natured, loving and cordial exclamation, 'Poor Goldsmith.'

68. Washington Irving comments on Goldsmith's life and writings

1825, 1840, expanded version 1849, New York, 1859

Washington Irving (1783–1859) first wrote a sketch of Goldsmith's life and writings in 1825 as one of the volumes in a series called *British Classics*. His interest in Goldsmith had been lifelong, and he once remarked that Goldsmith's writings 'were the delight of my childhood, and have been a source of enjoyment to me throughout life' (Stanley T. Williams, *The Life of Washington Irving*, 2 vols, New York: Oxford University Press, 1935, ii, p. 221). The first sketch was reworked and appeared as an introduction to an American edition of Goldsmith's selected works published in 1840 in New York. This introduction was expanded during 1849 into a full-sized biography which enjoyed widespread popularity both in England and abroad. While Irving's life does not reveal a singularly American point of view regarding Goldsmith, it does reflect an unusual understanding of the vicissitudes of his life and sympathy for his literary weaknesses. James W. Webb has discussed the history and reception of Irving's various versions of his *Life of Goldsmith* in 'Irving and his "Favorite Author," ' *University of Mississippi Studies in English*, iii, 1962, pp. 61–74. The passages printed here are found on pp. 161–247 of the expanded version of 1849.

'What reception a poem may find,' says he [Goldsmith], 'which has neither abuse, party, nor blank verse to support it, I cannot tell, nor am I solicitous to know.' The truth is, no one was more emulous and anxious for poetic fame; and never was he more anxious than in the present instance, for it was his grand stake. Dr. Johnson aided the launching of the poem[1] by a favorable notice in the *Critical Review*;[2] other periodical works came out in its favor. Some of the author's friends complained that it did not command instant and wide popularity; that it was a poem to win, not to strike: it went on rapidly increasing in favor; in three months a second edition was issued; shortly afterwards, a third; then a fourth; and, before the year was out, the author was pronounced the best poet of his time.

The appearance of *The Traveller* at once altered Goldsmith's intellectual standing in the estimation of society; but its effect upon the club,[3] if we may judge from the account given by Hawkins, was almost ludicrous. They were lost in astonishment that a 'newspaper essayist' and 'bookseller's drudge' should have written such a poem. On the evening of its announcement to them Goldsmith had gone away early, after 'rattling away as usual,' and they knew not how to reconcile his heedless garrulity with the serene beauty, the easy grace, the sound good sense, and the occasional elevation of his poetry. They could scarcely believe that such magic numbers had flowed from a man to whom in general, says Johnson, 'it was with difficulty they could give a hearing' . . .

Sixty guineas for the *Vicar of Wakefield*! and this could be pronounced *no mean price* by Dr. Johnson, at that time the arbiter of British talent, and who had had an opportunity of witnessing the effect of the work upon the public mind; for its success was immediate. It came out on the 27th of March, 1766; before the end of May a second edition was called for; in three months more, a third; and so it went on, widening in a popularity that has never flagged. Rogers,[4] the Nestor of British literature, whose refined purity of taste and exquisite mental organization, rendered him eminently calculated to appreciate a work of the kind, declared that of all the books, which through the fitful changes of three generations he had seen rise and fall the charm of the *Vicar of Wakefield* had alone continued as at first; and could he revisit the world after an interval of many more genera-

[1] *The Traveller.*
[2] See No. 1.
[3] Johnson's Literary Club.
[4] Samuel Rogers (1763–1855), about whom the author of the *DNB* life states, 'The more age impaired his originally limited productive faculty, the more homage he received as the Nestor of living poets.' Irving's paraphrase, if typical, probably distorts Rogers' actual statement; we have been unable to locate the original statement in Rogers' many miscellaneous works.

tions, he should as surely look to find it undiminished. Nor has its celebrity been confined to Great Britain. Though so exclusively a picture of British scenes and manners, it has been translated into almost every language, and every where its charm has been the same. Goethe, the great genius of Germany, declared in his eighty-first year,[1] that it was his delight at the age of twenty, that it had in a manner formed a part of his education, influencing his taste and feelings throughout life, and that he had recently read it again from beginning to end—with renewed delight, and with a grateful sense of the early benefit derived from it.

It is needless to expatiate upon the qualities of a work which has thus passed from country to country, and language to language, until it is now known throughout the whole reading world and is become a household book in every hand. The secret of its universal and enduring popularity is undoubtedly its truth to nature, but to nature of the most amiable kind; to nature such as Goldsmith saw it. The author, as we have occasionally shown in the course of this memoir, took his scenes and characters in this, as in his other writings, from originals in his own motley experience; but he has given them as seen through the medium of his own indulgent eye, and has set them forth with the colorings of his own good head and heart. Yet how contradictory it seems that this, one of the most delightful pictures of home and home-felt happiness should be drawn by a homeless man; that the most amiable picture of domestic virtue and all the endearments of the married state should be drawn by a bachelor, who had been severed from domestic life almost from boyhood; that one of the most tender, touching, and affecting appeals on behalf of female loveliness, should have been made by a man whose deficiency in all the graces of person and manner seemed to mark him out for a cynical disparager of the sex.

We cannot refrain from transcribing from the work a short passage illustrative of what we have said, and which within a wonderfully small compass comprises a world of beauty of imagery, tenderness of feeling, delicacy and refinement of thought, and matchless purity of style. The two stanzas which conclude it, in which are told a whole history of woman's wrong and sufferings, is, for pathos, simplicity and euphony, a gem in the language. The scene depicted is where the poor Vicar is gathering around him the wrecks of his shattered family, and endeavoring to rally them back to happiness.

[1] See No. 79.

'The next morning the sun arose with peculiar warmth for the season, so that we agreed to breakfast together on the honey-suckle bank; where, while we sat, my youngest daughter at my request joined her voice to the concert on the trees about us. It was in this place my poor Olivia first met her seducer, and every object served to recall her sadness. But that melancholy which is excited by objects of pleasure, or inspired by sounds of harmony, soothes the heart instead of corroding it. Her mother, too, upon this occasion, felt a pleasing distress, and wept, and loved her daughter as before. "Do, my pretty Olivia," cried she, "let us have that melancholy air your father was so fond of; your sister Sophy has already obliged us. Do, child, it will please your old father." She complied in a manner so exquisitely pathetic as moved me.

> 'When lovely woman stoops to folly,
>   And finds too late that men betray,
> What charm can soothe her melancholy,
>   What art can wash her guilt away?
>
> The only art her guilt to cover,
>   To hide her shame from every eye,
> To give repentance to her lover,
>   And wring his bosom—is to die.'

Scarce had the *Vicar of Wakefield* made its appearance and been received with acclamation, than its author was subjected to one of the usual penalties that attend success. He was attacked in the newspapers. . .

We have repeatedly adverted to his fondness for the drama; he was a frequent attendant at the theatres; though, as we have shown, he considered them under gross mismanagement. He thought, too that a vicious taste prevailed among those who wrote for the stage. 'A new species of dramatic composition,' says he, in one of his essays,[1] 'has been introduced under the name of *sentimental comedy*, in which the virtues of private life are exhibited rather than the vices exposed; and the distresses rather than the faults of mankind make our interest in the piece. In these plays almost all the characters are good, and exceedingly generous; they are lavish enough of their tin money on the stage; and though they want humor, have abundance of sentiment and feeling. If they happen to have faults or foibles, the spectator is

---

[1] *An Essay on the Theatre*: *Or a Comparison between Laughing and Sentimental Comedy*, published on 1 January 1773 in the *Westminster Magazine*.

taught not only to pardon, but to applaud them in consideration of
the gooodness of their hearts; so that folly, instead of being ridiculed,
is commended, and the comedy aims at touching our passions, without
the power of being truly pathetic. In this manner we are likely to
lose one great source of entertainment on the stage; for while the
comic poet is invading the province of the tragic muse, he leaves her
lively sister quite neglected. Of this, however, he is no ways solicitous,
as he measures his fame by his profits. . .

'Humor at present seems to be departing from the stage; and it
will soon happen that our comic players will have nothing left for it
but a fine coat and a song. It depends upon the audience whether they
will actually drive those poor merry creatures from the stage, or sit at a
play as gloomy as at the tabernacle. It is not easy to recover an art
when once lost; and it will be a just punishment, that when, by our
being too fastidious, we have banished humor from the stage, we
should ourselves be deprived of the art of laughing.'

Symptoms of reform in the drama had recently taken place. The
comedy of the *Clandestine Marriage*, the joint production of Colman
and Garrick, and suggested by Hogarth's inimitable pictures of *Marriage
a la mode*, had taken the town by storm, crowded the theatre with
fashionable audiences, and formed one of the leading literary topics of
the year. Goldsmith's emulation was roused by its success. The comedy
was in what he considered the legitimate line, totally different from the
sentimental school; it presented pictures of real life, delineations of
character and touches of humor, in which he felt himself calculated
to excel. The consequence was, that in the course of this year (1766),
he commenced a comedy of the same class, to be entitled the *Good
Natured Man*, at which he diligently wrought whenever the hurried
occupation of 'book building' allowed him leisure. . .

To the tender and melancholy recollections of his early days awakened
by the death of this loved companion of his childhood, we may attribute
some of the most heartfelt passages in his *Deserted Village*. Much of
that poem we are told was composed this summer, in the course
of solitary strolls about the green lanes and beautifully rural scenes of
the neighborhood; and thus much of the softness and sweetness of
English landscape became blended with the ruder features of Lissoy.
It was in these lonely and subdued moments, when tender regret was
half mingled with self-upbraiding, that he poured forth that homage
of the heart rendered as it were at the grave of his brother. The picture
of the village pastor in this poem, which we have already hinted, was

taken in part from the character of his father, embodied likewise the recollections of his brother Henry; for the natures of the father and son seem to have been identical. In the following lines, however, Goldsmith evidently contrasted the quiet settled life of his brother, passed at home in the benevolent exercise of the Christian duties, with his own restless vagrant career:

> Remote from towns he ran his godly race,
> Nor e'er had changed, nor wished to change his place.

To us the whole character seems traced as it were in an expiatory spirit; as if, conscious of his own wandering restlessness, he sought to humble himself at the shrine of excellence which he had not been able to practise:

> At church with meek and unaffected grace,
> His looks adorn'd the venerable place;
> Truth from his lips prevail'd with double sway,
> And fools, who came to scoff, remain'd to pray.
> The service past, around the pious man,
> With steady zeal, each honest rustic ran;
> Even children follow'd, with endearing wile,
> And pluck'd his gown, to share the good man's smile:
> His ready smile a parent's warmth express'd,
> Their welfare pleas'd him, and their cares distress'd;
> To them his heart, his love, his griefs were given,
> But all his serious thoughts had rest in heaven. . .

As we do not pretend in this summary memoir to go into a criticism or analysis of any of Goldsmith's writings, we shall not dwell upon the peculiar merits of this poem [*The Deserted Village*]; we cannot help noticing, however, how truly it is a mirror of the author's heart and of all the fond pictures of early friends and early life for ever present there. It seems to us as if the very last accounts received from home, of his 'shattered family,' and the desolation that seemed to have settled upon the haunts of his childhood, had cut to the roots one feebly cherished hope, and produced the following exquisitely tender and mournful lines:

> In all my wand'rings round this world of care,
> In all my griefs—and God has giv'n my share—
> I still had hopes my latest hours to crown,
> Amid these humble bowers to lay me down;
> To husband out life's taper at the close,

And keep the flame from wasting by repose;
I still had hopes, for pride attends us still,
Amid the swains to show my book-learn'd skill,
Around my fire an ev'ning group to draw,
And tell of all I felt and all I saw;
And as a hare, whom hounds and horns pursue,
Pants to the place from whence at first she flew;
I still had hopes, my long vexations past,
Here to return—*and die at home at last.*

How touchingly expressive are the succeeding lines, wrung from a heart which all the trials and temptations and buffetings of the world could not render worldly; which, amid a thousand follies and errors of the head, still retained its childlike innocence; and which, doomed to struggle on to the last amidst the din and turmoil of the metropolis, had ever been cheating itself with a dream of rural quiet and seclusion:

Oh bless'd retirement! friend to life's decline,
Retreats from care, *that never must be mine,*
How blest is he who crowns, in shades like these,
A youth of labor with an age of ease;
Who quits a world where strong temptations try,
And, since 'tis hard to combat, learns to fly!

69. Extracts from Joseph Cradock's *Literary and Miscellaneous Memoirs* dealing with Goldsmith

1826

Joseph Cradock (1742–1826) of Gumley was a friend and some-time collaborator of Goldsmith's. He had helped Goldsmith to sell his poems and wrote the epilogue to Goldsmith's play *She Stoops to Conquer*. These selections, printed here in condensed form, are culled from the London edition of Cradock's *Literary and Miscellaneous Memoirs*, printed for J. Nichols and Son, 1826, 4 vols, i, 228–36; iv, pp. 279–88.

I had not seen or heard from Dr. Goldsmith for a very considerable time, till I came to town with my wife, who was to place herself under the care of Mr. Parkinson, dentist, in Fleet-street, for rather a dangerous operation; and we took lodgings in Norfolk-street, that we might be in his neighbourhood. Goldsmith I found much altered, and at times very low; and I devoted almost all my mornings to his immediate service. He wished me to look over and revise some of his Works; but with a select friend or two I was most pressing that he should publish, by subscription, his two celebrated poems of *The Traveller* and *The Deserted Village*, with notes; for he was well aware that I was no stranger to Johnson's having made some little addition to the one, and possibly had suggested some corrections, at least, for the other; but the real meaning was, to give some great persons an opportunity of delicately conveying pecuniary relief, of which the Doctor at that time was particularly in need. Goldsmith readily gave up to me his private copies, and said, 'Pray do what you please with them.' But, whilst he sat near me, he rather submitted to, than encouraged my zealous proceedings.

I one morning called upon him, however, and found him infinitely better than I expected, and in a kind of exulting style he exclaimed, 'Here are some of the best of my prose writings; I have been hard at work ever since midnight, and I desire you to examine them.'—'These,' said I, 'are excellent indeed.'—'They are,' replied he, 'intended as an Introduction to a body of Arts and Sciences.'—'If so, Dr. Goldsmith, let me most seriously entreat, that as your name is to be prefixed, more care may be taken by those who are to compile the work, than has formerly been the case, when Knaresborough was printed for Naseby, and Yorkshire for Northamptonshire: and you know what was the consequence with Mr. Cadell.'

We entered on various topics, and I left him that morning seemingly much relieved. . .

I come now to the last day but one I passed with poor Goldsmith . . . whose loss (with whatever faults he might have) I shall ever lament whilst 'memory of him holds its seat.' At his breakfast in the Temple, as usual, I offered every aid in my power as to his works; some amendments had been agreed upon in his *Traveller*, and more particularly his *Deserted Village*. Some of the bad lines in the latter I have by me marked. 'As to my *Hermit*,[1] that poem, Cradock, cannot be amended.' I knew he had been offered ten pounds for the copy; and it was introduced into the *Vicar of Wakefield*, to which he applied himself entirely for a fortnight, to pay a journey to Wakefield. 'As my business then lay there,' said he, 'that was my reason for fixing on Wakefield as the field of action. I never took more pains than in the first volume of my *Natural History*; surely that was good, and I was handsomely repaid for the whole. My *Roman History*, Johnson says, is well abridged.' Indeed, I could have added, that Johnson (when Goldsmith was absent), would frequently say, 'Why, sir, whatever that man touches he adorns;' for like Garrick, when not present, he considered him as a kind of sacred character. After a general review of papers lying before him, I took leave; when, turning to his study-table, he pointed to an article I had procured for him, and said, 'You are kindest to me.' I only replied, 'You mean more rude and saucy than some others.' However, much of the conversation took a more melancholy tone than usual, and I became very uneasy about him. . .

Goldsmith and I (with great satisfaction I now speak it) never had a serious dispute in our lives; we freely gave and took. He rallied me on my Cambridge pedantry, and I hinted at illegitimate education; for, to speak on my mended judgment, Johnson, he, Garrick, and some

[1] 'Edwin and Angelina.'

others, had convinced me 'that all literature was not confined to our own academical world.' Goldsmith truly said, I was nibbling about elegant phrases, whilst he was obliged to write half a volume . . .

70. Sir Walter Scott writes about Goldsmith's works in *Biographical and Critical Notes of Eminent Novelists*

1827, 1829, 162–78

Scott's (1771–1832) view of Goldsmith's simplicity reflects some of the infatuation of the Romantics for his writings; and Scott's pronouncement on *The Vicar of Wakefield* reveals his own unconditional adoration: 'We read [it] in youth and in age, we return to it again and again, and bless the memory of an author who contrives so well to reconcile us to human nature.'

OUR biographical notices of distinguished Novelists were in some degree proportioned to the space which their labours occupy in the Collection for which these sketches were originally written. On that principle, the present subject, so interesting in every other point of view, could not be permitted long to detain us. The circumstances also of Dr. Goldsmith's life, his early struggles with poverty and distress, the success of his brief and brilliant career after he had become distinguished as an author, are so well known, and have been so well and so often told, that a short outline is all that ought here to be attempted. . .[1]

The publication of the *Traveller* gave the author all that celebrity which he had so long laboured to attain. He now assumed the profes-

[1] A four-page outline follows.

sional dress of the medical science, a scarlet cloak, wig, sword, and cane, and was admitted as a valued member of that distinguished society, which afterwards formed the Literary Club, or as it is more commonly called, emphatically, *The* CLUB. For this he made certain sacrifices, renouncing some of the public places which he had formerly found convenient in point of expense and amusement; not without regret, for he used to say, 'In truth, one must make some sacrifices to obtain good society; for here am I shut out of several places where I used to play the fool very agreeably.' It often happened amid those sharper wits with whom he now associated, that the simplicity of his character, mingled with an inaccuracy of expression, an undistinguishing spirit of vanity, and a hurriedness of conception, which led him often into absurdity, rendered Dr. Goldsmith in some degree the butt of the company. Garrick, in particular, who probably presumed somewhat on the superiority of a theatrical manager over a dramatic author, shot at him many shafts of small epigrammatic wit. It is likely that Goldsmith began to feel that this spirit was carried too far, and, to check it in the best taste, he composed his celebrated poem of *Retaliation*, in which the characters and failings of his associates are drawn with satire, at once pungent and good humoured. Garrick is smartly chastised; Burke, the Dinner-bell of the House of Commons, is not spared; and of all the more distinguished names of the Club, Johnson, Cumberland, and Reynolds alone escape the lash of the satirist. The former is not mentioned, and the two latter are even dismissed with unqualified and affectionate applause. *Retaliation* had the effect of placing the author on a more equal footing with his society than he had ever before assumed. Even against the despotism of Johnson, though much respecting him, and as much beloved by him, Goldsmith made a more spirited stand than was generally ventured upon by the compeers of that arbitrary Sultan of literature. Of this Boswell has recorded a striking instance. Goldsmith had been descanting on the difficulty and importance of making animals in an apologue speak in character, and particularly instanced the Fable of the Little Fishes. Observing that Doctor Johnson was laughing scornfully, he proceeded smartly; 'Why, Dr. Johnson, this is not so easy as you seem to think; for if *you* were to make little fishes talk, they would talk like whales.' . . .

Goldsmith, amid these more petty labours, aspired to the honours of the sock, and the *Goodnatured Man* was produced at Covent Garden, 29th January 1768, with the moderate success of nine nights' run. The principal character the author probably drew from the weak side of his own; for no man was more liable than Goldsmith to be gulled by pretended friends. The character of Croaker, highly comic in itself, and admirably represented by Shuter, helped to save the piece, which was endangered by the scene of the Bailiffs, then considered as too vulgar for the stage. Upon the whole, however, Goldsmith is said to have cleared five hundred pounds by this dramatic performance. . .

The reception given to the *Deserted Village*, so full of natural elegance, simplicity, and pathos, was of the warmest kind. The publisher showed at once his skill and generosity, by pressing upon Doctor Goldsmith a hundred pounds, which the author insisted upon returning, when upon computation he found that it came to nearly a crown for every couplet, a sum which he conceived no poem could be worth. The sale of the poem made him ample amends for this unusual instance of moderation. Lissoy, near Ballymahon, where his brother the clergyman had his living, claims the honour of being the spot from which the localities of the *Deserted Village* were derived. The church which tops the neighbouring hill, the mill, and the lake, are still pointed out; and a hawthorn has suffered the penalty of poetical celebrity, being cut to pieces by those admirers of the bard, who desired to have classical tooth-pick cases and tobacco-stoppers. Much of this supposed locality may be fanciful, but it is a pleasing tribute to the poet in the land of his fathers.

Goldsmith's *Abridgements of the History of Rome and England* may here be noticed. They are eminently well calculated to introduce youth to the knowledge of their studies; for they exhibit the most interesting and striking events, without entering into controversy or dry detail. Yet the tone assumed in the *History of England* drew on the author the resentment of the more zealous Whigs, who accused him of betraying the liberties of the people . . .

His celebrated play of *She Stoops to Conquer*, was Goldsmith's next work of importance. If it be the object of comedy to make an audience laugh, Johnson says that it was better obtained by this play than by any other of the period. . .

It must be owned, that however kind, amiable, and benevolent, Goldsmith showed himself to his contemporaries, more especially to such as needed his assitance, he had no small portion of the jealous and irritable spirit proper to the literary profession. He suffered a newspaper lampoon about this time to bring him into a foolish affray with Evans the editor, which did him but little credit.

In the meantime, a neglect of economy, occasional losses at play, and too great a reliance on his own versatility and readiness of talent, had considerably embarrassed his affairs. He felt the pressure of many engagements, for which he had received advances of money, and which it was, nevertheless, impossible for him to carry on with that despatch, which the booksellers thought themselves entitled to expect. One of his last publications was a *History of the Earth and Animated Nature*, in six volumes, which is to science what his abridgements are to history; a book which indicates no depth of research, or accuracy of information, but which presents to the ordinary reader a general and interesting view of the subject, couched in the clearest and most beautiful language, and abounding with excellent reflections and illustrations. It was of this work that Johnson threw out the remark which he afterwards interwove in his friend's epitaph,—'He is now writing a Natural History, and will make it as agreeable as a Persian Tale.' . .

Excepting some short Tales, Goldsmith gave to the department of the novelist only one work—the inimitable *Vicar of Wakefield*. We have seen that it was suppressed for nearly two years, until the publication of the *Traveller* had fixed the author's fame. Goldsmith had, therefore, time for revisal, but he did not employ it. He had been paid for his labour, as he observed, and could have profited nothing by rendering the work ever so perfect. This, however, was false reasoning, though not unnatural in the mouth of the author who must earn daily bread by daily labour. The narrative, which in itself is as simple as possible, might have been cleared of certain improbabilities, or rather impossibilities, which it now exhibits. We cannot, for instance, conceive how Sir William Thornhill should contrive to masquerade under the name of Burchell among his own tenantry, and upon his own estate; and it is absolutely impossible to see how his nephew, the son, doubtless, of a younger brother, (since Sir William inherited both title and property,) should be nearly as old as the Baronet himself. It may be added, that the character of Burchell, or Sir William Thornhill, is in itself extravagantly unnatural. A man of his benevolence would never have so long left his nephew in the possession of wealth which he employed to the worst of purposes. Far less would he have permitted his scheme upon Olivia in a great measure to succeed, and that upon Sophia also to approach consummation; for, in the first instance, he does not interfere at all, and in the second, his intervention is accidental. These, and some other little circumstances in the progress of the narrative, might easily have been removed upon revisal.

But whatever defects occur in the tenour of the story, the admirable ease and grace of the narrative, as well as the pleasing truth with which the principal characters are designed, make the *Vicar of Wakefield* one of the most delicious morsels of fictitious composition on which the human mind was ever employed. The principal character, that of the simple Pastor himself, with all the worth and excellency which ought to distinguish the ambassador of God to man, and yet with just so much of pedantry and of literary vanity as serves to show that he is made of mortal mould, and subject to human failings, is one of the best and most pleasing pictures ever designed. It is perhaps impossible to place frail humanity before us in an attitude of more simple dignity than the Vicar, in his character of pastor, of parent, and of husband. His excellent helpmate, with all her motherly cunning, and housewifely prudence, loving and respecting her husband, but counterplotting his wisest schemes, at the dictates of maternal vanity, forms an excellent counterpart. Both, with their children around them, their quiet labour and domestic happiness, compose a fireside picture of such a perfect kind, as perhaps is nowhere else equalled. It is sketched indeed from common life, and is a strong contrast to the exaggerated and extraordinary characters and incidents which are the resource of those authors, who, like Bayes, make it their business to elevate and surprise; but the very simplicity of this charming book renders the pleasure it affords more permanent. We read the *Vicar of Wakefield* in youth and in age—We return to it again and again, and bless the memory of an author who contrives so well to reconcile us to human nature. Whether we choose the pathetic and distressing incidents of the fire, the scenes at the jail, or the lighter and humorous parts of the story, we find the best and truest sentiments enforced in the most beautiful language; and perhaps there are few characters of purer dignity [who] have been described than that of the excellent pastor, rising above sorrow and oppression, and labouring for the conversion of those felons, into whose company he had been thrust by his villainous creditor. In too many works of this class, the critics must apologize for or censure particular passages in the narrative, as unfit to be perused by youth and innocence. But the wreath of Goldsmith is unsullied; he wrote to exalt virtue and expose vice; and he accomplished his task in a manner which raises him to the highest rank among British authors. We close his volume, with a sigh that such an author should have written so little from the stores of his own genius, and that he should have been so prematurely removed from the sphere of literature, which he so highly adorned.

71. Goethe on Goldsmith's irony and vision of man in *The Vicar of Wakefield*, in a letter to his friend Zelter

25 December 1829

Johann Wolfgang von Goethe (1749–1832), the great German poet and scientist, like Herder and Schlegel (see above, No. 13), had literally adored Goldsmith's *Vicar of Wakefield* from early manhood and regarded it as the finest novel of the eighteenth century. Several of Goethe's works reflect the influence of Goldsmith and there can be no doubt about the force of Goldsmith on his creative imagination and general mental development. This influence has been factually demonstrated by Lawrence M. Price in 'Goldsmith, Sesenheim, and Goethe,' *Germanic Review*, iv, 1929, pp. 237–47. The text here is taken from *Goethe's Letters to Zelter*, trans. A. D. Coleridge, London, 1887, p. 381.

. . . THE reason why I mention the worthy name (of Dr. Primrose) here, and illustrate my circumstances, by the picture of his family circle, I will now briefly explain to you. I lately chanced to fall in with *The Vicar of Wakefield*, and felt compelled to read the little book over again, from beginning to end, being not a little affected by the vivid recollection of all that I have owed to the author, for the last seventy years. The influence Goldsmith and Sterne exercised upon me, just at the chief point of my development, cannot be estimated.

This high, benevolent irony, this just and comprehensive way of viewing things, this gentleness to all opposition, this equanimity under every change, and whatever else all the kindred virtues may be termed, —such things were a most admirable training for me, and surely, these are the sentiments, which in the end lead us back from all the mistaken paths of life.

By the way, it is strange that Yorick should incline rather to that which has no Form, and that Goldsmith should be all Form, as I myself aspired to be when the worthy Germans had convinced themselves, that the peculiarity of true humour is to have no Form. . .

72. Anecdotes of Goldsmith by a friend and enemy, George Colman (the younger) in his *Random Records*

1830, i, 110–13

Dramatist George Colman the younger (1762–1836), son of the Colman who produced *She Stoops to Conquer* and who is known to have had serious reservations about Goldsmith's dramatic form, reminisces here about Goldsmith's life.

Oliver Goldsmith, several years before my luckless presentation to Johnson, proved how '*Doctors differ.*'—I was only five years old when Goldsmith took me on his knee, while he was drinking coffee, one evening, with my father, and began to play with me;—which amiable act I return'd with the ingratitude of a peevish brat, by giving him a very smart slap in the face;—it must have been a tingler;—for it left the marks of my little spiteful paw upon his cheek. This infantile outrage was follow'd by summary justice; and I was lock'd up by my

indignant father, in an adjoining room, to undergo solitary imprison-
ment, in the dark. Here I began to howl and scream, most abominably;
which was no bad step towards liberation, since those who were not
inclined to pity me might be likely to set me free, for the purpose of
abating a nuisance.

At length a generous friend appear'd to extricate me from jeopardy;
and that generous friend was no other than the man I had so wantonly
molested, by assault and battery;—it was the tender-hearted Doctor
himself, with a lighted candle in his hand, and a smile upon his countenance, which was still partially red, from the effects of my petulance.—
I sulk'd and sobb'd, and he fondled and sooth'd;—till I began to brighten.
Goldsmith, who, in regard to children, was like the Village Preacher
he has so beautifully described,—for

> Their welfare pleased him, and their cares distress'd,

seized the propitious moment of returning good-humour;—so he put
down the candle, and began to conjure. He placed three hats, which
happen'd to be in the room, upon the carpet, and a shilling under each:
—the shillings, he told me, were England, France, and Spain. 'Hey,
presto, cockolorum!' cried the Doctor,—and, lo! on uncovering the
shillings which had been dispersed, each beneath a separate hat, they
were all found congregated under one.—I was no Politician at five
years old,—and, therefore, might not have wonder'd at the sudden
revolution which brought England, France, and Spain, all under one
Crown; but, as I was also no Conjuror, it amazed me beyond measure.
Astonishment might have amounted to awe for one who appear'd to
me gifted with the power of performing miracles, if the good-nature
of the man had not obviated my dread of the magician;—but, from
that time, whenever the Doctor came to visit my father,

> I pluck'd his gown, to share the good man's smile;

a game at romps constantly ensued, and we were always cordial
friends, and merry play-fellows. Our unequal companionship varied
somewhat, in point of sports, as I grew older, but it did not last long;—
my senior playmate died, alas! in his forty fifth year, some months
after I had attain'd my eleventh. His death, it has been thought, was
hasten'd by 'mental inquietude;'—if this supposition be true, never
did the turmoils of life subdue a mind more warm with sympathy for
the misfortune of our fellow-creatures;—but his character is familiar
to every one who reads:—in all the numerous accounts of his virtues

and his foibles,—his genius and absurdities, his knowledge of nature, and his ignorance of the world,—his 'compassion for another's woe' was always predominant; and my trivial story, of his humouring a froward child, weighs but as a feather in the recorded scale of his benevolence.

73. Thomas Carlyle on the poetry of the eighteenth century—especially Goldsmith, in an essay on Goethe

1832, 1838, 1839, 1840

Thomas Carlyle (1795–1881), the prolific writer and author of many works including *Sartor Resartus* (1833–4) and *Past and Present* (1843), never wrote exclusively about Goldsmith but he did comment briefly on his niche in the British pantheon. In his essay on 'Boswell's *Life of Johnson*,' Carlyle compared Johnson ('Dr. Major') and Goldsmith ('Dr. Minor'): 'the Author of the genuine *Vicar of Wakefield*, nill he, will he, must needs fly towards such a mass of genuine Manhood; and Dr. Minor keep gyrating round Dr. Major, alternately attracted and repelled' (*Critical and Miscellaneous Essays*, 1888, iii, pp. 90–1). The selection included here, equally brief, is cited from Carlyle's *Critical and Miscellaneous Essays*, 4 vols, Boston, 1838, i, p. 214.

Our only English poet of the period was Goldsmith: a pure, clear, genuine spirit, had he been of depth or strength sufficient: his *Vicar of Wakefield* remains the best of all modern Idyls; but it is and was nothing more.

74. Henry Crabb Robinson on aspects of Goldsmith's writing and influence

1834-7

(a) On first person style in Goldsmith, 1 November 1834

(b) Recalling Mrs Anna Barbauld on Goldsmith's poetry, 29 December 1835

(c) On Goldsmith's influence on Wordsworth, 28 March 1837

Henry Crabb Robinson (1775–1867) kept diaries and wrote letters revealing his literary opinions and reporting those of his contemporaries, as in these selections about Goldsmith from *Henry Crabb Robinson on Books and their Writers*, ed. Edith J. Morley, London, 1938, i, p. 448; ii, pp. 472, 517.

(a)

Nov. 1st . . . The first person style does not suit the naïve character, and is the greatest fault in the *Vicar of Wakefield*. . .

(b)

Dec. 29th. I awoke early and read in bed what I finished soon after breakfast. This *Life*[1] has not much to interest me, because there is not much that interests me in Crabbe's poetry; I take no pleasure in his unpoetical representations of human life, and though no one can dispute that he had a powerful pen and could faithfully portray what he saw, yet he had an eye only for the sad realities of life. As Mrs. Barbauld said to me many years ago: 'I shall never be tired of Goldsmith's *Deserted Village*—I shall never look again into Crabbe's *Village*.' Indeed this impression is so strong that I have never read his later works —I know little about them. Of the *Life* the only parts that are attractive are the account of his extreme poverty and of his introduction to

---

[1] I.e., *Life of George Crabbe*.

Burke, who at once raised him out of his desperately forlorn condition and made a parson of him. . .

(c)

MARCH 28th . . . The views of the Loire which we afterwards enjoyed were of great interest to Wordsworth. Goldsmith's lines in *The Traveller* made an impression on him in his youth.

75. Goldsmith's first Victorian biographer: selections from James Prior's *Life of Oliver Goldsmith . . . in Two Volumes*

Printed for John Murray, 1837

(a) On Goldsmith's early display of poetic genius in *The Traveller*

(b) The originality of *The Vicar of Wakefield*

(c) On *The Deserted Village*

(d) Goldsmith's dramatic achievement in *She Stoops to Conquer*

Sir James Prior (1790?–1869), miscellaneous writer and Fellow of the Society of Antiquaries, wrote the first full-scale biography of Goldsmith. While it reflects many literary prejudices of his time (as any biography does), it nevertheless surveys Goldsmith's life as no previous biographer had. Only John Forster's (1812–76) biography, published in two volumes in 1854, can compare with it, and while both authors reflect Victorian assumptions about both Goldsmith and the eighteenth century, there is much to be said in favor of Prior's *Life* which is perhaps the more balanced and accurate of the two. Because it is the first attempt to evaluate all Goldsmith's writings in perspective, ample selections from it are quoted, especially sections critically appraising Goldsmith's major writings.

---

a)

It will be remembered that this work [*The Traveller*] was commenced by his own account in Switzerland, whence a portion of it, the *disjecta membra*[1] only we may believe, was transmitted to his brother in Ireland. For a time, the continued contest he had to sustain against

[1] I.e., dismembered limbs, from Horace's line (*Satire* iv, 62), "*invenias etiam disiecti membra poetae*,' translated: 'you would recognize, even in his dismembered state, the limbs of a poet.'

want by such productions as were more profitable in the literary market precluded serious attention to it, but as he became more at ease, such additions were made as his plan or genius suggested; the original outline, said by his contemporaries to have been more extensive than now appears, was contracted and filled up; and in this state though still imperfect and without the title (that of *The Philosophical Wanderer* was first suggested) being positively fixed, it was submitted to Dr. Johnson. He saw its merit at once, recommended it to be retouched and finished for publication, and towards the conclusion, voluntarily added a few lines of his own. The advice though not immediately followed, was not forgotten. A poem is one of those hazardous adventures in literature in which failure seems the rule and success the exception; we cannot therefore be surprised at his hesitation to publish, or the desire to give it all the benefit that time and care could impart; fully aware of the risk of turning his venture adrift on the ocean of public opinion, the precaution he adopted displayed prudence; for who would not, if he could, acquire the reputation not of a tolerable, but of a good poet?

The state of poetry at this period was such that a fair opening appeared to offer to a new claimant for its honours. The great masters who had charmed the preceding age had passed away, and none of equal powers had arisen to take their place. Young was advanced in life and expired a few months afterwards; Gray was indolent and fastidious; and excepting in a few of his pieces, several of the wits and critics, among whom Johnson even at this time was one, declared against him. Mason and Glover were scarcely popular. Johnson himself was silent. Churchill had just expired; one of those poets who though of such reputation among his contemporaries as to be termed in a memoir written in the preceding year 'the greatest English poet now living, or perhaps that this country ever produced,' is now if not forgotten at least neglected, his works rarely perused for the pleasure they afford, and even his genius indifferently estimated. Lloyd died nearly on the day of the publication of the new poem, but his reputation was not great. Falconer who had printed the Shipwreck two years before, was scarcely yet enrolled among the body of poets. Akenside, Armstrong, Smollett, Grainger, and Bonnell Thornton, all members of the medical profession, were otherwise occupied; and to this respectable list of five of the 'two-fold disciples of Apollo,' a term not unfelicitously applied to the former, was now to be added a sixth in the person of Goldsmith.

In sitting down to the composition of his poem, as well as in his general views of poetry, he had his eye fixed on the most popular models of the preceding age, which having undergone the test of time and given pleasure to every description of reader, he thought might be safely followed as the best. So likewise thought Dr. Johnson. Public opinion sided with both; and public opinion, as Aristotle and Cicero, and many others have told us, after a moderate time for deliberation, rarely mistaken in matters of taste. The opinions of Goldsmith on the art as well as his practice, are on record. In the *Life of Parnell* we find; 'He appears to me to be the last of that great school that had modelled itself upon the ancients, and taught English poetry to resemble what the generality of mankind have allowed to excel. A studious and correct observer of antiquity, he set himself to consider nature with the lights it lent him; and he found that the more aid he borrowed from the one, the more delightfully he resembled the other. To copy nature is a task the most bungling workman is able to execute; to select such parts as contribute to delight, is reserved only for those whom accident has blessed with uncommon talents, or such as have read the ancients with indefatigable industry. . .'

The plan of the poem is in great measure new, though it is possible that Addison's *Letter from Italy* suggested the idea. Travels in prose had been often told; but to array them for the first time in the garb of poetry, promised something of stronger interest to the reader, while the situation in which the *Traveller* was projected and commenced, entitles its author in all probability to the honours of originality. But it is in the execution of such things we must seek for the merit that gives them popular favour; to do this well requires poetical powers of a high order, good taste, a philosophical spirit of observation, and that nice discrimination which seizes only upon such points as mark national peculiarities in the strongest manner, and are immediately intelligible to the general reader. It is so far different from what is called *local* poetry, such as Denham's Cooper's Hill, which may have given the hint to Addison, that it overlooks in great degree the scenery of countries to fix upon and describe the moral characteristics of the people. Human nature is always difficult to pourtray [sic] in poetry with condensation and accuracy: but he who accomplishes this, is beyond question no ordinary poet.

We have proof at once of the judgment of Goldsmith, and of the plan being adapted to poetry of the highest order, in Lord Byron pursuing it in Childe Harold, which in all its leading points may be considered a kind of *Traveller* on a more extended scale. We find a similar survey of the people and countries through which they pass; the same attention to their distinguishing moral features; the same philosophical spirit of reflection, varying indeed with the opposite natures of the writers; many noble sentiments, and ideas of great moral sublimity, mingled with what is still more peculiar, the same reference to personal circumstances, feelings, and recollections; both identifying themselves in a peculiar manner with their subject. Lord Byron, however, by amplifying the design, has gained a stronger hold upon the reader. Goldsmith looks down as from a height upon the countries under his eye, with the large and general views of a philosopher whose business is not with detail. Lord Byron travels more extensively and tells his travels with more of the minuteness of a tourist; he is more various and diversified, yet scarcely more vigorous, and certainly not more condensed: both are ethical; and both indulge freely in their respective political views. In Goldsmith we find not one objectionable sentiment, nothing that assaults or pains the religious or moral feelings of the reader; the same cannot be said of the author of Childe Harold. The main purpose of the former is to show that by the benevolent ordination of Providence, the sum of human happiness is in most countries, however varying in natural position, capabilities, or form of government, nearly the same; that content belongs to the mind and disposition of the individual, more than to the circumstances by which he is surrounded. Lord Byron, who had probably set out with no fixed plan in view, is willing to tell of all that interested him; not of moral characteristics only, but of manners, localities, and the associations derived from historical events; he therefore perhaps carries with him general readers more. The one is general in his philosophy, the other more local and particular. If Lord Byron be more various and interesting, we find in Goldsmith purity of thought and that high moral feeling pervading all his writings, the want of which is so often to be lamented in those of his noble successor; while in vigour and sublimity whenever occasion requires it, he is rarely inferior.

True poets probably differ little in their conception of what should be good subjects for the exercise of their art, as Thomson, by another coincidence, appears to have thought well of the design which Goldsmith lived to execute. . .

A comparison between his description of Italy and that of Addison occurs immediately to the poetical reader; and if the same thought was suggested to himself, no tone of depreciation or jealousy appears to have been the result. The *Letter from Italy* is thus fairly and judiciously characterised a few years afterwards in one of his compilations for youth, the *Beauties of English Poesy*:—'Few poems have done more honour to English genius than this. There is in it a strain of political thinking that was, at that time, new in our poetry. Had the harmony of this been equal to Pope's versification, it would be incontestably the finest poem in our language; but there is a dryness in the numbers which greatly lessens the pleasure excited both by the poet's judgment and imagination.' . .

Addison dwelt little on what Goldsmith has been compelled by the pre-occupation of topics to make his principal theme. In comparing the one hundred and sixty-eight lines of the former with the sixty of the latter, they will be found as the range of the former was unlimited, to display more imagination and vivacity. In Goldsmith as his purpose was more philosophical, we find more of the depth of such an observer, equal vigour of description, more condensation of thought, and infinitely more smoothness of versification. Both unaccountably neglect to notice the chief delight of modern Italy, its music; for this in the hands of either, particularly of Goldsmith, who had a taste for it, might have been made the vehicle of some fine poetical painting and pointed remark. But his ingenuity deserves praise in furnishing a sketch after such a master, at once philosophical, spirited, and original. . .

The interval between the period of a publication issuing from the press, and the moment when public favour towards it seems no longer doubtful, is necessarily an anxious one for an author. To Goldsmith, notwithstanding some affected indifference expressed in the dedication, it could not be an unimportant matter; it was the first production to which he had put his name, as well as the greatest adventure in which he had hitherto embarked; and the stake was to him not merely reputation, but in some measure subsistence. Dr. Johnson, who knew the anxious feelings of his friend, made an immediate effort to relieve them by a recommendatory notice which appears in the *Critical Review* for December 1764.[1]

Offices of this kind proceeding from kind intentions need not necessarily be laudatory; they are often more in the nature of advertisements to announce existence than to disseminate praise, and prove frequently useful to works of admitted merit. It is not that the public cannot unassisted discover and reward such productions without a

[1] See No. 1.

director to guide its taste, but in the multiplicity of publications, some which are good may for awhile escape observation; and it is thus that the early notice of a judicious friend may do quickly for its fame what would otherwise be a work of time. This obviously was the idea of the great critic whom it may be interesting to trace in his friendly endeavours; he says indeed little, leaving the poem to speak for itself in the quotations, which amount to a fourth part of its number of lines. It was evidently written in haste: the remarks are of the utmost possible brevity, and not being included in some editions of the works of its writer although enumerated by Boswell among his productions, will be found in a future volume. . .

The number of lines in the first edition was 416; in the last, being the ninth printed during the life of the author, 438; making an addition of twenty-two to the original number; but as fourteen of the first edition were thrown out, the total number of new lines amounted to thirty-six.

Such as may be strictly called additions, from conveying thoughts or illustrations not in the first edition, are the following:—

> With food as well the peasant is supply'd
> On Idra's cliffs, as Arno's shelvy side.
>
>   *   *   *   *   *
>
> Where wealth and freedom reign contentment fails,
> And honour sinks where commerce long prevails.
>
>   *   *   *   *   *
>
> While nought remain'd of all that riches gave,
> But towns unmann'd, and lords without a slave.
>
>   *   *   *   *   *
>
> The self-dependent lordlings stand alone,
> All claims that bind and sweeten life unknown.

And that animated apostrophe to freedom of sixteen lines, commencing with

> And thou, fair Freedom, taught alike to feel
> The rabble's rage, and tyrant's angry steel:

and ending with

> Except when fast approaching danger warms.

Those deemed less fit by the author to retain their station in the poem, and therefore finally rejected, were

> 'Twere affectation all, and school-taught pride,
> To spurn the splendid things by heaven supply'd:

for which he substituted

> Say, should the philosophic mind disdain
> That good which makes each humbler bosom vain?

For the following passage which was thrown out—

> And yet, perhaps, if states with states we scan,
> Or estimate their bliss on reason's plan,
> Though patriots flatter and though fools contend,
> We still shall find uncertainty suspend;
> Find that each good by art or nature given,
> To these or those, but make the balance even;
> Find that the bliss of all is much the same,
> And patriotic boasting reason's shame:

now appear six lines, commencing

> And yet, perhaps, if countries we compare,

and ending with

> To different nations make their blessings even.

Immediately succeeding the lines where by the anecdote previously related, the Poet seemed to bestow divided attention between his verses and his dog, and which glance at the political apathy of Italy, a couplet, now omitted, continued the idea.

> At sports like these while foreign arms advance,
> In passive ease they leave the world to chance.

After the lines

> Yet think not thus when Freedom's ills I state,
> I mean to flatter kings or court the great,

came

> Perish the wish; for inly satisfy'd,
> Above their pomps I hold my ragged pride:

which were replaced in the amended edition by

> Ye powers of truth that bid my soul aspire,
> Far from my bosom drive the low desire, &c.

Among a variety of verbal alterations, a few of the chief as indicating his care in the revision, may be noticed:—

> A weary waste expanding to the skies,

stood originally

> *expanded* to the skies.
> Blest be those feasts with simple plenty crown'd,

was

> *where mirth and peace abound.*
> Amidst the store should thankless pride repine,

was

> *'twere thankless to repine.*
> Boldly proclaims that happiest spot his own,

was

> Boldly *asserts that country for his own.*
> And though the rocky crested summits frown,

was

> *rough rocks or gloomy* summits frown.

In the description of Italy, the lines

> Till more unsteady than the southern gale,
> Commerce on other shores display'd her sail.

stood thus,

> *But more unsteady than the southern gale,*
> *Soon Commerce turn'd on other shores her sail.*

Again,

> Yet still the loss of wealth is here supply'd,
> By arts, the splendid wrecks of former pride,

is changed from

> *Yet though to fortune lost here still abide*
> *Some splendid arts, the wrecks of former pride.*

And

> Each nobler aim represt by long controul,

was written

> *When struggling virtue sinks by long controul,*

Speaking of Holland—

> Industrious habits in each bosom reign,

was

> *breast obtain.*
> Here by the bonds of nature feebly held,

replaces

> *See, though by circling deeps together held.*
> Nor this the worst: as nature's ties decay,

was

> as *social bonds* decay.

Of England, as we are told,

> Where kings have toil'd and poets wrote for fame,

stood

> *And monarchs toil, and poets pant for fame.*

Of America,

> And the brown Indian marks with murd'rous aim,

stood

> *takes a deadly aim.*

There are but two instances of the transposition of lines; one in the
description of Holland, where in allusion to her embankments to keep
off the inroads of the sea, the lines

> Onwards methinks and diligently slow,
> The firm connected bulwark seems to grow,

immediately follow the couplet which they are now made to precede.
 The second is in the noble and animated sketch of our countrymen
so much admired and repeated by every good judge of poetry and so
great a favourite with Dr. Johnson. In the first edition it is—

> Stern o'er each bosom Reason holds her state:
> With daring aims irregularly great,
> I see the lords of human kind pass by,
> Pride in their port, defiance in their eye:—

which on further consideration is more judiciously arranged—

> Pride in their port, defiance in their eye,
> I see the lords of human kind pass by.

In a few passages, thoughts are repeated which particularly pleased him in prose, and were thought capable of strong poetic painting or expression, their previous use being probably forgotten. Thus the beautiful and affecting image—

> And drags at each remove a lengthening chain,

had been employed in the third letter of the *Citizen of the World*:—

> The farther I travel, I feel the pain of separation with stronger force; those ties that bind me to my native country and you are still unbroken. By every remove I only drag a greater length of chain.

And the lines—

> Each wanton judge new penal statutes draw,
> Laws grind the poor, and rich men rule the law,

correspond with a passage in the *Vicar of Wakefield*:—

> What they may then expect, may be seen by turning our eyes to Holland, Genoa, or Venice, where the laws govern the poor and the rich govern the law.

And again the simile—

> ——like the circle bounding earth and skies,
> Allures from far, yet as I follow, flies,

appears likewise in the novel:—

> And though death, the only friend of the wretched, for a little while mocks the weary traveller with the view, and like his horizon still flies before him, &c.

Again in speaking of the Dutch—

> Heavens! how unlike their Belgic sires of old,
> Rough, poor, content, ungovernably bold;
> War in each breast and freedom on each brow.

(b)

The *Vicar of Wakefield* secured friends among every description of readers; with the old by the purity of its moral lessons, and with the young by the interest of the story. It had the merit of originality by differing from nearly all its predecessors. With the popular productions before him of Fielding and Smollett, he studiously avoided their track by excluding variety of adventures, immoral scenes, and licentious intrigues, which under the plausible plea of exhibiting human nature, give us not only the worst parts of it, but almost necessarily corrupt the minds of youth by familiarising what it is never prudent wantonly to display. He was equally regardless of the example of Richardson, of his prolixity and sentimental refinements, however he may have honoured his morality. He had determined that his novel should not be too long to be perused with ease, and what was read should leave no taint of impurity behind.

But its great charm, as of all the productions of Goldsmith, is close adherence to nature; nature in its commendable, not vicious, points of view; we find little in incident or character overstrained, excepting perhaps the moral turpitude of Thornhill, and this scarcely exceeds what was common among fashionable rakes in the novels of the time. The Primrose family is a great creation of genius; such a picture of warm-hearted simplicity, mingled with the little foibles and weak-nesses common to the best specimens of humanity, that we find nothing like it in the whole range of fiction. Each of the individuals is nicely discriminated without apparent art or effort; we can anticipate what either will do, and almost will say, on any given occasion. The unwearied benevolence and submission to the will of Providence under all his distresses of the good pastor; the self-satisfied cleverness and little female devices to accomplish favourite purposes, of his wife; the liveliness and indiscretion of Olivia; the more considerate and sedate turn of Sophia; the pedantry yet simplicity of Moses; and goodness of heart of all, present a piece of moral painting of great beauty and of rare skill.

The other characters as they interest us less, please us less, from the disguised Burchell down to Jenkins the instrument of young Thorn-hill's vices. The conduct of the story has the merit of never once leading us from the main design of exhibiting the family in all their trials from the commencement to the conclusion, excepting the episode of the adventures of the son. The style is peculiarly easy, perspicuous, and simple, free from all attempt at fine writing or ambitious ornament, and without even one of those epigrammatic smartnesses which the apprehension of being considered dull led him occasionally to introduce into his Essays. This, among its other merits, has contributed to render the *Vicar of Wakefield* perhaps the most popular of all English books on the continent of Europe.

Few tests of the merit of a work of fiction are probably better than the admiration of foreigners, for it forms pretty good evidence that in the characters or circumstances of the story, our general nature, not the mere manners of a country, is happily pourtrayed. Fictions may be written and acquire a large share of success among ourselves, yet signally fail in securing favour among other nations; but popularity abroad as well as at home leaves less doubt of the existence of true genius in the writer. It is thus with the romances of Cervantes and Le Sage; and if we seek for higher examples they are to be found in the writings of Homer and other great masters in poetry. So likewise with the tale of Goldsmith. In France they enumerate seven different translations which have passed through innumerable editions; in Germany it is little less popular;[1] in Italy also familiarly known; and in these countries, as well as in the north of Europe, it is the first English book put into the hands of such as learn our language.

Critical wisdom however is seldom satisfied without discovering defects; and as we fancy ourselves privileged to speak freely of all we love, this may be done in the present instance without diminishing our regard. Of the existence of such he himself had obvious misgivings. 'There are a hundred faults in this thing,' he tells us in the advertisement, 'and a hundred things might be said to prove them beauties. But it is needless. A book may be amusing with numerous errors, or it may be dull without a single absurdity.'

The character of Mrs. Primrose, though rendered amusing by her foibles, is drawn in education and manners beneath what is usual in an intelligent clergyman's wife, but this objection seems anticipated by the words put into her husband's mouth, that he chose her, as she did her wedding gown, 'not for a fine glossy surface, but such qualities as would wear well.' Olivia's conduct in submitting to be married by a popish priest, which she is injudiciously made to admit she knew not to be binding, is not satisfactory. Sophia comes less frequently forward to exhibit her good sense and prudence in conversation than we wish. About Sir William Thornhill there is a coldness that wins little of our regard; possessed of power, wealth, and reputed benevolence, he takes no steps to assist a worthy and benevolent man struggling with poverty, whose hospitality he enjoys and to whose daughter he exhibits attachment, but leaves the family to the machinations of his nephew, in consequence of an error on their part, arising as he must have understood, from justifiable indignation towards him whom they conceived

[1] Although the best German critics seemed more enthusiastic than the best French critics.

guilty of treachery and ingratitude. His disguise near his own estates, cannot be reconciled with probability. Neither can we believe that one so avowedly virtuous, would entrust a large portion of his fortune to a nephew capable of appropriating it to the worst purposes, and of whose character he could not, from previous admissions and the report of the country, be ignorant. A few inadvertencies and legal errors, though of no moment, required little trouble to amend. Thus George Primrose is told on departing to join his regiment, to emulate his grandfather, who fell in the same field with Lord Falkland; this if taken literally would make the Vicar more than a century old. In a threat of Burchell it is assumed, that simply breaking the lock of a pocket book found near their habitation, subjected the parties upon complaint to a justice of peace, to be 'all hanged up at their own door.' We find also that sending a challenge though it be not accepted, is a capital offence; that a justice of peace on his sole authority can free a culprit from a criminal charge by representing it in a different light to the committing magistrate; and that a gaoler would permit a coiner imprisoned for trial, to quit his custody on verbal authority from the same magistrate; mistakes which as they may mislead foreigners, would have been better avoided. But when criticism enumerates these, it has done its worst; the feelings of the reader rise up in judgment against the critic, he throws aside the lucubration, and turns to re-peruse what has given him so much pleasure. . .

(c)

The journals devoted to literature hailed it [*The Deserted Village*] with the warmest applause; the author was gratified by his good fortune; the public pleased by the addition made to its sources of pleasure; and if some of the newspaper writers used their customary privilege of finding fault on some unimportant points, others were as loud in its praise; and attention was more drawn to a work which possessed merit enough to find a few enemies among a multitude of friends.

The previous reputation of the author as a man of unquestioned genius, tended no doubt to aid its immediate rise into notice; but in addition to intrinsic merits there were other causes which had effect in accelerating its success. The subject was domestic; the supposed evils to which it adverted, easy of comprehension; the scenes and incidents, more particularly those allusive to youth, such as almost all men have participated in and fondly remember; while the characters were of that familiar description that we could easily believe we had seen or known the individuals, and they came therefore before us with all the claims of old friends. The feelings were interested by a tale of grievances so eloquently and pathetically lamented, although few as he admits in his preface, had seen or could believe the fact of their existence. The distresses of the poor and their supposed oppression by the rich, which whether true or otherwise is ever a popular theme, on this occasion enlisted all the generous feelings on the side of their advocate. By designing men this is sometimes made a source of mischief by nurturing something of unjust prejudice among such as are lower in the scale of wealth against those who are higher; by Goldsmith it was merely another evidence of that amiable yet morbid sensibility which kept him in all his writings tremblingly alive to any scene or tale of distress in the humbler classes of life. There were likewise those pictures of rural life which always please in the description; sentiments of a generous and benevolent character; a tone of pathos and melancholy in the recollections of favourite scenes regretted as having fled for ever; similes of high beauty; a versification singularly easy and natural, perfectly musical to the ear without any straining or inversion of language to obtain it; and several of those personal allusions that always add to the interest of a poem, such as the reference to his wanderings—his cares and griefs—and even his poverty. These, amid other admitted excellencies, contributed to give it not merely momentary but permanent favour; for in all the fluctuations of taste since, it has never for a moment declined in public esteem.

Two years are commonly said to have been employed in its composition and correction; an error if meant that he was exclusively devoted to the work sufficiently obvious, as in that period we have seen he had written several volumes. Occasional hints, as he seems to admit in the dedication, might have been gleaned in country excursions during a few previous years; but the chief parts were written and the arrangement and revision no doubt effected by snatches, the result more of moments of ease of mind and of such as he deemed favourable circumstances, than of constant application. Even in this way the labour bestowed upon it was very considerable; the aim of a Poet beyond every other description of writer is excellence; and any degree of labour by which this quality which is essential to his being is obtained cannot be considered misapplied. . .

The fruit of his application was great uniformity of excellence; for we find in it no unfinished passages, none of that obscurity of thought or expression forming one of the greatest and yet most general faults of poetry; no inversion of language; no weak, rugged, or unmusical lines; and no objectionable rhymes, excepting we be permitted to advert to one instance where sketching the village school-master we are told—

> Yet he was kind, or if severe in aught,
> The love he bore to learning was in fault.

But this may have been merely a remnant of that provincialism which occasionally clung to him in manner, accent, and in pronunciation; for in Ireland the word *fault* is frequently sounded without the letter l; a peculiarity which like many other pronunciations in that country, remains popularly unchanged since the reign of Elizabeth. . .

An error in natural history was objected to in the line

> Where crouching tigers wait their hapless prey,

as in America, to which it applies, that animal is not found; this was met by an appeal to the usual license of poetry, and by a quotation from Anson's Voyage,[1] where in one of the American islands some reference is made to the presence of tigers; a species of which though not so fierce or powerful as that of Asia, is common on that continent. The importance given to this description of criticism, would imply there was little in the detail of the poem with which to find fault.

Against the general positions taken by the Poet, there were stronger objections. Trade it is presumed never can be considered any evil in a trading country; nor is the oppression or depopulation of villages by force or violence of the owners of the soil a probable occurrence in one that boasts to be free. Volunteer patriots and philanthropists who require no spur to exertion but rather an occasional check to their zeal, are too endemic to our soil, and too much on the alert for objects to patronise, to overlook or not to resent such a tyrannical act should it take place. However popular therefore the tale of a grievance commonly is, the writer found few to agree with him; he nevertheless sturdily maintained his opinion, and it may be conceded that if he found but one village razed or depopulated from whatever cause, this was perhaps sufficient for his purpose.

To swear to the truth of a song is proverbially a work of super-erogation; nor is such a voucher perhaps necessary for the political doctrines contained in a poem. It is scarcely necessary therefore to

[1] George Anson, *A Voyage Round the World, in the Years MDCCXL, I, II, III, IV* . . . (London, 1748).

contest the point whether the main argument of the *Deserted Village*, the evils of luxury, be or be not, a fallacy. Poets in all ages, have conspired to make wealth and its usual concomitants a theme for censure; while statesmen who have been fortunate enough to introduce it among the people they govern, consider themselves the greatest public benefactors. Luxury, viewed in the abstract, may be an evil, or at least lead to the introduction of certain moral evils, but it has in fact no abstract existence; it is merely a symptom of general prosperity, an attendant upon a high degree of knowledge, riches, and civilization; so that the presence of the former, is an indication of the existence of the latter. It is only when luxury is in excess, when the gifts of Providence are abused and made the means of vicious or inordinate appetites and indulgences, that it becomes justly amenable to the censure of the moralist. Restrained within due limits, the stimulus which it gives to human ingenuity must be advantageous to all communities aiming at more than mere animal existence. Nations have been always found to become luxurious as they become rich and intelligent; and it seems therefore idle to regret what is the strongest proof of their advance in the scale of social existence. Of this truth, whatever cause he may have had to change his opinion, none had been more convinced than Goldsmith a few years before. . .

The beauties of the poem offered something for the gratification of every taste; favourite passages found general circulation; but perhaps the most quoted is the celebrated one so much in harmony with the spirit and tendency of the argument—

Princes and lords may flourish or may fade.

The similes of the hare returning to her haunts, the bird teaching her young to fly, 'the tall cliff that lifts its awful form,' the description of the village schoolmaster, the apostrophe to poetry, all found advocates. But more especially the picture of the village preacher fixed attention for its excellence, as being at once minute and comprehensive in the characteristics, skilful in their selection, true to nature in general effect, and as forming not only the most finished specimen of a Christian pastor, but one of the most admirable pieces of poetical painting in the whole range of ancient and modern poetry. . .

(d)
Few will hesitate to admit that the success of the play [*She Stoops to Conquer*], although the humour may be occasionally broad, and

some of the situations bordering upon farce, was well deserved. The leading incident of the plot, the mistaking a gentleman's house for an inn, by a trick played off upon the credulity of travellers, is a novel contrivance, yet scarcely more improbable than the various blunders and involvements which comedy frequently exhibits; and if the fact ever occurred, of which it is said there are more instances on record than the mistake made by Goldsmith himself in travelling to school at Edgeworthstown, it is sufficient for the purposes of the dramatist. Several of the characters seem new, or nearly new to the stage. Tony Lumpkin is certainly original, and allowing for some coarseness, and the usual degree of comic embellishment, not far removed from nature; young Marlow has likewise claims to novelty; and Mr. and Mrs. Hardcastle differ in several shades from the customary old country gentleman and indulgent mother, familiar to the eye of an audience. The business of the scene is active and diverting, the interest sustained throughout, and the dialogue lively from the equivoque produced by the mistake of some of the characters with regard to their position with others. . .

76. Elizabeth Barrett Browning on the poetry of Goldsmith, in a letter to Hugh Stuart Boyd

1842[?]

This letter by the well-known poetess is quoted from the *Unpublished Letters of Elizabeth Barrett Browning to Hugh Stuart Boyd,* ed. by Barbara P. McCarthy, New Haven, 1955, pp. 250–1. It was probably composed in 1842 when the correspondents were having a friendly quarrel over the literary merits of Wordsworth.

As for your blasphemies against such of the gods as dwell near Helvellyn, it would certainly be prudent not to sit near you under any sort of *tree* while you utter them—for fear of a thunderbolt. My controversial answer to them all, is here in my 'article'—which you are not obliged to read because I send it. And to claim a like liberty for myself, I am not obliged to believe that *you* believe what you say or intimate of the great poet of our times! Pope-Goldsmith! Measure out broad praises to either!—but for genius, for philosophy, for various and expressive language and cadence,—for *poetry,* in brief— you cannot seriously place Wordsworth below *them.* Oh surely, surely not!

77. The anonymous author of 'Table Talk' in the *Morning Post*, London, comments on Goldsmith's indifference to sublime nature in *The Traveller*

18 December 1844, 5

On 9 December 1844 William Wordsworth, the poet, wrote a letter about the Kendal and Windermere railway to the editors of the *Morning Post*. This letter, discussing the effects of the proposed railway on the natural landscape beauty of the Lake District, provoked some commentary. Among the replies to Wordsworth was the anonymous author of 'Table Talk,' a daily column in the *Morning Post*. While most of this reply deals with the effects of the new railway on the poor of the Lake District, several paragraphs comment on the tradition of poems about the destruction of landscape—especially Goldsmith and Wordsworth.

It is indeed a very curious and noticeable circumstance, though unobserved upon, so far as I know, until Mr. Wordsworth's letter of the other day,[1] that the appreciation of beauty and loveliness in the wild sublime scenery of nature is but a modern delight among us, and was not known even to cultivated men, and to the poets of a century ago. Of this fact he [Wordsworth] offers some striking instances. May I venture to add another, and, as it seems to me, rather an important one. The simple and gentle-hearted Goldsmith, who had an exquisite sense of rural beauty in the familiar forms of hill and dale, and meadows with their hawthorn-scented hedges, does not seem to have dreamt of any such thing as beauty in the Swiss Alps, though he traversed them on foot, and had therefore the best opportunities of observing them. In his

[1] Wordsworth's letter was published in the *Morning Post* on 11 December 1844. It is printed with commentary by the editor in Alexander B. Grosart's *Prose Works of William Wordsworth . . . in Three Volumes* (1876), ii pp. 330-3.

poem *The Traveller*, he describes the Swiss as loving their mountain homes, not by reason of the romantic beauty of the situation, but in spite of the miserable character of the soil, and the stormy horrors of their mountain steeps—

> Turn we to survey
> Where rougher climes a nobler race display,
> Where the bleak Swiss their stormy mansion tread,
> And force a churlish soil for scanty bread.
> No produce here the barren hills afford,
> But man and steel, the soldier and his sword:
> No vernal blooms their torpid rocks array,
> But winter lingering chills the lap of May;
> No Zephyr fondly sues the mountain's breast,
> But meteors glare and stormy glooms invest.
> Yet still, *even here*, content can spread a charm,
> Redress the clime, and all its rage disarm.

Not one word does this fond admirer of cultivated nature say of the exquisite beauties of Alpine scenery, which are now the delight of perhaps two or three out of every hundred of the crowds of English who make the Swiss tour. He associated no feeling of delight with the awful sublimity of the snow-crowned mountains, or the sweet seclusion of the deep green vallies. He only thought of the barren soil and the severe climate. And that so many of us at the present day have escaped from this insensibility to the more secluded and awful forms of natural beauty we in a great measure owe to Wordsworth and his writings . . .

78. George Lillie Craik on Goldsmith's plot in *The Vicar of Wakefield*, in *Sketches of the History of Literature and Learning in England*

George Craik (1798–1866), long-time writer for the Society for the Diffusion of Useful Knowledge was, during 1849–66, Professor of English Literature at Belfast. Although a critic with limited vision, Craik, a thorough-going traditionalist, had actually read Goldsmith, especially *The Vicar of Wakefield*, and tried to understand him—a rare feat among Victorian readers. Craik concludes (on his p. 167) that Goldsmith was essentially of 'the school of Pope' and even surpassed that great poet in the quality of 'earnestness and cordiality.' For further information about Craik, see the *DNB*.

It has been observed, with truth, that, although Richardson has on the whole the best claim to the title of inventor of the modern English novel, he never altogether succeeded in throwing off the inflation of the French romance, and representing human beings in the true light and shade of human nature. Undoubtedly the men and women of Fielding and Smollett are of more genuine flesh and blood than the elaborate heroes and heroines who figure in his pages. But both Fielding and Smollett, notwithstanding the fidelity as well as spirit of their style of drawing from real life, have for the most part confined themselves to some two or three departments of the wide field of social existence, rather abounding in strongly marked peculiarities of character than furnishing a fair representation of the common national mind and manners. And Sterne also, in his more aërial way, deals rather with the oddities and quaintnesses of opinion and habit that are to be met with among his countrymen than with the broad general course of our English way of thinking and living. Our first genuine novel of domestic life is Goldsmith's *Vicar of Wakefield*, written in 1761, when its author, born in Ireland in 1728, was as yet an obscure doer of all work for the

booksellers, but not published till 1766, when his name had already
obtained celebrity by his poem of *The Traveller*. Assuming the grace
of confession, or the advantage of the first word, Goldsmith himself
introduces his performance by observing, that there are a hundred
faults in it; adding, that a hundred things might be said to prove them
beauties. The case is not exactly as he puts it: the faults may have
compensating beauties, but are incontrovertibly faults. Indeed, if we
look only to what is more superficial or external in the work, to the
construction and conduct of the story, and even to much of the exhibition of manners and character, its faults are unexampled and astounding.
Never was there a story put together in such an inartificial, thoughtless,
blundering way. It is little better than such a 'concatenation accordingly'
as satisfies one in a dream. It is not merely that every thing is brought
about by such sudden apparitions and transformations as only happen
at the call of Harlequin's wand. Of this the author himself seems to
be sensible, from a sort of defence which he sets up in one place:
'Nor can I go on,' he observes, after one of his sharp turns, 'without a
reflection on those accidental meetings which, though they happen
every day, seldom excite our surprise but upon some extraordinary
occasion. To what a fortuitous occurrence do we not owe every pleasure
and convenience of our lives! How many seeming accidents must
unite before we can be clothed or fed! The peasant must be disposed
to labour, the shower must fall, the wind fill the merchant's sail, or
numbers must want the usual supply.' But, in addition to this, probability, or we might almost say possibility, is violated at every step with
little more hesitation or compunction than in a fairy tale. Nothing
happens, nobody acts, as things would happen, and as men and women
would naturally act, in real life. Much of what goes on is entirely
incredible and incomprehensible. Even the name of the book seems an
absurdity. The Vicar leaves Wakefield in the beginning of the third
chapter, and, it must be supposed, resigns his vicarage, of which we
hear no more; yet the family is called the family of Wakefield throughout. This is of a piece with the famous bull that occurs in the ballad
given in a subsequent chapter:

> The dew, the blossoms on the tree,
> > With charms *inconstant* shine;
> Their charms were his, but, woe to me,
> > Their *constancy* was mine.

But why does the vicar, upon losing his fortune, give up his vicarage?

Why, in his otherwise reduced circumstances, does he prefer a curacy
of fifteen pounds to a vicarage of thirty-five? Are we expected to
think this quite a matter of course (there is not a syllable of explanation),
upon the same principle on which we are called upon to believe that
he was overwhelmed with surprise at finding his old friend Wilmot
not to be a monogamist—the said friend being at that time actually
courting a fourth wife. And it is all in the same strain. The whole story
of the two Thornhills, the uncle and nephew, is a heap of contradictions
and absurdities. Sir William Thornhill is universally known, and yet in
his assumed character of Burchell, without even, as far as appears,
any disguise of his person, he passes undetected in a familiar intercourse
of months with the tenantry of his own estate. If, indeed, we are not to
understand something even beyond this—that, while all the neighbours
know him to be Sir William, the Primroses alone never learn that
fact, and still continue to take him for Mr. Burchell. But what, after
all, is Burchell's real history? Nothing that is afterwards stated confirms
or explains the intimation he is made unintentionally to let fall in one
of the commencing chapters, about his early life. How, by the by,
does the vicar come to know, a few chapters afterwards, that Burchell
has really been telling his own story in the account he had given of
Sir William Thornhill? Compare chapters third and sixth. But, take
any view we will, the uncle's treatment of his nephew remains un-
accounted for. Still more unintelligible is his conduct in his self-adopted
capacity of lover of one of the vicar's daughters, and guardian of the
virtue and safety of both. The plainest, easiest way of saving them from
all harm and all danger stares him in the face, and for no reason that
can be imagined he leaves them to their fate. As for his accidental
rescue of Sophia afterwards, the whole affair is only to be matched for
wildness and extravagance in Jack the Giant-killer or some other of
that class of books. It is beyond even the Doctor of Divinity appearing
at the fair with his horse to sell, and in the usual forms putting him
through all his paces. But it is impossible to enumerate all the improbabilities with which the story is filled. Every scene, without any exception, in which the squire appears involves something out of nature or
past understanding—his position in reference to his uncle in the first
place, the whole of his intercourse with the clergyman's family, his
dining with them attended by his two women and his troop of servants
in their one room, at other times his association there with young
farmer Williams (suddenly provided by the author when wanted as a
suitor for Olivia), the unblushing manner in which he makes his

infamous proposals, the still more extraordinary indulgence with
which they are forgiven and forgotten, or rather forgotten without
his ever having asked or dreamt of asking forgiveness, all his audacious
ruffianism in his attempts to possess himself of the two sisters at once,
and finally, and above all, his defence of himself to his uncle at their
meeting in the prison, which surely outrants any thing ever before
attempted in decent prose or rhyme. Nor must that superlative pair of
lovers, the vicar's eldest son George and Miss Arabella Wilmot, be
forgotten, with the singularly cool and easy way in which they pass
from the most violent affection to the most entire indifference, and on
the lady's part even transference of hand and heart to another, and
back again as suddenly to mutual transport and confidence. If Goldsmith intended George for a representation of himself (as their adventures are believed to have been in some respects the same), we should
be sorry to think the likeness a good one; for he is the most disagreeable
character in the book. His very existence seems to have been entirely
forgotten by his family, and by the author, for the first three years
after he left home; and the story would have been all the better if he
had never chanced to turn up again, or to be thought of, at all. Was
ever such a letter read as the one he is made in duty and affection to
write to his father in the twenty-eighth chapter! Yet there is that in
the book which makes all this comparatively of little consequence; the
inspiration and vital power of original genius, the charm of true feeling,
some portion of the music of the great hymn of nature made audible
to all hearts. Notwithstanding all its improbabilities, the story not
only amuses us while we read, but takes root in the memory and
affections as much almost as any story that was ever written. In truth,
the critical objections to which it is obnoxious hardly affect its real
merits and the proper sources of its interest. All of it that is essential
lies in the development of the characters of the good vicar and his
family, and they are one and all admirably brought out. He himself,
simple and credulous, but also learned and clear-headed, so guileless
and affectionate, sustaining so well all fortunes, so great both in suffering
and in action, altogether so unselfish and noble-minded; his wife,
of a much coarser grain, with her gooseberry-wine, and her little
female vanities and schemes of ambition, but also made respectable
by her love and reverence for her husband, her pride in, if not affection
for, her children, her talent of management and housewifery, and the
fortitude and resignation with which she too bears her part in their
common calamities; the two girls, so unlike and yet so sister-like;

the inimitable Moses, with his black ribbon, and his invincibility in argument and bargain-making; nor to be omitted the chubby-cheeked rogue little Bill, and the 'honest veteran' Dick; the homely happiness of that fireside, upon which worldly misfortune can cast hardly a passing shadow; their little concerts, their dances; neighbour Flamborough's two rosy daughters, with their red topknots; Moses's speculation in the green spectacles, and the vicar's own subsequent adventure (though running somewhat into the extravaganza style) with the same venerable arch-rogue, 'with grey hair, and no flaps to his pocket-holes;' the immortal family picture; and, like a sudden thunderbolt falling in the sunshine, the flight of poor passion-driven Olivia, her few distracted words as she stept into the chaise, 'O! what will my poor papa do when he knows I am undone!' and the heart-shivered old man's cry of anguish—'Now, then, my children, go and be miserable; for we shall never enjoy one hour more;'—these, and other incidents and touches of the same kind, are the parts of the book that are remembered; all the rest drops off, as so much mere husk, or extraneous enwrapment, after we have read it; and out of these we reconstruct the story, if we will have one, for ourselves, or, what is better, rest satisfied with the good we have got, and do not mind though so much truth and beauty will not take the shape of a story, which is after all the source of pleasure even in a work of fiction which is of the lowest importance, for it scarcely lasts after the first reading. Part of the charm of this novel of Goldsmith's too consists in the art of writing which he has displayed in it. The style, always easy, transparent, harmonious, and expressive, teems with felicities in the more heightened passages. And, finally, the humour of the book is all good-humour. There is scarcely a touch of ill-nature or even of satire in it from beginning to end—nothing of either acrimony or acid. . . With many loveable qualities, he is charged with having had also some weaknesses and pettinesses of personal character; but his writings are as free from any ingredient of malignity, either great or small, as those of any man. As the author of the *Traveller* and the *Deserted Village*, published in 1765 and 1771, Goldsmith, who lived till 1774, also holds a distinguished place among the poetical writers of the middle portion of the last century. He had not the skyey fancy of his predecessor Collins, but there is an earnestness and cordiality in his poetry which the school of Pope, to which, in its form at least, it belongs, had scarcely before reached, and which make it an appropriate prelude to the more fervid song that was to burst forth among us in another generation.

79. Johann Wilhelm von Goethe on the influence of *The Vicar of Wakefield* on his whole life, in *The Autobiography (Dichtung und Wahrheit)*

1846, 208–11

See No. 71 for biographical material about Goethe, who continued to be influenced by *The Vicar*, as he himself states, throughout his early lifetime. Goethe is known to have remarked on 5 December 1824 (*Conversations*, trans. John Oxenford, London, 1930, p. 74): 'And, besides, our own literature is chiefly the offspring of theirs [England's]! Whence have we our novels, our tragedies, but from Goldsmith, Fielding, and Shakespeare?' And Frank F. Moore, an early twentieth-century student of Goldsmith's reputation, has written in *The Life of Goldsmith* (1910), p. 274: 'Goethe has become eloquent testimony to the effect it [*The Vicar of Wakefield*] produced upon him, when as a student in Strasbourg, it was read to him by Herder. To the end of his long career he affirmed that it had been the means of changing his ideals of life and drawing him closer to the truest literary forms.' During 1811–22 Goethe composed his autobiography, *Dichtung und Wahrheit*, in which he did not forget his debt to Goldsmith. This work was translated into English in 1824 from the French version by Aubert de Vitry. But it was not until 1846–8, when John Oxenford brought out his authentic and complete translation in two volumes, that Goethe's autobiography was read widely in England. The passage here appears in Oxenford's translation in Bohn's Standard Library Series (1846), II, pp. 208–11.

How far behindhand I must have been in modern literature may be gathered from the mode of life which I led at Frankfort, and from the studies to which I had devoted myself; nor could my residence in Strasburg [1769–71] have furthered me in this respect. Now Herder came, and together with his great learning, he brought with him many other assistances, and the later publications besides. Among these he announced to us the *Vicar of Wakefield* as an excellent work, with the German translation[1] of which he wished to make us acquainted by reading it aloud to us himself.

His method of reading was quite peculiar; one who has heard him preach will easily form an idea of it for himself. He delivered every thing, and this romance as well as the rest, in a serious and simple style, perfectly removed from all imitative-dramatic representation, and avoiding even that variety which is not only permitted, but even required, in an epical delivery; I mean that slight change of voice which sets in relief what is spoken by the different characters, and by means of which the interlocutors are distinguished from the narrator. Without being monotonous, Herder let everything follow along in the same tone, just as if nothing of it was present before him, but all was only historical; as if the shadows of this poetic creation did not affect him in a life-like manner, but only glided gently by. Yet this manner of delivery had an infinite charm in his mouth: for, as he felt it all most deeply, and knew how to estimate the variety of such a work, so its whole merit appeared in perfect purity, and the more clearly, as you were not disturbed by passages sharply spoken out, nor interrupted in the feeling which the whole was meant to produce.

A Protestant country-clergyman is, perhaps, the most beautiful subject for a modern idyl; he appears, like Melchizedek, as Priest and King in one person. In the most innocent situation which can be imagined in the world, that of a husbandman, he is, for the most part, united to his people by similar occupations, as well as by similar family relationships; he is a father, a master of a family, an agriculturist, and thus a perfect member of the community. On this pure, beautiful, earthly foundation, reposes his higher calling; to him is it given to guide men through life, to take care for their spiritual education, to bless them at all the leading epochs of their existence, to instruct, to strengthen, to console them, and, if present consolation is not sufficient, he calls up before them the hope and firm assurance of a happier future. Imagine to yourself such a man, with feelings of pure humanity, strong enough not to deviate from them under any circumstances, and by this already elevated above the many, of whom one can expect neither purity nor firmness; give him the learning necessary for his office, as well as a cheerful, equable activity which is even passionate,

[1] See the headnote to No. 67 for information about these German translations.

for he neglects no moment for doing good,—and you will have him well endowed. But at the same time add the necessary limitedness, so that he must not only labour on in a small circle, but may also, perchance, pass over to a smaller; grant him good-nature, placability, resolution, and everything else praiseworthy that springs from so decided a character, and over all this a serene condescension and a smiling forbearance towards his own failings and those of others: so will you have put together pretty well the image of our excellent Wakefield.

The delineation of this character on his course of life through joys and sorrows, and the ever increasing interest of the plot, by the combination of what is quite natural with the strange and the wonderful, make this romance one of the best which has ever been written; besides this, it has the great superiority of being quite moral, nay, in a pure sense, Christian, for it represents the reward of good intentions and perseverance in the right, it strengthens an unconditional confidence in God, and asserts the final triumph of good over evil, and all this without a trace of cant or pedantry. The author was preserved from both of these by an elevation of mind that shows itself throughout in the form of irony, by reason of which this little work must appear to us as wise as it is amiable. The author, Dr. Goldsmith, has without question great insight into the moral world, into its strength and its infirmities; but at the same time he may thankfully acknowledge that he is an Englishman, and reckon highly the advantages which his country and his nation afforded him. The family, with whose delineation he has here busied himself, stands upon one of the lowest steps of citizen-comfort, and yet comes in contact with the highest; its narrow circle, which becomes still more contracted, extends its influence into the great world through the natural and common course of things; this little skiff floats full on the agitated waves of English life, and in weal or woe it has to expect injury or help from the vast fleet which sails around it.

I may suppose that my readers know this work and remember it; whoever hears it named for the first time here, as well as he who is induced to read it again, will thank me. For the former I would merely remark, *en passant*, that the Vicar's wife is of that busy, good sort, who allows herself and family to want for nothing, but who is also somewhat vain of herself and family. There are two daughters; Olivia, handsome and more devoted to the exterior, and Sophia, charming and more given to her inner self; nor will I omit mentioning an industrious son, Moses, who is somewhat astringent and emulous of his Father.

If Herder could be accused of any fault in his reading aloud, it was impatience; he did not wait until the hearer had heard and comprehended a certain part of the details, so as to be able to feel and think correctly about them; he would hurry on immediately to see their effect, and yet he was displeased with this too when it manifested itself in us. He blamed the excess of feeling which overflowed from me at every step in the story. I felt, like a man, like a young man; everything was living, true, and present before me. He, considering only the artistic keeping and form, saw clearly, indeed, that I was overpowered by the subject-matter, and this he was unwilling to allow. . . Nor would he pardon us for not having seen at once, or at least suspected from the first, where Burchell is on the point of discovering himself by passing over in his narration from the third to the first person, that he himself was the lord whom he was talking about; and when, finally, we rejoiced like children at the *dénouement*, and the transformation of the poor, needy wanderer, into a rich, powerful lord, he immediately recalled the passage, which, according to the author's plan, we had overlooked, and then he read us a powerful lecture on our stupidity. It will be seen from this that he regarded the work merely as a production of Art, and required the same of us who were yet wandering in that state where it is very allowable to let works of art affect us just as if they were productions of Nature.

I did not suffer myself to be at all confused by Herder's invectives; for young people have the happiness or unhappiness, that, when anything has produced an effect on them, this effect must be wrought out within themselves; from which much good, as well as much mischief arises. The above work had produced a great impression upon me, for which I could not account. Properly speaking, I felt myself in unison with that ironical tone of mind which elevates itself above every object, above fortune and misfortune, good and evil, death and life, and thus attains to the possession of a truly poetical world. I could not, indeed, become conscious of this until later: it was enough that it gave me much to do at the moment; but I could by no means have expected to be so soon transposed from this fictitious world into a similar real one.

80. Leigh Hunt's pronouncements on Goldsmith the genius and writer, in *Wit and Humour, Selected from the English Poets*

1846 (2nd ed., 1846)

From the first sentence of his essay Leigh Hunt (1784–1859), poet and critic, presents his case regarding Goldsmith: 'Goldsmith excelled all his contemporaries in variety of genius but Voltaire.' Hunt proceeds to comment that Goldsmith may not have been as profound a thinker as Johnson but 'he was a greater humourist, and what is more, a greater poet.' Hunt's essay mirrors the early nineteenth-century fascination with Goldsmith—an attitude that involved isolating him from novelists of the eighteenth century and viewing him in a long line of great poets extending from Spenser and Milton to the early Romantic poets. Hunt, like Hazlitt writing in *The Spirit of the Age* (1825), was especially awed by the variety and breadth of Goldsmith's imagination and by his ability to write in all the literary kinds, poetry, history, natural philosophy, the novel, romance, and periodical essays. In this essay he dwells at length on Goldsmith's poetry and on two prose works, *An Essay on the State of Polite Learning* and *The Citizen of the World*.

GOLDSMITH excelled all his contemporaries in variety of genius but VOLTAIRE. If he was less of the profound thinker than JOHNSON, who scarcely ever thought otherwise than profoundly, he was a greater humourist, and what is more, a greater poet. The author, whose pen can move from novel writing to history, from history to poetry, and from poetry to natural philosophy, always with elegance, if not always with felicity, will boast a greater number of readers and consequently of admirers than him, who is greatest of the great in only one species of writing.

Though the chief excellence of GOLDSMITH is in prose, yet his poetry is so happily adapted to general understandings, that it is more universally admired. It is not however of the highest class: it always pleases with delicacy, and sometimes elevates with grandeur, but it never astonishes with enthusiastic daring. Of his first composition, the *Traveller*, Dr. JOHNSON said that 'there had not been so fine a poem since the days of POPE:' but this word *fine* is of so vague a meaning, that it is difficult to comprehend what the critic intended by his panegyric, when THOMSON had published the *Seasons*, and COLLINS had produced an ode that rivalled DRYDEN: if he designed to say, that there had not been so fine a poem in POPE's style, the praise may be allowed; it has all the flow of thought and clear exposition of that exact poet; its style is generally vigourous and melodious, and its metaphorical allusion easy and appropriate; in the *application* of epithets, which are the touchstones of true poetry, it would be difficult to find a more skilful master: but these beauties are difficult of *creation*: the '*bleak Swiss*' is surely a very violent illustration; to apply the elementary effect of winds and storms to the inhabitants of a stormy region is little better than to call the African the *electrifying negro*, because it perpetually lightens in Africa. GOLDSMITH's figures of speech however seldom start into this violence, though they are powerful upon powerful occasions: there are few metaphors so happy as that picture of a factious state, when

——— overwrought, the gen'ral system feels
Its motion stop, or frenzy fire the wheels.

But no heroic versifier since the days of POPE has been unchangeably vigourous in a long rhyming poem; SOUTHEY and COWPER, the most original poets of our time, are often unpardonably feeble in this respect, the one through an affectation of simplicity, and the other, singularly enough, of dignity. Metrical weakness is owing in most cases to paucity of emphasis; but GOLDSMITH in his *Traveller* is feeble in misplaced emphasis; for his words are of sufficient length and sound to be pompous in a better situation: he slides now and then into a kind of hurried halt, which is as lame as the feebleness of monosyllables. . . These debilities of verse could not have been the effect of negligence; for GOLDSMITH, though he was rapid in prose composition, polished his verses with the slowest attention: they must be reckoned among those infelicities of composition, which sometimes escape the self-love of an author fond of his first ideas. No poet however should hesitate to blot such lines; for what he may gain in vigour of thought, he loses in feebleness of language.

313

There is something peculiarly beautiful in what may be called the plot of the poem: the *Traveller* seats himself on Alpine solitudes to moralize on the world beneath him; he takes a mental survey of the character as well as landscape of different nations, and in such a situation is naturally inspired with serious and pathetic reflections on human nature; but he has caught the general melancholy of moralists, and his conclusions, like those of all systematic complainers, are not invariably just: he laments every thing, advantageous or unprofitable, happy or unhappy; if a nation is poor, it has the vices of poverty; if it is rich, it has the vices of riches: first the Swiss is lucky in his want of refinement, then he is unlucky; the Hollander is industrious, but then industry makes him avaricious; the Englishman is free, but then liberty makes him factious: thus in the first part of its character every nation is wise or happy, but in the next paragraph you find it both foolish and miserable. These descriptions of universal evil are always exaggerated; the generality of mankind will never think of their condition as irritable poets and gloomy philosophers chuse to think for them: at the very moment the author is endeavouring to prove that every man makes his own happiness, he judges of the happiness of others by his own idea of felicity, and pronounces them unhappy because he could not be easy in their condition. The fact is, that GOLDSMITH thought he was reasoning finely, when he was writing fine poetry only. It is the fault of poetical argument that the reasoner is apt to forget his logic in his fancy; he catches at a brilliant line, or a brilliant idea; his imagination fires; and his reason, that serves merely to overshadow its brightness, rolls from it like smoke. It is well for the generality of readers, that melancholy disquisitions in poetry have not the doleful effect of such disquisitions in prose. Poetry scatters so many flowers on the most rugged arguments, that the weariness of the road is insensibly beguiled. If the *Traveller* had been written in prose, or were stripped of its poetical ornament, it would allure no readers at all; and I am much afraid, that with the same alteration many an argument in DRYDEN and POPE would share the same fate. The nearer logic is allied to poetry, the faster it loses its strength to the greater power. How poetical, how wild is PLATO! How unpoetical, how rational is LOCKE!

But GOLDSMITH was attached to fictitious sorrows, and he could not help fancying a new subject of complaint for his *Deserted Village*. In this poem he describes a village depopulated by the grasping luxury of the neighbouring gentry, a circumstance which was much disputed in the poet's time, and notwithstanding the frequent oppression of enclosures, has never since been proved. Poetically considered, the *Deserted Village* is a more beautiful production than the *Traveller*. It is more original, more vigourous, more characteristic in its description. The strength of the poetry is not suddenly lost in those feeble lines that give his *Traveller* the air of an interpolated copy: it is full of the natural domestic images which endear the author to us as a man, while they recommend him as an observer of life. The village landscape, its sports, its domestic sounds, and its snug alehouse shining in all the comforts of clean sand and furniture, with the exception perhaps of the rural dances, which are rather French than British, must be familiar to every body who has been ten miles from London; the mock-heroic dignity of the schoolmaster, whose jokes are studiously laughed at by the boys, is superior to that of SHENSTONE's *Schoolmistress*, whose humour consists chiefly in externals. But the amiable cares of the parish curate compose the finest part of the poem. Though they occasionally rise into a grander spirit of poetry, they possess that simple pathos, which brings an unconscious smile upon the lips, while it reaches the heart. That affecting couplet,

> E'en children followed with endearing wile,
> And pluck'd his gown to share the good man's smile,

seems to me perfectly original; so does the noble simile that compares the holy preacher to a bird *tempting its new-fledg'd offspring to the skies*. But a critic should be cautious in bestowing the praise of poetical invention on GOLDSMITH. He has imitated all our best poets; and though he was indignant enough, when his ideas were copied without acknowledgment by others, he does not seem to have been eager in confessing his own imitations. The general idea of the parish priest is borrowed from DRYDEN, who improved it from CHAUCER; and the sublime comparison of the religious man to the mountain circled with clouds and topped with sunshine, is copied almost literally from CLAUDIAN. What he borrows however he never degrades; it is always excellently adapted to the nature of the production. He has beauties of his own too that might have been imitated by the best poets; the aged widow who picks water-cresses, and is the only inhabitant left in the desolated village,

> The sad historian of the pensive plain,

is a novel and picturesque image; and the six lines beginning 'Ill fares the land,' and those in praise of retirement, are as vigorous as the best moral verses of POPE. No poem is at the same time more decidedly marked with the manner of its author. GOLDSMITH throughout his works was very fond of repeating what he thought his happiest ideas. He so often uses some peculiar turns of language in which he delighted, that the reader who has discovered the trick sometimes fancies he has discovered an old idea, when it is nothing but an old peculiarity of manner. But he was also fond, even to an unpardonable vanity, of repeating his sentiments almost word for word. Dr. JOHNSON objected to the *Deserted Village*, that it was too often an echo of the *Traveller*; but the fact is, that all his productions are in some degree echoes of each other. Of three comparisons in the *Essay on the State of Polite Learning* he appears to have been particularly fond, and has introduced them with a trifling variation of phrase into three of his other works. GOLDSMITH should have been superior to this vain repetition, which is as little allowable to wit as it is to dullness. It is like one of those conversation humourists, who if they cannot labour a new pun or a new allusion to set your faculties at work, nail down your escape by some such recollection as 'By the bye, let me remind you of a deuced good thing I said upon a former occasion.'

Of his lesser poems the general character is tenderness and vivacity. The *Hermit*[1] is admired by readers of every age and intellect; it is one of the very few modern ballads which possess simplicity without affectation. Compositions of this kind are generally either elevated into a dignity incompatible with the ballad, or incongruously sprinkled with old English phrases and expletives, with *dids* and with *doths*, that have the feebleness without the respectability of age, and are helps to nobody's understanding but the author's. The *Hermit*, TICKELL'S *Colin and Lucy*, and SHENSTONE'S *Jemmy Dawson*, are the three best ballads in the language. . .

The *Stanzas on Woman* are exquisitely pathetic. Our language has no morsel that exhibits so true a simplicity of taste, while its effect is heightened with such poetical artifice. The question and answer so equally divided, so apparently artless, and the beautiful climax in the second stanza, are managed with a felicity that turns criticism into mere praise. These stanzas seem to have attained perfection; they are short, but they leave us nothing to desire. Pathos as well as wit is always more effectual, in proportion as it is more concise.

It appears surprising that GOLDSMITH, whose prose works abound with humour, should in his poetry have been so sparing of his first talent.

[1] 'Edwin and Angelina.'

He seems to have laboured at a prologue or an epilogue, and to have lost his more elegant vivacity, in adapting himself to the manner of its speaker. The epilogue however, spoken by Mr. LEE LEWES in the character of Harlequin, is vigorous, and well adapted to the occasion. Of all our prologue writers DRYDEN seems to have been the most witty, FOOTE the most humourous, and GARRICK, whose profession taught him every artifice of theatrical effect, the most generally pleasing. But tasks like these require very little genius; the writer has nothing to do but to make an audience good-humoured, and wit on such occasions is lost on three parts of the theatre.

Our author's pieces in professed imitation of SWIFT, possess neither the wit nor the ease of his model, whose social familiarity is more attained by the *Haunch of Venison*, which does not profess to imitate. But *Retaliation* would have been owned with pleasure by SWIFT himself; the style is perfectly easy, and the characters, especially that of GARRICK, exhibit much knowledge of human nature. The character of CUMBERLAND however, who is compared with TERENCE, and yet is said not to draw from nature, is dramatically inconsistent: GOLDSMITH disliked sentimental comedy, and therefore found it difficult to praise. The poem is also unfortunately divided into two characteristic descriptions, the one metaphorical, and the other personal; first his friends are dishes, then they are men. And lastly, it is still more unfortunate, that his company must be intoxicated before their epitaphs are written: the wise REYNOLDS, the good Dean,[1] and CUMBERLAND, the mender of hearts, make very awkward figures *sunk under the table*. But the general manner of the poem is certainly original; and the imitations it has provoked sufficiently prove its claim to reputation.

I do not know why I should criticise the comedies of GOLDSMITH among his poetical works, nor how those familiar dramas, which are poetry neither to the eye nor the imagination, can be called poetical. The ancient comedians, and those of the English who wrote metrically, may claim the title of poets; but if they who write mere prosaic dialogues for the stage are to be honoured with the appellation, you must call LE SAGE, RICHARDSON, and MISS EDGEWORTH poets, for some of their works are dialogues: upon this reasoning the *Devil upon Two Sticks* becomes a poem, for it is almost an entire drama, of which the Devil and the Student are the two persons. The only difference between such novels and most of our comedies is, that the former are never acted. If a work is not written in verse the only quality that

[1] Thomas Barnard, Dean of Derry. See No. 52.

can give it the name of a poem is imagination or poetical invention. Thus *Ossian* and *Telemachus* are called poems, because they want nothing but rhythm, which is the mere body, as imagination is the soul of poetry.

But the comedies of GOLDSMITH have nothing poetical about them: he seems to have avoided every studied ornament, in his dislike to sentimental comedy, from which he was anxious to divert the taste of the day. This taste however was so prevalent, that in his first comedy, the *Good-natured Man*, he restrained his acknowledged fondness for caricature and became more natural than I believe he was willing to be. There is much easy dialogue in this play, and most of the characters are to be found in nature; but the servant, Jarvis, like all dramatic servants, has too much sense and importance about him: from TERENCE down to the huge farce-writers of the present day, a footman is a very different being in real life and on the stage. The character of Croaker, who is always anticipating misfortunes, is an imitation of Suspirius in the *Rambler*: both the imitation and the original are caricatures, but the dramatic one is certainly the least unnatural; for he does utter a sentence now and then without misery in it. No character in nature ever confined his speech like Suspirius to one passion or one subject: there must be a time, when the common interests of life will compel him to accommodate his speech to his society. In the picture of the *Good-natured Man*, which is drawn with correctness and vivacity, there may be distinguished the usual fondness of GOLDSMITH for introducing himself into his works; he had gathered much experience during the wandering life he originally led, and was very skilful in applying it in a literary, if not in a practical way. I have no doubt that the *Good-natured Man* was a personification of his own accommodating careless temper: in his principal poems he is always an actor as well as a speaker; the adventures of the *Vicar of Wakefield's* son George are supposed to comprehend some of his own; and a ludicrous mistake which he made in one of his Irish journies formed the plot of his next comedy, *She Stoops to Conquer*, in which two gentlemen mistake an old country house for an inn, and are indulged in their error by the master of it, who is a humourist. Such a plot does not promise much nature either in the incidents or the characters, and in reality the production is merely a large farce with the name of comedy. Tony Lumpkin is certainly a most original personage; his subjection at home and his domination abroad, his uncouth bashfulness at the gallantries of his female cousin, and his love of mischievous fun, present an inimitable picture of broad rusticity: the natural contempt which he shews for his mother, who has indulged him till he is too old to play the child, enforces an excellent moral in the midst of the most laughable caricature. But the characters are exaggerated throughout, and most of the incidents are inconsistent and improbable. It is from this play and the grinning comedies of O'KEEFFE,[1] have arisen those monstrous farces of the present stage, which may, for ought I know, attain the end of comedy, for they are certainly satires on human nature.

It is from his prose works that GOLDSMITH will obtain his best reputation with the critic. In these his judgment becomes more correct, and he adapts his fancy to his subject rather than his subject to his fancy. If his sentiments in verse are little better than vehicles for poetical ornament, they become their own ornament in prose; they want no glare of dress to conceal poverty; their manner is chearful, their language unaffected and elegant. The style of almost every celebrated writer preceding GOLDSMITH is remarkable for some prominent quality, which is more immediately his own: thus SWIFT is plain, JOHNSON dignified, BOLINGBROKE ardent; and critics have said that a manner is as indicative of great authors as it is of great painters. But each of these writers wants the quality of the other, and certainly it were better to be distinguished by united than by individual excellence. ADDISON gained pre-eminence over all the writers of his age by an union of the qualities of style: he is deservedly celebrated for his simplicity; yet even ADDISON wants strength. It is most probable that his occasional weakness proceeded from affectation; for though his natural taste produced a style almost always unaffected, yet as he knew his talent, he might sometimes consider it too much, and the very wish to be artless would lead him into artifice: but a writer's artifice is always detected; if he escapes the criticism, he will be detected by the feelings of his reader. An author after all merely talks to his reader by signs instead of speech; and therefore the most perfect style seems to be that which avoids the negligence while it preserves the spirit of conversation. If no exclusive peculiarity of style would be proper in social intercourse,—if the majesty of JOHNSON would only awe his hearers, and the short decision of SWIFT intimidate them, an union of the elegant and the vigourous, of the attractive and the unaffected, is necessary to the beauty and the end of writing. This end seems to have been attained more nearly by GOLDSMITH than by

[1] John O'Keeffe (1747–1833), a minor comic dramatist who had written *Tony Lumpkin in Town* (1778–80) and *Wild Oats: or the Strolling Gentleman* (1791).

any single writer before or after him; and JOHNSON pronounced his own condemnation, when he characterised him as an author, 'who had the art of being minute without tediousness, and general without confusion; whose language was copious without exuberance, exact without constraint, and easy without weakness.' This is not mere eulogy; it is a criticism worthy its author and its subject. GOLDSMITH had united the chief beauties of his predecessors and contemporaries in a style the most adapted to miscellaneous writing: he had preserved all the ease of ADDISON, while he rejected his feebleness and indecision; he had shone in all the perspicuity of SWIFT, and added to perspicuity the ornament of elegance; and though his periods were sonorous and often grand, his friendship with JOHNSON had never led him to assume that studied loftiness which had become even fashionable. It was reserved for a future age however to conquer every minute feebleness of writing, to get rid of the *namelys* and *therebys*, of sentences ending with prepositions, and of relative pronouns that have no substantive relation. I have never met with a single author, who was invariably right in placing the adverb *only*: BLAIR, who detects its dislocation in ADDISON, uses it most unmercifully himself.

The earliest production of GOLDSMITH, an *Enquiry into the State of Polite Learning* in 1759, introduced him to the public in all his beauties of style and original turns of thought. Perhaps there never was an author who united such liveliness of manner with so melancholy a system of opinion. His writings abound with complaints on the unsuccessful toils of genius, and on the general misery of human life; and he began a literary career, which was to confer new laurels on the age, by writing an essay on the universal decline of letters. Much of this decline seems to have been imaginary: perhaps the despondent fancy was natural to a writer, who with all the consciousness of merit was struggling in obscurity to procure his daily subsistence. GOLDSMITH, like most writers vain of their genius, and impatient of the idea of censure, indulged in a contemptuous dislike of critics, whom he represented as 'the natural destroyers of polite learning:' but when he tells us that 'critics are always more numerous as learning is more diffused,' and that 'an increase of criticism has always portended a decay' of literature, he becomes feeble and inconsistent. Would it not follow, that when learning is not diffused, criticism would not be diffused; and therefore that when the 'natural destroyer of learning' no longer existed, the latter would revive in all its bloom?

England is perhaps of all countries the best adapted to vigourous knowledge. An Englishman not only thinks but speaks what he pleases; and therefore he excels in those arts which require a liberty of thought and speech, in political writing, in oratory, and particularly in logic: VOLTAIRE pronounced us the only nation in Europe who think profoundly. Such a nation wants nothing but the patronage of the great to excel in every department of literature; and GOLDSMITH might have allowed criticism a little respite from his rage, and attributed the decay of English genius to this simple deficiency. Some few of our latter writers indeed have received pensions from the state; but instead of receiving them as incentives to further exertion during the vigour of their health and powers, the money had dropped upon them when they have learnt to bear poverty and have almost lost both.

When literature wants patronage, men of taste become indolent and fall into imitation: from this cause has arisen that universal but elegant mediocrity of genius which characterises the present age. Every author imitates somebody's opinions or somebody's style; or if one more independent than the rest attempts to become original, he runs into the opposite extreme, and in his determination to remind us of no author good or bad, wanders into a vicious singularity. . . COWPER of all the poets of our age is the most correctly original; his thoughts were entirely his own, and therefore naturally produced a new style: he excels in domestic pathos; and in natural strength of reasoning may rank next to DRYDEN and POPE. But in his contempt of imitation he has fallen into the error of SOUTHEY: that air of candid familiarity, which his heart led him to indulge, feeling itself sufficiently at ease out of the fetters of rhyme, relaxed too often into the prosaic; and he has furnished another hopeless instance of the inefficacy of blank-verse in artless composition. The productions of this poet however have not developed his powers in all their strength: the distempered severity of his religious doctrines, nourished by the bigotry of mistaken friends, was perpetually at variance with his philanthropic mildness of spirit, and the struggle injured his genius while it was fatal to his repose; if he had felt less acutely for the follies of mankind, he would have become a great satirist. SHERIDAN is the best dramatist since the days of CONGREVE; his comedy of the *Rivals* is perhaps the only instance of broad humour uninjuring and uninjured by nature. With the exception of this writer and MURPHY, whose farce of the *Citizen* is the best in the language, our stage is wretchedly degenerate; but this degeneracy exhibits itself in a manner the very reverse of that which GOLDSMITH lamented in his time. Instead of the everlasting revival of old plays and the total disregard of living authors which he so feelingly laments, we are presented with the hasty comedies, or rather with nothing but the bloated farces of mercenary writers, who are in fact stipendiaries of the theatre, some of them being absolutely engaged by a permanent salary. Thus a modern dramatist [such as Goldsmith], who has nothing in view but the service of his employers and his own payment, is in the situation of a journeyman mechanic, with this simple difference, that the manufacturer of clocks or of cupboards is of public utility, while the manufacturer of plays is the depraver of public taste, and consequently of public morals. . .

As to the criticism of our reviews and magazines, which GOLDSMITH considers so alarming, the public do not rest so implicit a confidence in their authority as they used to do; a bad critic is as little regarded as a bad poet; we begin to judge by our feelings rather than our learning; and it is by appealing to taste and not to ARISTOTLE that the merits of a work are determined. At the same time, if the majority of our reviews are not worth attention, there have been lately some spirited attempts to rescue criticism from the charge of ignorance and corruption; it has lost much of that assertive and dogmatical tone which disdains to give a reason for its decision, and has become more philosophical and enlarged in its views. Criticism like this promotes literature instead of retarding it; a hundred reviews, thus combined to praise genius and to ridicule folly, would be nothing but a hundred incentives to merit; for though applause be compared to air, yet it is the air necessary to an author's existence. . .

I have been thus diffuse in criticising the *Essay on the State of Polite Learning*, because it was in some measure prophetically addressed to our own times. It possesses many individual beauties both of language and thought; its figures of speech are generally strong and well chosen; and that dry humour, which has so peculiar an effect in its own apparent unconsciousness, and which was afterwards proved to be GOLDSMITH's best originality, always catches at the proper objects of ridicule, and sparkles with ready illustration. The chapter on universities is full of judicious observation; it is almost a string of aphorisms, the more valuable as they were formed by experience, which is the logic of fact. It will be seen however that the prophetic warnings of the Essay have not generally become true, and that the effects which the author deplores are not always deduced from their real causes. His temper too often betrays itself, and leads him into conclusions without conclusion; he is too apt to confound false criticism with true, and decides too strongly from conjecture. In fact it is a very difficult, not to say an impossible task to settle the literary merits of contemporary nations, whose writers are often unknown beyond their native country; and the consciousness of this difficulty led the author into that unlucky assertion, which measured a country's *reputation* by writers who confer *fame on others without receiving any portion of it themselves.* GOLDSMITH by his own unconscious acknowledgement could no more pronounce on the contemporary literature of Italy or Germany than LOPE DE VEGA could have prounced on the literature of the contemporary English poets, of whom he knew nothing. . .

GOLDSMITH does not appear to have possessed an attention sufficiently persevering to pursue one individual subject through a long maze of reasoning. Hence he was fond of detached essays, into which he could throw the result of his meditations and his experience without tiring himself or his readers. Though he had such a host of predecessors in this species of writing, he seems to have imitated nothing either of their sentiment or style: in style he excelled them all; in sentiment he was sprightly yet sententious; and perhaps he is the only successor of ADDISON who indulges his readers in broad laughter while he gives them sound reason. The *Citizen of the World,* or as it was originally entitled, *Letters from a Chinese Philosopher in London to his Friends in the East,* affords the best specimen of GOLDSMITH's genius, both as an observer and a man of wit. The letters are upon the manners of the English; and in fact are merely a set of essays slightly connected by the supposition of an epistolary correspondence. Some of them possess nothing of the Chinese writer, and little of the epistolary form but the *address* at the beginning, and the *farewell* at the end; consequently the author, who was fond of seeing himself reflected in all his publications, printed many of them at various times, under the title of *Essays.* . .

As a Novelist GOLDSMITH has less faults perhaps than in any other species of writing. He seems to have introduced among us a new species of novel, the simple domestic: in no novel indeed is there an assemblage of characters so equally natural as in the *Vicar of Wakefield*: if there is a degree of romance about the pretended Mr. Burchell, it is well repaid by little touches of natural amiableness which endear this character almost as much to his readers as to the Vicar's little children. The contented liveliness, credulity, and good-natured disputes of the venerable pair, the Vicar's patient philanthropy and the wife's holiday vanity, the credulous importance of his logical son Moses, and the manly frankness equally credulous of George, with the beautiful contrast of the two sisters, the one overpowering with gaiety, the other winning with modest sensibility, compose a family picture unequalled in lively nature. The two first pages of the book present one of the best specimens of the author's dry simplicity of style, and the latter chapters abound with a domestic pathos, the more powerful as the writer seems unconscious of his powers, and we are reminded by no artifice of language or sentiment to keep our tears for a less designing pathos. The morality is unexceptionable: I know not a single novel, which could give young readers a better insight into the habits and follies of human life with less danger in the disclosure.

If GOLDSMITH were characterised in a few words, I would describe him as a writer generally original yet imitative of the best models; from these he gathered all the chief qualities of style, and became elegant and animated in his language while from experience rather than from books he obtained his knowledge, and became natural and original in his thoughts. His poetry has added little to English literature, because nothing that is not perfectly and powerfully original can be said to add to the poetical stock of a nation; but his prose exhibits this quality in the highest degree: if he was more of the humourist than the wit, it was not for want of invention; humour was the familiar delight, wit the occasional exercise of his genius. In short he is one of those happy geniuses who are welcome to a reader in every frame of mind, for his seriousness and his gaiety are equally unaffected and equally instructive.

81. George Lewes reviewing Forster's *Life of Oliver Goldsmith* (1848), in the *British Quarterly*

1 August 1848, viii, 1-25

In mid-1848 John Forster (1812–76), historian and biographer, published his scholarly biography of Goldsmith in four volumes. Forster, a friend of Lamb and Leigh Hunt, had been a literary critic for more than a decade and contributed to the *British Quarterly* and the *Edinburgh Review*. Not surprisingly, the volume was more than a biography: it attempted a thorough revaluation of Goldsmith's age and contemporaries, and it was also an experiment in literary biography. When George Lewes (1817–78), miscellaneous writer and later the virtual husband of George Eliot, reviewed it in the 1 August issue of the *British Quarterly*, he summarized its virtues and defects, and, perhaps more important, isolated the assumptions on which it was constructed. Because these Victorian assumptions are of considerable interest to Goldsmith's critical heritage, and because space does not permit our reprinting of passages from Forster's *Life*, we produce selections from the review rather than the original. The review ultimately presents the view of the 1840s and, furthermore, shows how a biographer used the life of a dead author as a pretext for writing about his own (the biographer's) age. Forster's *Life* was revised and reissued in two volumes in 1854 under the title *The Life and Times of Goldsmith*.

THERE are few biographies in any language to be compared with this minute, extensive, well-conceived, and entertaining work. It has been a labour of love; and, as the product of searching industry and generous enthusiasm, it will not only throw fresh light upon Goldsmith and upon Goldsmith's age, but will go far towards raising biography into something like the position due to it as an Art. Johnson said of some one, that he was 'a dead hand at a biography.' He might have extended the remark to biographers in general, who certainly have handled *their* subject with as little reference to its being the *life* of a man, as if they had the 'subject' on the dissecting table, and had to demonstrate the muscles of the back rather than the complicated mystery of vital existence. With such 'dead hands,' such droning 'demonstrators,' Mr. Forster has nothing in common. He holds biography to be the art of setting forth, in some imperfect representation, the life of a man: how he looked, spoke, acted, lived; what were his hopes, his aims, his follies, his virtues, his short-comings; in what element of circumstance he lived, and how that element was not the one in which *we* now live. The work is not mainly critical, not philosophical, not eulogistic,—although criticism, philosophy, and eulogy enter into its composition,—but *pictorial*. He does not attempt to dissect the man, but to represent him. He does not dissertate; he narrates. He does not eulogize; he loves.

To such a form as this, biography has of late been strenuously tending. Biography, like history, has within the last twenty years grown into higher importance, and is recognised as of wider scope, and demanding more artistic treatment than heretofore. A change has come over its spirit. We can now no more tolerate the wearisome pomp of academic eulogy, than the well-balanced periods of the 'dignity of history.' We look for something deeper than facts, dates, and anecdotes: we seek for glimpses of the man. Let any one, for example, compare Mr. Prior's laborious volumes[1] upon Goldsmith with this *Life and Adventures*, and he will see that Mr. Prior's diligence, praiseworthy though it be, has not in any shape succeeded in producing a *Life*; and that, even were his charges against Mr. Forster as correct as they are indubitably incorrect, the fact would still remain that Mr. Forster alone had written the *Life* of Goldsmith. . .

In Mr. Forster's picture of Goldsmith's times, he has, unhappily too often, and for too long, forgotten Goldsmith. Page after page (very amusing, it is true) may you read, without the slightest reference to the hero. Sketches of politicians and political movements are introduced by the author's discursive abundance, without a shadow of pretence. What was the Rockingham administration to Goldsmith, or he to it? He was not a politician—not a place-hunter—not even a political hack. He lived not in the troubled element of politics; rather

[1] See No. 75.

kept himself sedulously aloof from it. A few lines might have conveyed all the information necessary; but where the artist should have thrown in a few potent touches, he has 'made out' elaborate figures. Observe, however, that it is only as a fault in art we object to these discursive passages; in themselves they are excellent, and add to the entertainment of the book. One only asks, might they not have been elsewhere, and better elsewhere? . . .

. . . let us note in Mr. Forster's book the absence of any serious attempt to analyze Goldsmith's character. We speak not of failure, for he has not attempted. It came not within his mode of treating the subject. He has attempted to paint, and only to paint. So far he has succeeded. But in giving us this portrait, he would have added another charm if he could have let us see the workings of the poet's soul; in presenting this figure on the stage, it was in his power to have admitted us behind the scenes. We *see* the man, we do not *know* him yet. To know him we must ponder long upon his life and works; we must interpret the riddle for ourselves, with scanty aid from his biographer. Yet what a tempting subject for the psychologist! What strange apparent contradictions for the observer of moral phenomena to reconcile! In revising this book for a second edition, how gladly should we find Mr. Forster cutting away several repetitions—some pointless anecdotes—and some pages of mere digression, to substitute in their place some thoughtful pages of analytical exposition, in which Goldsmith's *mind* might be depicted as vividly as his appearance and ways are now presented to us.

As a fault against the truth and integrity of art must be noted Mr. Forster's *indulgence* towards his hero. True it is that he is less bitten by the *furor biographicus* than most writers; and we shall perhaps be accused of severity in noticing so modified a form of the malady, but the malady is there, and demands recognition. He does not exalt his hero into a demi-god; does not discover that his ugliness was beauty; his foibles, graces; his vices, virtues. There is no spurious enthusiasm, no 'got up' sensibility, no raving of any kind. The tone is manly and moderate; but it has not the severe beauty of truth. We do not object to his love for Goldsmith: let the biographer's love be as hearty as possible for his hero, but let his love rise superior to defects, not blind itself to them. Love the scarred face, if you will, and paint it; but do not make it smooth. The man in his truth is lovelier than in any colours of falsehood with which the adroitest artist can disguise him. Mr. Forster's sins on this head are comparatively small;

but they are, nevertheless, great enough to warrant notice, because great enough to interfere with the perfect truth of the delineation. Goldsmith had, perhaps, all the excellence which his biographer ascribes to him; but with it there was a large amount of human infirmity and moral deficiency, and this Mr. Forster does not so much deny, as slur over. . .

There may not [today], perhaps, be any one towering intellect—there may not be a Shakspeare, a Milton, a Bacon, or a Göthe: such men are rare, and always will be. But if we have not the one golden guinea, we have sixty shillings in silver; while in point of mere personal comfort and security, authors never were so enviable. Fancy Goldsmith or Johnson in our day! They would have had few struggles, little of that sordid poverty, still less of that necessity to work as mere drudges, when capable of creating works to charm the world. Now, unless it be argued that poverty is beneficial to authors and to literature, we cannot conceive how the present condition of authors is not on all sides a very decided gain. . .

How can we wonder that little Goldy was so generally despised? Was he not, in many things, somewhat despicable? Incontinent of speech, irrepressible in vanity, uncouth in manner, his bearing did not cover the defects of conduct. Over the patched beggary of his coat he could place his hat and conceal it—he had no such grace to hide the folly of his acts. People therefore spoke contemptuously of him; even those who loved him looked upon him as a child. His talents, his generosity, his open-heartedness, his light-heartedness, gained him the regard of Johnson, of Reynolds, of Hogarth, and others; but even they never spoke of him with *respect*. That his Irish animal spirits made him amusing, we can well understand; but there was great need of higher qualities to make him esteemed. Do not let us underrate his goodness—his sunny disposition must not be lightly spoken of—nor let us overrate it; for although, perhaps, the 'salt of earth,' sensibility and light-heartedness are by no means the staple food of life. To apply what Mr. Forster says of Honeywood, in the *Good Natured Man*, to Goldsmith, 'Not all our liking for good nature can prevent our seeing that there is a charity which may be great injustice—a sort of benevolence, for which weakness would be the better name; and a friendship that may be nothing but credulity.'

Mr. Forster, we repeat, is not the dupe of Goldsmith's showy qualities, and not to him are these observations addressed; but we doubt whether his readers will not carry away a false *impression* of Goldsmith's moral character, owing to the tone in which it is generally spoken of by his biographer. There is no suppression, but the whole is narrated with a delusive tenderness. With regard to the literary character, on the other hand, there is positive suppression. To this we alluded in the early part of our paper, and it is now time to specify it. In his account of Goldsmith's *Essays*, we only see the happy sallies and graceful writing; and, although he does not pretend to give a complete account of them, it is surely unwarrantable to suppress all mention of the mistakes and nonsense they contain. As a mere matter of literary history, it ought to have been recorded that Goldsmith pronounces Hamlet a 'heap of absurdities,' and ridicules the 'indecision' of the unhappy prince; nor should the preference for Pope over Homer, and all the analogous criticism, have been omitted. As they appear in this *Life and Adventures*, one would suppose that the *Critical Essays*, and the *Enquiry*, were masterpieces; as they appear in the *Works of Oliver Goldsmith*, they are very poor, and can be read only by the light of that interest which is thrown by a great reputation upon all early efforts. . .

The 'form of revenge' Goldsmith took was light-hearted indifference to the 'whips and scorns of time.' He threw himself fairly into literature, resolved to stand by that if it would stand by him. He did not do this very manfully, perhaps, but he did it thoroughly; and accordingly the next and greatest epoch of his life is called by his biographer, 'Authorship by Choice.' Much drudgery he had to undergo, no small amount of improvidence hampered his efforts, but yet, cheerfully struggling through all, he wrote, and worked out for himself an immortal name as the author of that simple, exquisite tale, *The Vicar of Wakefield*. It was a labour of love:

'Rather as a refuge,' says Mr. Foster, 'from the writing of books was this book undertaken. Simple to very baldness are the materials employed. But he threw into the midst of them his own nature; his actual experience; the suffering, discipline, and sweet emotion of his chequered life, and so made them a lesson and a delight to all men.

'Good predominant over evil, is briefly the purpose and moral of the little story. It is designed to show us that patience in suffering, that persevering reliance on the providence of God, that quiet labour, cheerful endeavour, and an indulgent forgiveness of the faults and infirmities of others, are the easy and certain means of pleasure in this world, and of turning pain to noble uses. It is designed to show us that the heroism and self-denial needed for the duties of life, are not of the superhuman sort; that they may co-exist with many follies, with some simple weaknesses, with many harmless vanities; and that in the improvement of mankind, near and remote, in its progress through worldly content to final happiness, the humblest of men have their place assigned them, and their part allotted them to play.

'There had been, in light amusing fiction, no such scene as that where Doctor Primrose, surrounded by the mocking felons of the gaol into which his villanous creditor has thrown him, finds in even those wretched outcasts a common nature to appeal to, minds to instruct, sympathies to bring back to virtue, souls to restore and save. 'In less than a fortnight I had formed them into something social and humane.' Into how many hearts may this have planted a desire which had, as yet, become no man's care? Not yet had Howard turned his thoughts to the prison. Romilly was but a boy of nine years old, and Elizabeth Fry had not been born. In Goldsmith's day, as for centuries before it, the gaol existed as the gallows' portal. It was crime's high school, where law presided over the science of law-breaking, and did its best to spread guilt abroad. This prison, says Doctor Primrose, makes men guilty where it does not find them so: 'it encloses wretches for the commission of one crime, and returns them, if returned alive, fitted for the perpetration of thousands.' With what consequences? 'New vices call for fresh restraints. Penal laws, which are in the hands of the rich, are laid upon the poor, and all our paltriest possessions are hung round with gibbets.' It scares men now to be told of what no man then took heed. Deliberate murders were committed by the state. It was but four years after this that the government, which had reduced a young wife to beggary by pressing her husband to sea, sentenced her to death for entering a draper's shop, taking some coarse linen off the counter, and laying it down again as the shopman gazed at her; listened unmoved to a defence which might have penetrated stone, that inasmuch, since her husband was stolen from her, she had had no bed to lie upon, nothing to clothe her children, nothing to give them to eat; perhaps she might have done something wrong, for she hardly knew what she did; and finally sent her to Tyburn, with her infant sucking at her breast. Not without reason did Horace Walpole call the country 'one great shambles.' Hardly a Monday passed that was not Black Monday[1] at Newgate. An execution came round as regularly as any other weekly show; and when it was that 'shocking sight of fifteen men executed,' whereof Boswell makes more than one mention, the interest was, of course, the greater. Men not otherwise hardened, found here a debasing delight. George Selwyn passed as much time at Tyburn as at White's; and Mr. Boswell had a special suit of execution black, to make a decent appearance near the scaffold. Not uncalled for, therefore, though solitary, and as yet unheeded, was the warning of the good Doctor Primrose. Nay, not uncalled for is it now, though eighty years have passed. Do not, he said, draw the cords of society so hard, that a convulsion must come to burst them; do not cut away wretches as useless before you have tried their utility. Make law the protector, not the tyrant of the people. You will then find that creatures, whose

[1] Easter Monday, allegedly the worst Monday of the year and especially perilous.

souls are held as dross, want only the hand of a refiner, and that 'very little blood will serve to cement our security.' '

The narrative of Goldsmith's theatrical experience reads like a chapter of contemporary history; the hopes of the dramatist, the exigencies of actors, the want of judgment in managers, are here pictured as if they occurred but yesterday. Will it be credited that Colman, a wit and a dramatist, was dismal in forebodings respecting so genuine and hearty a comedy as *She Stoops to Conquer?*—that comedy which Mr. Forster so felicitously calls 'a legacy of laughter.' One bit of criticism on this play we must not omit:

'There is altogether, let me add, an exuberant heartiness and breadth of genial humour in the comedy, which seems of right to overflow into 'Tony Lumpkin.' He *may* be farcical, as such lumpish, roaring, uncouth animal spirits have a right to be; but who would abate a bit of 'Cousin Tony,' stupid and cunning as he is, impudent yet sheepish, with his loutish love of low company, and his young squire sense of his 'fortin.'[1] There is never any misgiving about Goldsmith's fun and enjoyment. It is not obtained at the expense of any better thing. He does not snatch a joke out of a misery, or an ugliness, or a mortifica-tion, or anything that, apart from the joke, would be likely to give pain; which, with all his airy wit and refinement, was too much the trick of Sheridan. Whether it be enjoyment or mischief going on in one of Goldsmith's comedies, the predominant impression is hearty, jovial, and sincere; and nobody feels the worse when 'Tony,' after fearful joltings down Feather-bed-lane, over Up-and-down Hill, and across Heavy-tree Heath, lodges his mother in the horse-pond. *The laugh clears the atmosphere all round it.*'

That poverty was not the curse of Goldsmith's life becomes very apparent, as we trace it through these pages. Poor he was, but even in prosperity he was poor. When fame had given a value to his simplest writings, when booksellers were glad to advance large sums on works *to be* written—(five hundred guineas were paid and spent before a line of the *Animated Nature* was printed,) when literature might really have given him independence, he was just as much in debt and distress as when, a Grub-street hack he was glad of the loan of a few shillings. Incurable improvidence would always have kept him poor. His debts always outran his credit, and at his death he owed two thousand pounds. His love of ostentation, his reckless disregard of the future, his open-handed generosity, would have squandered thousands, and no income could have sufficed. . .

Mr. Forster's argument is strengthened by the very unpromising

[1] I.e., fortune.

appearance of his illustration. Goldsmith certainly was not a type of literary prosperity. He suffered all the ills which genius complainingly declares to be the 'badge of all its tribe;' but above and around all these ills Mr. Forster has shown us the bright halo which no suffering can dim. He has taken a notoriously unsuccessful case, to point out how, even there, genius achieved true success. Goldsmith was unhappy, it is true; but he was not unhappy *through literature*; it was not his genius which caused his sufferings. In any sphere of life he would have been as unsuccessful, as unhappy, if not incomparably more so. The sufferings he endured were the penalties paid by his weaknesses, they were not caused by his strength!

From this *Life and Adventures of Oliver Goldsmith*, we not only carry away with us much valuable information, but we also carry with us the conviction that literature is a great and sacred thing, and that men of letters have a calling in this world which nothing but the want of proper dignity in themselves can prevent the world from acknowledging. This is no small gain. If, as we said, the great and perhaps only practical remedy for the ills now affecting literature is to spring from respect, such books as this now before us are the heralds of a new era.

82. Henry George Bohn on Goldsmith's 'moral character' and its influence on his writings, prefaced to an edition of *The Works of Goldsmith*

1848, 1884 (with corrections), i, 64–76

Bohn (1796–1884), a bookseller and publisher, had published several libraries of standard works. His series of *British Classics* numbering to over 600 volumes had in 1848 not yet appeared; it was published in 1853 and soon became known throughout England and the Continent as 'Bohn's Classics.'

Of Goldsmith's moral character, it is difficult to speak either in terms of praise or blame. That his conduct, especially in the earlier part of his career, was highly irregular, is undeniable. It is probable, also, that at this period his religious principles were not more settled than his notions upon most other subjects; and it is certain, that he sometimes *talked* of sacred things with unbecoming levity . . . In his writings, he shews himself uniformly the friend of virtue, and the advocate of religion; and even those who are least disposed to look upon this as a sufficient test of a man's real sentiments, will find it difficult to believe, that the author of the *Vicar of Wakefield*, however much he may have erred in his own conduct, could have been otherwise than deeply imbued with belief in the truth, and reverence for the character, of religion. Possessing a warm heart and generous affections, he was at all times liberal to the distressed; of an unsuspicious temper, he often became the dupe of the designing and the worthless. He would rise from his bed at midnight, to relieve the wants of a street beggar; and perhaps finish the remainder of the night at a gaming-table, where he hazarded without scruple the money which properly belonged to some industrious tradesman, his creditor: yet no one has more happily ridiculed or more severely condemned the character of the man who is generous before he is just. His veracity has been called in question, and perhaps not without reason: nothing is more apt to lead to occasional departure from truth than inordinate vanity. His fictions, however, were harmless—so far as falsehood can ever be harmless—since they were generally intended not to injure others, but to convey an exaggerated notion of his own importance: they were also harmless in another point of view, since they were often so little plausible as to be easily detected. But while we must deny him the praise of virtue, we ought not to forget that his faults have been brought to the surface by his own simplicity, and that we need therefore make the less allowance for secret sins. As the generality of men are more wicked than they appear, so, on the other hand, it may be suspected of Goldsmith, that he appears more faulty than he really was; at least it may be surmised that his vices were not so much worse, or more numerous, than those of many who left a better character, as that he had less art to conceal them. His simplicity in this respect does, however, form no proper justification of his conduct; and it cannot be sufficiently lamented, that he who shewed himself so capable of appreciating the beauty of a virtuous life, should have indulged in irregularities which every good man must condemn. Yet such was the warmth of his affections, and the general benevolence of his disposition, that, in spite of his follies and his faults, he has more of our kindness than any of his contemporaries whose conduct may have been less exceptionable. . .

As a prose writer, Goldsmith is generally acknowledged to stand in the foremost rank of merit. He has the happy art of always engaging the attention, and communicating interest to whatever subject employs his pen: he never tires his reader by unnecessary minuteness, and seldom disappoints curiosity by superficial brevity. . . This style, too, it must be remarked, is peculiarly his own. . . Johnson himself disclaimed him as an imitator of his style; and, indeed, nothing can be more unlike the laboured pomp and massy state of Johnson's periods, than the easy grace and attic elegance of Goldsmith. As a writer of essays, he has had no equal since the days of Addison. From the judgment displayed in the few pieces of criticism which he has left, there is reason to believe that he would have excelled in this art, had he devoted to it a greater share of attention. His little tales are admirably told; but the subjects are generally borrowed, most frequently from the French writers. The story of Alcander and Septimius is one of the most exquisite pieces of composition in the English language. Of the *Vicar of Wakefield*, it is unnecessary to speak. It has been long an established favourite with the public, and if it can receive any addition to the praise which this extensive popularity implies, it must derive it from the circumstance of having elicited the following high eulogium from one who was himself the greatest master of fictitious narrative that the world has ever seen: 'The admirable ease and grace of the narrative, as well as the pleasing truth with which the principal characters are designed, make the *Vicar of Wakefield* one of the most delicious morsels of fictitious composition on which the human mind was ever employed. We read it in youth and in age—we return to it again and again, and bless the memory of an author who contrives so well to reconcile us to human nature.'[1] The *Citizen of the World*, written in imitation of Montesquieu's *Lettres Persannes*, is a work of great merit. It is equal to that of the French writer in the learning and judgment which it displays, and surpasses it in wit, humour, delicacy, and variety.

As a poet, Goldsmith ranks higher than any other English author who has written so little, with the exception, perhaps, of Gray. It has indeed been the fashion to decry that school of poetry to which he belongs, and of which Pope is the acknowledged head; and some ingenious critics have attempted to shew that its disciples have no just claim even to the name of poet. It is not necessary for us to enter upon this discussion. The common sense of mankind has declared for Pope and his followers: and if authority be required, it is surely not asking too much, that, in a question regarding poetry, the opinion of Dr Johnson and of Lord Byron, the best poet and the best critic of modern times, shall be allowed to have as much weight as that of Warton, and Bowles, and Sir Egerton Brydges.[2] Though Goldsmith has been included in the same censure with Pope, it may be observed that he possesses sufficient originality to distinguish him in many important respects from his school.[3] He is not more the pupil of Pope, than Pope himself is the pupil of Dryden: and if, in some respects, he falls short

[1] Sir Walter Scott, memoir of Goldsmith, see p. 276 above.
[2] All three had sharply and severely criticized Goldsmith's writings. Sir Samuel Egerton Brydges (1762–1837) was perhaps the most objective of the three, weighing Goldsmith's faults and balancing his limitations. For some discussion of his estimate of Goldsmith in *Censura Literaria* (1805–9, 10 vols), VII, see the Introduction.
[3] The ingenious critic of Ford's *Dramatic Works*, in the eighteenth volume of the *Edinburgh Review*, makes an honourable exception in favour of Goldsmith, from the sweeping censure which he passes on the English poets, from Dryden to Cowper, for what he terms their Frenchified taste. We mention this, not as approving of the reviewer's strictures, but in support of our position that Goldsmith ought not to be classed, whether for good or evil, with the imitators of Pope [Bohn's own note].

of his master, it must be admitted that, in others, he has greatly excelled him. In simplicity, elegance, and pathos, Goldsmith has no superior.

The *Traveller* is a noble production. It combines the highest beauties of ethic and descriptive poetry. Here is, indeed, little room for invention: but its absence is compensated by a variety of interesting pictures, and a succession of the most pleasing images. Imagination, which good critics are agreed in considering as essential to a true poet, Goldsmith possessed in a very high degree . . . Of the national portraits, the character of the Swiss is the most admirably drawn, and that of the Dutch is the least felicitous. The plan of the *Traveller* is obvious and simple; but such as it is, Goldsmith appears to have borrowed it. There is a forgotten poem by Blackmore, entitled *The Nature of Man*, in three books, octavo, 1711, which, in its preface, professes the following design,—'1st, To shew the influence of climate, &c. on faculties, dispositions, &c.; 2d, Bring down this general object to particular European nations; 3d, The causes enumerated which produce a generous or a worthless race of men.' We shall here quote part of the argument of the second book:—'The character of the French nation, their virtues and vices—of the Spaniard—of the Italians—of the Germans—of the United Netherlands—of the Britons—an episodical digression in praise of British liberty—the Briton's vices.' This poem our author must have seen; but it is scarcely necessary to add, that Goldsmith is indebted to Blackmore for nothing except the hint of his general plan.

The *Deserted Village* is more carefully finished than the *Traveller*, and this care has been successfully employed in adding to that character of simplicity which is proper to the subject. The remark of Horace, that the great perfection of art is to conceal all appearance of art, has never been more happily illustrated. The reader feels that the description here given, and the sentiments expressed, are the feelings and language most naturally suggested by the objects which were presented to the poet's view; yet the pleasure with which we dwell upon the individual features, and the vivid impression which they make, when grouped, upon the mind, are a proof of the genius which sketched out, and the fine taste which so happily executed, this enchanting composition. The *Deserted Village* is, however, inferior to the *Traveller* in the bolder flights of poetry; and it must also be admitted, that, with regard to particular sentiments, and the general train of thought, the author too closely resembles his former self. His principles of political economy led him to see in refinement, luxury, abused freedom, and the preference given to commerce over agriculture, the source of the greatest evil to nations in general, and to individual communities; and the reflections which are called forth in both cases, are therefore naturally the same. To compensate for these disadvantages, the *Deserted Village* exhibits more unity of subject, and a greater delicacy of finish; it has more exquisite touches of nature, it speaks the language of a generous heart, and conjures up, in all their freshness, those early associations upon which the mind ever delights to dwell. . .

The Hermit is a singularly beautiful ballad; but the original idea, and some of the sentiments, are borrowed from an old poem in Percy's *Reliques of ancient Poetry. The Haunch of Venison*, and *Retaliation*, were occasional poems, written in haste, and not published till after the author's death; yet, if we make some little allowance for the want of that correctness which they would probably have received, had Goldsmith himself revised them for the press, they are not unworthy of him. . .

In claiming for Goldsmith a very high place among English poets, we can ask that which public opinion has already assigned him. . .

Of his two comedies we have already spoken. *She Stoops to Conquer* was the more popular on the stage; but the critic will give the decided preference to the *Good-Natured Man*, which, for wit, elegance, and originality, is equal to the best dramas of Vanburgh and Cibber. . .

83. W. M. Thackeray and Thomas de Quincey on aspects of Goldsmith's genius and 'goodness'

1853–4

(a) Thackeray on Goldsmith's 'goodness,' in *English Humourists of the Eighteenth Century*, 1853, pp. 248–71

(b) de Quincey on *The Vicar of Wakefield* as a 'pure fiction' containing little of reality, in a postscript to *The Spanish Nun*, 1854

(c) de Quincey on Goldsmith as a novelist, in a review of John Forster's *Life of Goldsmith* (1848), first published in the *North British Review* for May 1848 and revised by de Quincey in 1857 for his collected works

Thackeray's (1811–63) volume on the *English Humourists* was originally published as *A Series of Lectures delivered in England, Scotland and the United States of America*. Containing essays on the 'wits' of the eighteenth century, Swift, Fielding, Goldsmith, Sterne, Smollett and others, Thackeray's vantage is somewhat different from his contemporaries'. He read widely and deeply each author included in his lecture series, as his chapter on Sterne and Goldsmith shows. In the essay on Goldsmith, for example, he views him as nearly mythical and calls him 'the most beloved of English writers, what a title that is for a man!' For purposes of brevity almost all Thackeray's voluminous footnotes have been omitted since they repeat material printed earlier in this volume.

Thomas de Quincey (1785–1859), Thackeray's contemporary, had a different view, one that focused on the atmosphere of reality within *The Vicar*. He had written sketches of various figures in Goldsmith's age including Dr Johnson and Chesterfield. In a revised edition of his tale *The Spanish Military Nun* (May–July 1847), he added the following 'Author's Postscript of 1854.' Here he comments on Defoe's novels and on Goldsmith's *Vicar* as romances 'counterfeiting so vividly the air of grave reality,' and describes an experiment made with Goldsmith's fiction. The passages quoted below are from *The Collected Writings of Thomas de Quincey*, edited by David Masson, 14 vols (Edinburgh, 1889–90), xiii, pp. 238–9; iv, pp. 288–9, 296–8.

(a)

. . . the career, the sufferings, the genius, the gentle nature of GOLDSMITH, and the esteem in which we hold him. Who, of the millions whom he has amused, does not love him? To be the most beloved of English writers, what a title that is for a man! A wild youth, wayward but full of tenderness and affection, quits the country village where his boyhood has been passed in happy musing, in idle shelter, in fond longing to see the great world out of doors, and achieve name and fortune—and after years of dire struggle, and neglect and poverty, his heart turning back as fondly to his native place, as it had longed eagerly for change when sheltered there, he writes a book and a poem, full of the recollections and feelings of home—he paints the friends and scenes of his youth, and peoples Auburn and Wakefield with remembrances of Lissoy. Wander he must, but he carries away a home-relic with him, and dies with it on his breast. His nature is truant; in repose it longs for change: as on the journey it looks back for friends and quiet. He passes to-day in building an air castle for to-morrow, or in writing yesterday's elegy; and he would fly away this hour; but that a cage necessity keeps him. What is the charm of his verse, of his style, and humour? His sweet regrets, his delicate compassion, his soft smile, his tremulous sympathy, the weakness which he owns? Your love for him is half pity. You come hot and tired from the day's battle, and this sweet minstrel sings to you. Who could harm the kind vagrant harper? Whom did he ever hurt? He carries no weapon —save the harp on which he plays to you; and with which he delights great and humble, young and old, the Captains in the tents, or the soldiers round the fire, or the women and children in the villages, at whose porches he stops and sings his simple songs of love and beauty. With that sweet story of the *Vicar of Wakefield*, he has found entry into every castle and every hamlet in Europe. Not one of us, however busy or hard, but once or twice in our lives, has passed an evening with him, and undergone the charm of his delightful music . . .

I spoke in a former lecture of that high courage which enabled Fielding, in spite of disease, remorse, and poverty, always to retain a cheerful spirit and to keep his manly benevolence and love of truth intact, as if these treasures had been confided to him for the public benefit, and he was accountable to posterity for their honourable employ; and a constancy equally happy and admirable I think was shown by Goldsmith, whose sweet and friendly nature bloomed kindly always in the midst of a life's storm, and rain, and bitter weather. The poor fellow was never so friendless but he could befriend some one; never so pinched and wretched but he could give of his crust, and speak his word of compassion. If he had but his flute left, he could give that, and make the children happy in the dreary London court. He could give the coals in that queer coal-scuttle we read of to his poor neighbour: he could give away his blankets in college to the poor widow, and warm himself as he best might in the feathers: he could pawn his coat to save his landlord from gaol: when he was a school-usher, he spent his earnings in treats for the boys, and the good-natured schoolmaster's wife said justly that she ought to keep Mr. Goldsmith's money as well as the young gentlemen's. . .

Nobody knows, and I dare say Goldsmith's buoyant temper kept no account of all the pains which he endured during the early period of his literary career. Should any man of letters in our day have to bear up against such, Heaven grant he may come out of the period of misfortune with such a pure kind heart as that which Goldsmith obstinately bore in his breast. The insults to which he had to submit are shocking to read of,—slander, contumely, vulgar satire, brutal malignity perverting his commonest motives and actions: he had his share of these, and one's anger is roused at reading of them, as it is at seeing a woman insulted or a child assaulted, at the notion that a creature so very gentle and weak, and full of love, should have had to suffer so. And he had worse than insult to undergo—to own to fault, and deprecate the anger of ruffians. There is a letter of his extant to one Griffiths, a bookseller, in which poor Goldsmith is forced to confess that certain books sent by Griffiths are in the hands of a friend from whom Goldsmith had been forced to borrow money. 'He was wild, sir,' Johnson said, speaking of Goldsmith to Boswell, with his great, wise benevolence and noble mercifulness of heart, 'Dr. Goldsmith was wild, sir; but he is so no more.' Ah! if we pity the good and weak man who suffers undeservedly, let us deal very gently with him from whom misery extorts not only tears, but shame; let us think humbly and charitably of the human nature that suffers so sadly and falls so low. Whose turn may it be to-morrow? What weak heart, confident before trial, may not succumb under temptation invincible? Cover the good man who has been vanquished—cover his face and pass on. . . . I have been many a time in the Chambers in the Temple which were his, and passed up the stair-case, which Johnson, and Burke, and Reynolds trod to see their friend, their poet, their kind Goldsmith— the stair on which the poor women sate weeping bitterly when they heard that greatest and most generous of all men was dead within the black oak door. Ah, it was a different lot from that for which the poor fellow sighed, when he wrote with heart yearning for home those most charming of all fond verses, in which he fancies he revisits Auburn—

> Here as I take my solitary rounds,
> Amidst thy tangled walks and ruined grounds,
> And, many a year elapsed, return to view
> Where once the cottage stood, the hawthorn grew,
> Remembrance wakes, with all her busy train,
> Swells at my heart, and turns the past to pain.
>
> In all my wanderings round this world of care,
> In all my griefs—and God has given my share,
> I still had hopes my latest hours to crown,
> Amidst these humble bowers to lay me down;
> To husband out life's taper at the close,
> And keep the flame from wasting by repose;
> I still had hopes—for pride attends us still—
> Amidst the swains to show my book-learned skill,
> Around my fire an evening group to draw,
> And tell of all I felt and all I saw;
> And, as a hare, whom hounds and horns pursue,
> Pants to the place from whence at first she flew—
> I still had hopes—my long vexations past,
> Here to return, and die at home at last. . .[1]

In these verses, I need not say with what melody, with what touching truth, with what exquisite beauty of comparison—as indeed in hundreds more pages of the writings of this honest soul—the whole character of the man is told—his humble confession of faults and weakness; his pleasant little vanity, and desire that his village should admire him;

[1] *The Deserted Village*, lines 77–96.

his simple scheme of good in which everybody was to be happy—no begger was to be refused his dinner—nobody in fact was to work much, and he to be the harmless chief of the Utopia. . .

Think of him reckless, thriftless, vain if you like—but merciful, gentle, generous, full of love and pity. He passes out of our life, and goes to render his account beyond it. Think of the poor pensioners weeping at his grave; think of the noble spirits that admired and deplored him; think of the righteous pen that wrote his epitaph—and of the wonderful and unanimous response of affection with which the world has paid back the love he gave it. His humour delighting us still; his song fresh and beautiful as when first he charmed with it: his words in all our mouths: his very weaknesses beloved and familiar— his benevolent spirit seems still to smile upon us: to do gentle kindnesses: to succour with sweet charity: to soothe, caress, and forgive: to plead with the fortunate for the unhappy and the poor.

His name is the last in the list of those men of humour who have formed the themes of the discourses which you have heard so kindly. Long before I had ever hoped for such an audience, or dreamed of the possibility of the good fortune which has brought me so many friends, I was at issue with some of my literary brethren upon a point—which they held from tradition I think rather than experience—that our profession was neglected in this country; and that men of letters were ill-received and held in slight esteem. . . A king might refuse Goldsmith a pension, as a publisher might keep his master-piece and the delight of all the world in his desk for two years; but it was mistake, and not ill-will. Noble and illustrious names of Swift, and Pope, and Addison! dear and honoured memories of Goldsmith and Fielding! kind friends, teachers, benefactors! who shall say that our country, which continues to bring you such an unceasing tribute of applause, admiration, love, sympathy, does not do honour to the literary calling in the honour which it bestows upon *you*!

(b)

THERE are some narratives which, though pure fictions from first to last, counterfeit so vividly the air of grave realities that, if deliberately offered for such, they would for a time impose upon everybody. In the opposite scale there are other narratives, which, whilst rigorously true, move amongst characters and scenes so remote from our ordinary experience, and through a state of society so favourable to an adventurous cast of incidents, that they would everywhere pass for romances, if severed from the documents which attest their fidelity to facts. In the former class stand the admirable novels of Defoe, and, on a lower range within the same category, the inimitable *Vicar of Wakefield*; upon which last novel, without at all designing it, I once became the author of the following instructive experiment:—I had given a copy of this little novel to a beautiful girl of seventeen, the daughter of a 'statesman in Westermorland, not designing any deception (nor so much as any concealment) with respect to the fictitious character of the incidents and of the actors in that famous tale. Mere accident it was that had intercepted those explanations as to the extent of fiction in these points which in this case it would have been so natural to make. Indeed, considering the exquisite verisimilitude of the work, meeting with such absolute inexperience in the reader, it was almost a duty to have made them. This duty, however, something had caused me to forget; and, when next I saw the young mountaineer, I forgot that I *had* forgotten it. Consequently, at first I was perplexed by the unfaltering gravity with which my fair young friend spoke of Dr. Primrose, of Sophia and her sister, of Squire Thornhill, etc., as real and probably living personages, who could sue and be sued. It appeared that this artless young rustic, who had never heard of novels and romances as a bare possibility amongst all the shameless devices of London swindlers, had read with religious fidelity every word of this tale, so thoroughly life-like, surrendering her perfect faith and loving sympathy to the different persons in the tale and the natural distresses in which they are involved, without suspecting for a moment that, by so much as a breathing of exaggeration or of embellishment, the pure gospel truth of the narrative could have been sullied. She listened in a kind of breathless stupor to my frank explanation that not part only, but the whole, of this natural tale was a pure invention. Scorn and indignation flashed from her eyes. She regarded herself as one who had been hoaxed and swindled; begged me to take back the book; and never again, to the end of her life, could endure to look into the book, or to be reminded of that criminal imposture which Dr. Oliver Goldsmith had practised upon her youthful credulity.

In that case, a book altogether fabulous, and not meaning to offer itself for anything else, had been read as genuine history. Here, on the other hand, the adventures of the Spanish Nun, which, in every detail of time and place have since been sifted and authenticated, stood a good chance at one period of being classed as the most lawless of romances.

(c)

. . . A man of original genius, shown to us as revolving through the leisurely stages of a biographical memoir, lays open, to readers prepared for such revelations, two separate theatres of interest: one in his personal career; the other in his works and his intellectual development. Both unfold concurrently: and each borrows a secondary interest from the other: the life from the recollection of the works—the works from the joy and sorrow of the life. There have, indeed, been authors whose great creations, severely preconceived in a region of thought transcendent to all impulses of earth, would have been pretty nearly what they are under any possible changes in the dramatic arrangement of their lives. Happy or not happy,—gay or sad,—these authors would equally have fulfilled a mission too solemn and too stern in its obligations to suffer any warping from chance, or to bend before the accidents of life, whether dressed in sunshine or in wintry gloom. But generally this is otherwise. Children of Paradise, like the Miltons of our planet, have the privilege of stars to 'dwell apart.' But the children of flesh, whose pulses beat too sympathetically with the agitations of mother-earth, cannot sequester themselves in that way. They walk in no such altitudes, but at elevations easily reached by ground-winds of humble calamity. And from that cup of sorrow which upon all lips is pressed in some proportion they must submit, by the very tenure on which they hold their gifts, to drink, if not more profoundly than others, yet more perilously as regards the fulfilment of their intellectual mission.

Amongst this household of children, too sympathetically linked to the trembling impulses of earth, stands forward conspicuously Oliver Goldsmith. And there is a belief current that he was conspicuous, not only in the sense of being constitutionally more flexible than others to the impressions of calamity, in case they had happened to occur, but also that he really met with more than his share of those afflictions. I am disposed to think that this was not so. My trust is that Goldsmith lived upon the whole a life which, though troubled, was one of average enjoyment. Unquestionably, when reading at midnight, in the middle watch of a century which *he* never reached by one whole generation, this record of one so guileless, so upright, or seeming to be otherwise only in the eyes of those who did not know his difficulties, nor could have understood them,—when recurring also to his admirable genius, to the sweet natural gaiety of his oftentimes pathetic humour, and to the varied accomplishments, from talent or erudition, by which he gave effect to endowments so fascinating,—one cannot but sorrow over the strife which he sustained, and over the wrong by which he suffered. . .

. . . In our days, if the *Vicar of Wakefield* had been published as a Christmas tale, it would have produced a fortune to the writer. In Goldsmith's time few below the gentry were readers on any large scale. So far there really *was* a disadvantage; but it was a disadvantage which applied chiefly to novels. The new influx of readers in our times, the collateral affluents into the main river from the mechanic and provincial sections of our population, which have centupled the volume of the original current, cannot be held as telling favourably upon literature, or telling at all, except in the departments of popularised science, of religion, of fictitious tales, and of journalism. To be a reader is no longer, as once it was, to be of a meditative turn. To be a *very* popular author is no longer that honorary distinction which once it might have been amongst a more elevated, because more select, body of readers. I do not say this invidiously, or with any special reference. But it is evident that writers and readers must often act and react for reciprocal degradation. A writer of this day, either in France or England, to be *very* popular, must be a story-teller—which is a function of literature neither very noble in itself, nor, secondly, tending to permanence. All novels whatever, the best equally with the worst, have faded almost with the generation that produced them. This is a curse written as a superscription above the whole class. The modes of combining characters, the particular objects selected for sympathy, the diction, and often the manners, hold up an imperfect mirror to any generation other than their own. And the reader of novels that belong to any obsolete era, whilst acknowledging the skill of the groupings, or the beauty of the situations, misses the echo to that particular revelation of human nature which has met him in the social aspects of his own day; or too often he is perplexed by an expression which, having dropped into a lower use, disturbs the unity of the impression; or he is revolted by a coarse sentiment, which increasing refinement has made unsuitable to the sex or to the rank of the character. How bestial and degrading at this day seem many of the scenes in Smollett! How coarse are the ideals of Fielding!—his odious Squire Western, his odious Tom Jones! What a gallery of faded histrionic masqueraders is thrown open in the novels of Richardson, powerful as they were once found by the two leading nations of the earth.[1] A

[1] England and France.

popular writer, therefore, who, *in order* to be popular, must speak through novels, speaks to what is least permanent in human sensibilities. That is already to be self-degraded. *Secondly*, because the novel-reading class is by far the most comprehensive one, and, being such, must count as a large majority amongst its members those who are poor in capacities of thinking, and are passively resigned to the instinct of immediate pleasure—to these the writer must chiefly humble himself: he must study *their* sympathies, must assume them, must give them back. . .

84. From Thomas Babington Macaulay's life of Goldsmith in *Encylopedia Britannica,* eighth edition

1856, x, 705–9

Lord Macaulay (1800–59), author of the celebrated multi-volume *History of England from the Accession of James II* (1849–61), wrote several lives which he contributed to the *Encyclopedia Britannica.* His interest in biography was made evident in 1857 when his various biographies were brought out as *Biographical and Historical Sketches.* While Macaulay praises Goldsmith's poetry and drama, he is harsh on his four historical works. This severity is not surprising when it is recalled that Macaulay was himself an accomplished historian and could select out wheat from chaff. Whether, however, he was as severe on all Goldsmith's histories as he is reported to have been on two of them, is unknown. Sir George Otto Trevelyan (1838–1928), Macaulay's nephew, quotes Macaulay as saying 'Goldsmith's *Histories of Greece and Rome* are miserable performances, and I do not at all like to lay out £50 on them, even after they have received . . . improvements' (G. O. Trevelyan, *The Life and Letters of Lord Macaulay,* 2 vols, 1876, i, p. 360). The strictly biographical portions of this sketch have been omitted.

GOLDSMITH, OLIVER, one of the most pleasing English writers of the eighteenth century. He was of a Protestant and Saxon family which had been long settled in Ireland, and which had, like most other Protestant and Saxon families, been, in troubled times, harassed and put in fear by the native population. His father, Charles Goldsmith, studied in the reign of Queen Anne at the diocesan school of Elphin, became attached to the daughter of the schoolmaster, married her, took orders, and settled at a place called Pallas in the county of Longford.

There he with difficulty supported his wife and children on what he could earn, partly as a curate and partly as a farmer. . .

He produced articles for reviews, magazines, and newspapers; children's books, which, bound in gilt paper and adorned with hideous woodcuts, appeared in the window of the once far-famed shop at the corner of Saint Paul's Churchyard; *An Inquiry into the State of Polite Learning in Europe*, which, though of little or no value, is still reprinted among his works; a *Life of Beau Nash*, which is not reprinted, though it well deserves to be so; a superficial and incorrect, but very readable, *History of England*, in a series of letters purporting to be addressed by a nobleman to his son; and some very lively and amusing *Sketches of London Society*, in a series of letters purporting to be addressed by a Chinese traveller to his friends. All these works were anonymous; but some of them were well known to be Goldsmith's; and he gradually rose in the estimation of the booksellers for whom he drudged. He was, indeed, emphatically a popular writer. For accurate research or grave disquisition he was not well qualified by nature or by education. He knew nothing accurately: his reading had been desultory; nor had he meditated deeply on what he had read. He had seen much of the world; but he had noticed and retained little more of what he had seen than some grotesque incidents and characters which had happened to strike his fancy. But, though his mind was very scantily stored with materials, he used what materials he had in such a way as to produce a wonderful effect. There have been many greater writers; but perhaps no writer was ever more uniformly agreeable. His style was always pure and easy, and, on proper occasions, pointed and energetic. His narratives were always amusing, his descriptions always picturesque, his humour rich and joyous, yet not without an occasional tinge of amiable sadness. About everything that he wrote, serious or sportive, there was a certain natural grace and decorum, hardly to be expected from a man a great part of whose life had been passed among thieves and beggars, street-walkers and merryandrews, in those squalid dens which are the reproach of great capitals.

As his name gradually became known, the circle of his acquaintance widened. He was introduced to Johnson, who was then considered as the first of living English writers; to Reynolds, the first of English painters; and to Burke, who had not yet entered parliament, but had distinguished himself greatly by his writings and by the eloquence of his conversation. With these eminent men Goldsmith became intimate. In 1763 he was one of the nine original members of that celebrated fraternity which has sometimes been called the Literary Club, but which has always disclaimed that epithet, and still glories in the simple name of The Club. . .

Before the *Vicar of Wakefield* appeared in print, came the great crisis of Goldsmith's literary life. In Christmas week 1764, he published a poem, entitled the *Traveller*. It was the first work to which he had put his name; and it at once raised him to the rank of a legitimate English classic. The opinion of the most skilful critics was, that nothing finer had appeared in verse since the fourth book of the *Dunciad*. In one respect the *Traveller* differs from all Goldsmith's other writings. In general his designs were bad, and his execution good. In the *Traveller*, the execution, though deserving of much praise, is far inferior to the design. No philosophical poem, ancient or modern, has a plan so noble, and at the same time so simple. An English wanderer, seated on a crag among the Alps, near the point where three great countries meet, looks down on the boundless prospect, reviews his long pilgrimage, recalls the varieties of scenery, of climate, of government, of religion, of national character, which he has observed, and comes to the conclusion, just or unjust, that our happiness depends little on political institutions, and much on the temper and regulation of our own minds.

While the fourth edition of the *Traveller* was on the counters of the booksellers, the *Vicar of Wakefield* appeared, and rapidly obtained a popularity which has lasted down to our own time, and which is likely to last as long as our language. The fable is indeed one of the worst that ever was constructed. It wants, not merely that probability which ought to be found in a tale of common English life, but that consistency which ought to be found even in the wildest fiction about witches, giants, and fairies. But the earlier chapters have all the sweetness of pastoral poetry, together with all the vivacity of comedy. Moses and his spectacles, the vicar and his monogamy, the sharper and his cosmogony, the squire proving from Aristotle that relatives are related, Olivia preparing herself for the arduous task of converting a rakish lover by studying the controversy beween Robinson Crusoe and Friday, the great ladies with their scandal about Sir Tomkyn's amours and Dr Burdock's verses, and Mr Burchell with his 'Fudge,' have caused as much harmless mirth as has ever been caused by matter packed into so small a number of pages. The latter part of the tale is unworthy of the beginning. As we approach the catastrophe, the absurdities lie thicker and thicker; and the gleams of pleasantry become rarer and rarer.

The success which had attended Goldsmith as a novelist emboldened him to try his fortune as a dramatist. He wrote the *Goodnatured Man*, a piece which had a worse fate than it deserved. Garrick refused to produce it at Drury Lane. It was acted at Covent Garden in 1768, but was coldly received. The author, however, cleared by his benefit nights, and by the sale of the copyright, no less than £500, five times as much as he had made by the *Traveller* and the *Vicar of Wakefield* together. The plot of the *Goodnatured Man* is, like almost all Goldsmith's plots, very ill constructed. But some passages are exquisitely ludicrous; much more ludicrous, indeed, than suited the taste of the town at that time. A canting, mawkish play, entitled *False Delicacy*, had just had an immense run. Sentimentality was all the mode. During some years, more tears were shed at comedies than at tragedies; and a pleasantry which moved the audience to anything more than a grave smile was reprobated as low. It is not strange, therefore, that the very best scene in the *Goodnatured Man*, that in which Miss Richland finds her lover attended by the bailiff and the bailiff's follower in full court dresses, should have been mercilessly hissed, and should have been omitted after the first night.

In 1770 appeared the *Deserted Village*. In mere diction and versification this celebrated poem is fully equal, perhaps superior to the *Traveller* and it is generally preferred to the *Traveller* by that large class of readers who think, with Bayes in the *Rehearsal*, that the only use of a plan is to bring in fine things. More discerning judges, however, while they admire the beauty of the details, are shocked by one unpardonable fault which pervades the whole. The fault which we mean is not that theory about wealth and luxury which has so often been censured by political economists. The theory is indeed false: but the poem, considered merely as a poem, is not necessarily the worse on that account. The finest poem in the Latin language,[1] indeed the finest didactic poem in any language, was written in defence of the silliest and meanest of all systems of natural and moral philosophy. A poet may easily be pardoned for reasoning ill; but he cannot be pardoned for describing ill, for observing the world in which he lives so carelessly that his portraits bear no resemblance to the originals, for exhibiting as copies from real life monstrous combinations of things which never were and never could be found together. What would be thought of a painter who should mix August and January in one landscape, who should introduce a frozen river into a harvest scene? Would it be a sufficient

[1] Lucretius, *De rerum natura*.

defence of such a picture to say that every part was exquisitely coloured, that the green hedges, the apple-trees loaded with fruit, the waggons reeling under the yellow sheaves, and the sun-burned reapers wiping their foreheads were very fine, and that the ice and the boys sliding were also very fine? To such a picture the *Deserted Village* bears a great resemblance. It is made up of incongruous parts. The village in its happy days is a true English village. The village in its decay is an Irish village. The felicity and the misery which Goldsmith has brought close together belong to two different countries, and to two different stages in the progress of society. He had assuredly never seen in his native island such a rural paradise, such a seat of plenty, content, and tranquillity, as his *Auburn*. He had assuredly never seen in England all the inhabitants of such a paradise turned out of their homes in one day and forced to emigrate in a body to America. The hamlet he had probably seen in Kent: the ejectment he had probably seen in Munster; but by joining the two, he has produced something which never was and never will be seen in any part of the world.

In 1773 Goldsmith tried his chance at Covent Garden with a second play, *She Stoops to Conquer*. The manager was not without great difficulty induced to bring this piece out. The sentimental comedy still reigned, and Goldsmith's comedies were not sentimental. The *Good-natured Man* had been too funny to succeed; yet the mirth of the *Goodnatured Man* was sober when compared with the rich drollery of *She Stoops to Conquer*, which is, in truth, an incomparable farce in five acts. On this occasion, however, genius triumphed. Pit, boxes, and galleries, were in a constant roar of laughter. If any bigoted admirer of Kelly and Cumberland ventured to hiss or groan, he was speedily silenced by a general cry of 'turn him out,' or 'throw him over.' Two generations have since confirmed the verdict which was pronounced on that night.

While Goldsmith was writing the *Deserted Village* and *She Stoops to Conquer*, he was employed on works of a very different kind, works from which he derived little reputation but much profit. . . These works he produced without any elaborate research, by merely selecting, abridging, and translating into his own clear, pure, and flowing language, what he found in books well known to the world, but too bulky or too dry for boys and girls. He committed some strange blunders: for he knew nothing with accuracy. Thus in his *History of England* he tells us that Naseby is in Yorkshire; nor did he correct this mistake when the book was reprinted. He was very nearly hoaxed

351

into putting into the *History of Greece* an account of a battle between Alexander the Great and Montezuma. In his *Animated Nature* he relates, with faith and with perfect gravity, all the most absurd lies which he could find in books of travels about gigantic Patagonians, monkeys that preach sermons, nightingales that repeat long conversations. 'If he can tell a horse from a cow,' said Johnson, 'that is the extent of his knowledge of zoology' . . .

85. David Masson on Goldsmith's 'English style,' from a memoir prefixed to the Globe edition of *Miscellaneous Works of Oliver Goldsmith*

August 1868, first published in 1883, then slightly changed in 1907, lviii–lx

David Masson (1822–1907), biographer, editor and Professor of English Literature at University College, London from 1853, did not include Goldsmith in his *Essays . . . on English Poets* (Cambridge, 1856), nor did he say much about *The Vicar of Wakefield* in *British Novelists and their Style: Being a Critical Sketch of British Prose Fiction* (Cambridge, 1859). But in 1883 he brought out a memoir of Goldsmith that was prefaced to a London edition of *The Vicar of Wakefield*. This memoir he altered somewhat for republication in 1907, the year of his death. Masson's four key points, as he calls them, argue that Goldsmith the Irishman intentionally turned everything he wrote into an 'English style' inhabited by 'English characters.'

And what shall one say now of Goldsmith's writings? Take four brief remarks:—(1) Not to be forgotten is that division of them, already dwelt on, into two distinct orders—*compilations* and *original pieces*. As the division was a vital one to Goldsmith himself—for his literary life consisted, as we have said, of a succession of glitterings of spontaneous genius amid dull habitual drudgery at hackwork—so it is of consequence in our retrospect of him. Probably much that Goldsmith did in the way of anonymous compilation lies buried irrecoverably in the old periodicals for which he wrote, and which are now little better than lumber on the shelves of our great libraries. But his compilations of English, Roman, and Grecian History, and his *Animated Nature*, once so popular, are still known, and are to be distinguished from that

353

class of his writings of which the present volume is a collection. Even in the present volume there are some small things that must be regarded as mere compilations, and may serve as minor specimens of Goldsmith in that line—the wretched shred called a *Life of Bolingbroke*, for example, and the better, but still poor, *Life of Parnell*, if not indeed also the *Memoir of Voltaire*, and the *Life of Beau Nash*. Deduct these, and in the *Inquiry into the State of Polite Learning*, the *Essays*, the *Bee*, the *Citizen of the World*, the *Vicar of Wakefield*, and the *Poems and Plays*, you have, in various forms, the pure and real Goldsmith. (2) In all that he wrote, his compilations included, there was the charm of his easy, perspicuous style. This was one of Goldsmith's natural gifts; with his humour, his tenderness, and his graceful delicacy of thought, he had it from the first. No writer in the language has ever surpassed him, or even equalled him, in that witching simplicity, that gentle ease of movement, sometimes careless and slip-shod, but always in perfect good taste, and often delighting with the subtlest turns and felicities, which critics have admired for a hundred years in the diction of Goldsmith. It is this merit that still gives to his compilations what interest they have, though it was but in a moderate degree that he could exhibit it there. '*Nullum ferè scribendi genus non tetigit; nullum quod tetigit non ornavit*' ('There was no kind of writing almost that he did not touch; none that he touched that he did not adorn,') said Johnson of him, in his epitaph in Westminster Abbey; and the remark includes his compilations. In *matter*, his History of England, for example, has become quite worthless; and if you want a good laugh over Goldy's notion of what sort of thing a battle might be, open the book at his descriptions of the battles of Cressy and Agincourt. What 'letting fly' at the enemy! and how it is the Black Prince in the one case, and Henry V. in the other, that settles everything with his own hand, and tumbles them over in droves! But read on, and you will see how the style could reconcile people to the meagreness of the matter, and keep the compilation so long popular. And so with his *Animated Nature*. Johnson prophesied that he would make the work as pleasant as a Persian tale; and the prophecy was fulfilled. The 'style' of Goldsmith—which includes, of course, the habitual rule of sequence in his ideas, his sense of fitness and harmony, the liveliness of his fancy from moment to moment, and his general mental tact—this is a study in itself. (3) In his original writings, where the charm of his style is most felt, there is, with all their variety of form, a certain sameness of general effect. The field of incidents, characters, sentiments, and imagined situations, within which the author moves, is a limited one, though there is great deftness of recombination within that horizon. We do not mean merely that Goldsmith, as an eighteenth-century writer, did not go beyond the intellectual and poetic range to which his century had restricted itself. This is true; and though we discern in Goldsmith's writings a fine vein of peculiarity, or even uniqueness, for the generation to which they belonged, there is yet abundant proof that his critical tenets did not essentially transcend those of his generation. Even more for him than for some of his contemporaries, Pope was the limit of classic English literature, and the older grandeurs of Shakespeare and Milton were rugged, barbaric mountain-masses, well at a distance. But, over and above this limitation of Goldsmith's range by essential sympathy with the tastes of his time, there was a something in his own method and choice of subjects causing a farther and inner circumscription of his bounds. All Goldsmith's phantasies, whether in verse or prose—his *Vicar of Wakefield*, his *Traveller*, his *Deserted Village*, his *Good-Natured Man* and *She Stoops to Conquer*, and even the humorous sketches that occur in his *Essays* and *Citizen of the World*—are phantasies of what may be called *reminiscence*. Less than even Smollett, did Goldsmith *invent*, if by invention we mean a projection of the imagination into vacant space, and a filling of portion after portion of that space, as by sheer bold dreaming, with scenery, events, and beings, never known before. He drew on the recollections of his own life, on the history of his own family, on the characters of his relatives, on whimsical incidents that had happened to him in his Irish youth or during his continental wanderings, on his experience as a literary drudge in London. It is easy to pick out passages in his *Vicar*, his *Citizen*, and elsewhere, which are, with hardly a disguise, autobiographical. Dr. Primrose is his own father, and the good clergyman of the *Deserted Village* is his brother Henry; the simple Moses, the Gentleman in Black, young Honeywood in the *Good-Natured Man*, and even Tony Lumpkin in *She Stoops to Conquer*, are so many reproductions of phases of himself; the incident on which this last play turns, the mistake of a gentleman's house for an inn, was a remembered blunder of his own in early life; and more than once his device for ending all happily is a benevolent uncle in the background. That of these simple elements he made so many charming combinations, really differing from each other, and all, though suggested by fact, yet hung so sweetly in an ideal air, proved what an artist he was, and was better than much that is commonly called invention. In short, if there is a sameness of effect in Goldsmith's writings, it is because they consist of poetry and truth, humour and pathos, from his own life, and the supply from such a life as his was not inexhaustible. (4) Though so much of Goldsmith's best writing was generalized and idealized reminiscence, he discharged all special Irish colour out of the reminiscence. There are, of course, Irish references and allusions, and we know what a warm heart he had to the last for the island of his birth. But in most of his writings, even when it may have been Irish recollections that suggested the theme, he is careful to drop its origin, and transplant the tale into England. The ideal air in which his phantasies are hung is an English air. The *Vicar of Wakefield* is an English prose-idyll; *She Stoops to Conquer* is a comedy of English humour, and Tony Lumpkin is an English country-lout: and, notwithstanding all the accuracy with which Lissoy and its neighbourhood have been identified with the Auburn of the *Deserted Village*, we are in England and not in Ireland while we read that poem. Goldsmith's heart and genius were Irish; his wandering about in the world had given him a touch of cosmopolitan ease in his judgment of things and opinions, and especially, what was rare among Englishmen then, a great liking for the French; but in the form and matter of his writings he was purposely English.

86. Frederic Harrison on Goldsmith's prose artistry

1883, 1912

(a) The age of Goldsmith as an 'Age of Prose' in 'A Few Words About the Eighteenth Century,' *Nineteenth Century*, xii (March 1883), pp. 399–400

(b) Goldsmith as the 'Mozart of English Prose,' in *Among My Books, Centenaries, Reviews, Memoirs*, 1912, p. 111

Frederic Harrison (1831–1923), author and positivist who was considerably influenced by the ideas of Matthew Arnold, refused for much of his life to consider himself a man of letters; but as he grew older his literary activity increased. A student of many literatures, his powerful intellect and wide reading exhibit themselves in his direct and pithy prose style. The second passage cited originally appeared in the *English Review*, xi, May 1912, pp. 178–9.

(a)

The weak side of the century was certainly in beauty; in poetry, and the arts of form. It was essentially the age of prose; but still it was not prosaic. Its imaginative genius spoke in prose and not in verse. There is more poetry in the *Vicar of Wakefield* than in the *Deserted Village*, in *Tom Jones* than in Pope's *Iliad*, and the death of Clarissa Harlowe is more like Sophocles than the death of Addison's Cato. The age did not do well in verse; but if its verse tended to prose, its prose ever tended to rise into poetry. We want some word (Mr. Matthew Arnold will not let us use the word poetry) to express the imaginative power at work in prose, saturating it with the fragrance of proportion and form, shedding over the whole that indefinable charm of subtle suggestion, which belongs to rare thoughts clothed in perfect words. For my part I find 'the vision and the faculty divine' in the inexhaustible vivacity of *Tom Jones*, in the mysterious realism of

Robinson Crusoe, in the terrible tension of Clarissa's tragedy, in the idyllic grace of the Vicar's home. This imaginative force has never since been reached in prose save by Walter Scott himself, and not even by him in such inimitable witchery of words. If it be not poetry, it is quite unlike the prose that we read or write to-day. . .

(b)

 In all English prose, no one to my mind can beat Goldsmith. I take the *Vicar of Wakefield* to be the high-water mark of English. It is free from that air of the Beau in full dress of *The Spectator*, and from the sardonic harshness of Swift. My *Works of Oliver Goldsmith* are in four volumes, 8vo, 1854, and I can read any part—even *The Citizen of the World*, the Comedies, nay, the Poems. To me dear 'Goldie' is the Mozart of English prose—the feckless, inspired ne'er-do-well of eighteenth-century art. He was a poor creature; and so were Sterne, and Lamb, and De Quincey—but they all four live by virtue of their unfailing charm, their ease, grace, and human feeling.

Select Bibliography

There are no bibliographies or checklists of Goldsmith criticism in the late eighteenth or early nineteenth centuries except John Knox Coulter's *Oliver Goldsmith's Literary Reputation 1757–1801* (Indiana University doctoral dissertation, 1965; see *DA*, xxvii. 1966, 767A), a brief work of less than two hundred pages in which the author discusses the possibility of present and future evaluation of Goldsmith, rather than performing a systematic study himself. Of invaluable aid are still Sir James Prior, *The Life of Oliver Goldsmith, M.B.* (1837) and John Forster, *The Life and Adventures of Oliver Goldsmith* (1848). Every student of Goldsmith's critical heritage needs to consult a few modern works: Temple Scott, *Oliver Goldsmith Bibliographically and Biographically Considered* (1928), Katherine Balderston, *The Collected Letters of Oliver Goldsmith* (Cambridge, 1928), R. S. Crane, *New Essays by Oliver Goldsmith* (Chicago, 1927), Ralph M. Wardle, *Oliver Goldsmith* (Lawrence, Kansas, 1957), Arthur Friedman, *The Collected Works of Oliver Goldsmith* (Oxford, 1966), Sven Bäckman, *This Singular Tale: A Study of 'The Vicar of Wakefield' and its Literary Background* (Lund, 1971). Roger Lonsdale's recent edition of *The Poems of Gray, Collins, and Goldsmith* (1969) is of unusual interest and importance, especially in the breadth of the editor's annotations. Of limited although considerable bibliographical use is Lawrence M. Price's *The Reception of English Literature in Germany* (Berkeley, California, 1932). A book on Goldsmith's reception in England, similar to Fred W. Boege's *Smollett's Reputation as a Novelist* (Princeton, 1947), remains to be written, as does another on his reception and reputation on the Continent.

Index

Note: The four indexes below are relatively comprehensive and have been compiled with the intention of aiding the reader in four general categories: I. General index of names, places, and works; II. Authors compared or related to Goldsmith; III. Individual works by Goldsmith; IV. Selected topics of Goldsmith criticism. Aspects of Goldsmith's life and career appear in the first general index.

I GENERAL INDEX

Abbey, Richard, in John Keats's letter to Fanny, 256

Abrams, Meyer, *Natural Supernaturalism: Tradition and Revolution in Romantic Literature*, 27 n. 55

Absolute, Captain, Sheridan's character in the *Rivals*, 75

Addison, Joseph, compared with Richardson, 4, 357; Goldsmith learned from, 15, 323; Hazlitt's opinion of, 24 n.26; Goldsmith excelled, 227, 320, 334, 358; style of, 245–6, 319; Reynolds on, 255; *Letters from Italy* and *Traveller*, 285–7; Thackeray praises, 342

Aeschylus, translated by Robert Potter, 104 n.1

Aetna, volcano in Italy, 140

Africa, in *Animated Nature*, 140, 145, 148; Hunt on, 313

'Age of Prose', Goldsmith's age an, 4, 7–8, 357

'Age of the Wits', Victorian distaste for, 4

Agincourt, Battle of, 354

Aikin, John, praises Goldsmith's work, xii, 226–36; scientist, 21; *An Essay on the Application of Natural History to Poetry*, 28 n.69, 226

Akenside, Mark, poet and physician, 284

Albouras, Asian volcano, 140

Alexander the Great, in *History of Greece*, 352

Allen, Elizabeth Jessie Jane, friend of Henry James, 65

Allestree, Richard, *The Whole Duty of Man* and *The Economy of Human Life*, 180

Alps in *Traveller*, 29, 36, 223, 302, 349

America, Goldsmith hopes to emigrate to, xxi; volcanoes in, 141; Dr Harrison, 258; Goldsmith's reception in, 263; in *Traveller*, 291; in *Deserted Village*, 297, 351

American poets, influenced by Goldsmith's landscape poetry, 6

Anderson, Robert, on Goldsmith's life, 213–25; *British Poets*, 227

Andes, in *Animated Nature*, 141, 143

Anne, Queen of England, Goldsmith's father during the reign of, 347

Anonymous, preface to American edition of Goldsmith's works, 251–2

Anson, George, *A Voyage Round the World*, 297

Anthony, Sir, Sheridan's character in the *Rivals*, 75

Antiparos, grotto of, 140

Apollo, sons of, should reside in London, 81; 'two fold', 284

Arequipa, American volcano, 141

Ariosto, Berni's modern adaptation of *Orlando Innamorato*, 203 n.2

tribute to a 'Universal Dictionary', 186, 197; to be one of Goldsmith's pall-bearers, 186; refuses Goldsmith's comedy, 188, 262, 350; Davies' memoirs of, 191–8; *Clandestine Marriage*, 267; relationship with Goldsmith, 271; prologue writer, 317

Garrick, Mrs David, Mme Riccoboni mentions, 50

Gay, John, Pope's epitaph on, 187; Fable X quoted, 194

Geneva, Goldsmith travels to, 214, 260

Genoa, in *Vicar of Wakefield*, 292

Gentleman's Magazine, praises *Traveller*, 33–4; unsigned review of *Good Natured Man* in, 28 n.60; translation of the jests of Hierocles in attributed to Johnson, 124 n.1

Georgians, Goldsmith most consummate prose stylist of the, 11

German flute, Goldsmith plays, 207, 214, 340

German romanticists, allude to Goldsmith, 11, 24 n.29; 'new critics' of the time, 17

Germany, documents about Goldsmith in, xix; Goldsmith travels in, xxi, 260; Goldsmith's reception in, 6, 24 n.29, 62, 214, 259, 265, 277, 294, 308–9; mentioned by Hunt, 323; in Sir Richard Blackmore's *Nature of Man*, 336

Gloag, John, *Georgian Grace: A Social History of Design from 1660–1830*, 23 n.14

Glover, Richard, *Authentic Anecdotes in Universal Magazine*, 22 n.4, 184; unpopularity of, 284

God, *Vicar of Wakefield* strengthens confidence in, 3, 54–6, 310, 329; capital punishment and, 53; in *Tears of Genius*, 164; ambassador of, 276; in *Deserted Village*, 341

Goethe, Johann Wolfgang von, praises *Deserted Village*, 114; on Goldsmith's influence on him, 3–4, 6, 24 n.29, 265, 277–8, 308–11; Goldsmith in

Carlyle's essay on, 280; discussed in introduction, 1, 10–13, 24 n.26; Lindau on estimate of Goldsmith by, 259; praised by George Lewes, 328

Goldsmith, Henry, Oliver's brother, dies, xxiii; in *Traveller*, 29–30, 33, 35, 215, 223, 283; preacher, 262; *Deserted Village* and, 267–8, 355

Goldsmith, Oliver, *see* Index III, Individual Works by Goldsmith

Goldsmith, the Reverend Charles, Goldsmith's father, xxi, 213, 347–8; dies, xxi; *Deserted Village* and, 268; model for Dr Primrose, 355

Gotter, Johann Friedrich Wilhelm, enthusiasm for *The Deserted Village*, 114

Graham, the Rev. George, master at Eton, 203

Grainger, James, M.D., translator of Tibullus, 93 n.2; publication of *Traveller* and, 284

Granville, George, Baron Lansdowne, Goldsmith excelled, 227

Gray, Thomas, Wordsworth studies the poetry of, 8; as poet of the third rank, 13, 335; style of, 25 n.40, 243; Goldsmith possibly influenced by, 108; praised by *Court Magazine*, 157; in *Tears of Genius*, 165; in Anderson's *British Poets*, 213; Aikin on the learning of, 228; at the time *Traveller* was published, 284

Greece, Victorians and the comedies of, 20; Goldsmith's history of, 21, 353

Green, Mrs Jane, plays Mrs Hardcastle in *She Stoops to Conquer*, 119

Greene, D. J., review in *Studies in Burke and his Time*, 23 n.6; translation of *Jests of Hierocles* should be attributed to Johnson, 124 n.1

Greenland, poetry would die in, 81

Griffin, R. J., *Goldsmith's Augustanism: A Study of his Literary Works*, 26 n.40

Griffin, William, Goldsmith contracts to write 'a new Natural History of Animals, etc.' for, xxiii; publishes *Deserted Village*, xxiii, 209, 218;

Nugent, Robert Craggs or Nugent, Viscount Clare, 1st Earl, *Haunch of Venison* addressed to, xxiv; Goldsmith becomes acquainted with, 215

Oakman, John, solicits money from Goldsmith, 237–8
Oelsnitz, Carl Edward von der, Goldsmith critic, 259
O'Keeffe, John, Hunt on, 319
Old Bailey, Goldsmith lives near, 185, 214
Ontario, Lake, in *Animated Nature*, 144
Osborn, James M., study of Johnson's Club, 23 n.10
Ossian, Hunt praises, 318
Otway, Thomas, language of, 228
Oxenford, John, translator of *The Autobiography of Goethe: Truth and Poetry: From My Own Life*, 113, 308; *Conversations*, 308

Padua, Goldsmith visits, xxi
Pallas, county Wesmeath, Goldsmith's probable birthplace, xxi, 182, 213, 347–8
Pambamarca, poets should not write about, 81
Pamela, Richardson's character, 10
Paris, Goldsmith visits, xxi; Goldsmith and Mrs Horneck travel to, xxiii; Mme Riccoboni lives in, 48
Park, Roy, *Hazlitt and the Spirit of the Age, Abstraction and Critical Theory*, 24 n.26
Parkinson, Mr, dentist, 270
Parnassus, in *Memoirs of Garrick* by Davies, 191
Parnell, Goldsmith's Life of, 218; Goldsmith excelled, 227
Parsons, Philip, 22 n.4
Patagonia, in *Animated Nature*, 352
Peak of Teneriffe, African volcano, 141
Peckham, Surrey, Goldsmith works at Rev. John Milner's school, xxi, 184, 214; returns to, xxii
Pennington, Lady Sarah, praises *Vicar of Wakefield*, 10, 51

Percy, Thomas, praises Goldsmith, 237–41; Goldsmith becomes acquainted with, xxii; describes meeting with Goldsmith and Johnson, xxii; critic of Goldsmith's verse, 14; *Memoir of Goldsmith*, 22 n.4, 196, 237, 251; founder member of Johnson's Club, 203; Goldsmith borrowed from *Reliques of Ancient Poetry*, 337
Philadelphia, Dr Primrose could not exist in, 60
Philips, Ambrose, Burke comments on, 15, 92
Philomela, in *Tears of Genius*, 164
physician, Goldsmith's practice in Southwark, xxi
Pinkerton, John, *Letters of Literature*, 19
Piozzi, Hester Lynch, on Goldsmith and Johnson, 202–4; *Thraliana*, 159; Fanny Burney on, 189
Pitman, J. H., *Goldsmith's Animated Nature*, 153 n.1
Plato, Hunt on, 314
Plautus, farcical moods of, 20; writer of comedies, 115
Pliny, Aikin on, 226
Pluche, Noel Antoine, *Nature Displayed*, 136
Plumb, J. H., historian of the Industrial Revolution, 18; *England in the Eighteenth Century*, 27 n.57
Plutus, temple of, 191
Po, in *Traveller*, 30
Pomfret, John, John Scott on, 93
Ponsor, Michael, xix
Pope, Alexander, *Iliad* and *Tom Jones* compared, 4, 357; a poor prose writer, 5; school of, 6, 8, 14, 17, 223, 303, 307, 335; Goldsmith and Johnson used the form of, 8, 15, 25 n.40, 230; in the second rank of great poets, 13; Hunt comments on, 14, 314, 316, 321; Burke comments on, 15, 92; temperamentally a satirist, 17; *Traveller* the best poem since the death of, 14, 33, 208, 211, 215, 223, 313, 349; quoted to describe

Watkinson, John, on Goldsmith's early life, 182–3

Webb, James W., 'Irving and his "Favorite Author"', 263

Wedderburne, Colonel, Mme Riccoboni on, 50

Weekly Magazine, Goldsmith's contributions to, xxii

Weinruth, Elizabeth, xix, 259

Westmeath, county of, probable birthplace of Goldsmith, xxi, 182

West, Jane, on *Vicar of Wakefield*, 10, 57–8

Westminster Abbey, Goldsmith to have been buried in, 186; Goldsmith's monument in, 209, 213, 220, 255, 354

Westminster Magazine, Goldsmith's contributions to, xxiv; *Humorous Anecdotes of Dr. Goldsmith*, 22 n.4

Westmoreland, de Quincey gives *Vicar of Wakefield* to a girl in, 343

Whigs, resentment of Goldsmith, 274

Whiston, William, in *Animated Nature*, 136

White, Neville, Southey writes to on Goldsmith, 25 n.31, 250–1

White's Club, George Selwyn and, 330

Whitefoord, Caleb, addition to *Retaliation* possibly written by, 170 n.1; knew Cumberland and Foote, 180, 249

Wilkes, John, Mme Riccoboni on, 49

Williams, David, *Voltaire: Literary Critic*, 123 n.1

Williams, Raymond, literary critic, 18; 'Literature and Rural Society', 27 n.51; *Culture and Society 1780–1950*, 27 n.51, 27 n.58

Williams, Stanley T., *The Life of Washington Irving*, 263

Willison, Ian, xix

Willoughby, Francis, naturalist, 153

Wilmotts, R. A., 'Goldsmith and Gray', 22 n.4

Winckelmann, Johann Joachim, German romantic critic, 24 n.29

Winterling, C. M., critic of Goldsmith, 259

Winters, Yvor, 23 n.7

Woodfall, William, attacks *She Stoops to Conquer*, 19–20, 28 n.66, 115–18; attacked in *Retaliation*, 75

Woods, John A., ed., *The Correspondence of Edmund Burke*, xix, 91

Woods, Sir Henry Trueman, *The History of the Royal Society of Arts*, 191 n.1

Woodward, Henry, actor at Covent Garden, 195

Woodward, Hezekiah, theory of the earth, 136–7

Wooll, John, *Biographical Memoirs of Joseph Warton, D. D.*, 206 n.1

Wordsworth, William, influenced by Goldsmith's landscape poems, 6, 8, 27 n.55, 282; revises notion of poetry, 8, 17; *Vicar of Wakefield* satisfies critical premises of, 11; second rank great poet, 13; a lyricist, 17; Browning on, 300; and *Morning Post*, 301–2

Woty, William, inscription by, 169

Wright, Andrew, Blake critic, 25 n.31

Yalden, Thomas, John Scott on, 93

Yale University Library, xix

Yeats, William Butler, paucity of Goldsmith criticism by, 8

Yorick, Mr, Goethe comments on Sterne's, 278

Yorkshire, incorrectly used in *History of England*, 231

Young, Charles Duke, Victorian, 23 n.15

Young, Edward, Goldsmith becomes acquainted with, xxii; *Deserted Village* and, 79; praised by *Court Magazine*, 157; in Anderson's *British Poets*, 213; old age of, 284

Zeck, George, role in Hungarian history, 215

Zeck, Luke, in *Traveller*, 215

Zelter, Carl Friedrich, Goethe's letter to, xiii, 3, 277–8

II AUTHORS COMPARED OR RELATED TO GOLDSMITH

III INDIVIDUAL WORKS BY GOLDSMITH

INDEX

The Good Natured Man, discussed in Introduction, 18–19; mentioned, 52, 73, 178, 180, 185, 189, 193, 216–17, 238, 255, 267, 328, 351, 355; reviewed, 70–1, 73–5, 318; commented on, 258, 262, 273–4, 337, 350; alluded to, 188

Haunch of Venison, mentioned, 236, 239, 317; commented on, 337
Hermit, see Edwin and Angelina
A History of the Earth and Animated Nature, discussed in Introduction, 21; reviewed, 135–56; mentioned, 179, 196, 219, 222, 239–40, 331, 353–4; commented on, 275, 352
History of England in Letters from a Father to his Son, mentioned, 179, 185, 194, 216, 219, 222, 348, 351
History of Greece, mentioned, 196, 219, 352
History of Rome, mentioned, 179, 217, 219, 271, 274

Life of Bolingbroke, mentioned, 219, 252, 354
The Life of Dr Parnell, mentioned, 179, 218, 222, 285, 354
The Life of Mr Beau Nash of Bath, mentioned, 179, 348, 354

Memoir of Voltaire, mentioned, 354
Miscellaneous Essays, mentioned, 216, 220, 222, 247, 329, 354–5

Poetical and Dramatic Works, mentioned, 220

Retaliation, mentioned, 75, 130, 132, 170, 196, 219–20, 223, 236, 239, 245; reviewed, 128–30; alluded to, 178, 199; commented on, 258, 273, 317, 337

She Stoops to Conquer, discussed in Introduction, 18–19, 21; mentioned, 73, 75, 178, 180–1, 185, 195–6, 218, 237, 248, 254, 274, 355–6; reviewed, 115–27, 298–9, 318–19; commented on, 118–19, 258, 262, 331, 337, 351; alluded to, 188
Stanzas on Woman, commented on, 316

The Traveller, discussed in Introduction, 6, 14–15, 17–18; reviewed, 29–43, 231–4, 283–92, 313–14; commented on, 34, 46, 110, 258, 264, 302, 336, 349; mentioned, 76, 108–9, 174, 178, 183, 185, 187, 189, 208, 210, 215–16, 220, 223, 230, 235, 243, 261, 270–2, 282, 304, 307, 315–16, 350, 355; alluded to, 168

Universal Dictionary of Arts and Sciences, mentioned, 197, 219

Vicar of Wakefield, discussed in Introduction, 2–3, 5–7, 9–13, 21, 22; reception, 51; reviewed, 45–50, 52–6, 58–61, 63–4, 275–6, 292–5, 303–7, 309–11, 329–30; commented on, 44, 56–8, 62, 258–60, 264, 323–4, 335, 339, 343, 345, 349; introduction to edition of 1900, 65–9; mentioned, 178–9, 183, 185, 189–90, 202, 209, 215–16, 222, 271, 277, 280–1, 318, 333, 350, 354–8

IV SELECTED TOPICS OF GOLDSMITH CRITICISM

Age of Prose versus an Age of Poetry, 4–5, 357–9
ambiguity, in Deserted Village, 102

biographical sketch, general comment,

213–25, 240–1, 260–3, 272–3, 278–80, 325–32, 333–4, 340–1, 347–8

characterization: Vicar of Wakefield, 44–7, 60; Good Natured Man, 70;

384